CEDRIC H. WHITMAN is Professor of Greek and Latin at Harvard University. He took his B.A. at Harvard in 1943 and his Ph.D. in 1947, and has been on the Harvard faculty since 1947. His *Sophocles: A Study of Heroic Humanism* was honored by an Award of Merit from the American Philological Association in 1952 and *Homer and the Heroic Tradition* received the 1958 Christian Gauss Prize from the United Chapters of Phi Beta Kappa. He has written a volume of poems entitled *Orpheus and the Moon Craters* and his study of Aristophanes is soon to be published.

Also in a Norton Library edition

THE ILIAD of Homer
translated and shortened by I. A. Richards

HOMER
AND
THE HEROIC
TRADITION

CEDRIC H. WHITMAN

The Norton Library
W · W · NORTON & COMPANY · INC ·
NEW YORK

Δ. Κ. Δ.

Books That Live
The Norton imprint on a book means that in the publisher's
estimation it is a book not for a single season but for the years.
W. W. Norton & Company, Inc.

PREFACE

AUTHORS do not, in all probability, create their books so much as books create their authors. The book here presented has won for itself, in the course of ten years, a life and will of its own which have made it a very different and far less conclusive thing from what was originally planned. It is not hard — rather it is almost inevitable — to ask such questions as: when were the Homeric epics composed, and under what circumstances? Was there a Trojan War, and if so, why was it fought? What was the meaning of such characters as Achilles and Odysseus to the ancient Greek world, and what is the innate force which keeps them before our eyes today? Was Homer one person or several, and, whichever he was, are the epics examples of "primitive" or "sophisticated" art? But the scholar who asks such questions has, in Bacon's phrase, "given hostages to fortune." He will never entirely retrieve his hostages, for these questions for the most part cannot be scientifically answered; not as yet, anyway, and perhaps never. The Homerist must live with these questions; but as he does so convictions grow, and the mid-twentieth century has brought such growing convictions almost to the point of ripe doctrine. Though the Old World largely maintains its scepticism, America has become the home of a new and firmly based theory of Homeric unity, which it is the purpose of this book to reveal and develop.

Polemics have little or no place here, on the whole. The researches of the last thirty-five years have provided so much that is new and compelling to think about, that the wish to prove small philological points or to dismantle the elaborated theories of others is forced to wait. What has been done in recent times in the fields of archaeology, linguistics, history, anthropology, and comparative oral literature, not to mention literary criticism itself, has put the whole Homeric problem in so new a light that now above all else the interested reader of Homer, whether he reads translations or the original, looks earnestly for a synoptic view, a framework by which he can shape his critical reactions within the bounds of rational and historical probability. What follows in the succeeding chapters is an attempt to formulate such a synoptic view, to bring together — for the first time, I believe — the results of modern specialized disciplines relating to Homeric studies and the kind of criticism which, twenty years ago, was called "New," but which now, in modified forms, has become simply this era's characteristic way of approaching such problems as imagery, action, and the poetic consciousness. Such criticism is belatedly making its way into classical studies, over the prostrate forms of some diehards; but it must come. All too long classicists have offered an occasional, and rather disinterested, left hand to the explicit "thought" of ancient poetry, a thing which, in the early poets at least, does not really exist. The unity of meaning and form, a truism in modern criticism, is nowhere more pertinent than in the critique of Homer, for whom form, intention, subject matter, diction, and versification were no more separable than the gases of the earth's atmosphere. Today, criticism and philosophy alike have turned toward a new approach, an approach to poetic creativity whole, as if its various aspects belonged together. The tendency is, in fact, to form a descriptive phenomenology of poetic experience which can take account of the interplay of the subjective and objective particulars of reality. Existentialism, as is well known, treats reality in a similar way, and by consequence, since it reacts against the Platonic and Aristotelian categories, opens many a vista upon the real motive energies in the poetry which preceded Plato and Aristotle.

The insufficiencies of this effort can be guessed easily, before the book be read. Not one of the special studies upon which it is based is in any sense complete; linguists, archaeologists, and the rest are all at work, and anything may happen, so that some chapters may be antiquated before they reach print. Nevertheless, the effort has seemed worthwhile, partly because new findings may at this stage rather modify than destroy the general theory, and partly because every book represents a phase of thought, which may stimulate the further thinking that will eventually supplant it. Certain students of mine, who in the past years have followed some of these ideas, are already now in advance of them. The Homeric field teems with ardent and sometimes inspired scholars, and this book, it is hoped, may assist them, either by advisements or by providing points of resistance. In particular, the historical chapters, Two through Four, require a word of warning: though most of the argument is now, I believe, beyond much question, especially as regards the transmission of the epic tradition in the so-called Dark Age, changes may occur. Least of all does Chapter II, dealing with Mycenaean history, lay claim to finality. Here well-known fact, controversial hypothesis, and pure guesswork are mingled in the attempt, by no means unprecedented, to adjust the quasi-mythical traditions of antiquity to archaeological, historical, and other scientific knowledge. Whether it will ever be possible to reach agreement in such matters seems dubious at best; and it is only to be expected that archaeologists (though I hope I have done their differences justice in my notes) and folklorists alike will object to my formulation. It is not my hope to enlighten either. On the other hand, it is my hope that, amid my own theories, I have made the whole fascinating problem of Homeric history and myth available and intelligible to the beginning student and the layman in the field. At least, I have tried to quote the authorities which all may read for themselves.

For the rest, it should be said that this book is almost wholly about the *Iliad*. In the beginning, it was the *Iliad* which raised the questions, and it was the *Iliad* which seemed to offer the answers. Now that the book is ready, the *Odyssey* points an accusing finger, and justly. The splendor of the *Odyssey* should not be overlooked in such fashion; its excellences are so numerous and so subtle that it deserves a book to itself, and not the mere final chapter and passing references which I have given it. But surely it will have it, for the *Odyssey* claims innumerable admirers in every generation, and will always do so, for it constantly adjusts itself to the flux of experience and the variety of human response. The *Iliad* is rigid. It is itself, and it is passionately Greek; mysterious, deathly, metaphysical, it requires far more than the *Odyssey* for sympathetic understanding. For one thing, it is far more dependent on its form than the *Odyssey*, on the exquisite balances of character, action, and especially imagery; secondly, it requires, for fullest comprehension, identification with a variety of characters by no means so instantly accessible as those of the *Odyssey*, characters whose motivations are isolated in remote archaic patterns of heroic comeliness and veiled in apparent or even real self-inconsistencies. In earlier antiquity, no doubt, the multiple and not necessarily consistent aspects of the Greek character found little difficulty in embracing spiritually, if not analytically, the supreme enigma of Achilles. Later, after Plato, Aristotle, Alexander, and the rise of Rome, it is perhaps not surprising, amid the general leveling of individual aspirations in the growing megalopolis, that it was the *Odyssey*, not the *Iliad*, which Livius Andronicus introduced to Rome as its first "cultural" schoolbook. Rome never really embraced the *Iliad*, nor did the Roman culture of the Middle Ages. But it slept in the Greek consciousness; traces of its wayward heroism reappear throughout the course of medieval oral poetry, in the Acritic and Klephtic ballads; and its bleak knowledge of humanity's most basic inner conflict flashes from the pages of some Modern Greek literature. The *Iliad* is the most Greek of all Greek poems, and we will understand it only when we set aside for the moment all the comforts of Greco-Roman and Christian humanism, and seek the Hellenic spirit pure.

I cannot by any means express how much this book owes to others. No one can read all the Homeric scholarship, but having read a great deal of it, I must acknowledge a large debt, even to those with whom I most disagree; and to those whose works I ought to have read but have not, I offer my apologies and the plea of human limitations. Clearly, my chief points of departure are the works of Milman Parry, Albert Lord, and James Notopoulos, the men who have done the most, by far, for the all-important doctrine of oral composition. Though it was never my privilege to know Parry himself, Professor Lord and Professor Notopoulos have both, in many a long conversation, afforded me the advantage of their direct experience with oral poets in Yugoslavia and Greece; and my thanks are also due to Professor Lord for a complete critical reading of the manuscript.

My debt is also great to many archaeologists. Foremost of these, I must thank Professor George Hanfmann, whose work on Ionia prompted much that I have written, and who, at a time most inconvenient for himself, combed my manuscript with a systematic criticism which only profound, conscientious knowledge and patient friendship can inspire. For whatever differences remain between our views, I commend all readers to his articles for a corrective. I am much indebted also to Professor George Mylonas, both for generously giving his time in many an instructive talk, and for personally initiating me into the archaeological mysteries of Eleusis. His recent work there, as well as at Mycenae, has done much to shape my own views. I must also cordially acknowledge the assistance of the staff of the American School of Classical Studies at Athens, especially Professor J. L. Caskey, Mrs. Caskey, Professor Eugene Vanderpool, Professor Homer Thompson, Mrs. Thompson, and Miss Lucy Talcott, who showed me every kindness during two periods when I was dependent on the School's library and other resources. In this connection, I wish to thank Harvard University also, for helping to finance those two trips to Greece, once by a grant in the summer of 1951, and once by a semi-sabbatical leave of absence in 1953. On both these occasions I worked on this study in its native air, luxuriating in what is surely the scholar's greatest joy, the pursuit of his interest combined with freedom from interruption.

Warm gratitude is also due to many other colleagues, students, and friends who have helped bring this book to completion. I wish to thank Professor Joshua Whatmough for introducing me years ago to the linguistic problems of Homer, and for his invaluable advice in my effort to deal with them. As always, too, I must thank Professor John Finley, no less for the unflagging creative interest he has shown in this study from the first, and the long conversations in which it was all talked out in advance, than for the acute and sympathetic reading which he gave it when it was done. His promptings and amendments are too numerous to mention, and his insight into ancient poetry set the key in which the work was originally planned. I owe much also to Professor A. M. Parry, both for his encouragement and for his substantive assistance in shaping a literary critique on the basis of the oral theory. Among more recent students, I must thank Drs. Kenneth Reckford and Anne Amory and Mr. Michael Putnam for their readings and criticisms of the manuscript, as well as Miss Anne Miller for help in proofreading and indexing. But it would be impossible to name all the students, graduate and undergraduate, who, during various curricula, have raised those significant points or asked those stimulating questions which make teaching such a productive occupation and, in the long run, a real help to scholarship.

It need scarcely be said that whatever perversities or mistakes remain in this book are in no way attributable to the people named, either above, or hereafter in the notes. Whoever formulates broadly upon the specific findings of others must take his own chances. It is the literary and critical part of this book which chiefly asks attention; the rest is framework, and the hope is that it is not too far wrong.

Some last words of thanks are in order: to my wife, Ruth, for her running stylistic criticism, chapter by chapter as the book was composed; to my two typists, Mrs. Ralph Matlaw and Mrs. Alfred Satterthwaite, who between them coerced an appalling longhand into legibility; and once more, to Harvard University, for a grant from the Clark Fund, whereby their exertions received reward. I am also very much indebted to the Department of the Classics, and especially the Chairman, Professor Eric A. Havelock, through whose kind offices I received a subsidy from the C. N. Jackson Fund for the preparation of the index. Finally, it is always a particular pleasure to acknowledge the beneficence of the Harvard University Press, its readers and editorial staff, as well as an unnamed outside reader, from all of whom I have had helpful suggestions; but above all, its Director, Mr. Thomas J. Wilson, whose warm personal interest has once more raised professional relations to the level of mutual creativity.

C. H. W.
Cambridge, Mass.
August, 1957

CONTENTS

The epic is the first flower — or one of the first, let us say — of a new symbolic mode, the mode of art. It is not merely a receptacle of old symbols, namely those of myth, but is itself a new symbolic form, great with possibilities, ready to take meanings and express ideas that have had no vehicle before.

Susanne Langer

I

THE MEANING OF UNITY

AFTER about twenty-five centuries, the *Iliad* and the *Odyssey* continue vigorous, both as landmarks and as question marks. Nothing is more certain than their artistic excellence and vitality, and few things outside the realm of theology have occasioned more controversy than the circumstances of their creation. It is unfortunate in the extreme that these two aspects of the poems, their triumphant art and their mysterious origin, have regularly been treated as two separate and unrelated studies: the literary critic has, as a rule, simply assumed, as did the ancients, the unity of authorship under the name of Homer, ignoring all controversy and devoting himself to interpretation, while the scholars who have squarely faced the so-called Homeric question have all too often been deficient in sensitivity to poetic processes and intention. The two approaches must be blended, for the two problems are really one. Manifestly, what is composed is the direct result of how and when it is composed; hence, literary criticism must make its peace with history, and the questions of date and authorship must look for solution not simply to logical or philological method, but also to real aesthetic responsiveness.

Happily, the smoke of battle between the "analyst" and "unitarian" schools has cleared away, and a new spirit of humility and careful research has succeeded the vituperations and positivism of the last century. In retrospect, it is not always easy to do justice to the efforts of those Homerists, by reason of both the quantity and the waywardness of their opinions. The unitarian, like every fundamentalist, tended to reject reason, and the analyst erred in overuse of it. If the analyst group was the more learned, on the whole, it was also the more deficient in literary feeling. For Wilamowitz, the *Iliad* as it stands was a "wretched patchwork." Deeply as one may deplore such a judgment, it is difficult to see how any better one could arise from the kind of rationalistic literary approach which the so-called Higher Criticism regularly employed. The fixed notion that repeated lines, or echoing phrases, offer evidence of tamperings and interpolations was simply out of place in dealing with Homer. More serious was the tacit assumption that poetry and prose have a similar logic, so that superficial failures of consistency in Homer could provide scientific criteria sufficient to prove the multiplicity — and the incompetence — of the compilers of the epics.

But Homer's work will never satisfy the many criteria, historical, philological, and linguistic, which the last century imposed on it. This is not to say that poetry may claim illimitable license in violating reason and consistency; it is to say that the unit of poetry is not idea, or fact, but image, and that where there is conflict, image must prevail. Poetry, conceived in image and executed through formal design, may reasonably ask to be analyzed in terms of its motivating forces and essential processes. Many of these, like speech itself, belong to the nonrational levels of human creativity, and some are almost wholly subconscious. Yet one need not indulge in deep psychological inquiry to perceive their results, for the terminus of every poetic process is the poetic image itself, in all its complex clarity. It is therefore in the logic of imagery, in the consistency of poetic conception, and in the formal structure that the unity or disunity of a poem must be sought. Analyzed from these points of view, Homer, far from disintegrating into a plethora of poetasters, reveals something of the stature which antiquity found in him. His formal structure shows a dazzling complexity, his imagery clusters into inevitable symbolic schemes of profoundest meaning, and above all, his basic and most central vision, the heroic self, imposes an ineradicable unity of ethos upon the whole design.

The unitarian position today rests upon a number of careful, specialized studies. It is no longer necessary to refute one by one the contentions of the old school, partly because in the long run the analysts, each with his own theoretical breakdown of the poems and perennially failing of agreement, argued the matter to rags, and eventually caused the whole method to die of its own ingenuity.[1] Yet a glance at the history of the Homeric Question is relevant, since, for all their final failure, the theories of Lachmann, Grote, Bethe, Fick, Kirchhoff, Wilamowitz, Leaf, and Murray, to name only a few great analysts, were the honest and perhaps necessary result of one of the greatest works of Homeric scholarship ever written, F. A. Wolf's *Prolegomena ad Homerum* of 1795.

Few books in modern times, least of all books written in Latin, can claim to have roused such intellectual turmoil or to have created such a widespread climate of opinion as this one. Though it is little read today, its conclusions are everywhere; the restless doubt which it occasioned about Homer's very existence still pervades the air to the extent that, until very recently, it was considered a token of simplicity to believe that Homer composed the Homeric poems. If the situation is changing at last, if scholars are again growing inclined to treat "Homer" as the name of a poet instead of a merely convenient short term for "all those who somehow composed and assembled Greek epic," Wolf nevertheless must still be honored as the founder, not merely of the school which disintegrated Homer into the work of many hands, but of all modern Homeric scholarship. We are still trying to answer Wolf's questions, and if our answers differ widely from his, they could scarcely be more regardful of available evidence; moreover, had he not asked these questions, we might still be conceiving Homer as the ancients did Orpheus, as a kind of demigod who one day arose, smote his lyre, and created literature.

The basic question was, "Could Homer write?" Wolf was the first to attempt a real reckoning with Homer's possible illiteracy, though the doubt had occurred before.[2] To answer that question in the negative at the end of the eighteenth century was only to draw a reasonable inference. No Greek inscriptions then known predated 700 B.C., and Homer was thought to be much older. If, therefore, Homer could not write, the *Iliad* and *Odyssey* were oral compositions, but of a length impossible even for the astonishing memories of antiquity; their episodes, or lays, must be the work of many bards, assembled later on in the age of Pisistratus, and worked into the two epics as we have them. The latter point was the weakest part of Wolf's theory, for the evidence about Pisistratean work on Homer is all late and self-contradictory, but in the face of the original question, it was the best recourse possible. Wolf hoped to develop the details of his thesis further in an edition of the epics but he died with the work unfinished, leaving only a book disturbing in the extreme, and for the time being irrefutable. Europe shuddered at the dethronement of the reverend figure of Homer, who had been to the eighteenth century a kind of creative "noble savage," a type of productive Nature herself. The pious turned their back on the whole matter, regarding Wolf as mere antichrist and his followers as iconoclasts. The more liberal minds took up the theory and were able to see that Nature, operating in mysterious folkways, could produce many original geniuses as easily as one. But on the purely scholarly level, the problem, in contrast to its many solutions, was a perfectly simple and clear one. Objectors to Wolf must prove either that writing was as old as Homer, or that the human memory could do incredible feats, and for the time neither course seemed possible. Hence, for over a century, scholars faced the problem bravely, trying to distinguish the layers of composition, the older from the younger, the work of "original" poets from that of compilers, interpolations of various ages, contradictions, anachronisms, and expurgations. By the time of Leaf's large edition of the *Iliad*, the chaos of Homeric scholarship made the Ptolemaic universe look simple. By creating an ever increasing confusion, the method had shown itself a failure, yet almost no one dared to return to a unitarian view. Indeed, in 1934, in the preface to the fourth edition of the *Rise of the Greek Epic*, Gilbert Murray wrote with some satisfaction that he could find "no unitarians left except Drerup."

It is ironical that Murray's preface also included a notice of the first monographs of Milman Parry, whose name marks the second great turning point in modern Homeric scholarship. Parry's achievement was to demonstrate what many had suspected or assumed, that Homer's poetic language is from beginning to end a traditional medium, a vast collection of formulae functionally designed to enable a singer to compose verses in his head, and thus narrate a traditional tale. In his two French theses, in his various articles, and above all in his great recorded collection of Serbian oral epics, only now being published by his colleague and continuator, A. B. Lord, Parry reverted directly to Wolf's original question, answered it anew, and outmoded with one lightning stroke a whole century of scholarship.[3] Homer did not have to write in order to compose the epics. The art of oral composition could be studied among the illiterate bards of Yugoslavia, and the inquiry proved the almost infinite possibilities of composition by formulae. Parry collected at least one poem of comparable length with the *Iliad*, and of considerable, if not quite comparable, quality.[4] The analogy was at hand, and it was no longer necessary to disintegrate the Greek epics into short songs in order to explain their creation in the absence of pen and ink. As Wolf had seen, the Muses were, in some literal sense, the daughters of Memory, but the ancient memory, aided by the formulae, was adequate to greater creative tasks than Wolf imagined.

Moreover, in the years between Wolf and Parry, many other changes, two of immediate relevance, had taken place in Homeric studies: the assumed date of Homer moved down from the eleventh or tenth century to the eighth, for reasons to be reviewed later, and the date of the introduction of writing was pushed up at least a century by the publication of the Attic Prize-Jug Inscription, the Hymettus *graffiti*, and other bits of early Greek script.[5] Hence it now appears that the Greek epic, oral though it is, belongs almost surely to a period when literacy existed. And indeed, the recent decipherment as Greek of the Minoan script called Linear B, characteristic of Cnossos, Mycenae, and Pylos, has even prompted the suggestion that the Greeks may well have preserved continual literacy from Mycenaean times.[6] The problem of Greek writing, however, affects in reality only the preservation of Homeric poetry, and not its creation. Despite attempts to disprove or modify it, Parry's thesis remains cogent, that the *Iliad* and the *Odyssey* are products of a purely oral technique of composition.[7]

The reaction of literary scholars at large to Parry's work has been that of people swallowing a bitter truth, rather than rejoicing in a revelation. As in the case of Wolf, Homer seemed again to have suffered a diminution of grandeur. Prejudice accounts for part of this mistaken feeling; but in part it is attributable to the fact that Parry himself never fully worked out his theory's implications for the literary criticism of the epics. Few Homerists have actually heard oral poets at work, and it is only human, perhaps, that men of a literate society tend to regard illiteracy in anyone, whatever the compensations, as an emblem of semibarbarism. To some, Homer's mastery appeared incompatible with illiteracy; hence the tendency to try to show that he must have used the writing which now appears to have been available to him. To others, and to some extent to Parry himself, the functionalism of the formulaic method seemed to bring Homeric art down to the level of the quasi-mechanical. One critic has even called Parry the "Darwin of Homeric studies." [8] The comparison is, in a way, apt, and possibly prophetic, though it might even better have been applied to Wolf: Darwin's threatening aspect has long since been absorbed in larger cultural vistas, and the oral theory of Homer will soon cease to appear at odds with his excellence. Oral poetry is neither primitive nor mechanical, nor does its traditional nature preclude the play of genius. Its methods may differ to a degree from those of written literature, and therefore Homer's greatness will not be found in imagined departures from oral technique, any more than Shakespeare's can be discovered by trying to envision those moments when he threw away his quill and chanted his verses aloud. A poet's native medium is his best artistic device. In seeking Homer's original genius, we must not seek the newly turned phrase, the nonformulaic line, or even the character who, we might somehow persuade ourselves, did not exist in previous tradition. It is not outside tradition that Homer has triumphed, but within it.

Yet Parry's theory raises certain real technical problems. He cannot be said to have demonstrated that unity of the Homeric poems in which he so fervently believed; indeed, it has been asserted that he demonstrated the precise opposite.[9] For when bards use the same traditional medium for many generations, how is it possible to distinguish the one from the many? Moreover, the songs collected in Yugoslavia for the most part approximate in length one book of Homer, rather than the whole of either epic. Under the conditions which Parry described, unity remained a large and seemingly groundless assumption.

An equally besetting problem centered, as already stated above, on the functionalism of the formula. Parry showed with great skill that the formulae of oral verse were, by Homer's time, metrically unique devices; that is, for a given idea and a given metrical space, one formula, and only one, was available.[10] Very few exceptions to this rule are observable, and such as exist are of little consequence. In a system of such stringent economy, therefore, it must follow that the poet has little choice about the phrases in which he must express his intention, and further, that to discover certain kinds of poetic meaning in Homer's phrases may be naive. For example, the famous formula "winged words," which recurs so frequently, was once explained as a poetically apt way of introducing animated speech. In a passage of withering analysis, Parry proved that the phrase never occurs in the same line with the name of the speaker, and that it is used only "when the character who is to speak has been the subject of the last verses, so that the use of his name in the line would be clumsy." [11]

The rebuke to poetic criticism is a real one. When one reflects that practically every phrase in Homer is formulaic, it becomes a question whether any should be criticized individually, or if so, in what sense. Parry himself suggested, as an artistic analogue, the formalized English poetry of the eighteenth century; [12] but a rereading of Homer soon lives down, by its sheer vigor and variety, any comparison with English Augustanism. "Winged words" is undoubtedly a functional formula, controlled by a compositional need; but its power is equally beyond denial, and its use is partly determined by the artist's wish to avoid clumsiness. As in contrapuntal music, the rules are strict, but they cannot compose the fugue by themselves. A phrase preserves freshness by its inevitability in the scheme, and "winged words" remain fresh; the expression does not, as Parry felt, lose all imagistic force because of its frequency and functional necessity. "Wingless words" also occur in Homer, denoting speech which strikes the hearer as odd or incomprehensible,[13] and the winged ones likewise do some poetic as well as metrical service.

Yet such problems make it impossible to approach the Homeric poems as one would approach the written text of any other author, especially if one is to deal with the details of language and imagery; and there are other matters too which affect literary criticism. In recent years it has become more and more clear that the full study of Homer is not the private preserve of the philologist. In place of the last century's detailed but narrow analysis of the text, the twentieth century has, characteristically, subdivided the Homeric problem among experts in various disciplines, of which the study of oral poetry is only one. Studies in the history and prehistory of the whole eastern Mediterranean, cultural and physical anthropology, comparative religion, comparative folklore, topography, papyrology, and above all, archaeology and linguistics have made enormous contributions to our knowledge of the times and circumstances of the Greek epic development. For the critic, the Homeric question, like so many other intellectual problems of modernity, consists in trying to extract not a conclusion, but a justifiable attitude, an honest approach, from the detailed findings of specialized researches, with all their doubts, reservations, and scientific suspension of judgment. To discover and clarify a poetic intention is to recreate synoptically a mind and a milieu; for Homer, the materials for such recreation lie far and wide.

Since Schliemann, Homeric archaeology has moved from the stage of providing realistic illustrations for the poems, and has gone far toward framing a sound chronology and cultural picture of Greece from the earliest times to the beginning of history in the Geometric Age, so-called from the characteristic ornamentation of the pottery of the eighth and ninth centuries B.C. The study of skeletal remains has thrown much light on the ethnic constituency of the prehistoric period. The history of art, particularly of vase-painting, has revealed the continuity and development of these early cultural epochs, while actual documents, such as the Tell el 'Amarna letters and the Boghaz-Keui tablets, have given a place, albeit sometimes a vague one, to many of the names and sites of Homer's world. Linguistic researches in the language of Homer multiply steadily, uncovering the meanings of obscure old words, throwing new light on metrical problems, and slowly unraveling the dialectal constituents of that unique artificial composite, the epic language. Most recently, the decipherment of the Linear B script of Cnossos has proved beyond doubt at last that the Mycenaean civilization was Greek and literate, that many of Homer's names and archaic forms are true epic survivals from the heroic age, and that this Mycenaean Greek, with its affinity with both the Arcado-Cypriote and Aeolic dialectal groups, was the language of the earliest songs about Troy and Argos, centuries before Homer.[14]

More knowledge is undoubtedly to come from these linguistic studies, and their efforts must be correlated with those of the theorists of oral poetry, and of editors of the Homeric text. It is known, for instance, that the Alexandrine scholars sometimes inserted particles in Homer to solve what seemed to be metrical lapses. Many of these "lapses," however, are now to be explained, at least with a degree of certitude, by the laryngeal theory, which can frequently account for apparent metrical lengthenings by the effect on the vowel system of old laryngeal consonants, lost in the Greek known to us. Parry, on the other hand, accounted for many of these irregularities by what he called the "play of formulae," a necessary function in oral composition, where the singer, in adapting a given formula to a new grammatical construction, must alter it a little in the inflectional ending, and sometimes thus commit a metrical breach. Certainly the play of formulae is an inevitable part of bardic practice, but its scope is perhaps to be defined more narrowly than Parry defined it, and possibly within limits perceptible through the laryngeal theory, No definitive study exists, as yet, of the relation between the lost laryngeal consonants and Homeric "metrical lengthening," but this problem and others related to it are pointing to a reassessment of Homeric textual problems as other than merely palaeographical, and putting a new demand on editors.[15]

To attempt to coordinate all these studies is no doubt premature, since investigations are still in progress and in many cases have given rise more to doubt than to clarity. But thinking proceeds in stages, and a justifiable literary approach to Homer cannot be based any longer on a single classical discipline. The world of Homer lies in many fragments, and will probably not be assembled perfectly for a long time. But it may not be too soon to see if some of the pieces fit, and, if they do, what may be the implications for criticism.

In the years since 1934, when Murray could find "no unitarians left except Drerup," there has been, in America at least, a consider-

able increase in the ranks of unitarianism. It has been called a change
in fashion, but it is more like a confession of renewed uncertainty,
after the failure of the last century's methods to produce a clear
doctrine. It marks a resurgence of literary intuition about two
highly polished works of art, in which flaws of consistency and
relevance, by which the activity of many hands might be detected,
are hard to find and impossible to prove. Large epics, the product
of literary agglutination from many sources, do exist, the *Maha-
bharata*, for instance; but the latter's fame rests upon its parts, the
tale of Nala and Damayanti, or the *Bhagavad-Gita*. The *Kalevala*
is equally an artificial assemblage, made in the nineteenth century,
of early oral Finnish poetry, and Dr. Lönnrot, who made it, showed
remarkable skill in the arrangement of the cantos which he col-
lected. But these works are nothing like Homer, whose poems,
traditional as they are, exhibit a structural unity and finesse com-
parable only to the most sophisticated and carefully devised works
of literature.

The argument from design has always been the Homeric uni-
tarian's chief recourse, and it is likely to remain so. Opponents
may deny it as overworked and even overimaginative, but it is more
probable that it has not been sufficiently exploited. The secret of
Homeric structure, of the *Iliad* at least, lies, as we shall see, in the
adjustment of oral technique to the psychology underlying the
Geometric symmetry of the late eighth century B.C. Its units are
the typological scenes and motifs which are the stock in trade of
oral poets, and Homer's finished design is far too authoritative to
suffer seriously from the small logical inconsistencies which have
sometimes been so fiercely denounced.

Logical inconsistencies in Homer fall into two classes, real and
imagined. To take an example of the latter first, it has been said
that the season shifts irresponsibly between winter and spring in
the later books of the *Odyssey*, but this is untrue.[16] Anyone who
has traveled in Greece may *feel* that it is early spring, but Homer
does not say what season it is, nor did he probably care. The sea-
sons, so dear to Hesiod's regulative scheme of the world, play only
a decorative part in Homer's similes, and never contribute even to
the backdrop of his primary action. In what season of the year does
the *Iliad* take place? Rationalism could excogitate a theory, but

Homer might look blank. Yet there are real logical impossibilities which raise the question of whether poetry is more concerned with fact or with fiction. In *Iliad* V, Sarpedon is badly wounded by Tlepolemus and carried off the field; only four days later he is back, not even convalescent, leading the Lycians in the assault on the Greek wall.[17] His wound is ignored or forgotten, in defiance of the facts of physiology; but is the fight between Sarpedon and Tlepolemus, therefore, a later insertion? [18] If so, then so must be the whole of the *Diomedeia*, and with it Books III–VII in general, for this whole section, as is well known, does not advance the action of the *Iliad* at all, and no more than the Sarpedon episode is any of it on the same time-level as the rest of the poem. It is all a tableau of traditional episodes, appropriately introduced by the panoramic Book II, where the lens widens to include more than the principal actors. Tradition had it that Sarpedon once lost to Tlepolemus of Rhodes, but survived and fought later. In compressing his material to fit his scheme, Homer had to leave out the time necessary for Sarpedon's recovery. He easily might have had a god produce a miraculous cure, but he did not bother, perhaps because all military operations of Books III–VII are singularly inconsequential, for all their sound and fury. Part of the meaning of these books, as will be shown later, lies precisely in their lack of sequential time and action; but their presence is indispensable both to the structure of the whole poem and to its conception of the characters.

The Sarpedon-Tlepolemus duel has been called an interpolation, on the further grounds that Tlepolemus is a Dorian (which, incidentally, he is not), whereas Dorians have no genuine part in Homer, and that the fight reflects conflict between Lycia and the Dorian colonists of Rhodes in the Dark Age after the Trojan War and the fall of Mycenae. If it actually does, then of course the duel belongs to a later layer of tradition than do episodes which can be properly placed in the Mycenaean Age. It does not, however, belong to a later layer of the *Iliad*, for Homer, who lived after both the Mycenaean and Dark Ages, could commit anachronism as well as any poet, and pluck his material from every tree in the garden of tradition. The particular point may be trivial, for the *Iliad* would not suffer gravely if this brief episode were expunged; but it illustrates a major question which has never been either posed or answered clearly. With what is the *Iliad* to be identified? Those who cast out "interpolations" make one of several tacit assumptions, either that it is to be identified with its oldest traditional material, or with the story of Achilles, or with a particular dialect, or with a conception of Zeus, or somebody else, which appears in one book and not in others; sometimes many of these assumptions are combined into an elaborate theory corresponding to nothing except its maker's preferential guesswork. All such attitudes attempt to impose a modern ideational unity upon the poem, at the expense sometimes of over half of it — a kind of unity which in fact no traditional poem ever could have. If, as is now generally believed, Homer came at the end of the long period of epic development, clearly he could retell anything that had gone before, altering to his purpose or not, as he chose. History and chronology would trouble him very little, for his concern would lie elsewhere. His poem, that is, the *Iliad* that we know, is not to be identified therefore with older or younger segments of the heroic tradition. Nor does he seem to have bent much effort toward making theologically consistent pictures of the Olympians; that was Hesiod's task. With character Homer was concerned, and here one may find the traces of a master hand, cultivating out of traditional soil something unique and new. For the rest, the *Iliad* is to be identified with its own inner unity of structure, textural or imagistic consistency, and the power and finesse of its deployment of formulaic speech. If one looks without prejudice at the *Iliad* for a unity possible to an oral poet, appropriate to a work of such dimensions, and comprehensible to the people of the eighth century B.C., such a unity can and does reveal itself. But one must cease expecting Homer to satisfy the standards of historical science, or even of certain kinds of rational logic; self-existence, not literal consistency, is the aim of poetry, and Homer lived four hundred years before logic of any kind was expounded.

The task therefore is to discover the intuitive, poetic logic of the *Iliad*, the cohesiveness which has given it its force as art for so many centuries. In the material which it uses, there is little inevitable unity; tradition is a farrago, and even the main thread itself, Achilles' wrath, need not by nature have been anything more than an episode. At least, it could have been treated as such, and probably had been by Homer's predecessors. When one asks what originality can belong to a poet whose subject matter and language are traditional common property, the answer must lie in conception and artistic method, or nowhere. Certain difficulties obviously bar the way: Homer's work is the oldest monument of Western literature, and beyond modern oral analogues in Greece, Yugoslavia, and elsewhere, we have little with which to compare it. Moreover, Homer's mind is the archaic mind, prephilosophic, primarily synthetic rather than analytical, whose content is myths, symbols, and paradigms.[19] It is not a primitive mind, however, for the archaic, preconceptual way of thinking has a maturity of its own, fully as valid as later modes, and, to judge from Homer, perhaps more valid. In any case, such mentality is a more fruitful source for poetry than the mind trained to logical and philosophical analysis, for its meanings cluster iridescently around nuclear images, with the complexity, and explosive power, of high-valence atoms. It is the function of poetry to compress meaning, where prose expatiates upon it, and the *Iliad* seems like a brief poem in the light of its meaning. Tolstoy, deeply impressed with it, and avowedly imitating it, spun *War and Peace* to infinitely greater length in prose. It is not always easy to trace the involuted and interwoven meanings — if indeed, they should even be called meanings — of ancient poetic symbols. Jungian analysis finds their significance in the "collective unconscious" of humanity, or of a culture, at large; but this is too general for our purpose. We are not in pursuit of a primeval archetype, but of the specific intentions of a specific poem. Our object is not the collective significance of myth, though this may play a part. Our object is Homer's meaning in using such material.

In the absence of other data, a poet's intention in his work identifies him. If the analyst school of higher criticism wrought confusion by trying to find "Homer" in certain parts of the epics and not in others, the theorists of oral composition have yet to distinguish him from the traditional medium in which he worked. To Parry, this distinction was essentially unnecessary: the man and the style were one, and Homer could have differed from his fellow bards only in a more developed skill at singing. Yet there seems to be more that should be said. Among the modern oral epics collected so far, only one compares with Homeric epic in size, and in power and subtlety, none. Some fine poems exist, but the *Iliad* and the

Odyssey are wonders of the poetic world. To say that Homer was merely a more skillful singer than the lost bards of antiquity seems to do little justice to the uniqueness which must have contributed to his preservation. It seems to be at least worthwhile to inquire into why and how Homer was more skillful, and to ask if possibly he conceived his work in terms hitherto unknown to the tradition and medium of his trade. Such questions may seem to be easy to ask and impossible to answer, since none of Homer's contemporaries left their work where we could find it. Yet, with the modern oral analogues to help, and with Homer's text before us, it is possible to see a little into the problem: it is possible, for instance, to see that in Homer, the formulae, stock lines, repeated passages, and traditional motifs have surpassed their own functionalism in the service of a vast controlling design; that repetitions are not mechanical, or even merely incantational, but architectonic; that imagery, action, and character form one unified poetic substance, molded around a vision of heroism which can scarcely, in its inimitable singularity, be anything but a personal and individual one. In these, and in similar aspects of his creativity, the poet of a traditional medium can, and must, reveal himself.

There is no evidence at all that the poet of the *Iliad* invented a single character or episode in his whole poem. He may not even have invented a single phrase. His invention was the *Iliad*. Parts of it he may have inserted verbatim from earlier poems which he had heard, and learned to sing himself, but if he did so, the power of the total *Iliad* bids one think that he did so advisedly, and not from poverty of inspiration. If there is one thing evident in the *Iliad*, it is the self-conscious control of a mature artist at the height of his power, disposing and concentrating to his purpose the chaotic funds of material in his mind. Nor should the formulaic nature of his language be a bar to seeing his creative originality. All speech is to an extent formulaic, and syntax itself is a formula of intelligibility. As is well known, the number of narrative plots is limited, and hence stories themselves are formulae, in the last analysis, mere frameworks for meaning, and often very inadequate ones. Homer's formulae differ only a little from the means which any artist must use, if he uses language; the units of narrative art are at best serviceable, at worst recalcitrant, to the meaning which the creator intends. The poet's task is, and always has been, to transform the serviceable into the symbolic, and for this purpose Homer's medium is no more restrictive than any other. In fact, as will be seen, it has distinct advantages.

Epic poems, by and large, suffer from a strong proclivity to end their days as exhibits in unvisited museums. To Poe, epic was "the art of being dull in verse." The exact opposite is true of the *Iliad* and the *Odyssey*, which, for all their antiquity, remain not only the most popular epics, but also among the most popular books, in Western literature. Though Homer can never, because of the formulae, be translated with real success, his power even in translation continues to find its way into receptive minds. The reason for this cannot lie in his simple-hearted adherence to an epic tradition whose original purpose was to glorify the deeds of a patron, or a patron's remote ancestor. Homer does record many deeds, of course, but it is a grave question to what extent he glorifies most of them. At a close reading, he appears to be more interested in examining them. Glory and praise by tradition abound in his pages, but the sum of those pages presents a view of action and the world somewhat broader and keener, to say the least, than the primitive warrior's guileless concern with his own magnificence. The stories of the two epics are of no import here. There is, in one sense, no such thing as a good story; there are only serviceable stories, from which meaning can be built. The basic story of the *Odyssey*, a highly serviceable one, recurs in countless folktales, all shorter and easier to read than Homer. The basic story of the *Iliad* seems not even very serviceable, for it has few parallels anywhere. Especially in the latter case, Homer's work is all, the transformation of the serviceable into the symbolic. To probe his intention requires first to find his symbols and discover how they become such; and this search will in no way resemble the antiquarian study of a fossil. It is the analysis of poetry whose vitality and effectiveness cannot with rationality be called into question.

To the ancient Greeks, Homer enjoyed a reputation as something between Holy Writ and an encyclopedia of universal knowledge; his art was deeply felt, but never analyzed, and the earliest critical approach, in the fifth and fourth centuries, was confined to solving naive questions of literal consistency, somewhat after the manner of Biblical Fundamentalism. Neither the textual work of the Alexandrines, nor the allegorizing interpretations of the Stoic school of Pergamon approached anything like a real poetic theory. Only the scattered remarks of the author of the treatise *On the Sublime* give any inkling of the artistic response in antiquity. Modern criticism has combed the epics with every kind of research, but literary studies have often suffered either from too great subjectivity, or from partiality toward certain famous scenes. This has been especially true of the *Iliad*, where the books dealing with Achilles, together with the favorite scene of all time, Hector and Andromache, are often selected for commentary while the rest of the poem is treated as mere plot-narrative, necessary for the continuity, but a little primitive, a little dull, and not quite worth critical treatment. Yet the *Iliad* is a far more closely knit work than the *Odyssey*, and suffers abridgment far less well. The seldom praised but magnificent battle which fills its central books is a triumph in the union of imagery and action; as a picture of war's terror and tragedy, it is unmatched in dramatic, emotive detail and epic objectivity. The *Catalog of Ships*, a ringing invocation to the mountains, valleys, and islands of Greece, is generally omitted by all save those who would solve the mysteries of its confused political geography. Books XX and XXI, generally thought fairly dispensable, contain a climax without which the *Iliad* could not be, as it is, a concentrated and dramatic mounting of the Trojan War entire, around the single incident of Achilles' wrath.

Aesthetic analysis reveals in the *Iliad* not merely unity of conception, but a unity everywhere articulated in the most minute details with perfected formal mastery of a crystallized traditional medium. And yet, as was said above, no framework of literary criticism can stand without some historical footing. It is of infinite importance to the understanding of Homer's intention to know whether his works took the form they now possess in the age of Pisistratus or two centuries earlier. It is equally indispensable to know whether the short text of Zenodotus or the canonical vulgate is more correct. The question of the epic's survival during the Dark Age will be found to be relevant to the whole matter of the cultural milieu of the poems. The attempt to formulate historically these periods admittedly involves hypothesis. But it may be long before any means other than hypothesis is at hand; meanwhile some probabilities and possibilities await exploration.

THE MEMORY OF THE ACHAEANS

IT was the common claim of ancient poetry, especially of epic, that great deeds, if unsung, perished from the mind. Yet, wherever it is possible to compare the events of an epic with their actual history, one sees that what is preserved in poetry bears only a special, sometimes slight, relation to fact, while it is quite normal for the places, dates, and even the characters of a recorded event to be magniloquently confused and distorted.[1] Sometimes, as in the case of court poetry, the motive for such distortion is the familiar one of flattery; but where much time has intervened between the facts and the poem, other motives must be sought, even beyond the mere fading of exact recollections. The function of the Daughters of Memory was to keep images before the minds of their hearers, images which often, even regularly, contained a larger proportion of wish and aspiration than of historical accuracy. History in a way supplants memory, at least the sort of memory possessed by the early archaic mind, which refabricates all experience into myth. Mnemosyne, the goddess of memory, was in actuality the goddess of myth, not of record; and if the Greeks regarded the *Iliad* and the *Odyssey* as true, one need not imagine that they regarded them as historically true. The concept of historical truth came late to the Greeks, and when it came, as the strictures of Thucydides show, it involved a critique of much hitherto accepted tradition. But until history was born, the truth which the Greeks found in their epics was that which lies in a myth's reenactment of the spiritual allegiances of a people. In such a process, little importance attaches to the factuality of events; in the context of myth, the only real fact is an action which, true or fictive, is inseparable from the moral and psychic meaning given it by the consensus of a living culture.

It may appear irrelevant to inquire, therefore, after such historical truth as may underlie the *Iliad* and the *Odyssey*. Yet the relation of a poet to his raw material offers evidence for the poetic process itself. In Homer's case, the first step toward understanding the poet is to understand as far as possible the history of his medium. Heroic oral poetry is not merely dependent on myth; even more, perhaps, it creates myth, and it is a question whether the figures and events which confront us in the epics possessed such a degree of archetypal stature before they had passed through the filters of a long bardic tradition, to arrive at last in the consummate hands of Homer. In subject matter and language it is seldom, if ever, possible to distinguish Homer from the tradition; but one may compare the tradition with history, as far as it is known for these remote periods, and thus observe, to a degree, myth in the making. This is not to say, of course, that myth is merely a poetic treatment of history. Myth may exist without any history at all; but the strong historical threads which run through the fabric of Greek folk-memory give it a peculiar concreteness, which doubtless accounts in part for the immediacy of Greek epic, that feeling of fact and veracity which led Schliemann, for instance, to search with almost evangelical conviction for the actualities of Troy and Mycenae.

Four centuries or more separate Homer from the dramatic date of his poems, which falls in the early part of the twelfth century B.C., in the last phase of the Mycenaean or Late Helladic Age. His tradition, however, embraces recollections reaching back much farther, a fact which suggests that the minstrels, or *aoidoi*, practiced an art nearly as old as the Greek language itself. The latter made its appearance in the Greek peninsula shortly after 2000 B.C., when a decisive archaeological break introduces the Middle Helladic, or "Minyan," phase of Greek prehistory.[2] These Middle Helladic people seem to have been warlike, for they destroyed the Early

CHRONOLOGY
(all dates approximate)

B.C. 3000   Early Helladic Period

2000–1800   Middle Helladic Invasion; first arrival of Greek speakers, cist grave burials, "Minyan" pottery (Gray Ware)

1800–1600   Middle Helladic Period

1600–1500   Late Helladic I; beginning of Minoan influence on the Greek mainland; shaft graves at Mycenae

1500–1400   Late Helladic II; Greek domination of Cnossos; "Palace" period in Crete; tholos tombs at Mycenae; Linear B

1400–1300   Late Helladic III A; destruction of Cnossos (1400); Mycenaean colonies in Rhodes and Cyprus; tholos tombs

1300–1200   Late Helladic III B; abridgment of Mycenaean trade; new fortifications at Mycenae and elsewhere; last tholos tombs; latest Linear B tablets (ca. 1200)

1200–1100   Late Helladic III C; "Granary" style pottery; fall of Troy VII A (1184); fall of Mycenae (ca. 1100, or slightly earlier)

1100–1000   Dorian Invasion introduces Iron Age; sub-Mycenaean pottery; historical distribution of dialects begins to take shape; refugeeism in Attica

1000–900   Protogeometric Period, centering in Attica; cremation burials; beginnings of colonization in Asia Minor and islands

900–700   Geometric Period; Homer (fl. ca. 725 ?); Dipylon Ware, 750–700

700–600   Proto-Attic and proto-Corinthian styles introduce the Archaic period in Greek art

Helladic sites systematically, and their culture, a highly unified one, brought sundry innovations. They practiced individual burial in stone cist graves, built houses around a central hall, or megaron, with a free-standing hearth, and at Tiryns and Mycenae, both of which had been occupied in Early Helladic times, they built the first fortifications. But the most marked feature of their culture was a distinctive kind of pottery, known as Minyan Ware, chiefly gray, though later yellow, red, and black forms of it appear as local varieties. Not until the Dorian, or West Greek, invasion, almost a thousand years later, does another such clear break occur; hence it is assumed that the Middle Helladic people brought the first Greek. They were not yet, of course, precisely Greeks, since that name is historically proper only to the composite people which resulted from the mixture of these Middle Helladic invaders with the Mediterranean population which had occupied various parts of the peninsula during the preceding centuries. They were, however, Indo-Europeans, and they came from the north, probably as part of a broader southward movement which carried Indo-European speech also into Asia Minor.[2a] After three or four centuries, when the old and new populations had intermingled, one may recognize in the Late Bronze Age the first genuinely Greek civilization in Greece. It begins about 1600 B.C., or a little later, with its center at Mycenae, and continues until the fall of the city, toward 1100. Its first two phases, late Helladic I and II, correspond roughly to the first two centuries of its duration, while the Late Helladic III phase, in which the city of Mycenae apparently exercised imperial scope and power, embraces the last two-and-a-half or three centuries. The characteristics of the period are well known, and though the two do not always agree in detail, both Homer and archaeology testify to the abundance and splendor of the Mycenaean Age, with its feudal organization, its bronze and gold, its chariot warfare, its megalithic fortresses and tombs, its vast trade protected by sea power, and not least, its refinements on the art of living, derived in great part from Minoan Crete.

Whereas many scholars had assumed that the Mycenaean civilization was Greek-speaking, there was no actual proof until recently, and opinion remained divided between those who saw in the Mycenaeans the early Greeks, whom Homer calls chiefly Achaeans, and those who believed that the Mycenaean world was a colony or outpost of the great, and clearly prior, Minoan culture brought to light by Sir Arthur Evans in Crete. The latter group even believed that both the rulers and the dominant language of Mycenae were in fact Cretan. The discovery at Pylos in 1939 of hundreds of clay tablets inscribed with the Minoan Linear script of Cnossos (Linear B) seemed at first to yield further evidence that the "Minoan" theory was correct; and if so, that Homer's tradition must either be translated, somehow, or else have nothing at all to do with the Mycenaean culture. But in 1953, with the decipherment of this Linear B as Greek by the late Michael Ventris, all doubt was removed, and while many difficult problems remain, two important historical points can be established: first, that Homer's Achaeans were indeed the Mycenaeans, whose language, still traceable in the epics, survived partially in the later dialects of Cyprus, Arcadia, and Pamphylia;[3] and second, that the last century or so of Minoan culture in Cnossos, from about the year 1500 or so to 1400, was dominated by these same Achaeans.[4] This fact also had been suspected previously; the masonry, for one thing, of the second palace at Cnossos recalls the rudeness of Mycenae rather than the refined ashlar of the Middle Minoan palace, and there are other resemblances as well.[5] The earlier palace at Cnossos, which fell by earthquake in the first half of the sixteenth century, is associated with the still-undeciphered Linear A script characteristic of Crete in general, and presumably the language of the Minoans. By 1450, this script and language had been replaced at Cnossos by Linear B, which is simply an adaptation of Linear A to the needs of writing Greek. Sometime between these two dates, the Mycenaeans had gained possession of Cnossos, and inherited the so-called thalassocracy of Minos. At this time also, Phaestos, Gournia, and Palaikastro in Crete were sacked, Cretan exports disappeared from foreign markets, while Mycenae attained her widest commercial expansion.[6] There can be little doubt that Greek epic tradition has its roots in history, when it recognizes a Minos II of Crete, an Achaean king, son of Zeus, whose grandson Idomeneus leads the Cretan contingent to Troy, and in the *Iliad* slays a man named Phaestos.[7]

The sack of this Greek-dominated Cnossos in 1400 remains something of a mystery. Despite attempts to exculpate Mycenae herself of the charge, she remains the most likely candidate. Egypt and the Hittites, the only other powers considerable enough, offer no records of such a campaign; both were temporarily confined by pressures from Mitanni, and the Hittites in any case were not a sea power. Pirates seem to be excluded by the tradition that Minos had swept the sea of pirates. A recrudescence of Minoan power on the island might be the answer; yet if this were true, it is surprising that so little sign of it continues after the fall of Cnossos, that the palace was not rebuilt, that the site was scarcely reoccupied, and that there was no return of the Linear A language. Linear B also disappears, to continue for two more centuries on the mainland.[8] If it was Mycenae that destroyed Cnossos, this would have been perhaps the first of those fratricidal struggles which seem to have brought about the decline of the Achaean world.[9]

Besides clarifying the question of Mycenae's relations with Crete, the decipherment of Linear B, by providing knowledge of Mycenaean Greek, has thrown light also on the linguistic constituency of Homer's tradition, and hence on the whole development of the Greek dialects. Homer's language, as is well known, is an artificial mixture of dialects, peculiar to epic poetry and corresponding to no spoken form of Greek. Linear B, on the other hand, no matter the provenience, records an apparently unified dialect, akin to Arcado-Cypriote and undoubtedly its ancestor. From these two facts it may be possible to frame some likelihoods about the formation of the Greek dialects, and the circumstances of their mixture in the language of the bards.

It is usually assumed that the Middle Helladic invaders around 2000 brought with them one of the three great subdivisions of East Greek: Ionic, Aeolic, or Arcado-Cypriote (Achaean). Ionic is the favorite candidate.[10] On the other hand, there have been those who favored Aeolic, and took refuge in the statement by Herodotus that the Ionians were not originally Greeks at all, but "Pelasgians," meaning presumably in this case the Early Helladic people.[11] The problem centers around the positing of three dialectical waves, with only one archaeological break by which to explain them. But Middle Helladic culture is singularly unified, and there is little reason to assume that it represents one dialect of Greek more than another. Indeed, especial difficulty lies in identifying it with Aeolic; for then the non-Greek Ionian predecessors would have had to learn their Greek from these Aeolians, and it becomes necessary to explain the Ionic dialect as a derivation of Aeolic, which it cannot possibly be. On the other hand, if Ionic and the Middle Helladic Gray Ware culture are one, then Aeolic is the derivative speech, which is equally unlikely, and meanwhile the Achaean dialect remains unaccounted for. It seems impossible therefore to equate the Middle Helladic stratum with any one dialect; it must represent all three somehow, and most likely it represents the ancestor of all three, namely Old East Greek at a predialectal stage. There is, in fact, no reason to assume that the historic dialects of Greece had formed themselves by the early centuries of the second millennium, while there is every reason to attribute this formation to the geographic regionalism of the peninsula of Greece itself. This way too, be it noted, lies the only possibility of finding truth in the statement of Herodotus about the Ionians. If they were not speakers of Greek to begin with, they would have to have learned their Greek not from such a dialect as Aeolic, but from a source more close to the mother tongue.

It was said earlier that the language of Linear B resembles Arcado-Cypriote and is probably its ancestor. It should be added, however, that it seems to be fully as closely related to Aeolic.[12] If that is the case, the strong likelihood arises that the venerable tongue of the tablets is not the ancestor of one Greek dialect, but of all the East Greek dialects, including Ionic. If no traces of the latter occur, the answer may be one of two: either Ionic dialect may not have been distinctively formed in the period of the tablets (1450–1200, roughly), or else, the extreme limitations of the Minoan syllabary in expressing Greek sounds make dialectal distinctions, if existent, hard or even impossible to detect.[13] But in general, both archaeology and linguistics point not to three dialectal waves, but one, which might be called properly and simply Old East Greek, the language which survives basically in Linear B, and was only later diversified into dialects.

On the other hand, Homer himself gives evidence that the dialects are, in some form, as old as the Bronze Age. Epic language offers formulae involving Aeolic, Ionic, and Arcado-Cypriote elements, and a great many of them must be old, for heroic tales are born

soon after the events which they celebrate. It seems necessary, there-
fore, to assume that, at least by the last phases of the Late Helladic
period, some dialectal differences, though not as yet detectable in
Linear B, were sufficiently marked so that they showed in oral
verse, and that the Bronze Age minstrels in various places sang their
songs in their own individual dialects, formulaic fragments of
which were sometimes borrowed and adapted — a process which
must have increased greatly in the Dark Age after the fall of
Mycenae. The dialects of the Bronze Age would not, of course,
have achieved their familiar historical forms, and precisely how
they were distributed is not wholly certain. But the probability is
that the Mycenaean Age marks the beginning of Greek dialectal
formation.

Legend and history contribute a few more details to the ethnic
and linguistic picture of the Mycenaean world. The Ionians, for in-
stance, seem to have enjoyed a wider sphere in the Bronze Age
than later. Herodotus and others record their presence in the Pelo-
ponnesus,[14] and there is also a curious tradition about an earlier
Athens and Eleusis in Boeotia, which sank beneath the waters of
the Copaic Lake.[15] Modern drainage of the lake has not revealed
these sites, but it is by no means unlikely that the Ionians may once
have occupied Boeotia, before being pushed into sterile Attica.

When they were forced thither and by whom is unknown, but if
the name Ionian in this early period really does indicate, as Herod-
otus suggests, the Early Helladic people, then one must attribute
their displacement to the arrival of the Middle Helladic wave
shortly after 2000. If, on the other hand, the Ionians formed part
of the latter invasion, they must have been slowly compressed into
a narrower sphere by their more warlike compatriots who later
occupied Boeotia and Thessaly, and called themselves Aeolians.
There is something to be said for the former alternative, in view of
the Athenians' claim to being autochthonous on the soil of Greece;
but the fact that the Middle Helladic pottery of Athens is undiffer-
entiated from other Minyan Ware makes it more likely that the
Ionians — if, indeed, the name even existed so early — came with
the other Greek-speakers.

As for the Aeolians, they may be properly identified with the
mythological families descended ultimately from Aeolus, Hellen,

and Deucalion, in all probability. Tradition associates them not only
with Boeotia and Thessaly, but also with Messenia, for Nestor, king
of Pylos, is of Aeolic ancestry.[16] They seem also to have been in
Phocis, Locris, Aetolia, and even Corinth.[17] Central and North
Central Greece, therefore, and in some sense Messenia, would have
been ethnically, perhaps also dialectally, Aeolic by Late Helladic
times, while the northern Peloponnesus, the Isthmus, and Attica
would be Ionic. Of the other parts of Greece which show monu-

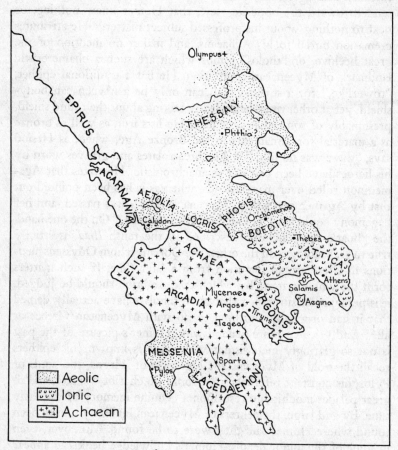

Probable Distribution of Dialects in the Mycenaean Age

ments from the Bronze Age, Argolis, Elis, Arcadia, and Lacedae-mon remain, and here, presumably, was the home of those Myce-naeans whose language, sometimes called Achaean, became in his-toric times Arcado-Cypriote, and was confined, after the fall of Mycenae, to Arcadia and colonies overseas.

Homer's actual knowledge of the Mycenaean world has been estimated variously, to say the least. To Schliemann, every word was scientifically correct, and archaeology sometimes had to be tortured into agreement with it. More recent archaeologists have tended toward the opposite view, that Homer knew nothing, or next to nothing, about his professed subject matter.[18] He attributes cremation burial to his Achaeans, and makes no mention of the great beehive, or "tholos" tombs which are such a characteristic landmark of Mycenaean civilization. He has a traditional epithet, "towerlike," for a shield which can only be a Mycenaean body-shield; yet at other times he is clearly talking about the round shield, presumably of somewhat later date. He lists iron as well as bronze as a material for armaments in the Bronze Age, when, as Hesiod says, "there was no iron." [19] The breastplates and greaves worn by his heroes have been cast out as anachronistic. He states that Aga-memnon ruled over many islands, whereas it has been pointed out that by Agamemnon's time, Mycenae's zenith was passed, and her hegemony could have included very few islands.[20] On the one hand, the "boar's tusk" helmet, described in the tenth *Iliad*, is strictly true to archaeology; on the other, the Dorians whom Odysseus men-tions in Crete are an intrusion from a later time. If such matters form the whole criteria by which epic tradition should be judged, it is perhaps not surprising that some scholars have actually denied that it had originally anything to do with Mycenaean Greece at all.[21] And yet, in a more general way, Homer's picture of the past is not so glaringly inconsistent with what is known: his epithets recall the gold of Mycenae, the big walls of Tiryns, the sands of Pylos; his constant references to bronze, to chariot warfare, and to great palaces indubitably rest upon a genuine memory of the early time. By and large, the centers of Mycenaean civilization have been found where Homer said they were to be found. Moreover, even in some of the minor details, Homer's knowledge begins to appear more accurate than was once thought. Iron, for instance, was not totally unknown in the Late Mycenaean period.[22] The round shield appears on the Warrior Vase from Mycenae, and the famous breast-plate question, which once prompted the excision from Homer of all lines referring to such body-armor, was suddenly settled of late when descriptions of breastplates together with the word "thorax" were read in Linear B inscriptions.[23] It further appears, from the same invaluable source, that the Olympian gods, including the so-called latecomer Dionysus, were the gods of the Mycenaeans, and that many a Homeric personal name, such as Achilles, is entirely historical.[24]

These points illustrate to the full the tenacity of oral poetry to its cultural origins; a bard's formula was an excellent preservative for many of the little details of a vanished civilization. Where it was not so infallible was in chronology: cremation, in Greece proper at least, appears only in Protogeometric times, about the tenth century, and the presumptive date for Agamemnon may indeed be too late for him to have inherited the fullness of Mycenaean sway over "all Argos and many islands." The bards did not hesitate to conflate times and stories, and Homer's materials come from any and all periods which precede him, some being of Mycenaean, or earlier origin, some from the Dark Age after the fall of Mycenae, and some from the poet's own time in the eighth century.[25]

If such is the case with Homer's knowledge of Mycenaean Greece, much the same must be said about his knowledge of Troy. It is idle to ask whether Homer ever saw Troy with his own eyes.[26] Whether he saw it or not, he would have had to describe it in old formulae in any case. Hence what he actually tells us about Troy could have been said of almost any Bronze Age city: it had a citadel with palace on a hill, large walls, a main gate with a flank-ing tower, and outside the walls two springs and a tumulus or so. In short, as Homer describes it, Troy is laid out exactly as Mycenae and Tiryns are laid out; a few local place names — the two rivers, Mt. Ida, and the name Pergamon for the citadel — make the only real differences, so far as topography is concerned. With the excep-tion of the two springs, Homer's generalized picture has been sub-stantiated archaeologically in the city now numbered Troy VIIA, which was sacked and burned about 1200 B.C., almost exactly the date at which Greek traditional reckoning placed the fall of Priam's city.[27] If its ruins appear less impressive than Homer implies, its violent end may be in part accountable, though one may do well to remember also the acute observation of Thucydides, that a city's greatness is not always to be rightly estimated from its material remains. More important, epic tradition has probably confused it with Troy VI, the much longer lived city which preceded it and fell by earthquake about 1350. The gold which Schliemann found and called "Priam's Treasure" came from an even earlier level, but gold from all Trojan periods was probably given to Priam by the poets in the way that Agamemnon's many islands were transferred to him from his more potent predecessors.

Homer's picture of the Trojans, apart from the topographical question, accords also in a broad sense with what may be inferred from their material relics, and from such scraps of history as are available. It is well known, for instance, that Homer, who records differences of language where they existed, mentions nothing about language difficulties between Trojans and Achaeans.[28] Neither does he indicate any divergence in customs, religion, or material culture, the one exception being the polygamy of Priam, a royal vagary perhaps learned from neighboring orientals. The personal names of Trojans and Achaeans alike present a mixture of perspicuous Greek nomenclature and foreign, or at least unfamiliar elements. The comparison of this picture with what is known is suggestive. The "Trojan" names Hector, Antenor, and Tros have appeared in the Linear B tablets from Pylos, beside other names known only as Greek in the lines of Homer.[29] In Troy VI the predominating pottery is hardly to be distinguished from the gray Minyan Ware characteristic of Middle Helladic Greece, and by the sixteenth century Mycenaean pottery similar to that of the Argolid begins to appear; it is imported at first, but soon is imitated locally, and it increases steadily through the rest of Troy VI and VIIA.[30] The gray Minyan Ware, together with the fact that the domestic horse too was introduced into Troy at the time of the founding of the sixth city, has led the most recent excavators to the conclusion that the Trojans of Troy VI and VIIA were very closely akin in origin to the Middle Helladic people who brought Greek into Greece. Later the two cultures diverged; Troy never underwent the strong Minoizing influences which transformed Mycenae and the Greek mainland. But apparently Troy always faced the west, and maintained regular and vigorous relations with Mycenae. Skeletal remains also from Troy VI to VIII have been declared, with reservations due to scarcity of material, to be very similar to those of Middle Helladic Greece.[31] Finally, the megaron, or large hall with free-standing hearth, which used at least to be generally regarded as something which the first Greek-speakers brought with them into the Greek peninsula, has been found in the earliest levels of Troy — earlier, in fact, than on the soil of Greece itself.[32] It begins to look only reasonable to assume that the Greeks and the Trojans originally differed very little, and that whereas Troy VIIA has many characteristics which set it apart from the Mycenaean world, it was doubtless very closely associated with that world. As for language, no evidence exists, but the suspicion arises that the Trojans spoke Indo-European and, at least possibly, a form of Greek.[33]

This assumption receives additional support, for what it is worth, from legend and traditional genealogy. In Homer, Hector and Teucer are first cousins, as a result of the fortunes of Telamon in the earlier Trojan expedition of Heracles. But it should be no mere accident that the name Erichthonius occurs in both the Trojan and Athenian royal genealogies, that Athena, now established as a Mycenaean deity, is the tutelary goddess of both Athens and Troy, or that Echepolus, who rules Sicyon under Agamemnon, is a son of Anchises.[34] The connection, too, between the Trojans and the Arcadians is quite explicit. Dardanus, the first founder of Troy, has either a namesake or a double who was king of Arcadia,[35] and in the *Aeneid*, Vergil derives both the Arcadians and the Trojans ultimately from the giant Atlas.[36] This is doubly interesting, because Pelops himself was the great-grandson of Atlas, and thus the house of Pelops, traditionally of eastern origin, finds a family link with both the Trojans and the Arcadians. One story says even that Pelops' bones were somehow incorporated in the Palladium of Troy.[37]

Many uncertainties surround the question of Trojan identity, but that they might have been as closely related to the Greeks as Homer and tradition at large imply is suggested by further observation of the languages of Asia Minor. For the arrival of Greek with the Middle Helladic people is paralleled by the almost contemporaneous appearance of speakers of Indo-European in Asia Minor. Where the Hittites came from is unknown, but they were well established in central Anatolia by 1900 B.C., and shortly thereafter became masters of the whole region, until their collapse about 1200.[38] They rose to great power under King Suppililiumas in the fourteenth century, and challenged the power of Egypt itself at the Battle of Kadesh in the following one. Their language, though mingled with many words from neighboring Semitic lands, is clearly Indo-European in its morphology, and is either· a member of the western, or *centum*, division of the mother tongue, or else represents some form of the latter before the division took place.[39] Along with Hittite, the Luwian, Palaic, and Lycian languages possess similar linguistic features of the *centum*. Since these tongues cannot be anything but intrusive in Asia Minor, it would appear that the migration which brought the Middle Helladic Greek-speakers to Greece had also an eastern branch, at the same time or even earlier, which carried these related Indo-European languages, including Trojan, into Anatolia.[40]

But if the identity of the Trojans remains conjectural, so too there is no lack of mystery about the Mycenaeans of the Greek mainland. We are not even perfectly sure, for instance, what the Mycenaeans called themselves. Homer calls them Achaeans, Danaoi, and Argives interchangeably, his choice being determined by metrical demands alone. But there is no reason to conclude that they were originally synonymous. In this case, some historical evidence is at hand, and although perfect clarity cannot be extracted from it, it casts some light on the way in which the oral singers preserved the past while transmuting it.

Homer's favorite term, Achaeans, survived in the mainland of Greece only in the names of a small district of Thessaly and in the province along the south coast of the Gulf of Corinth. In historical times, the latter's dialect was Doric, and clearly had nothing to do with the East Greek language of the Mycenaeans, whose nearest dialectal descendants lay in Arcadia and eastward in Cyprus and Pamphylia. Now there is some reason to think that the name Achaean came originally from the east. Ancient Greek tradition had it that Cyprus was colonized by the Achaeans after the Trojan War, presumably as a result of the Dorian invasion, which drove some of them to the mountain region of Arcadia, and some over-seas.[41] Archaeology, however, shows that Mycenaean settlements existed in Cyprus in the fourteenth century and even earlier in Rhodes, where, however, subsequent Dorian occupation removed all trace of the earlier dialect. Yet the citadel of Ialysus continued to be called Achaea, while the north coast of Cyprus was always known as Achaeans' Coast.[42] Contemporary documents also bear out the presence of Greeks in Cyprus at an early date. Certain of the Tell-el-'Amarna letters imply that Cyprus was united under a Greek king in the middle of the fourteenth century, thus lending substance to remarks in both the *Iliad* and the *Odyssey* about Cypriote kings.[43] Clearly, if the Achaeans fled before the Dorians to Cyprus after the Trojan War, they migrated to no unfamiliar territory.

But there is also other evidence, this time in the official contemporary documents of the Hittites, for associating the Achaean name with the east at an early date. Several of the Boghaz-Keui tablets, between the middle of the fourteenth and the late thirteenth century, record the name Ahhiyawa, which has been identified, though not without much dispute, with Achaea.[44] Other identifications include Hittite Millewanda–Greek Miletus, Laspa–Lesbos, Taroisa–Troy, Tawagalawas–Eteocles, Alaksandu of Wilusa–Alexander of Ilios; and somewhat less convincingly, Antarawas–Andreus, Assuwa–Assos, Mutallu–Mitylene, and Attarissyas–Atreus.[45] These conjectures are likely to remain controversial for some time, but they seem a little too numerous for mere coincidences; furthermore, none are historically impossible, and only one looks linguistically impossible — the most attractive one, unfortunately. Attarissyas can hardly be Atreus, albeit he occurs in a tablet of Tudkhalia IV, who ruled from 1250–1220, precisely the period when Greek genealogy would place Agamemnon's father. In any case, there can be little doubt that Ahhiyawa actually does equal Achaea, and Millewanda–Miletus appears to be equally certain.[46]

The real problem posed by the Hittite tablets is the location of Ahhiyawa. There is nothing in any of them to indicate the mainland of Greece, and certain of the contents tend to deny it.[47] The importation of the gods of Laspa and Ahhiyawa by the Hittite king Mursilis II, sometime in the last quarter of the fourteenth century, to assist in the cure of a royal disease, involved an odd pair of yoke-fellows if Laspa is Lesbos, and Ahhiyawa the whole rest of Greece. Moreover, in the records and letters of Mursilis II, including the long Tawagalawas letter, Millewanda and Ahhiyawa are clearly distinct, and though the latter is more remote, the former is occupied by and under the control of the Achaeans, including Tawagalawas himself, who was a relative of the Achaean king. This at least shows that Miletus was an Achaean holding in the late fourteenth century; and the range of power enjoyed by Tawagalawas, who could assist the Hittite king in suppressing revolts in Lycia, make demands on him, have disputes, and eventually, perhaps, become his vassal at his own request, indicates strongly that the Achaean influence on the coast of Asia Minor was not negligible. The later tablets, too, add a little to the rather vague picture. References to the king of Ahhiyawa himself in or on the borders of the Hittite empire, together with the campaigns of the turbulent Achaean leader Attarissyas, both in Hittite lands and in Cyprus, create the impression that Ahhiyawa must have been some nearer place than Greece proper.

Admittedly, the matter is a hazy one, and it has not been much clarified by the reading "to Achaea" on a Linear B tablet from Cnossos.[48] Ahhiyawa might be Greece. But, as said above, the name "Achaea" is as old as the fourteenth century in Rhodes and Cyprus, and it is highly possible that the Ahhiyawa of the Hittites too lay on or near the coast of Asia Minor. Crete has been suggested, partly on the grounds that the colonizers of the coasts of Caria and Lycia were traditionally Sarpedon and Rhadamanthys, the brothers of Minos.[49] But it is hard to make the chronology fit, since Cnossos, presumably the seat of the Greek thalassocrat Minos, was destroyed at least a half-century before the first mention of Ahhiyawa in the Hittite archives. Cyprus also is to be ruled out by the fact that the Hittites apparently knew it under the name "Alasya." Various possibilities remain; Pamphylia or Cilicia might be meant, or the Carian and Lycian coastal lands perhaps originally colonized from Crete. Unfortunately, in this whole region, archaeological material offers very little evidence for anything that might be called colonization, except at Miletus, Rhodes, and Cyprus. Traces of Mycenaean habitation have been claimed for other places, such as Colophon, Cos, Samos, and Mylasa, but real evidence has proved elusive. However, much digging remains to be done, especially on the mainland of Anatolia, and it is also possible that the adaptation of local architectural styles might make the strongholds of the Achaeans, if they are ever located at all, hard to distinguish. In such a degree of uncertainty, it is a permissible hypothesis that Ahhiyawa may have embraced several of the regions mentioned, both on the mainland and in the islands, and that the district around Smyrna and Mt. Sipylus also may have been included.

In any case, to the Hittites Ahhiyawa was, to begin with, a great power, and one in fairly close and friendly contact with them. Later, in the second half of the thirteenth century, during the predatory activities of Attarissyas in the Hittite lands, relations were badly strained, and Ahhiyawa appears to have been regarded as of lesser consequence than before.[50] It is interesting to note that about this same date — that is, about 1230 — the series of Mycenaean sherds at Miletus comes to an end, though part of the site continued to be occupied.[51] Throughout the whole Aegean and Near Eastern area, in fact, these years were a time of troubles which culminated for the Hittites in total collapse shortly after 1200, and for Egypt in the two great expeditions of the Akhaiwasha (Achaeans) and the Danuna (Danaoi), which assailed her coasts in 1225 and 1194.[52] For Mycenae herself, the whole century was one of decline; her commerce dropped off sharply, especially with Cyprus and Egypt, though Troy continued to import Mycenaean pottery.[53] Around 1250 Greece felt the first pressures of new invaders from the north, and at the end of the century Troy itself perished by fire. Amid such upheavals, the Ahhiyawa people lost their importance, and perhaps in some cases their footing entirely, in Asia Minor. Some may have emigrated; others, such as the vigorous Attarissyas, evidently turned to plundering the enfeebled marches of the Hittites. It is no wonder that King Tudkhalia IV did not consider the king of Ahhiyawa his equal any longer; Mycenaean influence abroad was on the wane. As for the two raids on Egypt, there is no reason to connect them with Attarissyas, but it is interesting to note that the first, that of the Akhaiwasha, was roughly contemporary with him.

So far then as documentary and other evidence is concerned, the name Achaean is associated from the first with districts east of Greece, from Miletus and vicinity, through various spots on the south coast of Asia Minor, to Cyprus. Material relics, it is true, have not appeared, but it is likely that Miletus was not the only Mycenaean outpost in the region. It is also tempting to think that the Achaean name actually originated there, as the tribal name of those Mycenaeans who, however they got there, lived on the borders of the Hittite empire, and the coasts and coastal islands of Asia Minor. If this is true, one may well ask how they became for Homer the inhabitants of Mycenaean Greece in general; and the answer to this may lie in what can be inferred partly from the monuments at Mycenae, Tiryns, and elsewhere in Greece, and partly from the extravagant hoard of legends in the epic memory.

Mycenae had its phases. At the opening of the Late Helladic period, beginning around 1600 or a little later, the city was ruled by a powerful dynasty whose principal monuments are the royal shaft graves, a direct development from the Middle Helladic cist-graves,[54] and now traceable in that period. By 1500, however, the characteristic royal tomb becomes the tholos, or beehive-shaped vault, a development of the rock-hewn chamber tomb, which continues in ever-increasing magnificence for almost three centuries.[55] These years mark the city's apogee of power and influence; the tholos-kings built also the Cyclopean walls, the Grave Circle within them, the Lion Gate, and the megaron of the palace. They also began the great system of roads north and south from the capital. Foreign trade flourished, and the colonies, or outposts, mentioned above belong to this period. Strongly Minoizing at first, Mycenaean art gradually adapted and conventionalized Cretan motifs into a characteristic style, somewhat as Minoan script was adapted to Greek needs in Linear B. The mastery of the seas, until 1400, lay in the hands of a Greek-ruled Cnossos; thereafter, Mycenae seems to have wielded it herself.

But in the next century some real changes occur, one of which, the sudden curtailment of trade, has already been noted. Tholos-tomb building comes to an end in the later years of the thirteenth century. Skeletal remains, such as they are, indicate no change of population, but distinctly new elements appear amid the general decline of elegance and luxury. One is the slashing sword, which supplants the thrusting rapier of Minoan design, and another is the fibula. More important perhaps is the appearance around 1250 of the human figure on vase painting, and particularly the human figure in armor, with chariots and other warlike appurtenances. The Warrior Vase of Mycenae and the Warrior and Chariot Sherd from Tiryns are examples.[56] These show a round shield, or almost round, and what appear to be fringed tunics or corselets, and spears with a butt-end spike. The last two elements have been thought to be of eastern origin.[57] The military implications of these motifs are further supported by the fact that around 1250 the Cyclopean walls of Mycenae were extended west and south; to the same period of building, apparently, belong the Lion Gate and the Grave Circle within the walls. Somewhat later, though exactly when is uncertain, the East Bastion and the secret underground cistern were built on the citadel in order to insure the water supply.[58] At Tiryns a similar precaution was attempted, as also at Athens, though Tiryns in other respects began to decay; the elegant bath chamber, for instance, ceased to be used except as a rubbish dump.[59] Evidently the castles of the Argolid had fallen into different hands. They were not foreign hands, however, for the Linear B tablets continue to record Greek down to about 1200. But these were men of war, not commerce and refinement. Their artistic and architectural achievements, full of the spirit of battle, give to the last phase of Mycenae a special stamp, one which is hinted at in Homer, and one which bears a grim resemblance to the tumults which rocked the whole eastern Mediterranean in the thirteenth and twelfth centuries.

It is a long-honored custom in Homeric studies to try to bridge the gaps of history with the slender wisps of legend. Some of these have occasionally turned out to be more solid than they looked. For instance, the Return of the Heraclids, as the Dorian invasion was called in antiquity, supposedly took place in two acts. The first attempt, led by Hyllus and repulsed at the Isthmus of Corinth by Atreus and Echemus, king of Arcadia, ended in a treaty by which the Dorians agreed to stay out of the Peloponnesus for a hundred years.[60] When the time was over, they returned, sacked Mycenae and her allied outposts, and took possession of all southern Greece. As it happens, the above-mentioned defensive fortifications

added at Mycenae and Tiryns date from just about a century be-
fore the fall of Mycenae, and since this is the case at Athens too,
it appears as if they were constructed in fear of a northern invader,
and not one from the sea. Little as all this may prove, it tends to
give the appearance of history to the legend of the two Dorian
attacks, separated by a hundred years.

There is also a story to the effect that the last dynasty of Myce-
nae, the Tantalid, or Pelopid, house, came from Asia Minor. Tan-
talus and his children, Pelops and Niobe, lived traditionally in the
vicinity of Mt. Sipylus in Phrygia, or Lydia, where their tombs,
the throne of Pelops, and the petrified form of Niobe are still to be
seen. Pelops, however, migrated to Greece, defeated Oenomaus in
a chariot race at Olympia, thus winning his daughter Hippodameia
and a throne. His descendants, Atreus, Agamemnon, and finally
Orestes, supplanted the Perseid dynasty as rulers of Mycenae.
Pelops himself is rather a complex figure, combining elements of
heroic legend with the myth of death and resurrection; slain by
his father and served as a feast to the gods, he was restored to life
by them, and given an ivory shoulder to replace the one absent-
mindedly eaten by the sorrowing Demeter. Many other tales are
told of him also which make it obvious that he is a rather extreme
case of the steady accretion of folklore about a famous name.[61] Yet
two details catch one's attention: the ivory shoulder, and the mi-
gration from Asia. Ivory is certainly easier to come by in Asia than
in Greece, so that one may presume that if the story had originated
in Greece, the gods might have been confined to the local ma-
terials.[62] As for the migration, it should be remembered that Pelops
was the grandfather, or in other versions the great-grandfather, of
Agamemnon, who sacked Troy traditionally in 1184. Agamem-
non's *floruit*, then, may be put roughly at 1200, and Pelops should
have gone to Greece sixty or ninety years before. A date in the
first half of the thirteenth century for the migration of Pelops ac-
cords well with the evidence from the Hittites, whose relations
with Ahhiyawa show a marked change, as we have seen, through-
out the thirteenth century, and seem to imply that it was losing its
former status. If some of the Achaeans turned marauder, like At-
tarissyas, others may have migrated to Greece proper, and it is at
least possible that their departure was symbolized in the legend

of Pelops' migration. The latter's son Atreus, according to Thu-
cydides, came to Mycenae, and having cultivated the favor of the
people, succeeded Eurystheus as king when the latter fell in battle
with the Dorians in their first assault around 1250.[63] As the first
ruler of the new dynasty, he perhaps began the great building pro-
gram which eventually produced the most striking of Mycenae's
architectural monuments. According to the most recent dating,
even the last two tholos tombs, the finest of all, belong to the time
of the first Pelopids. Their arrival may have been attended by a
struggle, for the earlier palace was destroyed by fire.[64] In any case,
most of their energies seem to have been directed toward fortifica-
tion, as if the city were under threat, as indeed it was, according
to legend. Such matters are incapable of proof, of course, but there
is a plausible consensus here between archaeology and tradition that
the sons of Pelops were the warlike rulers of Late Helladic III B
and C, under whom the city achieved a grim, final magnificence,
not long before its fall. And indeed, what we know of the house of
Atreus is by no means inconsistent with a period of decline, war,
and the fear of invasion.

If the slight changes in armament noted at Mycenae do indeed
show eastern influence, that influence could best have come with
Achaeans from Asia Minor. Pelops' victory in a chariot race recalls
the Hittite record of an Achaean prince traveling to the capital of
the Hittites to learn chariot-driving from them.[65] The name of
Pelops' charioteer, Myrtilus, has been compared to the Hittite Mur-
silis, with good reason,[66] and the Hittite rock-carved statute of the
Great Mother on Mt. Sipylus, sometimes called the Niobe, shows
that Pelops, a native of that region, need not have traveled far to
profit by Hittite culture. At least, a strong hypothesis arises that
Pelops was one of the Achaean princelings of the Anatolian coast,
who, when the time of disturbances began, sought new lands and
founded the last dynasty of Mycenae. It is also suggested, some-
what tentatively, that he, or others like him whose migrations have
been merged in story with his, brought to Greece the Achaean
name, long familiar to the Hittites, and later to the Egyptians, when
the Akhaiwasha and their allies attacked the Delta around 1225.
That Pelops and his descendants were peculiarly popular with epic
singers needs no demonstration, and perhaps explains why the epic

so strongly prefers to call the Mycenaean Greeks "Achaeans."

If it be asked what the preceding dynasties of the shaft and tholos tombs called themselves, Homer's other name for them, "Danaoi," naturally presents itself. Here again, contemporary records offer some help. Numerous documents from Egypt continue to record the name "Danuna," almost certainly meaning Greeks (Danaoi), from the first half of the fifteenth century to the beginning of the twelfth. As early as the reign of Thothmes III, about a century before the first Hittite mention of Ahhiyawa, an Egyptian hymn refers to the islands of the Danuna, and around 1412, an inscription of Amen Hotep III names the Danuna as among the piratical raiders of the sea. Since this is the period in which Minos II supposedly suppressed piracy, one is tempted to ask whether he did not, perhaps, monopolize it. Be that as it may, a little later, King Abimilki of Tyre wrote to the Pharoah Akhnaton of the death of the king of Danuna and of the peaceful accession of his brother. Though the Karnak inscription of Merneptah mentions Akhaiwasha without the Danuna among the invaders of Egypt in 1225, the Danuna are prominent among the Peoples of the Land and Sea in the Medinet Abu inscription of Ramses III.[67] Thus through the era of the tholos tombs to the time of the Trojan War, the Danaoi are well known to the rulers of Egypt and Tyre. Twice they are mentioned as hostile seafarers, once around the time of the sack of Cnossos, which corresponds to the zenith of Mycenae, and once in the great unsuccessful raid on Egypt, which took place when her power was declining. Surely these Danaoi are the earlier masters of Mycenae, the builders of the shaft graves, the earlier beehive tombs, and the Cyclopean walls. There seems to be no reason to distinguish the shaft and tholos builders as two distinct dynasties, as has been suggested; the change was a change of fashion, no more.[68] The history of the Danaoi is noticeably longer than that of the Achaeans, who mingle with them only in the last hundred and fifty years or so before the Dorian invasion.[69]

Again, for what it is worth, mythic pedigrees offer support. It has been noticed that the legendary houses of early Greece show two types of family pedigree, long and short.[70] The Pelopids of Mycenae have a short one, as do the Aeacids and the house of Odysseus. The longer ones, such as those of the Abantid, or Perseid, kings of Argos, the Cadmeans of Thebes, or the Erechtheids of Attica, reach many generations back before ultimately deriving themselves from Zeus. The theory is that the short ones, which spring from Zeus within three or four generations, denote families who came from overseas, and left their ancestry along with their ancestral tombs behind them. In the case of Pelops, at least, this is a likely explanation, and at all events it is a striking fact that the most distinguished of Homer's Achaeans have short genealogies. On the other hand, the family history of the Abantid kings of Argos is one of the longest of all, counting six generations before Io, the antediluvian ancestress of the house. This was the ruling house of the Argolid before Pelops, and Perseus, its most distinguished scion, was the "founder" of Mycenae; that is, the building of the first Cyclopean wall, around 1350 was associated with his name. His mother was Danae, and one of his ancestors Danaus. Particularly in the latter case, the name may be significant, for Danaus' brother was Aegyptus, which places both names under the suspicion of being eponyms. Precisely how Aegyptus can be eponymous is a question, of course, but the two names together, inevitably implying Egyptian and Greek, fit nicely with the Egyptian habit of calling the Greeks Danaoi.

When the Achaeans came, they married princesses of the old native dynasties, thus probably authenticating their right to rule. Hence it is, incidentally, that the rape of Helen, whose Tyndarid ancestry was doubtless a large part of Menelaus' royal patent, still provides a better excuse for the Trojan War than Priam's gold, or any other economic reason. Matrilinear descent has been widely attributed to early Greece, and is known to have been the rule in Lycia also.[71] The latter is, indeed, one of the few countries with which Pelops, variously called a Phrygian, Paphlagonian, or Lydian, is not associated. Nonetheless, Greek connections with Lycia were numerous; the Hittite tablets record the Achaean Tawagalawas' aid in keeping peace in Lycia, while in Homer, Sarpedon, by genealogy a Greek descended from the Cretan colonizer of Lycia, leads the Lycians with his cousin Glaucus.[72] The latter in turn is closely bound to Diomedes by old ties of mutual hospitality, and the story of Bellerophon in the sixth *Iliad* amply illustrates the maintenance of contact between the Achaeans overseas and the old families at home. To the Danaoi, the Achaeans may have been *parvenus*; they may have needed the support of state marriages to gain their thrones; they may have insinuated themselves into the older society by such methods as Thucydides hints at when he says that Atreus cultivated the favor of the people, but they were not strangers. Their inheritance of Mycenae involved no struggle, and the long series of Mycenaean imports into Anatolia indicates nothing but the same friendly relations between the two regions, at least down to about 1300, as Homeric tradition paints.

Such connections may also be traced, though dimly, in some of the cults of Arcadia.[73] If the Arcadians, as said above, are related in legend to the Trojans and in language to the Achaeans, it can hardly be meaningless that the story of Tantalus, who served his son to the gods, who in turn restored him to life, is almost exactly repeated in the story of King Lycaon of Arcadia. The Thyestean feast may be a kind of continuation of this myth, and so, possibly, may be the story of Idomeneus' sacrifice of his son. Lycaonia, usually known as the hinterland behind Caria and Lycia, is given also as an old name for Arcadia.[74] Wolf cults, or at least the folklore of werewolves, are common in both Arcadia and Lycia, centering about the cult of Zeus (or Apollo) Lycaeus. The "Lycian" Apollo, with associations both in Argos and in the east, seems to have been a wolf-god,[75] and one is reminded of his destruction of the Rhodian Telchines in the form of a wolf. Such correspondences are not to be pressed too far, yet it appears that, while the Danaoi of the mainland were absorbing the refinements of Minoan Crete, the Achaeans were learning things from the peoples of Anatolia, chariot driving from the Hittites, and some rude cults from the mountain lands back of Lycia, which survived along with their language in Arcadia until classical times.

When and how the Achaeans got to Asia Minor is not entirely evident. If the Trojans could have been part of an eastern arm of the Indo-European migration of 2000, so, presumably, might the Achaeans have been. On the other hand, their short genealogies, their easy attainment of realms by marriage in Greece, together with the various ancient traditions of colonization in Cyprus, Lycia, and elsewhere, suggest that colonization is the more likely answer. If the Hittite sources or Linear B ever yield clear knowledge of where the king of Ahhiyawa lived and how long he had lived there, the question may be answered. But in the absence from Asia Minor of anything resembling Middle Helladic culture, except at Troy VI, it is better to assume colonial expansion in the fourteenth century, corresponding to the spread of Mycenaean commerce.

Homer's other name for the Greeks, "Argives," is not really a problem, any more than it is a problem why Agamemnon is king of both Argos and Mycenae. Besides using "Argos" to mean the whole Peloponnesus and even the whole of Greece, epic tradition confused Argos the city and Mycenae for the simple reason that they are inseparable. The whole Argolid, including Tiryns and Asine, is too geographically unified to admit of more than one great power, nor did it ever have more than one in historical times, namely the city of Argos. If this was true in the classical period, when the city states depended upon regional isolation for part of their defense, it must have been even more true in the Mycenaean Age, when the imperial city, far from fostering regionalism, built roads throughout the passes to pull together the districts under its hegemony. A city of the Argolid which controlled also the Isthmus region could hardly have tolerated a separate power in her own plain, the whole of which was and is visible from her acropolis. Argos and Mycenae, for all practical purposes, were one; and Argos the district included the Argive Larisa, Tiryns, Midea, Dendra, and Asine, a system of fortified castles designed for the defense of the great central city in its nook of the mountains. These castles would be pointless in themselves without Mycenae, and for Tiryns, for instance, to have been independent, was strategically impossible, in whatever stage of feudal fragmentation the world lay. Diomedes' "kingdom" of the *Catalog* can only have been a baronial estate held under the Mycenaean overlord.[76]

Homer's use of the three names, therefore, appears to be in part historically justified, in part a case of the false perspective characteristic of epic. In the last century of Mycenaean civilization, when the Achaeans had mingled with the Danaoi, there was no reason to distinguish them; and if the Achaean designation preponderates, that is no more surprising than that the Plantagenets were known as "Angevins" rather than as "Poitevins." The dominant element gives its name to the whole, and a real analogy arises in the second century B.C., when the Achaean League was responsible for the Roman protectorate of Greece being called "Achaea." It is perhaps surprising that in 1194 the Egyptians still refer to their invaders as "Danuna," though the Achaeans, whom they had distinguished in 1225, could scarcely have been absent. But an explanation may again be found in the practice of the Romans, who never abandoned the term *Graeci*, from the small West Greek tribe with whom they had had early contact. To call all the Greeks "Argives," or Greece itself "Argos," can only have been prompted by the preeminence in epic tradition of the great cities of the Argolid.

The picture thus drawn shows the Mycenaean world at its height not unlike the classical Greek world, whose geographic center was not the mainland of Greece, but rather the Aegean itself. Its eastern settlements on the shores of Anatolia and adjacent islands sometimes fell under the suzerainty of the current empire of the interior, as the later Ionian cities fell under the yoke of Persia, and sometimes asserted independence. As in classical times, the cultural and ethnic connections between the Bronze Age settlements on both sides of the sea must have been strong, although, as with every system of feudal principates, the political federation was weak and subject to the predilections of ruling lords. The two *Catalogs* of the second *Iliad* must be really traditional poems, though like all else in oral poetry they were recomposed for the occasion.[77] There could scarcely be a clearer example of how bardic memory works than in these ostensibly factual passages, where an old survey of Mycenaean Greece, consistent enough in its broad outlines with feudal organization in general and with much specific archaeological knowledge, nevertheless includes a Sparta unfounded at the dramatic date, and a settlement at Larisa in Aeolis which looks suspiciously like the one founded by the migrating Aeolians in the Dark Age. The Carians of Miletus and the landlocked Arcadians of the *Catalog* also suggest times later than the fall of Mycenae. At the same time, certain features of its tradition show a strict concern, if not with real chronology, with the chronology of legend: Thebes, for instance, is not mentioned as such among the Boeotian cities, but is called "Hypothebes," doubtless because in the years preceding the Trojan War, it had been sacked by the Epigoni, and little was left of it. There may even be more than legend in the fact that the Greek *Catalog* includes only the Dodecanese contingents as allies from Asia Minor and vicinity, while many clearly Greek names appear in the Trojan *Catalog*, sometimes as leaders of native local contingents. Herein one may understandably read a reflection of the collapse of the mainland's contact with what had formerly been fiefs and outposts, before the disintegration began shortly after 1300. By the time of the Trojan War, Sarpedon and Glaucus (the lords of Lycia) or Euphemus (the Troezenian leader of the Ciconians) may well have felt a closer military connection with Troy than with the cities of Greece, howbeit in the case of Glaucus, as said above, the personal claims of Diomedes still had a residual authority.

How far the Achaeans were causative or merely symptomatic of the disturbances of the time can only be guessed, but they were clearly involved in them. The cohesiveness of the earlier days was gone, and if one may justly find a connection between the new warlike spirit in Mycenaean art and the legends of the Achaeans, lurid with bloodshed and turbulence, and forming the world's greatest treasury of plots for tragedies, it looks as if the age fought against itself, and went down in a series of mutually destructive wars which flung the Aegean area into an era of isolation and darkness. The Trojan expedition, now almost universally admitted to contain a kernel of historical truth, can have been only a part of the general crumbling of the whole Mycenaean structure. Even as early as 1400, one probably sees traces of this fratricidal struggle in the sack of Cnossos. Under the Achaeans this kind of activity seems to have grown intense, and eventually to have withered the magnificence of Mycenae, leaving her too weak to repel the Dorian invaders. A passage in Hesiod perhaps reflects the change: after describing the Bronze Age, Hesiod inserts an Age of the Heroes, unfamiliar to the old myth of the Ages, heroes who died at Thebes and Troy.[78] These can only be the Achaeans, whom he distinguishes from the other Bronze Age men. The latter he depicts as a violently destructive people, but says that the Heroes were much better, and were taken to the Islands of the Blest after their deaths. More likely it was the other way around; but it is interesting that he draws any distinction at all. Perhaps his view was influenced by the Achaeans' own vainglorious songs.

Homer, on the contrary, though his pages ring with the glory of his heroes, offers probably some real insight into the Achaean temperament and mode of life in certain passages which are hard to explain as anything but true reflections of the period. In the *Odyssey*, Menelaus tells Telemachus that he was so fond of Odysseus that had the latter only come back from Troy, he would have sacked one of his own cities and given it to him.[79] This is a rough sort of friendship gift, conceivable only in a feudal world where carelessly destructive overlords handed recalcitrant fiefs back and forth freely, but bloodily. One wonders what might have been involved in Agamemnon's offer of seven cities to Achilles.[80] More pointed even are the remarks of Odysseus to Agamemnon in one of the latter's frequent moods of discouragement:

> Ah, would that you ruled some other, some worthless host,
> Not over us, whom Zeus has appointed from youth to old age
> To wind the skeins of heavy wars, till we perish all.[81]

The tragic self-consciousness of Odysseus in these lines, like the *Odyssey*'s melancholy retrospect on the heroic world, can scarcely be attributed to anything but the poet's own synoptic insight into the times which he was reconstructing. If some of his details, especially the chronological ones, were confused by the tradition which he followed, he was nonetheless in accord with the spirit of an age four centuries older than himself. Bardic memory, embalmed in formulae, could keep the general outlines of a culture clear; and though factual details and history in the modern sense were never its chief concerns, wherever such were relevant to the pattern of spiritual reconstruction, they might survive with surprising accuracy. Oral poetry regularly lays claim to unerring and unchanging truthfulness; yet in both Homer and Hesiod, standing as they do at the end of the oral epic tradition, there is evidence of a growing consciousness of epic's mingling of fact and fiction. Hesiod makes his Muses say:

> We know well how to speak many false things resembling true;
> Yet we know, when we wish, how also to speak the truth.[82]

Similarly Odysseus, whose conversation has been compared earlier in the *Odyssey* to the enchanting utterance of the bards, in the firelight scene of Book 19 "caused many lies to seem like truth as he spoke." [83]

Epic is a transforming medium. It is like trying to draw a tree's roots from the appearance of its branches to try to recover history from the *Iliad* and the *Odyssey*. Where historical controls exist, Homer's picture of the Mycenaean world can be largely verified: his principates are in the right places, his local and personal names, or many of them, appear in the archives of Mycenae, Pylos, and Cnossos; the organization of his feudal society is loose and minimal, while the individuals are just such savage and tremendous aristocrats as one would expect to tread the stone ramps and Cyclopean walls of Tiryns and Mycenae. For all its conflations, confusions and *montages*, epic has given us a picture of Mycenaean reality, corroborated and refined, rather than denied, by increasing historical knowledge. Above all, however, it has given us the picture of Mycenaean reality which the Mycenaeans themselves wished to have transmitted to posterity — "a subject of song for generations to come." Since they kept archives of contracts, inventories, and accounts, clearly the Mycenaeans could also have kept chronicles, but they did not. Instead they kept singers, taught by the Muses to transmit their annals through the mirrors of imagery and myth, and they could have found no better way of communicating their own historical attitude. "Poetry," says Aristotle, "is more philosophic than history," and therefore the Homeric poems are no doubt, for us as for the Achaeans, the truest history of the Mycenaean Age.

III

ATHENS, 1200–700

UNTIL recently it has been habitual, in giving account of prehistoric Greece, either to omit all mention of Athens, or to say little beyond the observation that she was not very important in the early period. The Mycenaean civilization obviously centered in the Argolid, whose wealth of archaeological treasures tended to overshadow such few Mycenaean objects as appeared on Attic soil. And in fact, aside from the "Pelasgic," or Cyclopean, walls of the Acropolis, and a couple of stones suspected of having once belonged to a late Helladic palace, there was little enough to controvert the general impression of Athens' insignificance.[1] Moreover, on the surface at least, Homer's testimony would seem to bear out that impression. Athens is mentioned only a few times, the Athenian leader is not especially distinguished, and in addition to these undeniable facts, the widespread belief that the works of Homer were collected, or at least edited, by Pisistratus has spread a veil over Homeric criticism and made it all but customary to regard most, if not all, of the references to Athens or Athenians in the epics as late interpolations, dating from the end of the sixth century.[2] The latter notion is still very popular, and archaeology alone cannot dispose of it. But, since the 1930's, with the American excavations in the Athenian Agora, archaeology has begun to draw a very different picture of early Athenian history, and thereby to create a disposition to find Athens' place in epic, rather than to exclude her from it.

If the prehistoric phase of Athens is not so brilliant as that of Mycenae, it starts earlier and continues later. Excavations by the Italians on the south slope of the Acropolis revealed a Neolithic settlement, just about where Thucydides says the first inhabitants of Athens lived.[3] Neolithic strata have also appeared on the north side of the Acropolis, below other layers representing all periods down to Mycenaean times.[4] In particular, the Middle Helladic phase, well represented by both the matt-painted and Minyan gray ware, seems to have been very prosperous.[5] From the Mycenaean period, numerous figurines have turned up; [6] and, in addition to the tholos tombs long known at Menidi near Athens and at Thorikos,[7] recent excavations of chamber tombs in the Agora, and of a particularly rich, doubtless royal, one on the north slope of the Areopagus, have created an impression of considerable opulence and importance in this period of Attic history.[8] After the Mycenaean era, the chief evidence comes from the Outer Cerameicus cemetery, where the progressions from sub-Mycenaean, through Protogeometric to Geometric styles of vase painting illustrate an unparalleled continuity of culture in the Dark Age.[9] This continuity was strikingly confirmed by the exploration of a secret fountain dug deep under the north walls of the Acropolis, corresponding in purpose to the secret cistern at Mycenae; the pottery in this fountain, dating from 1250 to 1150, leads without break to the sub-Mycenaean ware of the Cerameicus.[10] By 1940, it was possible to state beyond a doubt that Athens, as such, had existed before 2000 B.C., and that there was more than mere legend in the Athenians' classical assertion that they were autochthonous, and had never been driven from their land.[11]

Yet for the Homerist, the importance of Athens does not lie primarily in her history in the Mycenaean period, nor in the probable authenticity of the so-called "Athenian" passages; it lies rather in Athens' position during the so-called Dark Age. During the twelfth century, Greece and the whole Aegean area were shaken by the tumultuous movement of hostile peoples pressing down from the north and occasioning repercussions throughout the more settled regions of the south, even to the coasts of Syria and Egypt. The relationship is not very clear between this Dorian Invasion, as the

movement was called in Greece, and such events as the fall of the
Hittite empire and the two great raids on Egypt of the Akhaiwasha
and the Danuna. The most likely view is that the Dorians formed
one element, the westernmost, in a large movement of northern
barbarians whose southward thrust dislodged more civilized peoples
and drove them to piratical seafaring and the soldiery of fortune.
In any case, the arrival of the Dorians in Greece rang the death-
knell of the Bronze Age; in site after site, the late Mycenaean strata
are divided from those of the Early Iron Age by a layer of charred
ruin. The fall of Mycenae herself is usually placed around 1150, or
somewhat after. The civilization which had supplied the subject
matter and developed the basic technique of epic song disappeared.
Yet, some four hundred years later, the epic is in full flower in
the *Iliad* and *Odyssey*, its tradition unbroken and its form perfected.

How the epic survived is no longer much of a problem: oral epic
will survive as long as there are bards to sing and audiences to listen.
The question now is where they sang and who was left to listen
during the four hundred years of semibarbarism which followed
the clean sweep of the Dorians. It cannot be assumed that the latter
were much interested in the heroic traditions of the people they
conquered, especially since, with a few exceptions which are ob-
viously anachronistic,[12] no mention of the Dorians or their settle-
ments occurs in Homer, who was not even introduced to the men
of Sparta, according to Greek tradition, until the time of Lycur-
gus.[13] When the Dark Age ends, around 700, Greece already pre-
sents the familiar historical distribution of dialects: various forms
of Doric in the Peloponnesus and southern islands, except for
Arcadia and Cyprus, where the old "Achaean" dialect survives in
new forms; Attic around Athens, with Ionic in the Cyclades and
central coasts of Asia Minor; Aeolic in Lesbos, the Troad, and
around the Adramyttian Gulf, with an Aeolic mixed with North-
west Greek in Boeotia and Thessaly; in Phocis, Locris, and Elis,
Northwest Greek. In such a picture, the problem of the survival
of epic is reduced to a very few possibilities. Cyprus and Arcadia,
for instance, the direct heirs of the Achaean language, must be
excluded at once, because the epic language that appears in Homer
contains only faint traces of this language, which would surely
have been the dominant one if either Cyprus or Arcadia had been

the chief preserver of the tradition. Aeolic lands offer a better possibility, for there is considerable Aeolic in Homer; Achilles himself comes from Thessaly, where Aeolic of sorts was spoken, and many of his exploits seem to have been transferred to him from the later Aeolic colonization of the Adramyttian Gulf.[14] Yet, for all the theory that Homer was originally sung in Aeolic,[15] and although some Aeolic poems underlie parts of the *Iliad*, the language of the epic as we have it remains overwhelmingly Ionic in appearance, with a certain sprinkling of Atticisms generally attributed to surface corruption in the sixth century and later. This fact, together with the almost universal belief of antiquity that Homer was an Ionian and lived in Chios, Ios, or one of the Asiatic cities, accounts for the long-held view that Ionia was the place where the epic tradition survived the Dark Age.

This opinion was entirely reasonable in view of the belief that Greek colonization of the eastward regions began, according to the somewhat vague designation of ancient historians, "after the Trojan War." [16] Moreover, it accorded well with the brilliant development which colonial Greece underwent in the seventh and sixth centuries, when mainland culture was deeply in debt to the inventiveness of the Ionians. Homer was looked upon as the earliest fruit of the same tree from which sprang the poetry of Callinus, Mimnermus, and Anacreon, the bright new modes of sculpture, architecture, and "Orientalizing" vase-painting, the earliest geography and history, and finally philosophy itself. All intellectual and artistic power seemed to have gone to Ionia "after the Trojan War," or after the Dorian Invasion, where it lay fallow for a while, then blossomed and reinvigorated the mainland.

Yet if this explanation were the true one, the Ionian cities ought to show the usual evidence of continuous habitation, or at least of early habitation, by the Greeks. Pottery and house walls from the centuries between 1100 and 800 ought to lie below the classical levels, but this is precisely what has not appeared. Excavations in Ionia and Aeolis are by no means complete, and as yet all conclusions, especially chronological ones, are subject to doubt. But recent archaeological surveys have so far failed to reveal evidence for the continual Greek occupation of a single Ionian, or Aeolic, site.[17] Even Mycenaean remains are scanty enough in these places, and where they do appear, they are followed not by sub-Mycenaean and Protogeometric levels, but as a rule by native Anatolian layers. When Greek pottery does appear, it must be dated not much earlier than 850 in most places, and often later. This is true for Smyrna, Ephesus, Samos, and probably Colophon. Miletus offers more complex difficulties, but there still appears to be only a slight bridge between the last Mycenaean traces, around 1200, and the first clear evidence of Greek occupation around 700.[18] As said above, the exact dates are subject to considerable future revision; but while further digging on lower levels may well uncover the traces of a more widespread Mycenaean occupation than is now assumed, it is at least unlikely that the gap between the Mycenaean and the Geometric levels will be filled by any convincing evidence of Greek culture. And the reason for this lies not simply in an argument from silence, but in the fact that the earliest Geometric pottery from Ionia shows little sign of originality, and every sign of being either imported from the mainland or at least dependent on mainland models.[19] It emerges therefore, as our knowledge increases, that Ionia in the ninth and eighth centuries was not a luxurious haven of Greek culture which had been quietly developing through the Dark Age and preparing the renaissance of the classical world, but rather a frontier movement, maintaining itself, perhaps with great difficulty, against neighboring, and often hostile, mountaineers of the hinterland. By the beginning of the sixth century this frontier had, indeed, become a civilization with some breath-taking accomplishments, but earlier than that its reliance upon the mother country, especially in the matter of vase-painting, seems established beyond a doubt.[20]

So far as they are known, therefore, the facts indicate that only toward the end of the Dark Age, and not soon after the Trojan War, the Greeks went to Ionia, and even then in no great numbers, to reoccupy sites where their ancestors had perhaps been in Mycenaean times. If that is the case, it is no longer possible to believe that the epic tradition survived in Ionia, though it doubtless went there with the first settlers. Aeolis, though traditionally settled earlier, actually offers no better conditions for the continuity of the epic than Ionia.[21] By the negative process of elimination, one must conclude that the memory of the Achaeans was preserved on the mainland, and not in the colonies, which did not yet exist. But there is abundant positive evidence also, and, much as it varies in intrinsic value, it all points toward Attica.

It was mentioned earlier that recent excavations have begun to reveal the extraordinary continuity of the civilization in Athens. Some of the details now become relevant, especially those relating to the military strength of the Acropolis, and to the slow but uninterrupted evolvement of successive styles in vase-painting and other arts. The advance of the Dorians, which annihilated so many Mycenaean fortresses, halted before the Athenian Acropolis. On its flanks, a series of hastily abandoned and burnt houses testify to the presence of the invader, but the steep and heavily fortified rock itself shows no trace of having fallen.[22] Indeed, the secret fountain under the north walls of the Acropolis proves quite the contrary, with its deposit of sherds dating continuously from the middle thirteenth century through the next. This fountain is of almost exactly the same date as the similar one at Mycenae, built by the last great dynasty there. At Athens, this device kept the defenders of the citadel supplied with water, while the natural defenses and the formidable Cyclopean Walls were, not very surprisingly, adequate to repel the enemy. The parallel defense measures adopted at Tiryns, Mycenae, and Athens around 1250 clearly suggest a general invasion and one from the north.[23] As stated earlier, there were apparently two assaults, separated by a hundred years, the first a failure, the second widely successful. But the success of the second attack did not extend to Athens. As the most recent excavator of these regions summarizes:

There is sufficient evidence to prove that no general destruction of the Acropolis took place when these dwellings on the North Slope were abandoned. Tradition has it that Athens was spared the fate that overtook the rest of Greece, and the ceramic evidence points to a continued development from late Mycenaean times to the early Iron Age. This is amply demonstrated by the contents of some early graves recently discovered in the German Excavations at the Kerameikos. The prehistoric settlement in Athens may have been sacked more than once by invading hosts from near or far, and its inhabitants may have had to abandon their houses temporarily, but the same people apparently returned to their old homes or established themselves in the near vicinity. The continuity of their race, which was a matter of great pride to the ancient

Athenians, can be demonstrated by archaeological evidence to be established fact.[24]

Of equal significance to the stratification, and perhaps of even greater moment for Homeric criticism, is the evidence of steady development in ceramic arts, for these testify not merely to the maintainance of foothold against invasion, but also to a civilization with leisure and resource to progress. The small votive figurines shift so gradually in style between Mycenaean and Geometric times that it is often not easy to distinguish them out of context.[25] In these, hieratic conservatism doubtless tended to preserve a pose and manner ultimately traceable to Minoan models.[26] Vase-painting offered greater freedom, and herein the full creativity of the Athenian mind revealed itself for the first time. The Dark Age in Athens is no longer very dark. Such abundant, and such clear material has now been reclaimed from the north slope of the Acropolis, from the Agora and from the Cerameicus, that it requires little or no technical knowledge to follow step by step the ingenious workings of the Athenian potters and painters from the twelfth century (or before) to the eighth. Herein lies the chief evidence for Attic culture in these centuries, and its real relevance to the Homeric question.

Nothing like a full description of the growth of Geometric art from the Late Mycenaean can be given in this brief summary, but a few details may serve as illustrations. One of the most prominent motifs of Protogeometric ware is that of concentric half-circles, often resting on a band running around the shoulder of the jug. These half-circles, carelessly drawn freehand, appear often enough on Late Mycenaean and sub-Mycenaean vases, but in Protogeometric times they are drawn more and more frequently with the compass, and finely adjusted to the size and curvature of the vase.[27] Full concentric circles, arranged vertically along a center line and framed by border patterns, are found commonly on Protogeometric pots, and also on some Mycenaean ones from the Acropolis fountain.[28] Numerous other motifs, from periods which employed in any case relatively few, can be traced in their continuance, or development, for four hundred years: the spiral, the dotted outline pattern, the slanting rope-design, and the omnipresent double-axe motif, stylized in Geometric art to the "butterfly" design of two triangles with a common apex.[29] One critic is even tempted to see in the familiar Geometric motif of a chevron filled with cross-hatching a formalization of the Mycenaean "mountain and tendril" design, thought to be symbolic of the marriage of Zeus and Hera.[30] Examples could be multiplied, such as the long preservation and slow transformation of the stirrup-jar shape, or the recrudescence of Mycenaean armaments, rapier and figure-eight shield, on late Geometric vases, or the occasional reappearance of a ridged foot, reminiscent of Middle Helladic design, in the eighth or ninth century.[31] The point lies in two features upon which all are agreed: the unbroken continuity of this pottery, and the vigorous creative originality which it evinces.[32]

From the degeneration of the last phase of Mycenaean decoration, with its "close" style as seen in the Granary class pottery of Mycenae, the early Protogeometric artists took refuge at first in an extreme simplicity. Much reserved space, broken only by the usual half-circles or a wavy band, characterizes the early style. Then gradually old designs are reformed and reintroduced, till the ripe Protogeometric arrives about the middle of the tenth century, a triumph of rhythmic, organic art. Yet it is interesting also to note that even as early as the Granary period (first half of the twelfth century) Athenian potters resisted the chaotic *horror vacui* of the Granary style,[33] and that even then, perhaps, restraint and a certain chastity had made their homes at Athens. In any case, from the tenth century on, there is a distinct consciousness of the relationship between the decoration and the space to be decorated, a profound intuition of the dynamics of a curve and the geodesic properties of a line. Instructive contrasts can be drawn between Attic ware and the pottery of any other region during the whole Geometric period: nowhere else is such tectonic rhythm observable, nor such tactful adjustment of older elements and fine workmanship.[34] Both the continuity and the ingenuity seem to be Attic.

There is something at once Hellenic and Homeric in such originality in the handling of traditional material. This point will be taken up again; here it is important to note only that the history of Protogeometric and Geometric pottery of Attica displays, with clinical precision, the growth of the Hellenic spirit, from its roots to its first masterpieces, in one art form. The growth of the Homeric epic from the old Achaean heroic tale, to judge from what we know of Homer's verse and from what we can guess about his predecessors', cannot have followed a very different course. The intuitive refinement and formalization of representationalism is everywhere inherent in Geometric art, and so is it, too, in Homer. It further appears that the genius which created Geometric art not only was preserved during the Dark Age in Attica, but also originated there. It has recently been shown, from a study of all Protogeometric pottery, that the style began in Athens, and that Athenian pots were widely exported throughout the Cyclades as far east as Cos and Lesbos, as well as to the Argolid and Corinthia, where they gave rise to the local styles.[35] The implications of these facts are wide: they imply not merely a local artistic leadership, but also a considerable commercial sphere for Athens in the tenth century. The eastward limit of that sphere, indeed, is still the islands, and as yet hardly touches Asia Minor, a point which is important in regard to the spread of the Ionic dialect. But it becomes an inescapable conclusion that Athens in the Dark Age was not only culturally and politically independent, but also commercially dominant.[36]

Such vigor on the part of Athens, however, at a time when the rest of Greece still staggered under the recent upheavals, was not necessarily or wholly due to native spontaneity, or the mere fact that the people had managed to resist invasion. The Protogeometric period witnessed a considerable increase in population in Attica, which cannot have been due to a mere rising birth rate.[37] Skeletal material, never too abundant for prehistoric Greece, is nevertheless sufficient in the case of Attica to show that during the Dark Age, the typical Mycenaean skull, of basically Mediterranean type with absorbed Nordic characteristics, underwent certain changes which in turn led to the blended type of classical times.[38] Although the intrusive elements in the sub-Mycenaean era include European Alpine and Nordic-Iranian, suggesting the possible presence of Dorians, yet the strong maintainance of Mediterranean types seems to indicate a bolstering on the other hand of this earlier stratum, perhaps from the Peloponnesus.[39] In any case, though some of the subspecies are new, both Nordic and Alpine elements had been present in Attica and elsewhere in Greece since the Middle Helladic invasion, at which time their appearance doubtless corresponds to the introduction of Greek. These skulls, therefore, need not be specifically Dorian.[40] They are much more likely, indeed, to have belonged to Achaeans or Aeolians, dislodged from their lands by the Dorians, and seeking refuge in Attica.

The assumption that they came from outside finds some support in the rather sudden introduction of cremation burial in the Protogeometric period. Once thought to have originated with the Dorians, cremation seems now curiously linked to the rise and expansion of Protogeometric from 1100–950, and may perhaps have originated in Attica.[41] On the other hand, it does occur elsewhere,[42] and the more likely explanation is that it was employed by sojourners on foreign soil as a mode of disposal which would be available to those without land in which to cut the chamber tombs which served as family vaults.[43] Especially in Attica, where land was scarce in all periods, refugees could hardly have acquired much, at least not for a long time, and elaborate tombs cut in another's land might be unwelcome. On the other hand, ashes in an urn required only an inconsiderable space which could be either publicly devoted to the purpose, or privately granted. The question of where the Greeks may have learned cremation in the first place perhaps leads back to the Trojan War. Cremation was almost universal in Troy, and it is possible that the Achaeans, as Homer narrates, adopted the custom out of necessity; a beachhead offers little room for the stately tombs which the Mycenaeans constructed on their own territory.[44] The absence of all Homeric reference to such great tombs may be due to the simple fact that no Greek whose funeral is described ever dies on home soil, with two exceptions, where the evidence is ambiguous: the shade of Anticleia, Odysseus' mother, implies that her body was burned indeed; but that of Amphimedon, in referring to the funeral he hopes to receive, makes no mention of fire.[45] It is possible that in the case of Anticleia, the epic generalization of cremation has taken precedence over the specific situation, in the same way that a generalizing epithet, even if none too appropriate, has a formal right to stand with any heroic name.

When the Dorians came, the Mycenaean people fled their homes, and if the dialects of Arcadia, Cyprus, and Pamphylia indicate where some of them went, there is much to indicate that a great number went to Attica. The remark of Thucydides about Athens' reception of refugees after the Dorian invasion is well known.[46] Pausanias is more specific. He tells how the Achaeans, driven out by the Dorians, tried to invade the lands of the Ionians in the northern Peloponnesus. The latter appealed to Athens, who received them, not so much because they cared about the Ionians as because they thought they would be an added bulwark against the Dorians.[47] The finely balanced motives already suggest typical Athenian temperament, in whose piety there was always an understandable grain of interested foresight. But if the chronology is not altogether mixed up, the Ionians were not the first exiles to come. The king who received them was Melanthus, the great-grandnephew of Nestor of Pylos, and he himself had been driven from Messenia to Attica, where he supplanted Thymoetes, the last of the Theseids.[48] The tradition is a little confusing here, for presumably the Theseids had been supplanted a century or so earlier by Menestheus with help from Laconia; indeed, what happened to the sons of Theseus is a hopeless tangle. But all authorities are agreed that the last dynasty of Athens was a Neleid one, consisting of Melanthus, his son Codrus who died fighting the "Peloponnesians" (Dorians), and his grandson Neleus, who led a colony to Miletus. That refugees came also from the north, from Orchomenos and Thebes, seems a reasonable inference, though the mixture of West Greek with the native Aeolic of those regions prompts the thought that perhaps in part the Aeolians received the Dorians more peacefully and intermarried with them. But amid the many confusions, it is at least evident that Athens provided a natural haven from the Dorians for all who could get there. Aristotle says that the Athenians were generous with their citizenship in these years.[49] The fame of Athens as receiver of the suppliant, so dear to the dramatists of the fifth century, has its roots in very early times.[50] For Homer, even Orestes found refuge from his murderous mother not in Phocis, but in Athens.[51]

No exact chronology can be worked out, of course, for these events. The date of Codrus is a problem, though the four generations which separate him from Nestor should bring him into the eleventh century, which is reasonable.[52] The Neleids in the eleventh and the Erechtheids in the two preceding centuries, or longer, bring

Attic royal history far into the Mycenaean age; and there are even traces of two dynasties before the Erechtheids. Myths and legends do not, of course, represent precise history. But they do represent patterns of behavior and collective aspirations, and in terms of such general formulations, the legendary events of Attica may be seen as true. And these present a picture consistent with archaeological findings: that Athens, with her long royal pedigrees and her boast of autochthonous origin, was, if not the most famous, at least the longest-lived of the Mycenaean states; that she survived the Dorian assault, and received suppliants from cities which did not survive; that as a result of this not wholly disinterested assistance to her neighbors, she suffered land-poverty, though in other respects the cross-fertilization may have been culturally stimulating; and that by 900, or perhaps earlier, overpopulation led her to undertake the colonization of the islands and the coasts of Asia Minor. The tradition that Neleus, son of Codrus, led a colony from Athens to Miletus need not be taken literally, but its essential elements, a foreign leader in Athens being somehow responsible for a colony overseas, fits exactly with what can be known with certainty, however the exact dates and circumstances may be dim.[53]

One or two remaining points may further illustrate how dim the connection was between the Ionian colonies and the direct stream of Mycenaean bardic tradition. The colonists, for instance, do not seem to have been Ionians in the earlier sense of the name. Herodotus lists a most heterogeneous group of emigrants, even including some Dorians,[54] and indeed the emigrants ought, in view of the times, to have been heterogeneous. Later Herodotus, attempting to say what an Ionian is, concludes that they can be distinguished only on cultural grounds: all those who spring from Athens and keep the Apaturia are Ionians.[55] These two points in themselves make it clear that Ionia was settled by Athens, at least primarily; the Apaturia is a strictly Attic feast. Whoever the Ionians were who came to Athens under Melanthus, the Asiatic Ionians owed their very identity as such to the mother city, and were in every cultural and national sense its product. Perhaps this is the reason why Homeric epic fails to distinguish Athenians from Ionians. The latter are mentioned only once, and then it is clear that the Athenian soldiers of Menestheus are meant.[56] Such a confusion, if it is a confusion, could hardly have arisen if the epic had been preserved in an Ionia that had flourished independently throughout the Dark Age. It must have arisen at a time when the Ionians of the Peloponnese and the Athenians had merged themselves to a degree, that is, in the period of migration, or a short while before in the period of foreign asylum at Athens. It has been wondered why the Ionians, if the Homeric poems belonged to them, should be mentioned once only, and then vaguely, and the conclusion seemed to follow that the poems had been originally Aeolic. But the Aeolians are not mentioned at all, and by this argument have even less right to the epic than the Ionians. The *Iliad* and the *Odyssey* are the terminations of a long agglutinative tradition, not the product of any single dialectal group.

Unless the evidence just reviewed is completely misleading, there should be little remaining doubt that Athens, and not Ionia, was the cradle of the Greek epic, after the fall of the Achaean states. Oral poetry requires, as a *sine qua non* of survival, a continuous tradition of bard instructing bard in the formulaic techniques, and Athens is unique in providing the necessary conditions. Of the refugees who came to Attica, clearly some of the most distinguished would have been singers. To their former patrons, the bards had been sacrosanct; to the Dorians they may not have been. More important, the bards needed an audience who would listen. For a while after the fall of Mycenae, audiences could doubtless have been found in small enclaves of the older population wherever they had been able to maintain themselves. But as the subjugation of the Peloponnesus and parts of the north became more complete, such enclaves, at least from the cultural point of view, must have shrunk to nearly nothing, while those who could remove themselves to the safe bastions and liberal promise of Athens. In Boeotia and Thessaly, where a strong Aeolic element continued, more of the old culture and the old songs may have survived than in the Peloponnesus. Yet, if Boeotia and Thessaly had been the chief preservers of the epic, epic dialect would indeed have been chiefly Aeolic, and by the eighth century it would have been mixed also with the Northwest Greek which penetrated those lands, for oral verse slowly acquires dialectal habits from its environment. But Northwest Greek is totally lacking. A further point is that had the epic tales survived only in obscure places, the creation of such a work as the *Iliad* would have been unlikely. Those who study today the survival of oral epic in Yugoslavia and Greece find remarkable songs, but chiefly short ones. The atmosphere needed to produce the *Iliad* out of the old Achaean lays was one which not only preserved tradition but refashioned it into a shape appropriate to the world which was rising out of the old Achaean world. Only in the development of Athenian Geometric pottery is such an atmosphere evident. Whatever scraps of the tradition survived in Cyprus, or Aeolic lands, these were isolated and abortive. The center of the world, and with it the bulk and the real life of epic poetry, had shifted to Athens.

In the history of Homeric scholarship, the thought has occurred sporadically that Homer should be associated with Athens.[57] Aristarchus and Dionysius Thrax even thought that Homer was an Athenian.[58] The theory has always been decried on three principal grounds: the dialect, the "Pisistratean recension," and the dependency of Athens upon Ionia until the late sixth century. Archaeology has now come near to disposing of the last of these arguments completely. The Pisistratean theory has long been the incubus of Homeric studies, but internal evidence and a real reckoning with the nature of oral verse may make it clear that Pisistratus recognized, and did not create, in the *Iliad* the national poem of the Athenians. As for the dialect, it is really not so great a problem, if the facts be consulted. Once termed "Old Ionic," to fit the belief in Ionian origin, the epic dialect is now correctly analyzed as a mixture, basically Ionic, with strong Aeolic elements and a sprinkling of Arcado-Cypriote and Attic forms. Although oral poetry regularly shows a tendency to dialectal mixture, because of the borrowing of phrases by singers of different districts, the case with Homer seems to be a little more extreme than most. Moreover, the elements are closely welded, especially the Ionic and Aeolic elements, so that no stratification of the poems is possible: any dialectal form can turn up anywhere, and all are used with equal ease. This fact implies that, however various were the origins of the epic language, by the time it was used for the *Iliad* and the *Odyssey* it had become a crystallized, unified vehicle, whose formulae preserved useful and effective expressions from many periods and places, the fashioning of generations of bards. Two principal questions arise in connection with it: first, what circumstances can account for such an extraordinary blending of heterogeneous speech into an artificial unity; and second, what is the nature of the chief component, usually called Ionic?

The answer to the first question is probably to be found in the events which took place in Athens in the period between the fall of Mycenae and the end of the eighth century. If Attica received the singers exiled from the fallen courts of the Achaeans, it must be assumed that numerous representatives of the three chief dialects of the Late Bronze Age were brought into closer contact than ever before. The princely *aoidos*, or minstrel, as pictured in the *Odyssey*, is a rather stationary fixture in contrast to the wandering rhapsode, his classical descendant. Although the *aoidoi* doubtless heard each other on occasion in the earlier time and perhaps borrowed phrases, with the uprooting of the tradition and its regathering in Attica, epic language must have entered a new phase. Now Achaeans, Aeolians, and Ionians must sing in each others' presence, profiting to the extent of collecting into their repertories many new phrases, and building still others by the vigorous exercise of analogy. The process would have taken a long time, but there are about four centuries in the Dark Age, and that is certainly enough. Meanwhile, the audience also grew slowly accustomed to the mixture, which is an important point. For if any singer had suddenly presented his audience with the epic language as we have it, it would have seemed almost as outlandish as it does to the beginning student. Such a blend demands special sociological conditions which are to be found only in Attica between 1150 and 750. Not only the language demands these conditions. The subject matter itself, with its profusion of stories from all different periods and regions, requires a transcendence of local predilections. Finally the whole conception of the large, ecumenical epic must have its roots in some mingling and concentration of ethnic traditions in a limited territory. The Homeric view of the past embraces local tales from everywhere in Greece, the islands, and Asia Minor, and sees them all as parts of a great whole. Tne welding of these requires, in its rudiments, more than the fire of a single genius. It requires a crucible in which the ingredients are forced to mingle for a sufficient time.

If Athens had fallen to the Dorians, Greek epic poetry, if it survived at all, would have been a very different thing.

As it is, besides the blend of stories from everywhere, there is also the blend of dialects in Homer, with a predominance of what is usually called Ionic. The next question is what this Ionic really is. Historical Ionic is known from inscriptions of the seventh century onward, from the pages of Herodotus and Hippocrates and the earlier Ionian poets, Archilochus, Callinus, Semonides of Amorgos, and Anacreon. Its distinguishing features are, primarily, (1) the use of eta for an inherited long ā, even after epsilon, iota, or rho; (2) open spelling of unlike contiguous vowels which were probably pronounced with contraction; (3) a tendency to inflect athematic verbs as if they were contract verbs; (4) the use of kappa for pi in indefinite and relative pronouns and adverbs; and (5) in Eastern Ionic, the loss of h (psilosis). Of these, (1) and (2) occur regularly, but not universally in Homer; (3) occurs, but is balanced by an almost equal occurrence of the Aeolic tendency to inflect contract verbs like athematic ones; (4) never occurs, and (5) is confined to a very small number of words, from which the h may have been lost when the epic was first transliterated from the uncial Attic alphabet, which had an h, to the Ionic, which did not. But the real question is, when did Ionic get these characteristics? The usual view is that they are very old, that Ionic dialect is the oldest in Greece, and that Attic is a younger derivative of it. But even on the face of it, the assumption is unlikely, when one considers that it involves dating back dialectal characteristics without change some four hundred years, from the seventh century to about the eleventh, when we first hear of Ionians, as separate from Attica, coming from the Peloponnesus to Athens under Melanthus. What these particular Ionians spoke is likely to remain a mystery, but it is a safe guess that it was not much like the language of Herodotus. Even if it had been, they could not have kept it pure in Attica for a few centuries and then planted it in the eastern colonies. The case of Aeolic has created a false analogy. The Aeolic of Lesbos and Asia Minor is, indeed, purer than that of the mainland in historic times. But Aeolis was doubtless colonized somewhat earlier than Ionia, and before the mixture of mainland Aeolic with Northwest Greek took place; and furthermore, the Aeolian colonists doubtless did not pass through the melting pot of Attica. Some Aeolians probably came to Attica, but these joined the Ionic colonies, not the Aeolic, even as Herodotus says.[59]

There has never been reason to believe that the Ionic dialect arose in the shape we know it before the colonization of Ionia, and the late date now indicated for that event equally indicates a late date for the dialectal development. This fact must put a new light upon our view of the relationship between Attic and Ionic, and upon Homer's relation to both. Ionic is a branch of Attic, not the other way around, and the dialect of Homer took shape in an Attic atmosphere, dialectally as well as otherwise, and not in an Ionic one. The Ionic characteristics listed above can all be shown either to be late developments, or to represent old practices which must once have been shared by Attic at an early stage. Strabo says that the early Ionians and Athenians once spoke the same dialect,[60] and the statement has usually been taken to mean that they both spoke an Ionic from which the pungent Attic characteristics later emerged. But it must mean that they both spoke an East Greek dialect which did not as yet contain the full roster of characteristics of either of its historical branches. The name does not matter, but since it must have been spoken on Attic soil almost exclusively for some centuries before Ionia was founded, it seems only just to call it Attic.

Certain specifically Attic forms, corresponding to later practise, have long been known in Homer. Most of them are regarded as late modernizations of the text dating at earliest from the time of Pisistratus. Zenodotus changed some of them to what he felt was proper Ionic. But Aristarchus, who thought Homer an Athenian, left them alone, and one of the greatest of modern linguists writing on the subject has said:

Perhaps, if the possibility arises of seeing a wider range of activity in the epic on the part of Attic bards, many difficulties of Homeric speech will be quietly removed, and therewith analysis may reach a stopping point. In any case, the attempt must be made.[61]

It is time we reckoned with the Athenian bards. One may not be willing to believe with Aristarchus that Homer himself was an Athenian. One must, however, recognize that the Attic dialect, much as we know it, must have been current in Athens by the eighth century, and that for sometime before, its characteristics were beginning to emerge. Epic speech is conservative and admits colloquial elements slowly, but it does admit them. If eta for inherited long ā is almost universal in Homer, so was it in earlier Attic.[62] Yet long ā does occur, as in Attic, after epsilon, iota, or rho, and such an occurrence is to be explained as the casual effect of early Attic colloquial speech upon the epic tradition. The phenomenon of *diectasis*, or reopened contractions with altered vowels, can only be traced to earlier contractions, and at that, the characteristic Attic ones. The scarcity of psilosis in Homer bespeaks a period before the loss of h in Eastern Ionic, possibly through contact with Aeolic speech. The prevalence of open contiguous vowels rather than contracted ones is an epic conservatism due to the metrical demand for dactyls, though the frequency of synizesis points to the regular spoken practice of contraction in both Ionic and Attic. It requires far more manipulation and guesswork to maintain the old theory than to explain both the Ionic and Attic phenomena of Homer as an essentially truthful representation of epic dialect in the eighth century, a dialect basically Old Attic with many absorbed Aeolic and Achaean formulae, and influenced to a degree by some features of the newer, contemporary speech of Athens and Ionia.[63] Actually, it is difficult to find in Homer any form or word which must be only Ionian and cannot have been also early Attic.

A minor degree of corruption may have taken place. But it is poor method to assume a corruption if the text as it stands can be explained. To assume that the Ionic of Homer is of an Attic and not of a colonial variety, is only consistent with the archaeological and anthropological evidence and with the historical and legendary tradition. The doctrine that Homer had been modernized in the sixth century and later, partly for political reasons and partly by accident, was once perhaps, the only recourse. Now that the role of Attica in preserving the traditions of the Achaeans can be adumbrated with such probability, it becomes far more natural to conclude that Attic phenomena in the text, whether dialectal or involving subject matter, are old and genuine and do not postdate the time of Homer himself. Pisistratus may well have enshrined the *Iliad* and *Odyssey* as inevitable parts of the Panathenaic festival, but he did not have to put them together, modernize them, or nationalize them for the purpose. They owed a large part of their existence to Attica from the first.

This is not to say that Homer was Athenian. When the Greeks did go to Ionia, they could not have left the epic behind. Homer himself, as the conflicting claims to him indicate, could have lived anywhere within certain limits, and we shall certainly never know much more than that. The claim of Chios has received specious support from the mingling of Aeolic and Ionic dialects in that island, and from the famous close of the *Hymn to the Delian Apollo*. But the admixture of Aeolic in the epic language must long predate the mingling of dialects in Chios. As for the *Hymn to the Delian Apollo*, the author of that decorative and charming poem is as clearly an Ionian as the author of the grave *Hymn to Demeter* was Athenian. Homer's work differs greatly from both, but his spiritual affinities are essentially Attic. If the Ionians later found in him models for their own vivid, delicate, and often pessimistic poetry, it should not be forgotton that also for Sappho the Aeolian, Homer offered visions to her taste — Helen, Hector, and Andromache. Homer was universal in classic Greece, and even the Spartan Tyrtaeus found what he wanted there. Yet the truly distinguishing mark of Homer, of the *Iliad* in particular, is something which recurs only in the Athenian poets, Solon, Aeschylus, and Sophocles: that is, the great metaphysical questions of the bases of individual identity, of justice, time, and the imbalance between action and result. These are the questions which impelled Athenian culture toward its greatest achievements, and they are likewise the forces which underlie the vast energy of Homer's heroic conceptions. The general voice of antiquity, which connects his name with Ionia is probably justified. He may well have lived in a colony. But his works, like every other early Ionian work of art, belong in the cultural milieu of Athens, with the masterpieces of Dipylon vase-painting, with the earliest records of Greek writing, and with the first stirrings of the austere intuition of tragedy.

IV

FESTIVALS, PISISTRATUS, AND WRITING

THERE is a vaguely defined but widely current conception that either Pisistratus, or his son Hipparchus, or both of them, in the late sixth century, did something to the text of Homer which accounts for the shape in which we have it today. The full-blown form of this conception, which some still believe, is that Pisistratus, or perhaps Hipparchus, was the first to collect the songs of Homer, which hitherto had been orally disseminated in different parts of the Greek world, to write them down, arrange them into the *Iliad* and the *Odyssey*, and have them performed by rhapsodes at the Panathenaea as a legally established part of the festival. Not everyone believes all this, but most people believe that Pisistratus, or one of his friends, at least interpolated a few verses, and almost all agree that the lines of the *Catalog*, which associate Ajax with Athens are a falsification, inserted for political reasons in the time of Pisistratus, to justify Athens' recent seizure of the island of Salamis from the Megarians. Intermediate variations on the theme are innumerable, but in any form it involves some grave misapprehensions. The most grave are that the Attic aspects of the poems, whether dialectal or otherwise, are inconsistent and late, and that the *Iliad* as we have it represents the taste and outlook of the sixth century; and finally that the vulgate text is a hopelessly corrupted affair through which we can never penetrate to what Homer really said.

The Pisistratean theory, first formulated in modern times by Wolf in 1795, was documented by him from ancient sources, which, though they conflicted greatly, all pointed to Pisistratus' having done something to Homer.[1] Believing as he did that Homer lived long before writing was invented, Wolf could find no other way to explain the survival of the epics in written form. We now know, through the energetic fieldwork of Parry and others, that oral poetry does not behave according to his suppositions, and that the operations of Pisistratus are not only unnecessary, but even impossible. But the Pisistratean theory still enjoys wide popular currency.

Even in antiquity, where Wolf first found it, the theory seems to have been a popular, not a learned one. One of our earliest sources states that Hipparchus first brought the poems to Attica; but the same author says that Hipparchus was the elder son of Pisistratus, a belief which Thucydides says was popularly, but falsely, held by most Athenians.[2] The whole story sounds like the mere echoing of a folktale. The Greeks loved a first discoverer for everything, and if the real one could not be found, they invented one. The Spartans claimed that Homer had been introduced into their city around the year 700 by the half-mythical Lycurgus.[3] It seems dubious, to say the least, that Sparta should have been blessed so early, and that Homer, who had been imitated for nearly two centuries by many poets, including Solon, had to be introduced to Athens by Hipparchus. For a century and a half or so, Athens had indeed suffered social and economic retard, while Corinth, Sparta, and the Ionian cities took the lead. But she must have ceased to exist, for the Hipparchus story to be true, for it presumed a Homer already complete and well known in Ionia and elsewhere. Athens was not so backward or so isolated as that. Aristotle, who describes Hipparchus' literary patronage, mentions Anacreon, Simonides, and others, but not Homer.[4]

The other, even more popular story, that Pisistratus first collected the scattered remains of Homer's poetry and arranged them in writing, rests principally upon an amalgam of the testimony of Cicero (nearly half a millennium after the event), Flavius Josephus, the historian of the Jews, Pausanias, and an epigram in the Greek Anthology, of uncertain date, no authority, and clearly tendentious import.[5] Some illustrious names in scholarship can be found subscribing to this belief. Its inherent difficulties, which have been well analyzed by Wilamowitz,[6] scarcely need repetition, since it flies so vehemently in the face of both oral theory and the real aesthetics of the Homeric poems. Like the story of Hipparchus, it is a legend, and its growth as such has recently been clearly spelled out.[7]

But even those who reject all other forms of the Pisistratean theory generally admit that Pisistratus interpolated the poems to a degree. The ancient testimony for this belief is more respectable than the rest, but it affects only a very few passages, notably those dealing with Athens, which are supposed to have been added for nationalistic reasons. The suspicion of Athenian interpolation, usually attributed to Pisistratus, but sometimes to Solon and sometimes to flattering rhapsodes, seems to have grown steadily from the time when the Megarians, smarting under the loss of Salamis, first accused the Athenians of having added the lines in the *Catalog*, which connect the Salaminian Ajax with Athens. They had their own version of these lines which connected him, and especially Salamis, with Megara. From this point on, suspicion has grown around almost every mention of Athens or of Athenian heroes in Homer, and "Pisistratean" tampering has been found everywhere. Even the son of Nestor in the *Odyssey*, whose name unluckily is Pisistratus, has been thought to be an imposter.[8] Yet the whole idea ultimately stems from the accusations of a political enemy, and our most direct knowledge of it hangs by the conjectural completions of a lacuna in a remark by the otherwise unknown historian Dieuchidas of Megara, as quoted by Diogenes Laertius in the third century A.D.![9] Even the *scholia* which deal with these lines must go back to this, or a similar Megarian source.

It is perhaps time that we look at the Salaminian passage in a different light, and ask, in particular, if it is really inconsistent, as is usually said, with the rest of the *Iliad*, or if the wish to see in all Homeric references to Athens belated attempts to usurp a place in Holy Writ may be, to say the least, a prejudice. If we examine Mycenaean Athens in the light of its Cyclopean walls, Palace, water supply, royal tombs, pottery, gold, ivory, and other obvious wealth, it is clear that the city was by no means insignificant, and that the occasional references to her in Homer are not, on the face of it, likely to be counterfeits. Neither the Athenians nor their leaders, Menestheus, Iasus, and Stichius, do anything sufficiently wonderful to justify a forgery, and the only lines for which any reasonable motive for such can be found are the Salamis lines. The Athenians did indeed take Salamis from Megara in the days of Solon, and they may have tried to authenticate their claim by an appeal to the *Iliad*. But did they have to invent the relevant passage, or was it there? It is sometimes asserted, for instance, that Ajax is nowhere else in the *Iliad* associated with the Athenians.[10] But this is not true. In three good-sized passages of the Great Battle, Ajax fights together with the Athenians,[11] and his brother Teucer has a bow-carrier with the singularly Athenian name of Pandion.[12] These passages in the *Iliad* show perfect harmony with other tradition. The Athenian tribe Aiantis, the Athenian cults of Ajax and Athena Aiantis, and the family which derived itself from his grandson Philaeus could scarcely all have been invented by Pisistratus.[13] After the death of Ajax, legend has it that Teucer pleaded his cause with Telamon from a boat in the Piraeus, not in Salamis — a judicial technicality which hints significantly that the administrative center of the district was in Athens.[14]

Moreover, geography, legend, and what little can be inferred from material remains make it highly likely that Salamis was closely associated with Athens in the Mycenaean period. Less than a mile of water separates the island from the Attic mainland, so that as in the case of Tiryns and Mycenae, it would appear impossible from a military point of view for a small independent state to exist so close to one so heavily fortified and so flourishing as Athens. Late Helladic sites on Salamis have not been excavated, but it would be very surprising if any turned out to be comparable to Athens. The states of the Saronic Gulf must have been unified under the leadership of Athens. The tradition of her early rivalry with Eleusis reflects precisely what must have happened between the two principal cities of the region. Already at Eleusis in the Late Bronze Age, a temple stood on the site of the Telesterion of the Mysteries, and other contemporary remains indicate a flourishing city.[15] The defeat of the Eleusinians by Erechtheus seems to have brought Megara also under the sway of Athens eventually. In any case, Pylas, king of Eleusis, bequeathed the town to the Athenians, who lost it only later in Codrus' war with the Peloponnesians.[16]

The case of Megara may not be dissimilar. The burial of the Athenian king Pandion in Megara, and that of the Megarian king Nisus in Athens point to a close connection between these two cities also in pre-Dorian times.[17] In its very early period, Megara is supposed to have fought and lost a war with Minos of Crete; the Cretans took down the ring wall of the city, which was not restored until the time of Alcathous.[18] This Cretan conquest of Megara may provide the origin of the story of the Athenian girls and boys sent as tribute to the Minotaur. No evidence exists for believing that Crete ever dominated Athens,[19] whereas there is a story that Periboea, daughter of King Alcathous of Megara and mother of Ajax, went with Theseus when he sailed to Cnossos.[20] Later the story was told that the tribute consisted of Athenian youth, but it is possible that originally they were Megarians, whom Theseus rescued. Theseus, after all, had mastered the whole Saronic region in his early years.

Returning now to the *Catalog*, one finds that neither Eleusis nor Megara receives any mention, while Salamis has only the two lines about Ajax. The picture which emerges is the perfectly credible one of Athens around 1200, under King Menestheus, dominating the whole Saronic Gulf, with Ajax of Salamis as the most distinguished warrior of the contingent, even as Diomedes is the most distinguished warrior of the Argolid. Several strands of tradition bind this whole Saronic regime to the rest of the Achaean world. On his mother's side, Ajax was the grandson of Alcathous, son of Pelops, who slew the lion of Cithaeron, married the daughter of King Megareus, and became king of Megara.[21] Like so many other Achaeans, he owed his throne to an exploit and a state marriage, and like other Tantalids, he seems to have murdered his sons.[22] On the paternal side, Ajax is an Aeacid, and a kinsman of Achilles. His half-brother Teucer's Trojan mother, not to mention his traditional colonization of Cypriote Salamis and his very name, perhaps point to the eastern background of the Achaeans proper. As for Menestheus himself, although of Erechtheid stock, he seems to have usurped the throne from Theseus, with the help of the sons of Tyndareus.[23] Such political interference from the Peloponnesus, together with the presence of Tantalid princes in Megara continuing down to Hyperion, "son of Agamemnon," [24] and half-Tantalids in Salamis, suggests precisely the sort of loose federation of a feudal world whose leadership maintains itself by ennobling marriages and intrigue. Without taking the tradition too literally, one may be permitted to see herein the spread of Achaean rule in Attica and the Megarid in the thirteenth century, with its center on the Acropolis. The old Aeacid rule of Aegina, where a Late Helladic palace stands, magnificent in design and workmanship, gives way to the half-Aeacid, half-Tantalid rule of Telamon and Ajax in Salamis; Eleusis is long since conquered; Megara falls under Tantalid sway, while Menestheus, with help from the Peloponnesus, masters Athens, and is regarded in Homeric tradition as the rightful overlord of the whole district. There seems little reason to doubt Ajax' associations with this Saronic federacy; and one need not look to Menestheus for a figure to gratify Athenian pride at recitations of Homer. Ajax is the great Athenian hero of the *Iliad*, even if he actually lived in Salamis, and his fame was second only to Achilles'.

If the above formulation seems fanciful, and dependent largely upon fable and legend, at least there is more to support it now than there was twenty years ago. Mycenaean Athens can no longer be called insignificant. Her pottery, as said earlier, shows wide commercial connections, as well as characteristic local designs.[25] Her other monuments suggest a degree of power which must have unified the Attic peninsula; and indeed, there may be more than fable in the tradition that it was Theseus who first accomplished the political union of Attica.[26] Homer, for instance, never speaks of Attica or Atticans, but always of Athenians, even when he is talking about Sunion.[27] The *Catalog* has been thought to be strongly influenced by later Athenian poets because of the omission of Megara, Thebes, and Aegina, and the belittlement of Corinth and Salamis.[28] Actually, the *Catalog* seems to represent the situation rather as it should have been: Megara and Aegina must have been under Athenian control; Salamis is mentioned only for Ajax' sake; Corinth was not particularly important in the Mycenaean period, and in any case her relations with Attica were slight.[29] As for Thebes, even elsewhere in the *Iliad* she is only mentioned in connection with events that took place there in the past, such as the expedition of the Seven, the stories of Heracles or Semele, or the funeral of Oedipus. The reason is that Thebes had been very recently sacked by the Epigoni, and had no importance any longer, so that her omission from the *Catalog* is entirely consistent with the rest of the poem.[30] There is actually no more reason to think that any hand has tampered with these *Catalog* entries, to the greater glory of Athens, than there is to exclude Ajax from his rightful position, or to take exception to any of the so-called Athenian passages.[31]

The whole treatment of Athens in the *Iliad* and *Odyssey* seems to be about what one might expect from what we now know of her material culture, and what we may plausibly infer from her long tradition. If not so much is said about her as one might expect about an important city, be it noted that a great deal more is said about her than about Tiryns, for instance, whose importance is never doubted. It is perhaps a matter of wrong perspective; Athens dominates so much later on in Greek history, that one is tempted to underestimate her greatness in the Mycenaean period by comparison, and thus arrive at the feeling that all epic references to her must be later forgeries. It is high time the prejudice was abandoned, difficult as it may be to blow away the mist of doubt, once the cry of forgery has been raised.

The Pisistratean theory of Homer, especially in the form which makes Pisistratus the collector, and in some sense the creator of the two great epics, has attracted many because it seemed to fit compelling facts and settle burning questions. It explained why the vulgate text sprang from an Athenian archetype; it explained the writing of hitherto oral poetry; it associated the *Iliad* and *Odyssey* with the establishment, or revival, of the Panathenaea in the sixth century,[32] which fitted with what we know of their performance at that festival later;[33] it explained the Attic forms reasonably as late infiltrations, and the references to Athens as, in good part, falsifications. But examined closely, it raises more difficulties than it seems to solve. In the first place, the tradition is not really consonant with itself: Pisistratus (or Hipparchus) did something, but it is not clear whether he (or they) imported a manuscript into Attica, or collected the scattered oral remains of the poet, or first made the poems part of the Panathenaea, or merely doctored them to the national taste, or forced the rhapsodes to sing them in the correct order.[34] The first importation of a manuscript by Hipparchus seems a clear impossibility for reasons given above.[35] The interpolation theory, in view of the internal evidence of the poems, and the new archaeological evidence for Athens, makes sense only as a political slander, analogous to the exchange of unpleasantnesses between Athens and Sparta in 431.[36] Thus the collection theory is left, and the Panathenaea.

Regarding the former, three extremely difficult questions must be raised. First is the question of the relation of Pisistratus' supposed text to the vulgate as we have it. The papyri of Homer indicate that until the time of Aristarchus, both epics were burdened with a varying number of interpolated verses, (mostly of neutral value and hence probably spurious,) a fact which has led some scholars to believe with Wolf that the vulgate was essentially the creation of Aristarchus.[37] Yet where did these verses come from if Pisistratus had established the canon before 510 B.C., and the official text existed at Athens? Irresponsible improvisation by rhapsodes at the festivals has been offered as an explanation,[38] but this will hardly do, for improvisations, or lines invented to temporize with a lapse of memory or flatter a special audience, are not scrupulously written down by waiting secretaries. An official text could not prevent their occurrence in performance, but it could prevent their being recorded, even if anyone wanted to record them. Moreover, a recent investigator of this problem is now convinced that the Pisistratean archetype was essentially not the text of Aristarchus, but that of Zenodotus — hundreds of lines shorter than the vulgate, and lacking the Shield of Achilles! [39] If that is the truth, we must somehow reconcile such opposing attitudes as are implied in the idea of an official state text, the conception of antique Holy Writ, and the lighthearted tamperings and additions of numberless poets between 510 and 150 B.C., in a couple of poems which everyone knew almost by heart.

We shall return to the problem of the longer and shorter texts; but first we must ask how Pisistratus could have collected Homer. If the poems were still unwritten, he must have invited bards to come sing for him from various parts of the Greek world. Most of these would doubtless be found in Ionia, yet, strange to say, they showed in their epic language none of the more extreme elements of the Ionic dialect which had already spread into elegy. Instead, they showed a certain infusion of Attic. Not all Atticisms in Homer are to be attributed to the mere spelling of the scribes who took the poems down; some are distinctly different forms.[40] Furthermore, bards from different regions sing the same song differently. Yet these scattered bards had a peculiar collective instinct for a harmonious whole. In their case, there must have been an inspired, temporary suspension of that habitual Greek feeling that the bard (or anybody else) who lived on the other side of the mountain was, unless he was a relative, an ignoramus and an imposter, who could scarcely speak Greek and certainly did not know the song right. Somehow these bards had preëmpted the laws which required them to sing in order, unless, of course, what they sang was a chaos of traditions, with numerous beginnings, middles, and ends; in which case, we owe the *Iliad*'s wonderful Geometric structure to Pisistratus, two centuries after the close of the Geometric Age.

Moreover, there is the question of the alphabet. One of the strongest defenders of the theory explains that although the Ionic alphabet was already the alphabet of literature, the official text of Homer was written in the old official script of Attica, unserviceable as it was for the purpose, and then mostly disregarded by the improvising rhapsodes.[41] In such a picture, the concept of officialdom seems at once omnipresent and ineffectual. That the epics were originally written down in the old Attic alphabet lies almost beyond a doubt, for certain spellings in our text could only have arisen from mistakes made in the course of transliterating from the Attic to the Ionic alphabet. But if the *Iliad* were truly an Ionian poem, sung by Ionians, with the Ionian alphabet already in existence, as it had been for almost two centuries, and if it really had been the alphabet of literature, it is hard to believe that official chauvinism would have led Pisistratus to insist on the local lettering. Especially if he had had any interest in establishing an authentic text, he would have chosen the Ionic, which would represent things better. It would seem far more natural to believe that the *Iliad* and *Odyssey* were first written in the Attic script because it was the only script available at the time. Whether or not the Ionic script, when it was officially adopted in 403, had been in private use already for some time is not entirely clear; inscriptions on stone and on vases indicate the contrary, yet on the other hand the evidence for alphabetical transliteration of the tragedians, or Pindar, or even the Homeric *Hymns*, is far from conclusive.[42] It is hard, therefore, to decide when Homer was first transliterated into Ionic script; but whenever this process took place in Attica, it seems necessary to believe that the Ionian Homeridae already had texts of the poems, and that they were likely enough in Ionic letters. The most plausible time for such Ionian copies to be made is certainly the late seventh or early sixth century.[43]

The question of the Panathenaea remains. There seems to be little doubt that Pisistratus either instituted the Great Athenian four-year festival, or else refurbished it with enhanced splendor. The latter is more likely, perhaps; in any case, he may perfectly well have arranged for the first time the formal and complete presentations of the epics which later appear as regular events. A law governing such recitations is known, and though there is some doubt as to its origin,[44] it is unlikely that the poems could ever have been formally given without a few provisory rules. One may probably conclude, therefore, that Pisistratus made, or at least enforced, a law instructing the rhapsodes to sing in order. There are two other things he may have done: he or his son may have purchased a manuscript of Homer from a rhapsodic guild in Ionia, but it was certainly not the first ever seen in Attica, and its function cannot be conjectured. Secondly, Pisistratus may, as the Townley *scholia* suggest, have decided to include the *Doloneia* in the festival performances. There is no compelling reason to believe this, but if true, it is his one contribution to Homeric textual history.

If Pisistratus did this much for Homer, it is surely sufficient to provide the seed of truth necessary for the growth of the legend. It is not to be supposed that a tyrant, however benign, creates a great epic from nothing. Augustus ordered the *Aeneid*, but he ordered it from a well-known and clearly able poet. The two great national epics of the Greeks — whether "national" is taken to mean Panhellenic or Panathenian, and in some sense they are both — could never have been born from the devised cultural program of a despot. They must have arisen from a long-prepared, direct relationship between the poet and his audience, in whom the Hellenic spirit had grown in ways that are at least partly traceable. Athens owed much to Pisistratus, especially an economic and social stability which had been lost for almost two centuries. The political *coup d'état* of Clisthenes was only the last in a series of changes which were to free the Athenians for the realization of their cultural potentialities. But the accomplishments of the twenty eventful years between the fall of Pisistratus and the battle of Marathon were not a birth, but a rebirth. Athens had been great before, in the prehistoric Iron Age, when the other states of Greece were feeble. Her Dark Age came late, in the seventh century, when the abuses which Solon tried to heal became rife. During the next hundred years, Solon and Pisistratus rediscovered and reshaped the Attic spirit to a degree. Their figures may be looked upon as in a way symbolic of two great motivations which characterize fifth-century Athens, the one visionary, architectonic and austere, reflecting profoundly upon the nature of the individual self and political justice, the other the spirit of vivid enterprise, strongly colored by the brilliant new culture of Ionia, with its luxurious love of the decorative, its intellectual vigor, and its hardheaded pursuit of fact. Yet, both Solon and Pisistratus were Athenians; both spirits were native essentially, and both can be seen in Homer and in the Geometric world. When Pisistratus reorganized the Panathenaea to include orderly performances of epic, he did little more than elaborate and glorify what was already a deeply rooted social practice. Though all classical poetry bears a relation to political life, it was never the business of the statesman to create poetry. It was his business to regulate its public performance, under the office of *leitourgia*, and above all, to defray costs. This Pisistratus was in an excellent position to do, and this he probably did, no more. And if he recognized that the *Iliad* had a special appropriateness in Athens, it was not because it celebrated Athens directly, for of course it did not, nor did he try to make it do so. More likely, in the sixth century, when tragedy and comedy were taking shape, the Homeric poems, as prototypes, commended themselves spontaneously to the Athenian mind, with its new leisure and its heightened creative instinct. It is even possible that the Athenian transmission of epic tradition during the Dark Ages had not been totally forgotten,

and that early manuscripts in old Attic characters, the guarded
possessions of rhapsodes, were still visible on occasion, testifying to
Athens' earlier leadership of all things now called Ionian, and to the
near kinship of Homer to the masters of the Dipylon Geometric
style.

It seems highly probable, therefore, in view of the Panathenaic
law, that performances of the *Iliad* and *Odyssey* were regular parts
of the Panathenaea in Pisistratus' time. This association of the poems
with a festival has been pushed even farther, until often it is as-
sumed that Homer actually composed them for a festival and sang
them there. The creation of a long, closely knit epic from a loose
and scattered tradition requires, it is argued, the kind of audience
which can be found in Greece only in the *panegyris*, or large open
festival.[45] Such gatherings were not confined to the people of one
city, but were ecumenical, as is the Homeric epic. Also, they lasted
several days, which would allow sufficient time for a full perform-
ance, and a three-day program of the *Iliad* has been reasonably out-
lined for the Panathenaic presentations.[46] But unless the Panathenaea
was founded in very early times, the *Iliad* must have been composed
for an older festival, perhaps the great one at Delos, or the Panionia,
held on the mountainous promontory of Mycale.[47] The relative
dates, however, of the Ionian and Athenian festivals are a matter
of guesswork.[48] The important point is the connection between the
panegyris and the long epic, a connection which was certainly
real in historical times, and may possibly have been real as early as
Homer.

On the other hand, there are difficulties. It is easy, for instance,
to say that the large, panoramic epic arose, through combination
and reworking, out of the short heroic song; it is less easy to show
how and why it did. Writing is a further problem. The Homeric
poems were orally composed, and if Pisistratus did not have them
written, who did, and when, and why? Most important, perhaps,
is the question: how could the *Iliad*'s great bulk ever have been pro-
duced at a festival or anywhere else by a single singer in three
days? An oral poem is the possession of many bards, in outline
and scenario, but the treatment is the singer's own; Homer's work,
a marvel of design and unity, cannot be anything but the work of
one singer. Yet, the shortest time necessary for a single bard to

produce so much is, by the recent estimate of a collector of oral poetry, two weeks.[49] There are, as yet, no real answers to these questions, but, as always in Homeric scholarship, there is speculation.

In the *Odyssey*, the songs of Demodocus and Phemius give us some idea of the court poems of the Achaeans, although not a very exact one. Homer has summarized and approximated, and the language is his own. In Achilles' self-accompanied song in the *Iliad*, he has represented a nonprofessional version of the same kind of poetry, no doubt. Between these telling, but not very detailed, vignettes of the Achaean times and the product of Homer himself lies a broad artistic and social gulf, fully as striking as that between Mycenaean pottery and the Geometric mastery of the Dipylon style. The promptings which led a poet of the eighth century to evolve a monumental unity out of an unschematized mass of material can, of course, only be guessed at. But the example of Geometric art was more than an example; it was a symptom of the spirit of the age which saw the rise of the city state, and the foundation of those principles of rational order which the Greeks imposed upon themselves. Amid the growth of ethnic self-consciousness, a festival involving people from many different cities and districts might also create a demand for a poetry of a new kind, a Panhellenic kind, which could celebrate the past of all the listeners in a form consistent with the new age. We must assume that poets tried to do this before Homer; oral poetry depends even more directly upon its audience than does written. We may probably assume that poets, attending the festivals like everyone else, sang there at first quite informally, and not at all as an official part of the program. Any gathering of people was a possible audience, and before festival gatherings, oral poetry could begin to evolve from its courtly phase and local concern by degrees into a civic and ethnic organ, until at length it was invited to take its place formally in those public expressions of ethnic unity, the *panegyreis*. And throughout this period, the nascent Hellenic intuition of passion illuminated by order would have been refining, and designing with architectonic consciousness, as in the case of vase-painting, the long and closely cherished tradition of the heroes.

All those early bardic efforts have perished; Homer alone survives. One reason for his survival may be his superior excellence. But his excellence would surely have perished with him but for one fact, the fact that somehow, and for some reason, his work was written down. An oral poem can be infinitely reproduced, as we know, in some sense of the word, and bards claim that they always sing it exactly the same way. But field experiments prove something very different.[50] Each rendition is a recomposition, and the more time intervenes between singings, the more changes occur. Also, epic speech, though conservative, does gather accretions of new elements slowly. Long poems can, indeed, be memorized from a written text and recited with almost perfect exactitude; and poems can be orally, and quite differently, recomposed on the basis of a written text.[51] But without any text at all, the teller of a poem has no choice but to shift and adapt the poem to the developments of taste, language, and style; for of such is the original creativity of the oral singer. Had Homer's works survived only by mouth until the time of Pisistratus, they would have been far more tinged than they are with Attic neologisms; the metrical effect of the digamma would have been felt far less, as it is in the later Homeric *Hymns*;[52] finally, their structure would have had much more in common with the rhythms of Attic black-figure than with the Dipylon style. As it is, the first manuscript must date from the late eighth century, from the time, if not from the hand, of Homer himself.

It is now no longer a matter of any doubt that alphabetic writing was known in Greece by the late eighth century, and probably for a good while before. Its earliest monuments, the Dipylon Prize-Jug and the Hymettus sherds are Attic, and the reasonable inference is that the alphabet was an Attic import from Phoenicia dating from the time of the widespread distribution of Protogeometric pots, that is, about the late tenth and early ninth century. By the early seventh *graffiti* of casual informalities in Thera, as well as scratchings and formal inscriptions from Perachora, Naxos, and elsewhere, testify to long usage and considerable familiarity. Pleasantly enough, the very earliest Attic examples, insofar as they can be read, are all in dactylic hexameter, and the inscriptions of the Dipylon Prize-Jug in particular has a characteristic Athenian flavor of festivity and charm:

Whoever of the dancers disports most gracefully, to him this
[jug or prize?]

The alphabet was no hieratic secret guarded by priests, or confined
to archival accounts, records, or business operations. It was a fairly
public accomplishment by the late eighth century, and people al-
ready wrote verse with it.[53]

It has been suggested that the alphabet was adopted by the
Greeks for the specific purpose of writing epic verse, whose syllabic
constituency cannot be adequately rendered in such a medium as,
for instance, the Cypriote syllabary.[54] Before renouncing such a
theory as too good to be true, it should be admitted that of all the
peoples of antiquity, the early Athenians are most likely to have
conceived the uses of the alphabet as primarily artistic. Homer
probably was written down for the first time by an Athenian hand,
either in Athens or in one of the new colonies. But such a com-
modity as the alphabet finds so many purposes that it is superfluous
to select a single one, such as the writing of epic, as the primary
reason for its introduction. What is even more important, the un-
derlying psychology of oral verse-making is inherently antipathetic
to the idea of writing.[55] The regular assumption of epic singers, that
the song is always the same, even if actually it is not, baffles in
advance the desire for the stabilization which writing imposes. The
song is the possession of a singer, and it requires some basic social
changes to conceive it as reposing in a book. Parry once wrote that
writing destroys the primitive element in early, oral poetry, and
"accounts for the growth of a new form of society in which there
is no longer any place for the old heroic ideal." [56] More precisely,
the heroic ideal never really lost its place in Hellenic society, but
it did constantly suit itself to varying phases, and Homer himself
perhaps represents such a self-adaptation.

In the sense that he is at once the climax of the oral tradition
and the beginning of written literature, Homer is a transitional
figure.[57] There is not much that is still primitive in Homer, but
whether his refinement and sophistication point to the effects of
writing is a dubious matter.[58] Homer's mode of composition seems
to be, from beginning to end, strictly that of the oral poet. To
assume that he simply took a pen and wrote what he had often sung

is to assume a change which has not yet been observed by any who have ever studied oral poets at first hand; hence the suggestion that Homer dictated to a scribe.[59] This seems the most likely possibility, though at least one example does exist of a man who, from total illiteracy, became an eminent writer, the Greek revolutionary general Makriyannis. Yet Makriyannis did not write what he had sung: while illiterate, he had practiced oral verse-making, but when he learned to write, he wrote prose memoirs.[60] He does not provide the full example which is desired, therefore, of an oral poet transferring his efforts to paper, but he does prompt one or two suggestions about the motivation underlying the writing of the epic. Makriyannis' wish to write a prose account of his activities in the revolution registers in some sense a dissatisfaction with the improvised accounts in verse which he had formerly sung to his companions. In an age when the art of writing has gone far toward thrusting back the boundaries of illiteracy, it can hardly fail to strike a creative artist sooner or later that the medium of pen and paper has something new to offer. One might even say that, with writing, a new idea of permanence is born; oral communication is shown for what it is — inaccurate and shifting. Writing has a godlike stability, and to anyone with an eye for the future, its significance is scarcely to be mistaken. In the case of Makriyannis, we know, from the series of paintings of his own and others' exploits which he had made, reproduced in copies, and circulated to all the courts in Europe, that he entertained some respect for his own future fame. Painting, like writing, procures fixity of form, and it can be made to reach large audiences. If one seeks the motivation for the transference of oral verse to written form it must lie in the disseminated knowledge of writing itself, in its disintegration of the belief that unwritten songs never change, and in the promise of real fixity. One ought, therefore, to associate the great epic, in contrast to the short epic song, not only with festival audiences, but also with writing, not because writing is necessary for its creation, but because the monumental purpose of the large epic is profoundly served by anything which bestows fixity of form. In the century which saw the rise of the city state, the festivals, and the first flowering of the great colonial movement, the Greek mind cannot have failed to recognize that written characters have a peculiar permanence, whatever had been commonly believed about the immutability of oral tradition.

But it is possible to envision an even more functional and inevitable reason for the commitment of the Homeric poems to writing. If the festivals had become, around the end of the eighth century, popular though informal centers for bardic singing, Homer might well have felt a natural interest in displaying his own work there. Yet, if his chef-d'oeuvre were a poem which required two weeks at least to sing, the problem of presenting it in its entirety at a three-day festival became insurmountable. Homer himself might sing parts, but one of the *Iliad's* chief glories is its sustained dramatic unity. Sojourning in a village, his own or strangers', the poet might claim his audience day after day, till the work was done, but if the performance was to be compressed into three days, the singer's voice would fail, and he must have help, even as at the Panathenaea, the rhapsodes relayed each other. If, therefore, the *Iliad* was sung at the Panionian, Delian, or other festivals in Homer's time — and no audience would be more appropriate to such a poem — it must have been performed by a series of singers, just as it was later. Yet, if these singers were all bards in their own right, they would, as oral singers do, recreate in their own way, doubtless with much emulation, and the unity of the poem would be, to a degree, lost. Little Homers must instead be trained to perform the master's work, and in order to restrain their creativity, a fixed text was required. Homer could dictate, the scribe could write, the pupils could learn; and thus the midpoint between oral and written literature could occur.

This is perhaps the origin of the Homeridae, and the first distinction between the *aoidoi*, or oral poets, such as may be observed today in Greece and Yugoslavia, and the rhapsodes of classical antiquity. Oral singers, though they learn from each other, do not normally found guilds, yet the Homerids of Chios were apparently just that. Such a formation requires a special circumstance, and one need not assume that later rhapsodes who called themselves Homeridae were claiming to be either actual descendants of the poet, or were speaking in terms of pure self-adulatory metaphor. They simply preserved a term which doubtless originated to distinguish those singers who were trained to sing Homer's works solely from those who learned the improvisational art of oral composition. In order to train them to sing Homer's words instead of their own inventions, a text was necessary, and this could only be obtained from Homer himself, probably by dictation. This then would be the occasion for the first writing of the Greek oral epic — a "publication" through festival performance by a group of adjutants to the poet, who could not sing the whole thing himself, nor trust others to sing it in his inimitable way without the written word.

This is not to say, however, that the use of writing accounts for the superiority of Homer. For all we know, some of his predecessors may have committed their work to paper somehow. The advantage which a singer gains from dictating his text to a scribe, at a slower pace than usual and consequently with increased opportunity for self-editing, has been observed and described, and one may allow Homer this much advantage from writing.[61] The minor lapses and inconsistencies which dot all oral poetry are remarkably few in Homer, especially considering the size of the poems. Excellence of this sort can be reasonably attributed to the deliberate speed of dictation and, possibly, correction upon review. But one does not need writing to conceive the character of Achilles, to create a glowing simile, or even to construct a long narrative with consummate skill. The thread of poetic creativity lies in successions of images, which for Homer are deeply bound to the formulae of the oral method. Homer's imagery shows a general consistency of pattern which reveals and illustrates the tenor of his poems; but viewed in its details, the imagery is a mass of fluid interplay and half subconscious suggestion, having many of the qualities expected in any impromptu. No one today has ever heard what was a miracle of the eighteenth century, an improvisation by Mozart; but a couple of his fantasias may convey some idea of what it was like.[62] Certainly the concept of structure and unity in these pieces is an intuitive one, quite different from the schematized method of the more formally composed works. Indeed, Mozart, with his extraordinary gift for composing long works in his head and then writing them down whole with scarcely a correction later, offers what may not be the worst analogy to Homeric methods of composition.

To summarize, then: the newly established festivals of the eighth century created a new kind of audience, representative of all

Greeks, more or less, and thus put the heroic tradition under the necessity of abandoning its parochial confinements, and of adapting itself to an early Panhellenism. Herein may be seen the germ of the synthetic and somewhat rationalized picture of the Achaean past which Homer paints. Perhaps others besides Homer attempted large epics of synoptic canvas. In Homer's work, at least, the synoptic world-view was spread behind a dramatic core in a way sufficient to explain the survival of this poet among all the others. Scholars have often assumed earlier *Iliads* than ours, and surely they are to be assumed. But they must have all been by Homer, for the *Iliad* is a profoundly personal creation. He must have sung it many times before the work was committed to writing, for the benefit of the Homerids, the poet's performers.

We may now return briefly to the problem of the vulgate text, and its longer and shorter variants. The idea of an official state text of Pisistratus is, as we have seen, inconsistent with the facts and alien to the times. Homer's original dictated text was official enough, in one sense, but precisely how soon it became official for the ancient Greeks is a problem. We do not know which version, if there were several, Pisistratus favored for his Panathenaic performances; Plato in the fourth century sometimes seems to quote an unfamiliar version, unless he simply quoted from an inaccurate memory.[63] To reconstruct an archetypal text some four to six centuries older than our earliest scrap of papyrus is not likely to be a very rewarding task; yet without some theory, we cannot begin to know whether we read in Homer the poet himself, Pisistratus, Aristarchus, or a fortuitous potpourri of them all.

Certain presumptions present themselves at once: Homer's work shows the unmistakable hallmarks of eighth-century art, and little or nothing that need be later; in order for that to be the case it must have been crystallized in that form in the eighth century and not later. How, therefore, does one explain the wide variations in the textual tradition of the papyri before Aristarchus? His predecessor Zenodotus, for instance, athetized or omitted altogether whole large sections of the *Iliad*, including the *Shield of Achilles*. It has recently been promulgated that Zenodotus had before him the sixth-century text of Pisistratus, and that the larger version of Aristarchus admits a spate of later interpolations.[64] Yet the *Shield*, omitted by Zenodotus, was one of the first sections of the *Iliad* to be recognized as consistent with the structural instincts of the Geometric Age.[65] Moreover, there are crucial spots in the text of Zenodotus which clearly anticipate or summarize a longer version.[66] Surely the answer to such a problem can only be found among the probabilities attendant on the oral theory. For the first writing of the *Iliad*, however it preserved what Homer sang, did not compel anyone, except the Homerids, to recite it exactly the same way. The later laws restraining rhapsodic virtuosity prove that. More important, the advent of writing could not have exterminated oral verse-making all at once, and the latter's survival in Greece to the present day leads one to believe that the art has never died out in Greece.[67] Any illiterate bard who heard the *Iliad* sung at a festival could go home, and, provided he had reasonable skill, recreate the poem at will, but not with exactitude. The more often he heard it, the less he might deviate, but what singer deserves condemnation if he felt unable to reproduce at all the verbal peculiarities of the *Shield*? That was indeed a special creation conceived for a special function, and elaborated with the most lavish skill. Many of its formulae are not in the common repertoire, and it was easier to leave it out.[68] So too with the *Catalog*, which is omitted from many manuscripts. Here no technical difficulty arises, but a change of taste. Catalog literature had no such fascination for later periods as it did for the age of Hesiod. Oral reproduction would omit it.

It is usually assumed that for a time at least, early texts of Homer were jealously guarded by the Homeridae of Chios, the real or supposed descendants of the poet. If that is true, or even if texts were scarce, as they must have been until the middle fifth century, certain sections of the Greek world would have to depend on oral versions of the *Iliad*, by no means canonical, and often much shorter than the original. It is unlikely that they would be much longer. Each poet who sang would undoubtedly assert that he alone sang the correct version, and wherever oral singing continued vigorous, the statement would carry weight. Nothing prevented the dictation, eventually, of these local versions to local scribes, and the desire for such written copies may well account for the origin of the "city" texts, with their far-flung provenience, and their considerable variations. When Zenodotus faced a collection of these in Alexandria, together with good Athenian exemplars, he concluded that the latter were interpolated. Aristarchus, partly no doubt because he thought Homer an Athenian, preferred the Athenian texts. The official text which he left is not his creation; it is a restoration, probably as good a one as we shall ever get, of the original. If it involves some imperfections and dubieties, yet the vulgate is closer than any of the shorter texts to what one expects of an eighth-century poem. And there is no reason to doubt that, among the texts before Aristarchus around 160 B.C., there was one or more which represented with reasonable faithfulness the original eighth-century version. But before this first real recension, it is not surprising if Greece as a whole lacked the concept of an official, canonical text.

The dating of Homer to the latter part of the eighth century is now more widely accepted than the dating of the first manuscript to that time. The oral epic tradition cannot have continued in the main cultural centers as a primary creative medium much after 700, when it faded before the spread of elegiac and lyric forms; and on the other hand, though writing must have come earlier, its earliest extant monuments belong to the last quarter of the eighth century. This fact, together with Homer's all-important affinity with high Geometric Art, creates a strong likelihood that the composition of the poems took place some time between 725 and the very early years of the seventh century. The guesses of antiquity are not very helpful. Herodotus' statement, that Homer lived 400 years before his own time, has recently been interpreted as the estimate of a maximum, computed on the basis of a genuine genealogy of the poet.[69] Eratosthenes places Homer a century after the Ionian migration, which gives the latter half of the eighth century, but only if the archaeological evidence be consulted, and not Eratosthenes' date for the latter event.[70] Generally speaking, it is clear that antiquity, in its lack of a sound chronological system, did not know just when Homer lived. Yet one vague indication has been somewhat overlooked. Arctinus of Miletus, probably the author of the *Aethiopis*, was born in the eighth Olympiad, or about 740.[71] His *floruit*, therefore, would be about 700, exactly right for a pupil of Homer, which he is supposed to have been.[72] Many other points have been urged as indicating the late eighth century for Homer: the dependency of the early lyric poets, not to mention Hesiod, upon the *Iliad* and *Odyssey*,[73] the emphasis upon the Phoenicians in the latter poem, and the general world-view, which seems to correspond to what we know of the eighth-century world.[74] But the really cogent evidence lies in the poems themselves, and in the *Iliad* in particular, as the chief artistic glories of the Geometric Age.

V

HOMER AND GEOMETRIC ART

IF it is true that the *Iliad* and *Odyssey* are in some
sense the terminations of an "Attic" period of epic
development, a period which began sometime after the fall of
Mycenae and reached its climax toward the end of the eighth cen-
tury, it is reasonable to expect that the art of Homer should have
something in common with the general cultural atmosphere of the
Attic peninsula around 725. Many studies now exist, demonstrating
the similarities between Homeric poetry and Geometric art; [1] what
is not always remembered in these studies is that in this period Geo-
metric art means Athenian art primarily. Boeotian fibulae have been
found bearing what must be taken as illustrations of epic tales, but
by and large it is Athenian Geometric, specifically the Dipylon
ware, which has provided the analogy. And this, as we have seen,
was a local Attic development, which arose out of a long period of
preparation, whose history is recorded chiefly by the vases of the
Outer Cerameicus cemetery, beyond the Dipylon Gate of Athens. [2]

Pottery with so-called geometric design is found in various early
cultures. In Greece it makes its first appearance in some late vari-
eties of Mycenaean ware. [3] But the latter reveal at most the rudi-
ments out of which the potters of the Protogeometric period laid
the foundations for the great style known as the High Geometric.
Such early geometric patterns may be looked upon as natural and

even inevitable for primitive times. But the High Geometric with which we have to deal is anything but primitive; it is an extremely elaborate decorative mode, embodying a clear aesthetic theory, and, perhaps for the first time in Greek culture, that peculiar rationale of artistic types, at once general and individual, which later earned the name of "Classic." As one critic describes it:

The Geometric period, represented chiefly by pottery, but also by figurines of clay, bronze and ivory, as well as by elaborate jewellery and metal ware, is clearly a period not only of great technical ability but also of developed artistic sense. The pictures drawn on the vases give some intimation of the life lived by their makers, and even of the myths and poems with which they were familiar. The distribution of the vases themselves shows that already considerable intercourse and commerce existed between the different parts of Greece, even suggesting in certain cases the trade relations of some of the cities. Crude inscriptions scratched on the walls of the vases give evidence that knowledge of the alphabet and of writing was already spreading. The Geometric culture, then, is the earliest flowering of the Greek genius.[4]

Since the Mycenaeans are now known to have been Greeks, the last phrase should perhaps be altered to "Classic genius." For though both Geometric art and the Homeric epos are in some sense archaic and have roots in the Mycenaean past, the salient elements of both, from the purely artistic point of view, are forward-looking, and have much more in common with the austere gravity of the fifth century than they do with the megalithic, feudal world of Mycenae.

The relationship between old subject matter and new treatment is perhaps most clearly seen in the Homeric similes. Schliemann's discovery of the actual sites and objects which Homer describes created a natural disposition to see in the similes reflections of that world, and to draw analogies between his descriptions and the pictures on Mycenaean walls and vases. Warriors, bulls, lions, and horses do, of course, occur in abundance, both on Mycenaean monuments and in the pages of Homer. But more recent scholars have begun to trace the all-important distinction between the naturalistic, descriptive style of Mycenaean work ultimately derivable from Minoan art, and the formalistic and essentially emotive intention which is shared by Homer and the Geometric artists. Thus on the famous Mycenaean dagger blade which shows a lion hunt, the lions are easily recognizable as such, while, in fulfillment of the general ornamental purpose, they appear as rather arch, decorative beasts, with the emphasis laid upon their grace of stance and movement. By contrast with such lions, those on the Geometric vases are not at all naturalistic, but simply visions of terror, conceived wholly in terms of toothy jaws, glaring eyes, and bristling mane — precisely, in fact, the details which Homer invariably emphasizes in the lion similes.[5] The image is not therefore simply a decorative addition: it is a narrative element, charged with the emotional force of the scene in which it stands, and developed accordingly. The variations are rather subtle, for though all Homeric lions are fierce, they are seen differently at different times: some are ravening and monstrous, some handsomely irresistible, some nobly defiant, some balked and retreating sulkily. As compressed psychological commentaries, they enrich the scene more by advancing it than by merely ornamenting it. So narrative verse uses the visual image to its dynamic purpose, and conversely, the visual art of the Geometric vase-painter is at times narrative: lions appear attacking deer, some of the deer being half eaten, yet showing no signs of discomfort. Naive as this may seem, it is one way of showing the contrast between the peaceful world of deer and the wild world of lions, of saying, in fact, the deer were grazing, and the lions came and ate them.[6] Much in the same way, the *prothesis*, or funeral scenes of Dipylon ware are the narratives of funerals, time being ignored by the painter as it is often by Homer. The painter shows successive stages of the action as if they were simultaneous, even as Homer often shows simultaneous actions successively.

All this is in contrast to the Minoan and Mycenaean procedure, where the subject matter regularly does not violate the time sense. Minoan art represents a pictorial concept in a single and perfectly plausible moment. There is no straining for the dramatic. A comparison between a Cretan horse and Geometric horse again illustrates the difference of concern: the Cretan horse is a vision of solid magnificence, the Geometric is all legs, equipped only for motion.[7] For the one, reality lies in the actual appearance; for the other, it lies in action and inner nature, and there can be no question as to which view is nearer to Homer's. Homer almost never describes anyone's actual appearance. His method is strictly dramatic, emphasizing always deed, motive, and consequence. By both epic and Geometric painter, the traditional themes have been transformed from static external shapes into symbols of active process.

The simplicity of a highly formalized surface, animated by psychological and metaphysical preoccupations, is a token of classical Hellenic art. In its later periods, the surfaces became filled with images of humane grace, whose tensions, revelatory of the motivating passions, are often too subtle to make themselves at once apparent. In the Geometric period, there is less ambiguity. The human figure, constructed of sticks and triangles, is barely recognizable as human, yet its movements are widely expressive. It is not yet the exquisite blend of repose and action which characterizes fifth-century work; it is the paradoxical phenomenon of rigid elements busily active, the flicker of frozen gestures betokening war, joy, lamentation, or surprise. Yet if the blend is not yet perfect, if the polarities of form and action are still an unsolved, and even undreamed-of, riddle, the classic spirit is nevertheless to be recognized in this rudimentary symbolism. If the stick-and-triangle figure is the last crystal of a primitive tradition, soon to be supplanted by the early representationalism of the seventh century, the underlying conceptions of Geometric art are anything but primitive. The figures are used as half-abstract elements in a unified and perspicuous design, vast in scope and sophisticated in execution. It is perhaps not surprising that in the age of the alphabet the Greeks achieved their first triumphs of analytic design, and learnt to spell their architectonic ideas in irreducible elements. We have here the first evident use of *stoicheia*, elements, self-consciously deployed with rational control and aesthetic intensity. Like the Homeric formulae, the conventionalized birds, horses, men, and ships of Geometric vases have a long traditional history. But something new is being said with them. They have been organized into larger wholes, whose outlines in turn have been conceived and controlled by the ceramic surface which they are to fill. The vividness of a Geometric ship lies partly in the curvature of the vase on which it sails. Large separate scenes, or metopes, of war or funeral regularly occupy the broadest parts of the vase; the slenderer parts more often are filled with repeated motifs, rows of marching spearmen or birds; foot, shoulder, and neck frequently content themselves with frets

shaped to the plastic purpose, triangles pointing in or out, or me-
anders, whose possibilities of almost infinite expansion and con-
traction lend themselves, like Homer's stock-motifs, to adjustable
treatment in transitions between major episodes.[8] Backgrounds are
likely to be dotted with stars, flowers, circles, or swastikas, in some-
what irregular array.

From the point of view of a strict artistic economy, there is noth-
ing to compare with Geometric art except the Homeric epos. Ho-
meric formulae are, like the motifs of Geometric vases, basically
stiff traditional elements, irreducible building blocks of oral epic.
A degree of individual remolding hardly alters their essential nature
or reveals much about the poet's personality any more than do the
slight variations observable in the different hands of individual vase
painters. It is the architectonics that count. If Homer's big scenes
are more effective and more developed dramatically than those on
Geometric pots, it should be remembered that his tradition is even
older, and that poetry might be expected to lead the plastic arts in
the history of any culture. The methods are parallel, and are more
observable in the less striking parts of both media. When Homer
shifts his scene, he does so with a line as traditional and as nearly
neutral as the meander fret which separates the friezes of a vase:

> Thus they fought in the likeness of blazing fire.

As it happens, this particular line, with its image of fire, is drawn
into the general artistic scheme of the *Iliad*, so that its neutrality
vanishes at length and it becomes meaningful in context. But so too
does the meander fret, in the hands of a skillful artisan, become part
of the articulation of the total ceramic design. It expands or con-
tracts to its surface, as Homer's image of fire can be a passing refer-
ence or the substance of a scene. In similar fashion, the rows of
marching warriors so frequent on Geometric ware recall the battle
books, with their countless reiterations of the motifs of heroic war-
fare. Yet here again Homer, though methodologically similar, is
more advanced, and by his sheer tact in deployment and selection
has given momentary individuality to scores of names, otherwise
mere anonymities of mythic genealogy. Such individualization is
rare on Geometric pottery, but not unknown. In a pair of balanced
figures, one may have a sword, the other not; or a group of mourn-

ers may all hold their hands to their hair except for one, who extends his toward the corpse.[9] It is easy to overinterpret such moments of asymmetry, but it is perhaps not too much to say that herein is some concern with the particular as distinct from the species. It is more important to note that, whatever the degree of individualization or asymmetry in both Homer and Geometric painting, the traditional elements are not disturbed in their essence. There are no radical departures. All is done by means of minute, refined motifs which gradually construct a planned and unified total.

The art of the eighth century, whether visual or verbal, looks both forward and backward. In its emotional subtlety, in its rational concern with total pattern, in its early effort to individualize the specific within the type, it looks forward to the great Classic age. In its use of formalized traditional motifs, and concomitant refusal to approach representationalism it leans toward the past. The outlines of the Geometric warrior can be seen as early as the Warrior Vase of Mycenae, though the latter shows a style of debased realism foreign to the elegant and vigorous spearmen of the eighth century. And indeed, all early Geometric motifs originate in Mycenaean ones; their spirit is their own. One critic writes:

Although it came into being as a result of processes set in motion at an earlier date, and although every element in Protogeometric decoration is present in an embryonic form in late Mycenaean art, the artistic conception expressed in the pottery of the new style differs as widely from that of the Mycenaean period as Geometric art differs from the art of the seventh and sixth centuries.[10]

Yet in some earlier Geometric ware, traces of old Mycenaean naturalism are occasionally visible, or heraldically placed figures will recall a favorite compositional mode of the Late Helladic times.[11] More clearly traditional, and much more frequent, of course, are certain points of subject matter, especially of armament. Scenes representing heroes struggling with animals recall far-off days of myth, in the spirit of Homer's "and they fought with mighty beasts of the mountains, and mightily they overcame them."[12] Warriors mounted in chariots or armed with figure-eight shields could hardly have been a regular feature of eighth-century warfare; yet these appear, traditionally preserved, on many a Geometric vase, side by side with hoplites, carrying round shields.[13] The so-called "Dipylon" shield, itself a conventionalized rendering of the Mycenaean figure-eight shield, does not receive specific mention in Homer; but Homer's epithets for shields include some which are appropriate only to the Mycenaean body-shield, a vanished implement in his time. The long-argued question of the Homeric shield is really a simple one: body-shields, or at least their epithets, survived in the tradition, if not in fact, and round shields had entered it probably more recently. The occurrence of both on Dipylon vases testifies to the lofty disregard for historicity in the artists of the time, and helps to explain Homer's apparent inconsistency.

Transformation of actualities into communicative conventions is a basic function of all art, and one of the difficulties of Homeric scholarship has been to reconstruct the actuality from the convention. The shield is only one problem; burial customs present an even greater complexity. In the Homeric poems the dead are burned, and funeral games are conducted when the pyre has died down. But though it has been persuasively argued that the Mycenaeans held funeral games,[14] they certainly did not cremate the dead; neither did the Greeks of Homer's own time, although somewhat earlier, between 1000 and 800, the practice, at least in the neighborhood of Athens, seems to have been regular.[15] The full difficulties of the historical question need not be canvassed here: archaeology alone can decide it. What is clear is that, however they got there, the motifs of cremation burial and of funeral games existed in the epic tradition, and that Homer combined them, with or without historical accuracy, for a definite and extremely effective purpose in the twenty-third *Iliad*. Such use of traditional motifs to an architectonic end is wholly in line with the spirit of the Geometric period.

Motifs could come from any time and any place, and for the most part it is nearly impossible to remake them into fact and history. When Athena goes to the "house of Erechtheus,"[16] the line has been interpreted variously as proof that a Mycenaean royal-house cult existed there,[17] or that this whole part of the *Odyssey* is of Attic origin.[18] Both statements might be true, but they cannot be proved from what lies before us in the poem. At most, the passage indicates that by Homer's time a temple of Athena existed, doubtless where the Erectheium now stands, and that it suited the poet's fancy to send her there. We shall probably never know why or when that temple entered the bardic repertory, but we may guess at why it stands where it does in the poem. Athena, moving lightly in and out of the action at this point, smoothes the way before Odysseus and creates an atmosphere of peace and safety. After leaving Nausicaa she departs to a singularly peaceful and serene heaven.[19] The atmosphere germane to her is consistent with the atmosphere which she is creating for her favorite. If, then, Athens was the haven of peace for refugees in the period preceding Homer, Athens may here be symbolic, as the previous description of heaven is symbolic, of a divinely perfect refuge.[20] The gods' actions usually parallel that of the heroes in some way. Odysseus goes to Alcinous' palace, Athena goes to Erechtheus'. Both stand in safe places. Total design, not particularity of motif, is the end in view.

It is the same with all the rest of the traditional heritage. It has been suggested that the stories of Achilles' raids on the neighboring towns of Troy reflect the penetration and colonization of the Adramyttian gulf by the Aeolians from northern Greece, and that Nestor's tale in the eleventh *Iliad* of cattle raids in Elis, with its reference to the heroic Siamese twins, Actorione-Molione, is a brief form of an old tale about wars between Pylos and Elis in the Protogeometric period.[21] If these suggestions are correct, as they well may be, they only further emphasize the agglutinative quality of the tradition, and its total lack of concern with chronology. Both historical events would be anachronistic, in that they took place long after Troy, but both have been transformed and pressed into service, the one to emphasize the unrewarded energy of Achilles, the other as one of Nestor's earnest, and characteristically lengthy, paradigms of warlike virtue. As for the Actorione-Molione mentioned by Nestor,[22] they seem to have been a favorite motif in the Geometric period, occurring on several vases, in particular on a curious wine decanter recently excavated from the Athenian Agora.[23] The story of the Siamese twins may have come to Attica with the descendants of Nestor; certainly they entered the repertoire both of the bards and of the Geometric vase-painters as a frequent motif.

And like all mythic motifs, its meaning was not fixed, but varied within limits to accord with the larger purpose of the artist.

Clearly the oral epic, gathering in all things as it went, could not represent the Mycenaean world, or anything else, with strict historicity. If the palaces described by Homer correspond by and large to the palaces excavated at Tiryns or Pylos, there is at least one other building reference which is difficult to take as referring to anything but Geometric structure. In their wrestling match, Odysseus and Ajax are said to resemble the rafters of a house.[24] The image seems unintelligible except for the Geometric house models from Perachora and the Argive Heraeon,[25] whose quasi-Gothic arched roof would correspond to the wrestlers' arched necks and shoulders, while their locked arms would resemble the rafters spanning the distance between the walls. But the affinity between Homer and Geometric art does not lie in references to contemporary phenomena within the actual subject matter; rather the opposite. With the exception of the *prothesis*-scenes, which reflect the funerary nature of the vases which bear them, both painting and epic are concerned primarily with mythic subjects. Such vases as present actual scenes offer chiefly illustrations, sometimes quite specific ones, of the body of epic narrative which we know, in a later form, as the Epic Cycle.[26] It is perhaps significant that scarcely one before 700 can be assigned a position as an illustration of Homer himself: if these vases and the epics are approximately contemporary, it is impossible that the vase-painters should have been influenced as yet by the pre-eminence of the *Iliad* and *Odyssey*, which dramatize actually rather obscure events in the Trojan story; it is far more likely that they would choose their subject matter from among the more central happenings of the whole war — the Rape of Helen, the Wooden Horse, or Ajax with the body of Achilles. The fact that the vase subjects are so drawn is all the stronger proof of the concern of the Geometric period with the heroic tradition in general, and an illuminating commentary on the state of mind of Homer's first audience. They dwelt in these myths; their conception of art was retrospective of a heroic past whose Helladic actualities they knew little about, but whose Hellenic possibilities they instinctively foresaw. In Homer's own case it was no different: he led the old Achaean ruffians into the first phase of classical Hellenic shapeliness.

As the classical spirit progressed, selectivity increased, and the formalism became more subtle. In Geometric art, formalism is as complete as possible, though rigid and at times forbidding; but conservatism, rather than selectivity, is to be seen in the limited number of motifs and scenes presented. Indeed, the high Geometric style marks the peak of a development of ever-increasing fullness of patterned detail. Yet the principle which conceives design as a total covering is not necessarily a token of the primitive, and certainly is not in Greece. "Close" Geometric was preceded by more open styles, including especially the extremely restrained and open Protogeometric. Rather the tendency is symptomatic of the artistic spirit of the age, and its analogue is to be found in the fullness of the epic, with its continuous time and its infinite wealth of detail.[27] Details of battles, spears, feasts, helmets, horses, and love affairs lay in the epic stockpile; the challenge was to organize them. The growth of the Close Geometric from earlier styles shows the painters steadily answering the challenge to arrange larger and larger masses of these in more perfect wholes. Nothing could be more tactful than the disposition of designs on a Dipylon vase. The basic ceramic shape is felt as a controlling rhythm to which all the painted parts are subordinated, so that the whole emerges as an organic unity, not indeed a unity achieved by the domination of a single interior curve, or other compositional principle, as in later work, but the unity of exterior outline fully expressed and motivated by hundreds of discrete, stylized contributors.[28] And of such a kind, also, is the unity of the Homeric epic, whose diverse traditional constituents have been compressed, as it were from the outside, by an imposed dramatic theme, as well as by a completely arbitrary structural system which, as will appear, is characteristically Geometric. Masses of old heroic incidents have been arranged and subordinated to a major shape, and made to appear as if they created that shape, as the triangles and meanders of the vases seem to accent and encourage the curves of the clay. Of the two basic principles, structure and texture, the former surely is the more peculiar classical concern, and here in the eighth century, for the first time to our knowledge, structure has achieved its first triumphs. In the case of pottery, the triumph is known to be specifically Athenian. In no other Geometric art does this supremely organic quality obtain. Impressive as are the Boeotian raised relief funerary jars, for instance, they possess nothing of the total authority and stance of Dipylon ware. Their designs could be hung on any object with equal effect. But not so in Attica. Already the Attic spirit, with its austere grace, rational control, and structural intuition — a kind of Gestalt psychology penetrating the emotional force underlying form — is at work. And as one looks about early Greece and the Geometric art of other districts, it is hard to associate the formal elegance and structural power of Homer with anything but this early Athenian spirit.

The relationship between Homer and Geometric painting has been long recognized, to a degree. But its full extent, and the fact that it is Attic ware exclusively which is applicable, have perhaps been underemphasized. "Ring-composition," a term used to describe the framing of an incident between similar or identical formulae, has been studied as a structural principle in Homer,[29] and it has been shown that many Homeric scenes are broadly subject to classification by types.[30] Yet one may go further along these lines. Homer's scenes, besides being typological specimens, are disposed and developed in the poems with subtle reference to character, thus gaining a particular, psychological aspect which participates in the motivation of the total action. They are, furthermore, placed, especially in the *Iliad*, in balancing positions, echoing each other either through similarity or contrast. The most obvious example, of course, is the balance of the Quarrel in Book I of the *Iliad* by the Reconciliation in Book XXIV.[31] Thus there is a circular composition also of scenes themselves, scenes framing scenes in concentric rings around centerpieces, exactly as central motifs are heavily framed by borders in Geometric painting.[32] Concentric circles are a universal device in Geometric art, and an especial favorite in Athenian Protogeometric; and the principle of balance around a central point which is implied in concentric circles is far and away the dominating formal principle in the *Iliad*. The poem as a whole forms one large concentric pattern, within which a vast system of smaller ones, sometimes distinct and sometimes interlocking, gives shape to the separate parts.

It has been suggested that such "onion skin" design arose from a device originally mnemonic. The oral poet, having mentioned A, B, and C, picks them up later on in the order C, B, and A, since it is natural to reconstruct a train of thought backwards.[33] This may well be true, especially in passages of moderate compass, and the technique appears chiefly in paired speeches where a series of questions is answered in reverse order. A fine example occurs in the underworld scene of the *Odyssey*: speaking with the shade of his mother, Odysseus asks (1) after the manner of her death, (2) after his father, (3) his son, (4) the state of his own position in Ithaca, and (5) after Penelope. Anticleia answers these questions precisely in reverse, gracefully expanding or contracting the thematic phrases of Odysseus with haunting effect, like the clear but altered tones of an echo.[34] But if the device was originally mnemonic and functional, such a purpose is clearly superseded when it becomes the structural basis of a fifteen-thousand-line poem such as the *Iliad*. It has become an artistic principle. Even as in the scene just mentioned it has imparted a forcefully lyric effect, so too as the chief patterning device of the *Iliad* it imposes shape and articulates the limbs of the dramatic material. It is a commonplace in ancient art for technical devices which are functional in one medium to be transferred to another medium where they are purely ornamental. Many large earthen vases, votive ones, have handles too slender, for instance, to be practical on anything but a metal jar, and Minyan gray ware is thought to have been based on metal models.[35] By a similar insinct, perhaps, the use of "hysteron proteron," giving the effect of concentric circles, was gradually transformed from a mnemonic device to an architectonic one. Such a process is wholly in keeping with what has been said of the Geometric approach to the creative act: like all Greek art, it conserved, while it transformed, and tended to keep in mind the matrix of any formal element, however widely its experimental variations might range.

The *Iliad* is a poem which was by no means clearly implied by the mere existence of the epic tradition, any more than the High Geometric masterpieces were implied by the concentric circles and half-circles, meticulously drawn with the compass, on Protogeometric ware. A special concern was necessary, an emotional conviction compelling enough in both poet and audience to motivate so grand a scheme. And again, as it seems, the spiritual motive for the *Iliad* must be traced to Athens. The colossal urns found near the Dipylon Gate were evidently grave markers in the Cerameicus, regularly bearing scenes of *prothesis*, or lying in state, the body on its bier, surrounded by processions and lamentation.[36] Sometimes as much as five or six feet high, these chefs-d'oeuvre are completely covered with finely drawn figures and designs in rhythmic friezes, fired to a rich color and varnished to a deep gloss. Citizens' grave memorials at once so intricate and so stately are difficult to find elsewhere. In dealing with the figures of the dead, which are regularly painted larger than the other figures, one critic compares them to Homer's phrase, "large, large stretched out," of fallen heroes.[37] But further than that, the urns themselves betray a monumental concern with individuals, a willingness to see them heroically enlarged, isolated amid flickering but ordered masses, in much the same way that Homer views his main figures against their backgrounds. In both Homer and the Dipylon vases, reality is a vision of formal symmetry, within which emotion lives in muted but effectual details. In Homer, the primitive has been reduced to form. Magniloquent sagas of old kings and warriors, once conceived for self-praise and self-perpetuation, have yielded to a refined and tragic retrospect, in which the figures walk in formal patterns of passion and despair, and the enormous self-conceptions are dominated by the quiet existence of the total picture. Such a view was typically Athenian later, and the Dipylon vases show it to have been Athenian in the eighth century. They stand to Homer precisely as the fifth century steles stand to the drama of Sophocles. Nowhere else in Greece was the heroic spirit ever so much at home as in Athens. And if there Geometric pottery achieved heroic proportions while maintaining its finesse, balance, and delicacy of detail, it seems impossible to associate Homer, who did precisely the same for the epic, with any other cultural atmosphere.[38]

From all we know of later Ionian art, it must be admitted that there is nothing Ionian about the art of the *Iliad*. The qualities commonly called Ionian in Homer, such as the sense of the decorative and the loose style (*lexis eiromene*), involve misunderstandings. Homer's decoration, presumably his similes, have been shown to exist not for their own sake, but for the sake of the action in which they occur, and are therefore highly organic.[39] The style is indeed the "strung" style, so far as sentence structure goes. But it is hardly to be compared with the style of Herodotus, which is often fairly periodic in its sentences, and "strung" primarily in the sequence of ideas or subjects. Homer's style is almost the exact opposite: if the sentences are simple, and strung together, the motifs in the large show a strong subordinating syntax, not, indeed, in their direct relations with each other, but in relation to the design of the whole. The real analogue of Homeric style is Geometric art, whose discrete but sequential motifs find their unity in the external shape in which they stand, and very little in their subordination or interplay with each other. Linear syntax is not necessarily Ionian, and the author of the *Iliad*, wherever he came from, had the Attic Geometric spirit, not the later Ionian spirit, in his heart. Above all, he had the heroic, and tragic, spirit, and therein he was certainly more Attic than Ionian.

The life-span of the High Geometric style seems to have been short. The older view, that it reached far back into the Dark Age and began to wane in the eighth century, has now generally been supplanted by a chronology which compresses the height of the style into the last quarter of the eighth century.[40] Toward the end of the century, the first Orientalizing motifs appear, and for the next two centuries these dominate the art of Corinth. In Athens, however, High Geometric is succeeded more directly by a type of sub-Geometric, known as proto-Attic, in which the close economy of the earlier work is already breaking down, and a new representationalism begins, sometimes with a kind of wayward grace and spritely freshness, sometimes hopelessly faltering. The extreme virtuosity of the Dipylon style is gone, and the new mode is not yet achieved. All analogies may be pressed too far, but if the *Iliad* reflects the close organization, fine subtlety, traditional conservatism, and, above all, the retrospective heroic outlook of the best Dipylon urns, it might be suggested that the *Odyssey* already shows signs of the two new styles which made their appearance around 700, or shortly thereafter. The baldric of Heracles in the eleventh *Odyssey* has been said to represent late eighth-century Orientalizing ornamentation.[41] There is, moreover, something strikingly suggestive of the *Odyssey* in numerous vases of the proto-Attic style.[42]

Finally, the question of rationalism enters. Geometric art, it was said, is rational in that it employs a formal and intellectual extension of such principles as balance, responsion, contrast, and repetition, in an orderly syntax. The *Iliad* too is rational in this sense. But in the *Odyssey*, where the rationale of pure formalism has yielded to more plastic design, for the first time one meets the rationalism of *idea* in the moral and theological scheme of justice which is presented. The form therefore becomes dependent on the controlling concept to a degree, while the imagery tends to lose some of its structural function, and to pass over into the illustrative and ornamental. Although many matters, such as the basic language, style, and conception of the Bronze Age culture, remain the same in both poems, there are also fundamental changes in the artistic and intellectual approach of the *Odyssey*, and these changes, whatever else they prove, assuredly mark the end of the Geometric Age.

VI

IMAGE, SYMBOL, AND FORMULA

IT is a commonplace of criticism to observe that Greek poetry is more direct than English poetry, in the sense that the Greek poets, with the notable exception of Pindar and Aeschylus,[1] make far less use of metaphor and other forms of figurative language than do the English. Even English prose of the simplest sort is full of metaphors and metonymy, such as the "flow of time" or a "torrent of abuse," which have, of course, lost nearly all their figurative force and have become mere trite circumlocutions. Rendered into Greek literally, these would be all but unintelligible, for although all the forms of Greek poetry have clichés which are peculiar to their own idioms, they are seldom imagistic. The reason for this fact cannot be found in the neoclassic doctrine of "suitability," which began with Aristotle and culminated in Boileau and Pope. The Greeks were not afraid of bold or far-fetched images; indeed, when they do use images, they generally use bold ones, and some of the metaphoric flights of Aeschylus and Pindar dazzle even the modern reader, when they do not make him wince. One could more easily imagine Aeschylus adopting Eliot's "coils of light spiralling downward to the horror of the ape," than using such a phrase as the "flow of time." Perhaps the latter is too tame. More likely, the Greek poet ordinarily felt no need to transform his language in this way, but used imagery for more specific ends than the general one of keeping his language indirect and poetic. By and large, he presented his thoughts in a language which is as direct as it is concentrated and intense.

Modern criticism tends to find the essence of poetic speech in metaphor, and to regard the art of poetry as primarily imagistic, while the more external elements of the form, meter, rhyme, and even the other rhetorical figures, are purely secondary. If this view is true, a serious question arises about Greek poets, especially Homer: how to account for the power of a poet who has always been found so singularly lacking in metaphor? It has been estimated that there are only twenty-five real metaphors in the whole first book of the *Iliad*, which has six hundred and eleven lines.[2] At the rate of one metaphor in each twenty-four-and-a-half lines, few poems would be effective. Either metaphor cannot be so central, or else Homer has been overestimated. But there is a third alternative, that Homer may be indeed more metaphoric than has been thought. The directness of Homer's language is striking, but it is very far from the directness of prose. If it lacks metaphor in the modern sense, it is nonetheless a tremendous imagistic texture, and metaphoric in the sense that all language is, in a way, metaphoric. In order to make clear what is meant, it will be necessary to explore the meaning of metaphor and of poetic speech in general. It must also be borne in mind that in Homer we are dealing with an oral, traditional style, and that the problem therefore differs somewhat from the problem as found in written literature. This is not to say that the poems do not exhibit many of the virtues found in written literature; they do. Even a purely literary approach reveals many of their profound vistas. But the question of metaphor well illustrates the limits of the method. In the Homeric epic we have to deal with something which established many of the literary assumptions of Western culture, but which in its oral, traditional origins was modally different from all subsequent poetry.

Even on the surface, Homer is by no means lacking in figurative language. The most evident kind is, of course, the great epic simile, rising like a prismatic inverted pyramid upon its one point of contact with the action. Metaphor occurs, though sparsely: when fighters fall, they "sleep the brazen sleep," or "night wraps their eyes." The Achaeans are subdued by the "scourge of Zeus."[3] The somewhat mysterious "bridges of war" may be metaphor.[4] Among the lesser figures, one can find examples of metonymy, synecdoche, apostrophe, anaphora, personification, onomatopoeia, and probably others.[5] But even if these were more numerous than they are, they would not explain the power of the Homeric style which Matthew Arnold described as simple, rapid, and noble. Homer is unique in the ability to call things by their right names — helmet, ship, or shield — and make them strike the ear as rich and strange. Thus what might be called the "first level" of the poems, the rational, factual level, has an intense beauty of its own, which perhaps partly explains Homer's appeal to children. In any case, it makes him the most sensuously vivid of all poets; whatever extended implications may exist, it is never necessary to grasp these before one can feel the poetic fire of a scene. The simplest statements of fact or action have a compact vitality and immediacy which put all naturalistic modes of realism to shame. For all his scarcity of the more familiar types of figurative imagery, except simile, Homer's lines are as sharply imagistic as it is possible to conceive; all is clear, pure, and detailed. What is the secret of such a poetic method, which seems to do without so many of the poetic modes of other literature, and why is there no prosaic dross in these long narratives which seem to have so much to record in the way of plain fact, common action, saga, genealogy, and catalogue? To answer the question, one must examine the components of the epic style itself, and see in what way it is related to the imagistic and symbolic procedures of poetry in general.

It is not easy to find satisfactory definitions for the terms "symbol" and "image" as used in literary criticism. In general, however, the poetic symbol is a word or phrase which carries a larger meaning than that which it denotes, and this larger meaning is determined and limited by the contextual associations of the work in which it stands. Such association is clearly distinct from the "free association" of psychoanalytical method; and similarly the poetic symbol, in being more fluid, is distinct from the more or less fixed Freudian symbolism of dreams, though it may make use of the latter. An image, on the other hand, is primarily a word or phrase devised to evoke sense impression, visual, auditory, or any other. Images may, and easily do, become symbols by association, and how rapidly this can happen is well illustrated by Shakespeare's:

Put out the light, and then put out the light.

But the first function of an image is a direct appeal to that part of the mind which recognizes sense-experience.

The term "direct appeal" demands clarification, for it is precisely the direct appeal of Homer's narrative method which is the immediate object of this inquiry. Since both symbols and images appeal directly to the mind — the latter primarily to sense, the former to wider realms of association — it will be necessary to explore briefly the psychology underlying this appeal, and to seek the wider meanings of symbolism. The clearest and most convenient formulation is that of Susanne Langer, in her brilliant *Philosophy in a New Key*. According to Mrs. Langer, the chief function of the brain is to select, classify, and transform by recombination the data of sense-experience. This function, which she terms "symbolic," or "symbolific transformation," terminates in two modes of expression, the discursive and the presentational.[6] The discursive mode is the logical, syntactical symbolism of language, and it relates primarily to the process of logical, rational thinking. Its communications require time, and they depend for intelligibility upon a selective series of articulate sounds and a systematic syntax. The presentational mode is that of the visual arts, whose syntax, if so it may be called, lacks the systematic aspect of language, requires no time to be envisioned whole, and relates primarily to the intuitive side of the mind.[7]

In these two contrasting modes, clearly two contrasting types of symbolism are represented, the one mediated by time, and controlled by the denotative limits of words and the framework of logic, the other immediate, supralogical, and controlled only by the structure evolved by its own intention. It is the latter which is essentially the mode of art, but two major arts offer odd combinations of both modes. Music, though consisting basically of tones, which are presentational, requires time to be heard entire, and employs in the laws of harmony and counterpoint an extended syntax analogous to that of language. And poetry uses, as its only medium, the discursive mode of language. Yet when we speak of the "direct appeal" of an image or symbol, we mean that it appeals as an image of painting or sculpture appeals to the mind, that is, presentationally, and without the intermediate office of any extended, or rational, syntax. We may well ask how, in any art whose entire medium is discursive, it is possible to achieve symbols or images whose effect is presentational. Where the symbol or image consists of a single word, the problem scarcely arises, for no grammatical syntax is involved, and the amount of time required to pronounce one word is scarcely sufficient to intervene between it and the mind's response to its meaning. Indeed, in one of Saroyan's plays, a character writes poems consisting of one word only, such as "Tree" or "Is." But while it must be admitted that this character understood the basic problem of poetry, the amputatory method is not the answer, for poetry aims at more than monosyllabic images. It aims at images in series and in relation to each other, all functioning in the service of a complex total meaning, toward which its vehicle of words and grammar are not by nature ideally conducive.

"All art," said Nietzsche, "aspires to the condition of music," meaning that all art aspires to achieve its end through pure form. In the twentieth century, nonobjective painting and the "nonthinking" school of poets, led by Gertrude Stein, attest the challenge of other arts to music's primacy in the sphere of pure formalism. Yet these answers are somewhat like that of Saroyan's poet. Form in painting implies a struggle with subject matter, and form in poetry implies a reckoning with the intellective reference of words. To remove the problems implicit in the raw materials of an art is not to solve them. The chief symptomatic difference between poetry and prose is that the latter, in using a discursive symbolism to a discursive end, has its problem of the adjustment of form and content already solved: grammatical syntax corresponds to logical (ideational) syntax. The poet's problem is to make grammatical syntax correspond to the presentational syntax of his intended work of art. If grammar wins the day, his work is frigid, or prosaic. The problem is even further complicated by the fact that poetry is not to be divested wholly of its discursive quality, which is implied by the medium. Attempts to do so, such as those mentioned above, are, like the attempts of Bernini and other artists of the Baroque to transcend their media, manneristic. Whatever their success or partial success, they are very foreign to classical Greek poetry, and differ from it in much the same way that Bernini's pontifical tombs, where marble is made to resemble silk, differ from the classical sculptor's acquiescence to his material. The answer is not to annihilate

the discursive quality, but to transform it. Any poet, especially an
epic poet with a story to relate, must deal with words in gram-
matical relationships, but these grammatical relationships must con-
stantly create the presentational, formal syntax of the poem, the
artistic life and meaning which it must, as poem, possess apart from
the strict denotation of its words and the logical sequence of its
ideas.

It is by means of the image and the poetic symbol, as defined
above, that language is made presentational. Any word alone may
be imagistic, except perhaps colorless modal auxiliaries, and any
word may be a poetic symbol, hence presentational. But when a
group of grammatically related words become presentational, it is
because some technique has been employed to suppress their gram-
matical symbolism in favor of a presentational symbolism. The im-
portance of the time element is consequently also diminished, since
the sense of evolving thought is transcended by the imagistic unity
of the total phrase. The techniques which so tend to identify groups
of words with artistic rather than logical syntax are familiar: meta-
phor and the other figures, departure from colloquial order of
words, actual omission of some grammatical factor which can easily
be understood, meter with its effect of contrapuntally modifying
the normal sound of words, rhyme which tends to emphasize sound
over sense, and finally diction itself. For when we praise a poet's
choice of a right or inevitable word, we must remember that it is
chosen in reference to the poem's artistic end, and not for its dic-
tionary meaning. Language thus used becomes imagistic and sym-
bolic in a new sense. As a picture of a cat is a symbol of a cat, but
not a definition of a cat,[8] so too poetic language is a symbol of the
thing represented, but not its definition.[9] It must now be asked,
how far can the process go? Can poetic economy be so complete
that every word in a poem will be presentational, or must there
be always some dross?

In the *Four Quartets*, Eliot seems to have admitted that, in cer-
tain poetic forms at least, there must be some dross, a residue of
unavoidable discursiveness which one may as well treat as frankly
unpoetic. But a glance at three lines from Shakespeare will show
that even the humblest words can be drawn by a skilled hand into
a symbolic scheme:

O Westmoreland, thou art a summer bird
That ever in the haunch of winter sings
The lifting up of day.[10]

Here the isolation of *a* bird of joy against *the* given fact of winter grief completes the metaphor with a special poignancy. If the position of the two articles be exchanged, this poignancy totally disappears, and the image becomes an optimistic one of perfectly expectable, even inevitable, rescue from casual misfortune. The limits of meaning of the definite and indefinite article are here used to frame a psychic attitude characteristic of the aging and guilt-laden Henry IV.

Any word, therefore, even the indefinite article, may become symbolic in a poetic scheme, that is, it may contribute presentationally and not merely grammatically to that scheme. Imagery does so in that its very diction, carefully selected, prompts a unified, though perhaps highly complex and articulated, sensory response. Symbols, in the full sense of poetic symbols, do so by virtue of their accumulated contextual meanings in the poem. To illustrate: in the first book of the *Iliad*, the image of fire occurs in the burning pyres of those dead of the plague.[11] It is simply an image, and a vivid one. But in the course of the poem fire takes on a host of associations, and becomes in a sense the symbol of the chief action of the poem. Such a process is possible only in an art which employs a medium where meaning is both denotative and connotative. In spite, therefore, of the grammatical, discursive problem, words, with their specific denotative force and their power of almost infinite semantic expansion through connotation, offer perhaps the richest soil of all for artistic symbolism. Synonyms, for instance, by virtue of identical denotation, and even homonyms, or near-homonyns, through similarity of sound, may both contribute to the symbolic structure.

To return now to the *Iliad* and the *Odyssey*: it has sometimes been felt that the formulaic, oral style which Homer inherited from the epic tradition could not, since it was not his own creation, have anything to do with his genius, which was to be sought instead in his departures from oral method. But besides the fact that we cannot point to a single certain departure from the method, it must be said that Homer's genius is profoundly involved with the tradi-

tional style, and we shall not understand his unique power without
first understanding the aesthetics of the style itself. This whole
aspect of formulaic verse has been ignored, partly because Parry's
studies in epic technique emphasized the functionalism of the for-
mula, and its origin in the long, slow work of multitudinous sing-
ers.[12] That the formulae are traditional and functional is granted.
What else they are remains to be seen.

One of the chief characteristics of the epic formula is that it
regularly occupies a given metrical position in the hexameter. The
proper name with its epithet is many times more frequent at the
end of a line than at the beginning. The word χείρ, "hand," is very
frequent in the *Iliad*; in the nominative or accusative plural, if modi-
fied by ἄαπτοι or ἀάπτους, "invincible," it invariably closes the line;
but the phrase ἐν χείρεσσι, "in his hands," always begins the second
foot of the hexameter. A glance at the Homeric concordance could
multiply examples of such practice almost to infinity. A formula
is, in fact, a semantic unit identified with a metrical demand, and
it is a testimony to the extraordinary strictness and economy of the
singers that there are so few duplications, or formulaic alternatives
with the same meaning and metric.[13] There are a very few excep-
tions, and certainly a word changes position more easily than a
phrase does, but in general both words and phrases are fixed in def-
inite metrical positions.[14]

Another peculiarity of the epic formula is the semantic unity of
its parts. This is especially true of noun-and-epithet combinations,
such as "Agamemnon king of men," "swift-footed horses," and
"rose-fingered dawn." These are not meant to be heard analytically,
but more as names given in full; they are the equivalents of Aga-
memnon, horses, and dawn, and, often repeated, fall on the ear as
units. Yet they are ornamental units also, and richer than the mere
nouns alone would be. Furthermore, such unity is not confined to
phrases involving nouns with epithets. The battle books of the *Iliad*
abound with a bewildering variety of formulae, all metrically dif-
ferent, but all conveying the fall of a warrior who has his death
wound: "his limbs were loosened," "he seized the earth with his
palm," "night wrapped his eyes," "his armor rattled upon him"
(as he fell), and a great many others. All frequently recur, and
once their meaning is known, the ear no longer distinguishes the

words so much as accepts the phrase whole. "So speaking, he sat down" crystallizes to a single image. Some formulae even fill whole lines, yet their essential unity is not lost:

Thus he spoke, and brandishing hurled a long-shadowing spear.

One may break this down into words, but one tends to read it, or hear it, simply as one expression, embodying the act of ceasing to speak and hurling a long spear. The line is a unity, and even the strongly imagistic word "long-shadowing" does not dominate its force, which is kinetic and narrative. The mind's singularly unified response to the formula is observable in the beginning student's frequent ability to translate a formula correctly, though he may have forgotten which word means what. The process can extend even to those passages of many lines, such as the descriptions of a feast, launching a ship, or arming for battle. Such nonanalytic unity of meaning also is functional in origin. The singer wanted a phrase with a certain meaning and devised it; once devised, it could be reused, but only as a whole. To break it up or alter it was possible, but then one made another whole. The formula, not the word, was the epic unit. And the same is true of the longer repeated scenes. They might be lengthened or shortened, but they were units, to be used as such.[15]

One might, therefore, describe the epic formula as an artificially devised unit of semantic, grammatical, and metrical functions. As such, it has clearly transcended the discursive function of speech, and has become a vividly presentational medium, in short, an art form. Whether or not a given formula embodies an actual metaphor, it is nevertheless always imagistic, and appeals directly to the senses. Its artificially devised union of metric and meaning subordinates its grammar and suppresses the time sense, so that from the materials of a discursive symbolism has been made a building block of a presentational symbolism. The formula is functional, therefore, not merely in the sense that it assists in creating verse, but also because it is a sort of poetic atom, a fragment of technically transformed speech whose structure is already that of art, not logic.

Oral epic is not, then, in a sense composed of words at all; its formulae are not the words of speech, but units of poetry and song. The paucity of metaphor is perhaps best explained by this fact alone; for all poetic speech is an artifice aiming at the subordination of logical relationships to the symbolism of artistic form, and the task is equally well performed, if not better performed, by a specially devised series of formulae as it is by metaphor. It appears, in fact, that metaphor is only one of many techniques employed by the formula for making images.

Since our knowledge of ancient Greek oral technique comes from two Homeric poems alone, it is difficult to state with certainty the extent of the formulaic system. For all the fixity of the combinations of noun and epithet, the crystallization of frequent phrases, and the all but complete absence of duplication among formulae, there is also an enormous amount of variation in Homer's phraseology, and the vocabulary of the poems is staggeringly large. It may well be asked how much of all this can be formulaic. It was Parry's conviction that everything in Homeric style was traditional and formulaic, though he recognized that without more evidence certainty was impossible.[16] But two internal facts of the Homeric poems themselves tend to justify Parry's opinion. First, it is clear from the concordances to Homer that, for all the variations, almost every word (not to mention whole phrases) has a preferred position in the line, or two preferred positions, and not more as a rule. In the case of words and phrases occurring only once, of which there are many, the greatest doubt arises. Yet even these phrases are often formed on the analogy of other phrases whose formulaic nature is apparent, and often enough the word which occurs alone but once occurs in an otherwise well-known formula. The second fact which leads one to believe that the whole style is formulaic and traditional is the dialectal mixture. No attempt to separate the various contributions of Aeolic, Ionic, and the others has ever been successful. Any dialectal form may turn up anywhere, which would certainly not be the case had Homer, who presumably spoke one dialect, altered the traditional epic idiom to any appreciable extent.

It is more than likely, therefore, that essentially everything in Homer is formulaic, and that to look for Homer's verbal contribution is vain. He doubtless made some. But creativity of this sort took place totally in terms of formulae, some of which were often the special possession, or even personal creation, of individual singers;[17] it would be most difficult, without the discovery of other contemporary epics, to put one's finger on a single phrase which is Homer's own, though one may suspect the *Shield of Achilles* of containing not a few. But Homer's own genius could not have lain chiefly in the devising of new formulae; in a traditional style there is little premium upon verbal, or even formulaic, novelty. It is the genius of the style itself, more than it is Homer's genius, which appears in the splendor or aptitude of individual phrases.

In actuality, when one considers the extent of the formulaic method, it is clear that the functional purpose which gave birth to it was far transcended in the phase of its greatest development. The wide range of phraseological variation, while it confirms rather than upsets the oral theory, also proves that mere convenience was only a minor consideration to a really skilled singer. Homer could say anything. A poor singer might have only a few formulae, comparatively speaking. But Homer's immense range shows what the traditional style was to one who really commanded it. It was a language within a language, and must have been learned as a language is learned, by ear and use. It was a presentational, imagistic, and highly formalized language also, in which each unit had been turned on the lathe of generations of poetic artificers, into a perfected and inevitable device, satisfying both the functional and the artistic needs of the poet.[18] Grace and accuracy of observation characterize the mosaic pieces of this language, and each is itself the symbol of an idea, an image, or an action. Yet, since the whole is still a language, it conducts in a kind of disguise the necessary minimum of discursiveness.

When words are set to music, they become not merely groups of meaningful syllables, but syllables whose meaning, by being adjusted to a tonal pattern, is modified by the formal effect of the union, and suspended in time until the pattern is complete. Something of the sort happens in the making of words into formulae. And if analogies to the technique of Homer have been found in Serbia and Greece itself, it is difficult to find anything analogous to the effect of Homer, in whom the style achieved an extraordinary degree of perfection. Something similar is perhaps to be found in the style of Mozart. Based as it is on a developed aristocratic tradition, whose compositional elements are largely formulaic, the eighteenth-century manner became in Mozart's hands, through sheer skill of deployment, a medium of surpassing emotional and artistic authority, whose impact is of such intimately combined force and elegance that it is hard to say which predominates.

Oral tradition had already, then, provided Homer with a language which needed no further artistic transformation; it was an art-language, and the analysis of it so far has had little to do with Homer as an individual poet. Yet every singer was a creator within the formulaic limits, and therefore Homer's genius should reveal itself in the same way that any creative genius does, in the use of the medium, and in the propriety of the parts to the whole. Only in Homer's case the limits and possibilities of oral technique must be kept in mind.

In general, the combinations of proper names with their epithets stand in Homer as they must have stood in the tradition, and though every epithet may have sprung from an individual source,[19] it ends as a heroic generality whose reference is to the whole heroic world.[20] Any man might be called "mighty," for instance, and any woman "white-armed." These are ideal abstractions of the heroic view of things, symbolical in a way of the sexes, the one as strength, the other as beauty. If the epithet "good at the war cry" seems to be all but confined to Diomedes and Menelaus, it nevertheless does not indicate their particular ability to shout war cries, for it is used, though rarely, also of Hector, Ajax, and Polites, to answer a metrical need. It happens simply because the names Diomedes and Menelaus are metrically equivalent in Greek, and the whole formula fills the second half of the hexameter after the feminine caesura, and never occurs elsewhere. Some heroes, indeed, tend to appropriate to themselves certain particulars of the heroic apparatus, as a large planet collects families of comets. Thus, partly for metrical reasons, but also by reason of special characteristics, Odysseus is "many-counciled," and Achilles is "swift of foot." These two, incidentally, are metrically equivalent, but never exchanged, and indeed it is no mere chance. Odysseus is not principally famed for his swiftness of foot, and Achilles admits his lack of subtlety in council.[21] These, then, are specific character-epithets. Agamemnon's "king of men" epithet may be of similar kind.[22] But it is a question whether they can be regarded as Homer's characterizations, or, like patronymics, regular and traditional for the most famous heroes.[23]

Only a very few epithets, uncommon ones for the most part, seem to be used with reference to the specific context in which they stand, such as "much-traveled," used only twice of Odysseus, and "cowardly," used of Aegisthus.[24] For the most part, epithets merely complete names, and their symbolic force, such as it is, lies only in their relating the names to the large tradition of the heroic past, and giving them thereby an added dimension.

On the other hand, since everything in the epic is formulaic, though highly varied formulaic speech, the functional aspect cannot in the large be the determining factor. Functions are functions of something, and in this case, of the poet's intention. The oral poet, like any other, must plan his lines, and he must have some notion of what the end will consist of when he sings the beginning. It is not beyond the oral singer to do so much. The text of Homer may have its little failures, which are due to traditional intrusion of a formulaic word which is actually not at all appropriate.[25] But Homer won fame not for his noddings but for his triumphs. The problem in oral composition was not to invent a new phrase, at least not as a rule, and certainly not unless it was absolutely necessary. The problem was to adjust the building blocks of the poetic speech with reference to association and design.

Another example of the use of a common formula in an uncommon way can be found in the *Patrocleia*, where Patroclus, attempting to scale the Trojan wall, confronts Apollo, and rushes at him, "equal to a god." [26] The phrase is traditional enough, but here it takes on more than a merely honorific force. Patroclus is struggling with Apollo, and, as appears later, he is anything but Apollo's equal. Yet the poet has made it clear just before that Patroclus' great burst of courage is due to the direct inspiration of Zeus, and that this inspiration is yet a "calling unto death." [27] The heroic association of divine valor with death involving a god is implied in the epithet, which moreover recalls Patroclus' first moment of involvement in the action which led to his death. This is the moment when, summoned by Achilles, he comes out of his tent "equal to Ares," and "it was the beginning of his woe." [28] From here on till his death, Patroclus' epithets take on a divine context. One might multiply instances, but at the risk of seeming to isolate special moments of propriety, and obscuring the all-important fact of Homer's con-

sistent felicity in the arrangement of formulae. Each one that seems
singularly well chosen depends for its effect on hundreds of lines
of texture which have prepared it.[29] No one, for instance, can fail
to notice the effect of the common phrase, "glorious gifts," which
ends the *Patrocleia*, as the immortal horses of Achilles, "glorious
gifts" from the gods to Peleus, carry the charioteer Automedon to
safety, leaving Patroclus dead on the field. Its commonplace ring
now takes on a peculiar irony, since all Achilles' glorious gifts here-
after will be vain and stale, mere commonplaces of his heroic posi-
tion. Here it is almost impossible to draw the line between the poet
and the style itself, yet the effect is there, an effect of terrible bitter-
ness. Indeed, the whole line, unnecessary for the action alone, seems
to have been added to emphasize the connection of Achilles with
the Olympians who have espoused his cause and permitted the death
of his friend. In Homer's scheme, instead of wearing themselves
out, the formulae keep gaining symbolic weight, like rolling snow-
balls. Achilles is often compared to a lion, but when he strides out
the door of his tent "like a lion" after threatening Priam, the image
reflects in particular the helpless king's view of him;[30] it cannot,
in that moment, remain mere epic ornament. Even such a cliché as
the rose-fingered Dawn, who mounts Olympus, passes from the
functional to the symbolic by constant reference to the airy world
of the gods and their circumambient scheme of divine scatheless-
ness, against which the deadly human drama is played. As one critic
aptly remarked, everything becomes symbolic in the hands of a
good poet.[31]

In Homer this transformation is as nearly complete as it can
possibly be, partly by virtue of the oral style itself, partly by
Homer's use of it. When one approaches some of the larger forms
of Homeric imagery, the hand of the poet himself becomes more
distinguishable. The similes, as is usually said, rise from a single
point of comparison with the action, and thereafter go their own
way. This is partly true, yet their way is controlled by the larger
pattern to an extent, for if it were not, the extra clauses which
regularly expand the similes would be, for all their formulaic im-
mediacy, hopelessly discursive. To continue with lions, for example,
they behave variously. It is like a desperate lion that Odysseus
emerges from the underbrush and meets Nausicaa:

Forth like a lion bred in the mountains he started, trusting in
  strength,
One that strides rain-soaked and blown by the wind, his eyes
Blazing; and forthwith comes among cattle or sheep,
Or among wild deer; and his belly bids him
Come to assail the flocks, even to the sturdy steadings.[32]

Here the added details give fullness to the picture, but the image is
controlled within the limits of the main characters' situations, the
wild, sea-battered, and hunger-driven hero in relation to the domes-
tic and defenceless young Phaeacian girls. This rain-and-wind-lashed
lion wins a good deal more sympathy, for all his terror, than does
the ravening beast to which Agamemnon is compared when he
slays two sons of Priam.[33] And these are but two of many variants
on the lion theme. The simile may begin at a pinpoint of external
similarity, but it ends in character. When Odysseus is compared to
an octopus, his two chief characteristics are implied — tenacity and
deviousness.[34] Again, in the Phaeacian episode, where the song of
Demodocus makes Odysseus weep like a woman captured in the
sack of a city,[35] the long-developed image raises a host of implica-
tions. Throughout the whole entertainment held in his honor, the
mystery of Odysseus, and particularly his striking difference from
the Phaeacians, has been subtly implied. They have been testing
him, and have found him singularly sufficient and challenging, but
his superiority has remained so far an unexplained, half-hidden fire,
which has been slowly revealing itself. Now with the simile of the
captive woman, Homer suddenly injects a graphic and terrifying
vision of the world from which Odysseus comes, a world of burnt
cities, slain men, and women dragged to slavery, the old turbulent
Achaean world, which to the Phaeacians is just a song for an eve-
ning's amusement.[36] The latter, especially Alcinous, have been try-
ing to impress their guest, but now the tables are turned. Before
the shattering reality of Odysseus, the long-sufferer, this fairy-tale
world of Phaeacia fades to a humble, attentive background. Al-
cinous questions Odysseus anxiously, and the hero begins his great
narrative. But the simile has brought to a dramatic head the con-
trast between those who are simply favored by the gods, and those
who meet their challenge on sea and battlefield.

Such a dramatic use of the simile at once invades the proper function of the scene itself. Another example is the quiet image of the stars at the end of *Iliad* VIII. There the watchfires of the quiescent but still threatening Trojans are compared to the numberless stars on a clear night; but scene and simile are both nightpieces, and they blend almost imperceptibly, creating a momentary abatement of the intensity of war, and preparing the way for the nocturnal interlude which takes place before the battle is resumed. Here the image is not controlled by character, but by a total dramatic situation. It does not exist wholly for its own sake, handsome as this particular one is. Like a fountain, it rises from its point of comparison, fire and stars, but falls back into the larger basin of meaning. For the fire is a deadly symbol in the *Iliad*, while the stars stand in the world of the gods, the placid air; and images of divine peace alternate throughout the poem with pictures of war and strife. At the end of Book VIII, this intrinsic and consistent contrast unites the image of peaceful stars and the description of the embattled watchfires into a strange union with each other and with the whole poem.

Thus images become action; and the scene is an image dramatized. This process, though common in the epic, is so germane to the more concentrated form of tragedy that one or two examples from the latter will help to illustrate it. The self-blinding of Oedipus for instance is the active climax of a whole series of images dealing with the symbolic implications of sight and blindness; earlier it was dramatized in the scene with Teiresias. The manacles which are put on Philoctetes are simply a dramatized image of the paralyzing volitional paradox in which he finds himself. The net and the seapurple carpet in the *Agamemnon* are very familiar. In the case of the manacles and the net, the treatment of the plot seems to have bred the symbols. In the *Oedipus*, one might argue that the crucial symbol of sight versus blindness preëxisted, or at least coexisted with the treatment. Epic, with its more diffuse action, offers few examples of imagery so tightly knit with action. But if Homer's method is different, his practice is just as symbolic, and one may see a little into his types of creative association. Women's weaving, for instance, seems to have exercised power over his imagination. Helen's great web is woven with pictures of the war for her sake,[37] and becomes in an instant the symbol of her self-conscious great-

ness and guilt, paralleling her speeches to Hector, Priam, and Aph-
rodite. How different is Penelope's weaving, the token of her
filial piety toward Laertes and her fidelity to Odysseus! [38] And it
has been said with insight that Andromache's weaving of a purple
fabric with flowers, while Hector is fighting his last battle, does
not occur by chance; purple is the epithet of death, and flowers
are grave-offerings.[39] It might be added that the flowers are per-
haps in character for Andromache. These are weavings with a fatal-
ity in them, and they prompt the wish that Homer had described
the patterns on Calypso's loom, and Circe's. But perhaps it is just
as significant that he did not. Calypso and Circe are goddesses with-
out fatalities, and their weaving is merely decorative. But with
Arêtê, the Phaeacian queen, there is middle ground. What she
weaves is not described, but her yarn is a "sea-purple," as it should
be for the queen of a great seafaring people.[40] And when Helen
reappears in the *Odyssey*, spinning, though not weaving, is the
motif which signalizes her return to domestic propriety.[41] Her
equipment is singularly gorgeous, and she is compared to the most
chaste of goddesses, Artemis of the Golden Spindle. It is not per-
haps surprising that Homer should have pushed his traditional
images of spinning and weaving into fatal or characteristic symbols.
Even that early, the Moirai were regarded as spinners; and one
"weaves" both trickery and council.[42]

In an age and in an art form where the "stream of consciousness"
has not yet become a regular method, the emotional springs of a
scene tend to objectify themselves in things and people. Homer
does, indeed, use the soliloquy, often with tremendous effective-
ness, as in Hector's last reflections by the Scaean Gate. But he also
dramatizes mood into action. In the scene where Poseidon comes
to the assistance of the Greeks while Zeus slumbers, there is a strange
passage where the Greek chiefs put on better armor, giving the
inferior arms to inferior people; then Poseidon leads them forward
with a sword like lightning in his hand.[43] To describe in such a way
the renewed courage of those who have courage to renew is simply
to dramatize a simile: "they counter-attacked like fresh men with
new armor." It surely has no realistic significance, for the battle
was in too desperate a stage to allow time for such maneuvers.[44]
It is difficult to know whether the passage ought to be read as

action or image. But the real point is that the distinction has broken down, as it often does in Homer. Since all his action is imagistic, it is no surprise to find on occasion that his images also act. Such passages are bold indeed; a few, such as the *Iliad's* Fight in the River, are unintelligible unless read as acting images. They announce the triumph of the poetic scheme over every naturalistic consideration. They are, in a way, like the poet's disregard of time in such a scene as the discovery of Odysseus by Eurycleia. There a flashback of seventy-six lines intervenes between the nurse's recognition of the scar and her gesture of joyous surprise.[45] No attempt is made to convey the quickness of the action. But there is no lack of narrative skill here. The poet solves the problem of describing the instantaneous by disregarding time altogether, and the whole picture of past and present collapses to a single imagistic point in the hearer's mind. Eurycleia's total memory was too big for a single formula, or even several. So Homer simply dramatizes her mental image, complete with speeches and even the boar-hunt, which incidentally she could not have witnessed.

The relation between certain of Homer's scenes and the image contained in a formula is sometimes so close and explicit that some episodes seem to be scarcely more than formulae acted out like charades. In the fourth *Odyssey* Menelaus relates how he was confined by adverse winds in the island of Pharos for twenty days, until the sea nymph Eidothea came to his rescue. He asks her which of the gods "shackles and binds him from his path." [46] The last two words of the formula recur, with a slight change, in *Odyssey* 5, where Athena stills the winds which have shipwrecked Odysseus:

> Then she bound the paths of the other winds.[47]

The metaphor of being "bound," or prevented from a journey by adverse winds, or, as in English, wind-bound, is reversed into an image of binding the paths of the winds, which is the function of a benign and favoring deity. So far, we meet here only formulaic variations on a basic metaphor. But in Book 10 of the *Odyssey* the metaphor becomes action, a little scene:

> And he [Aeolus] stripped off the skin of a nine-years' ox,
> Wherein he bound the paths of the blustering winds. . .

> And tied them in my hollow ship with a shining string
> Of silver, that not even a little might breathe through. . .[48]

What was originally a figure of speech is acted out, with the winds literally tied up in a bag with a silver string, which the companions later undo, in one of their occasional moments of insubordination. The episode comments eloquently on the psychological interpretation of metaphor and magic, poetic speech and poetically conceived action.

Again, the description of Odysseus' landing in Phaeacia and meeting with Nausicaa strikingly illustrates how a single formula with its image not only may underlie and mingle with the action, but also may externalize or objectify the internal states of the characters and embrace a dramatic situation whole. After the struggles of the shipwreck, the hero, exhausted, half-conscious, and vomiting brine, crawls ashore at the river mouth, in a place free of stones, where there was "a shelter from the wind." [49] The passage is full of an overwhelming sense of relief and salvation, but it arises not from anything Odysseus says about it, but from the nature of the things which he encounters. Of these — the land itself, the slackened stream, the lack of stones — none is so central to the feeling of benignity as the image of windlessness, the cessation of all rough elements.[50] The winds have had their will in the shipwreck. One of the two things Odysseus still fears now is that the wind will blow cold at dawn if he sleeps on the shore;[51] and he seeks the thicket of wild and domestic olive,

> Which neither the force of the damp-blowing winds
> Pierced, nor the flashing sun struck with his rays,
> Nor the rain poured through.[52]

There he falls asleep, like a spark hidden under ashes. This is logical enough, but it is also magical. A spark under ashes revives with wind, and presently there are winds; but with a subtle change. Homer is immersed in images of peace and safety, the focus of which is to be Nausicaa, herself an image of tender nurturing, peace, and every blessing of civilization. She cannot be a wind. At the beginning of Book 6, she is asleep, like Odysseus, but Athena, summoning her to his aid, comes into her safe chamber, through the closed doors, "like a breath of wind." [53] This wind which rushes toward the bed of Nausicaa is a presaging token of the impact which the experienced, weather-beaten Odysseus is to have upon the sheltered Phaeacians, especially Nausicaa, an impact which is vividly dramatized in Book 8. This wind has action and danger in it, nicely imaged in the simile of the weatherbeaten lion, when Odysseus comes out of the bushes toward the princess and tells her how wind and water brought him to Scheria.[54] By contrast, Phaeacia, the land blessedly remote from all enemies, is a windless paradise: "Assist his bath," says Nausicaa to her friends, returning to the formula which keeps repeating itself, "where there is shelter from the wind." [55] It is scarcely a wonder, in such an elaborate complexity of weather symbolism, that when Athena finally leaves Nausicaa in charge for the moment, she goes to an Olympus which, though it is much unlike the gods' dwelling as described elsewhere in Homer, is very like the safe thicket where Odysseus sleeps:

> Neither by wind is it shaken, nor ever wet by rain,
> Neither snow comes near it, but verily clear sky
> Cloudless expands, and a white gleam spreads over all.[56]

It is a mistake to think that Homer has climbed in this vision of supernal tranquility to a nobler conception of the divine kingdom than he had in the *Iliad*. He is simply following the course of his imagery, and developing in action and description the vision which is most briefly caught in the formula, "where there was a shelter from the wind."

An understanding of this method can sometimes lead to the real purport of a passage. In *Iliad* XX Aeneas tells Apollo how Achilles once chased him all the way down Mount Ida in a surprise raid; Athena, he says, "going before Achilles *made a light*." [57] Here "light," as elsewhere in the *Iliad*, is a metonym for victory; as such it occurs in various formulae.[58] In the beginning of the nineteenth *Odyssey*, however, one finds the scene where Telemachus and Odysseus are removing the arms from the hall by night, in preparation for slaying the suitors:

> And before them Pallas Athena
> Holding a golden lamp made a most beautiful light.
> Then spoke Telemachus to his father swiftly:
> "Father, here is a great wonder I see with my eyes;

The walls of the house and the fair panels,
The pine beams and the pillars thrusting upward
Gleam all round to my eyes as if with blazing fire.
Surely some god is within, of those who keep Olympus." [59]

Here, as in Aeneas' formula, Athena makes a light go before a hero
destined for victory. But the metaphor has turned into a miracle,
motivated, however, on the simple, logical level by Eurycleia's
earlier question: who will carry the light for you? The essence of
both the formula and the scene is the same image of divine light
going before, guaranteeing triumph, or better, foreseeing it from
the gods' timeless point of view.

Alexandrine critics questioned the genuineness of this passage,
because of the impropriety of Athena's doing so menial a task as
carrying a lamp.[60] But the lamp is merely a detail, like the silver
string tying up the winds, an adjunct to the light of triumph. The
ancient objection is transparently foolish in this case anyway, but
the formulaic analogy makes the meaning of the passage clear.

A comparable passage occurs at the end of *Odyssey* 20. Here the
suitors, guilty now of every possible breach of civilization, are sud-
denly bewitched by Athena; they laugh "with strange jaws," and
weep simultaneously, and the food that they eat seems streaked
with blood. The seer Theoclymenus perceives the phenomenon,
and more too:

Ah, wretches, what evil is this you suffer? In night your
Heads are wrapped, and your faces, and limbs below;
Lamentation flares out, your cheeks are wet with tears,
The walls are sprinkled with blood, and the fair panels.
Full is the forecourt, and the great hall of ghosts,
Making their way into Erebus under the darkness; the sun also
Perishes from heaven, and an evil mist spreads over all.[61]

This passage too has been suspected, and called "shamanistic," in
that it exhibits clairvoyance, and envisions as finished what is yet
to come.[62] But such clairvoyance into things to come, here the
deaths of the suitors, merely reflect, as often in Homer, the gods'
way of looking at things. The passage corresponds, as darkness cor-
responds to light, to the passage of Athena with the lamp; if that
betokened victory, this betokens death. And again, it is merely the

dramatization, in visionary terms, of formulaic motifs familiar enough elsewhere. When Theoclymenus says, "Your heads are wrapped in night," it is precisely parallel to the formulaic line:

Dark night wrapped his eyes about . . .[63]

The metaphor is a frequent one for death, and one which itself is developed in the *Iliad* into literal action when a darkness, caused by mist that blotted out the sun, gathers around the body of Patroclus in the thick of the battle.[64] Here too, the sun "perishes from heaven, and an evil mist spreads." The sprinkling of blood on the walls and meat, moreover, is not an unfamiliar image; it is one associated with impending but as yet unaccomplished doom: twice in the *Iliad* Zeus sheds a rain of blood, once when Sarpedon is about to fall, and earlier when Zeus himself intends "to hurl many brave heads into Hades." [65] All these motifs are recognizable elsewhere. The journeying ghosts, on their way to Hades, may seem to a degree irregular; yet these two lines only summarize what is narrated in the opening of Book 24, the so-called second *Nekyia*. All such use of poetic materials is entirely characteristic of Homer. It rests upon the compression or expansion of images whose smallest unit is the formulaic phrase and whose larger developments may grow to many lines. And in the vision of Theoclymenus, though its effect is unique and its atmosphere somewhat more macabre and uncanny than is usual in Homer, there is nothing innovating or shamanistic, nothing which is not native to the traditional imagery. Even the uncanniness finds some parallel in the crawling hides and mooing meat of the slain Cattle of the Sun.[66]

The episodes just described, however, contain a great deal more than the images mentioned, and, of course, not every scene can be read backwards into a formula. The character of Nausicaa, for example, is a chef-d'oeuvre quite apart from her symbolic function in the rescue of Odysseus. Her own existence as a poetic creation, a paradigm of the day on which a girl becomes a woman, is an especially appealing example of the genius of the Greek artist for generalizing upon the individual without destroying individuality. But all Homer's characters are equally universalized individuals, and his scenes for the most part dramatize them for their own sakes, within the limits of a totally conceived heroic world. Thus, though the poetic image is the genesis of the dramatic or narrative scene, their dimensions and functions differ.

Yet many of Homer's scenes, apart from their relation to formulae, are just as traditional poetic units as the latter, and doubtless all are modeled to a degree on types.[67] The battle books of the *Iliad* offer a dizzying variety of small combat scenes, whose recurrent motifs are combined and recombined into ever new situations, whose circumstances, like life itself, are always different, yet always coincide with others at certain points. It is a formal design corresponding to, but not specifically imitating, the natural world. Crystallized and formulaic, its life is not naturalistic but generic, its realism is classical, not that of photographic illusionism. The battle books, for instance, have been mistakenly neglected, for quite apart from their intimate connection with the whole structure, they better illustrate in one way Homer's skill with the oral style than do the more famous parts of the poem. Traditional as they are, Homer narrates them as images in a whole design. An image was defined originally as a direct appeal to sensory response, and in the formula, it was stated, a syntactical group of words gains the presentational power of an image through identification with the formal syntax of a fixed rhythmic pattern. When formulae are combined and recombined as they are in Homer's battle scenes, it is like the falling of glass chips in a kaleidoscope. Patterns constantly are formed, always with consistency of color, and always with pieces of the same shape, yet always different and always luminous with surprise. No matter how many are combined, the imagistic impact of formulae is not lost provided they are chosen with relevance to the total design which is aimed at. The poet's mind herein acts like the mirror in the kaleidoscope, constantly rounding the fall of formulae into an organic, larger unit.

The outlines of the larger units are, of course, determined by plot and character. Large scenes, like coral, are agglutinative organisms, made of smaller formulaic pieces. But they are also whole conceptions, subordinated in turn to the whole poem. They do not just grow; they grow by design, each with a presentational life of its own, that is, with the ability to impress the mind as a unit and not as a series. Thus the famous scene between Andromache and Hector has been finely analyzed as an interlocking of two main

images, the world of man and the world of woman, which are hope-
lessly separate save for the unifying presence of a child.[68] This is
one view and an important one. But there are also many other ways
of looking at it, for when an image is dramatized, it can never
again be compressed; it exists in its own right as a scene, an image,
but a kinetic one, an image of humanity in action.

But to speak of "images of humanity" leads to the most general
considerations, and the question of Homer's ultimate intention as
an artist. No mere analysis of the tools and technique of a poet can
explain his power. The structural elements of epic, scene, simile,
and formula, subserve a total concept which in Homer's case is a
vision of the heroic world of the past. Like all else Homeric, it is
in part traditional, the keepsake of generations of bards, the long
memory of the "glories of men." But it is also molded anew by each
new hand for each new poem. It differs a little, though only a
little, in the *Odyssey* from what it was in the *Iliad*, and hence it is
always a creation, or a re-creation, never a mirrored imitation. It
reflects nothing exactly, for it comes to being through the formulae
which are not realistically mimetic, but distillates of observation,
formalized units standing at a remove from reality in order to pre-
sent it imagistically. It took centuries to forge this medium, and
the pieces date from every generation of singers from the fall of
Troy, or before, to the eighth century. Hence it arises that Homer's
world is not the Mycenaean world, nor the world of the eighth
century. It is the epic world, a visionary structure whose chief pillar
is the heroic aspiration. Within that structure, all the elements
fit, though they may not correspond precisely to anything outside
it. Each refers broadly to the whole, reflecting a composite idea,
not a specific one. Parry said that the fixed epithet adorns the whole
of heroic verse rather than any specific person.[69] He might have
gone farther and said that every formula reflects a group of asso-
ciated notions seen in perspective within the heroic structure. Ar-
chilochus lost his own personal shield in battle. In Homer, every
shield, even Ajax's big one, is the universal heroic shield, seen
through centuries of admiring retrospect. It is "towerlike," or
"equal all round," or "well turned" interchangeably, not because
Homer forgot which kind of shield Ajax was carrying on a certain
day, but because the only shield his Ajax ever had was an epic

shield, symbolic of all that a heroic shield must be. It is a shield-metaphor, which changes with perfect unconcern from a Mycenaean body-shield to a round hoplite shield, reflecting any shape which had crept into the conventional speech by sometime being glorified in action. A completely plastic conception, the Homeric symbol, shield, whether it be called ἀσπὶς or σάκος, is always a metaphor, and in Book XVIII of the *Iliad* it undergoes a tremendous expansion and becomes a metaphor of the whole heroic world.

So too with helmets. For one trained in the bardic tradition, a helmet was conceived according to the metrical space it was to fill. At the beginning of a line it might well be αὐλῶπις τρυφάλεια. It seems impossible to identify this particular helmet, and one suspects it of being a composite helmet-image, with no counterpart in armory. It strikes the ear grandly,[70] but it seems to have no factual inevitability. When Apollo knocks the helmet from Patroclus' head, the phrase is used, but the same implement is also referred to as πήληξ and κυνέη, which presumably have different meanings.[71] But the distinctions have no importance for Homer. His phrase is a pictorial unit, encrusted with helmet images, the metaphor, not the name, of a helmet.

The two or three really specific descriptions of objects in Homer stand out in great contrast to the host of formulaic things. The boar's-tusk helmet, the cup of Nestor, and perhaps the breastplate of Agamemnon [72] protrude from the texture of the poem as they do just because they are decorative and definite, rather than stock in trade. Somehow, perhaps because they were considered peculiarly remarkable objects, they escaped falling into one generality or another, and their descriptions survive whole. So do the objects themselves, at least two of them. The boar's-tusk helmet has been reconstructed from Middle Helladic fragments — incidentally long antedating the man who wears it in the *Iliad* — and the cup of Nestor, though greatly disputed, is surely to be recognized in the dove-goblet dug up by Schliemann.[73] It is not impossible that Agamemnon's breastplate might somewhere turn up. But no one has ever found a shield like that of Achilles, and no one ever will. Metaphors are not found in excavations.

The answer to the problem of Homer's "directness," his apparent lack of metaphor, is now clear. His whole world is a metaphor, an enormously articulated symbolism of the heroic life. His apparent naturalness is the product of the exact opposite, a highly contrived convention. But poetic truth is artifice, and the more complete the artifice is, the more true is the poem. Frigidity and bathos proceed not from artificial causes, but from rifts and failures in the artifice. If metaphor flags and facts prevail, the presentational is lost, and the poem sinks to prose. But Homer's metaphor cannot ever flag. It is in great part identical with the very language he speaks. For no matter how poor a singer used this speech, there is one virtue he could never lack, the momentary vividness of image after image. He might arrange his images badly, or repeat himself too often and in the wrong way, and thus dull the edge to a degree and fail of any real supremacy. But the epic medium was an extraordinary one, with some special advantages which, in the hands of a great singer, could lead to the *Iliad* and the *Odyssey*. Yet what was required of such a poet, in order to use the epic language to the full and create such poems, still, as in the case of all great artists, baffles analysis. The metaphoric world of the heroes which Homer created lay in fragments like the chips of stone and gold before a mosaic is made. The pieces were ideally suited to the purpose, but it remained to conceive the total design around a central theme, and then, within that design, to set all the formal building blocks in such a way that they would pick up light and shadow from each other in a consistent symbolic scheme. If the scheme is right, everything within it will be symbolic; but everything must be seen symbolically for the scheme to be right. At this point, we must leave it to Homer.

VII

FIRE AND OTHER ELEMENTS

IT has been said that the oral poet feels no urge to coin new and striking phrases, as does the poet who writes.[1] The oral poet conceives his art, as indeed he must, as a continuous recombination of formulae. These formulae have already, as we have seen, partially solved the problem of making language presentational, leaving the poet more free to center his attention upon the arrangement and consistency of his poem. Since the whole is carried in the mind, and each unit is imagistic, in the sense defined in the last chapter, it is almost inevitable that certain images should group themselves systematically around leading ideas or characters; the creative process can be described in part as a movement from image to image, a movement controlled on one side by the demands of narrative, and on the other by the particular associations of the individual poet. Yet these images do not form a schematic set of deliberate correspondences; they change and shift constantly, according to the demands of the larger scene-image in which they stand, and the consistency which they show is the consistency of the whole design. By association with action and character, they grow into symbols, but like all symbols, they reflect in their unity a Gestalt, or organism of mental pictures and processes which do not correspond to any single concept. Their wording may change, but this basic set of associations, developing slowly throughout the narrated action, reveals the main threads of the poet's concern. If the formulaic method explains how an oral poet managed to compose at all, the image-patterns of the epic give the clue to his artistic plan. All poets plan their images, of course; but an oral poet's leading motifs must, to be manageable and communicable, remain austerely simple and strict in their economy. Herein the practical need of the performer and the meaning of his art serve each other, and well-nigh merge.

The total imagery of the *Iliad* exhibits the most extraordinary range of observation, especially in the formal similes, and the most startling of these, such as the comparison of the Achaean battle-line to an honest woman measuring wool,[2] or of Hector to a stone rolling down a cliff,[3] occur once only. But there are also numerous kinds of image which, as part of the more expectable vocabulary of a warlike tradition, recur many times: comparisons of advancing hosts to the waves of the sea, of heroes to fierce animals, tall trees, whirlwinds, cliffs, and eagles. These are stock in trade on the one hand; yet it is precisely in this type of imagery that Homer's poetic economy makes itself evident. These motifs are not used indiscriminately, but with great subtlety, always emphasizing and sometimes symbolizing the larger movements of the poem. For the most part, these images occur in groups, in limited parts of the poem, changing to reflect changes of action. Only one stretches from beginning to end of the *Iliad*, reflecting the progress of the main action. This is the image of fire.

In one form or another, fire occurs about two hundred times in the *Iliad*, and of these only ten can really be said to be casual uses, unconnected with the main scheme.[4] For the rest, fire itself, or comparisons of things to fire, forms a remarkable pattern of associations, all centering around the theme of heroic passion and death. Nothing could provide a more clinical case history of the working of a poet's mind upon a traditional theme than Homer's use of fire. For clearly, in the epic tradition, the motif existed chiefly in the form of men in armor flashing, or dashing, like fire. This is by far the most frequent form in which the image occurs, and there are numerous formulae for it, and sundry variations. Fire, or "heat" thus becomes a simple metonym for war, so that a battle with stones can even be referred to as "a divine-kindled fire of stones." [5] In

Homer's hands, however, not only do the heroes behave like fire; fire itself behaves like the heroes. With the exception of the few passages noted, every spark of flame, no matter how naturally and inevitably it is lit, is drawn eventually into the tragic symbolism.

It begins naturally enough with sacrifices and funeral pyres. The first fire we hear of is in the prayer of Chryses, who reminds Apollo of the sacrifices he has burned. Shortly thereafter the pyres of the dead blaze in the Greek camp; [6] Chryses' sacrifices were doubtless of a festive nature; but the fire of sacrifices to the gods takes on darker coloring as the poem proceeds. The next one is the propitiatory and repentant sacrifice of Odysseus at Chrysa,[7] and after that the sacrifices of the Achaeans on the brink of a disastrous battle, and of Agamemnon himself, whose prayers Zeus has refused.[8] While he entertains the Embassy, Achilles roasts meat for a meal; [9] but later in Phoenix' account of his wrath against his father, the image of meat roasting in the fire merges mysteriously with the watchfire of the guard set upon Phoenix, whose rage would not cool, so that the fire could not be quenched for nine nights. By this point in the poem, as we shall see, anger and fire are inseparably associated, so that a special meaning surrounds the later narrative of Nestor's earliest memory of Achilles in the light of a sacrificial fire.[10] Finally the idea of sacrifice becomes really doom-laden. Its last three occurrences are in contexts far removed from the festive. As he watches Hector fleeing from Achilles, Zeus says,

> My heart mourns for Hector who burned many thighs of bulls
> On the peaks of Ida of the many glens, and sometimes in the
>   acropolis.
> Now divine Achilles pursues him with swift feet round Priam's
>   city.[11]

The sight of the pious man whom he cannot save, driven to death on the site of his many sacrifices, may well move Zeus. The sacrificer becomes the sacrificed, and Andromache's burning of Hector's clothes is like the last of his profitless sacrifices.[12] It is in lieu of a funeral; in fact sacrifice and funeral have blended, in part, and they become actually identical when the twelve Trojan youths are immolated at the funeral of Patroclus.[13] Surely there is a consciousness here of an inverted order of things: Andromache burns Hector's empty clothes, while his corpse remains unburnt; Achilles sacrifices twelve living men to swell the pyre of Patroclus. The limits of funeral and sacrifice have somehow become confused, and their functions perverted.

Pyres for the dead are, of course, numerous in the *Iliad*, but in general they follow the action closely, appearing at climactic moments. They appear first as the direct result of Agamemnon's insult to Chryses, the germ of the plot. In Andromache's narrative to Hector, the pyre of her father enters as a poignant commentary upon her own tragic isolation, and incidentally upon the character of Achilles also.[14] At the end of the first day's fighting in the poem, the passage known as the Gathering of the Dead, with its long description of the Greek and Trojan funerals, seems to serve a special purpose.[15] As yet the Achaeans have suffered no special defeat, yet they decide, on Nestor's advice, to build a wall to defend themselves and their ships. The problem of Book VII is to bridge the gap between the victorious displays of Diomedes in V and VI, and the sudden worsting of the Greeks in VIII. A wall is needed to keep these reversals from becoming an immediate rout. And in order to motivate the wall adequately, the poet binds its construction closely to the taking up of the dead; Nestor proposes both the truce for burial and the wall-building in a single speech — a unique example of compendiousness on his part. But the reason for it is to create a specious motivation for this sudden act of defensiveness, and the burning and burial of the fallen provides just the imagistic atmosphere needed. From the logical point of view, there is a weak link in the structure here; Homer has tried to hide it in the dazzle of funeral pyres.

The funeral motif has two climaxes, the pyre of Patroclus and the pyre of Hector, and both reflect upon the character of Achilles. The burial of his friend takes place in an atmosphere of horror and savage grief. He delays it until he can carry out to the full his threatened vengeance; he repeatedly drags Hector round the bier, until the ghost of Patroclus himself begs for some haste with the formalities.[16] Something of Achilles' own feeling that he cannot do enough for his friend is reflected in the reluctance of the fire to burn; special winds must be summoned, and then at last the pyre flames.[17] The contrast between such scenes of wrenching agony and the long perspective on sorrow in Book XXIV is profound. When he restores the body of Hector to Priam, Achilles repeats his honorable treatment of Andromache's father, and his own fulfilled dignity is echoed in the long but restrained triptych of lamentation, as Andromache, Hecuba, and Helen conduct Hector's funeral. When the embers of this pyre die down, the tragic fire-motif which spreads wildly throughout the poem, somehow returns to its limits at last.

As one looks back from this point, lurid flame seems to start from every portion of the poem. The eyes of Agamemnon in the quarrel glare darkly like fire.[18] In the king's hope of victory, we foresee the flare of burning Troy.[19] As the marshaled host marches out, they are like wasting fire that burns in a wooded mountain glen,[20] the first of a famous chain of similes. Rage, destruction, heroic valor, and heroic honor are all fire. Sometimes the hero simply moves like fire; sometimes it is his eyes that burn terribly under the nodding helmet.[21] Achilles' own fierce choler sometimes blazes clear, and sometimes is compared to a growing cloud of smoke.[22] Athena drops from Olympus to the battlefield like a meteor shooting sparks;[23] sometimes she comes in a burning chariot.[24] When Hector smashes the Achaean gates with a stone and leaps inside the wall, he seems all clothed in fire, with his arms and eyes flaring; but it is a dusky, threatening flame, for he is also like the night.[25] Later, as he threatens to burn the ships, he is like a blazing eagle, so that in his most victorious moment, his fire is joined by the bird of Zeus, who gives him the victory.[26] Even proper names get caught significantly in the conflagration. As Hector begins his great attack, he addresses his four horses, two of which have fiery names, Aithon (Blazing) and Lampus (Torch),[27] and the first man slain by Patroclus as he drives the Trojans back from the ships is Pyraichmes, "Fiery Spearhead."[28] While images of tree-felling as a rule prevail in the pitched battle, forest fire is the regular image for a rout.[29]

But it is in connection with the wrath of Achilles and the plan of Zeus itself that the fire motif undergoes its principal development. In this connection it becomes symbolic, from simply imagistic, and thus gives to every passage involving it the tragic context of the hero himself. There could scarcely be a more apt symbol of Greek heroism, which turns upon the poles of divinity and death. The fire of the funeral pyres betokens one side of the heroic nature; the other reaches toward the gods through the lightning-flashes, which presently become the explicit sign of Zeus' acceptance of the hero's cause.[30]

The plan of Zeus to defeat the Achaeans in Achilles' absence does not actually begin to take effect until Book VIII, but at the end of the preceding book, the sign of Zeus' participation in the war begins. The Achaeans and Trojans are at their evening meal:

> All night long then the long-haired Achaeans feasted,
> And the Trojans also in the city, and their allies;
> And all night long Zeus the Councillor was planning evil against them,
> Terribly thundering; and pale fear seized them.[31]

It is not yet made clear to either side who is to be the object of Zeus' evil plan, but it soon becomes specific enough when the battle is joined next morning:

> While it was dawn and the sacred day was rising, steadily
> Missiles of both hosts flew to the mark, and the men were falling;
> But when the sun bestrode the midst of the sky,
> Verily then the father spread out the golden scales,
> Casting therein two fates of long and grievous death,
> Fates of the Trojans, masters of horses, and bronze-vested Achaeans;
> Taking the center he poised them; the Achaeans' day drooped fatal;
> Down to the full-nourishing earth the fates of the Achaeans
> Settled, and the Trojans' rose up toward the broad heaven.
> Mightily he himself thundered from Ida, and hurled a flaming
> Lightning-bolt at the host of Achaeans, and they perceiving
> Wondered aghast, and pale fear secretly stole over all.[32]

The use of the scales here symbolizes, as usual in Homer, fatality, meaning what must happen because of the nature of things. The scales never indicate a miraculous, unnatural, or supernatural event; their readings are, in Homer's phrase, "according to fate." Here they point to the inevitable weakness of the Achaeans without Achilles, and by their token the plan of Zeus is shown as grounded in fact and made organic with the human situation. The lightning flash which dismays the Achaeans is the direct reflex of Achilles' retirement. The action of the god and the inaction of the hero are essentially one.

On the other hand, the lightning flash itself presently takes on the appearances of a special, personal rebuke. Diomedes, flushed with recent triumphs, rescues Nestor from the tangle of his wounded horses, and turns against the Trojans with such fury that "they would have been pent up in Ilium like sheep," had not Zeus again hurled the lightning.[33] There follows a little tussle between Diomedes and Zeus, and the god has to hurl three more bolts before Diomedes will swallow Hector's taunts and retreat. Here lightning, the symbol of the necessity of Greek defeat, has become an actor on the scene, the agent of things as they are, according to the decree of the scales of Zeus. On the surface of it, this is direct interference, yet it is also in character for Diomedes. It would be impossible to allow Diomedes, whose brilliant exploits in Books V and VI have included the wounding of two gods and a bold resistance to Apollo himself, to yield too easily to a divine sign and turn his back on the enemy. His heroism has reached a high and inspired level, though not that of Achilles. Moreover, he is the least dismayed of all the princes by the retirement of Achilles, and on three occasions he recommends his own valor to Agamemnon, who would give up in discouragement.[34] It is in character, therefore, that he should give in least easily. His resistance to Zeus is coupled with that of the two goddesses who inspired him in V. Exactly as they came to Diomedes in V, Hera and Athena start on their way now, in a chariot to the battlefield, and they too have to be threatened individually with lightning.[35] The scene which follows on Olympus then dramatizes in terms of the gods' own personalities the passionate and wayward courses of the warriors below. Diomedes in a rage of frustration, had prayed for the earth to swallow him.[36] Hera, in a rage of frustration, trembles on her throne and shakes Olympus. But Zeus, unmoved, says that she may plunge into the depths of the earth, but he would not care.[37] The image of being swallowed up by the earth spreads from Diomedes to Hera.

But now the lightning flashes are understood by Hector as a sign of victory.[38] Hector calls to his fiery horses and drives the Achaeans steadily back toward the wall. As Agamemnon in terror appeals to Zeus for the army's safety, Homer brings in a new symbol. Zeus sends an eagle to reassure the king; the eagle has a fawn in its claws, probably a sign of the taking of Troy.[39] It is as if Zeus here indicated the limits of his plan; later on again, the ultimate victory of the Greeks is foreshadowed by an eagle, which goes unnoticed by the Trojans.[40] For the moment the lightning carries the day; fire is on the Trojan side, and burns threateningly in the form of the watchfires which at the end of Book VIII dot the plain, and burn throughout the succeeding night.[41]

Presently the threat takes a more definite form: Hector will burn the ships. This is his first thought when he recognizes the meaning of the lightning flashes; [42] throughout the Embassy, the essence of the Greeks' fear is the image of burning ships,[43] and during the whole central battle it remains the principal deed which Hector envisions in his victory, growing ever more imminent until at last he is at the ships and calls to his companions to bring the fire.[44] It is of course literal, physical fire which Ajax keeps warding away as he strides from deck to deck, battling desperately with a boathook for a spear; but the fire has not lost its connection with Zeus' intention and with Achilles: Idomeneus, at one point, feels sure that the Achaeans can hold off the fire, *unless Zeus himself* hurls it onto the ships.[45] Moreover, the frequent stock comparisons of Hector and the Trojans to fire now have the effect of identifying Hector and his threat as the agents of the Plan of Zeus.[46] War itself is fire, yet here the real fire which threatens is the blaze of the tragic wrath. Nor has the related thunder signal been forgotten; [47] one of the finest uses of it comes when Zeus thunders in answer to a prayer of Nestor's. The god meant to encourage Nestor, and Nestor understands the omen. But the Trojans, to whom now the omen of thunder and lightning is a token of their own victory, are equally encouraged; they set on the Greeks more fiercely, and drive them back even more.[48]

Such ambiguity is increased during the counterattack which the Greeks make, led by Poseidon. Fire still appears in connection with Hector and the threat to the ships,[49] but only while Poseidon's help must be in secret; when Zeus is deceived by Hera into napping, Poseidon assists the Greeks openly. But from the moment of the god's arrival, the fire shows signs of changing sides, and begins to play around Idomeneus, whom Poseidon directly inspires. Idomeneus comes to the battlefield like a lightning flash; [50] a little later he is again compared to fire, and further on to a wild boar with fiery eyes.[51] This is while Zeus is still awake; after he falls asleep, Poseidon takes the field openly, leading the Greeks with a sword which is like lightning.[52] Then comes the climax; the lightning which had been his sign of victory turns against Hector, and he falls beneath the stone of Ajax, like a lightning-blasted oak.[53] Thereafter, Zeus awakes and restores the order of the day; but this part of the action illustrates both the suppleness and careful economy of the fire image. Ambiguous and varied as it is, it goes by plan.

When the first fire actually falls on the ships, the motif passes from the momentary image into the action itself. This moment is most carefully prepared, and the poet gives it a separate, brief invocation of the Muses.[54] The breaking of Ajax' spear, which the hero recognizes as the direct work of the gods, is only the last of a series of such happenings, which include the lightning-flashes of Book VIII, the wounding of the chiefs, and the breaking of Teucer's bowstring.[55] With Ajax momentarily helpless, the Trojans finally set fire to the first ship, and Achilles sees it. The identification of the wills of Achilles and Zeus is hinted at in this moment, since not long before, Zeus was waiting to see the flame arise.[56] Both were waiting to see it, and both of course saw it, but Homer notes only that Zeus waited for it, and Achilles saw it. He smites his thigh and calls to Patroclus to hurry, for now for the first time he feels that the latter's urgency is justified. He repeats, in fact, Patroclus' own gesture when he hurried away from Eurypylus to rouse Achilles.[57] Thus in the single moment of the first firing of the ship, the two sides of Achilles' nature are brought into sharp confrontation — the intransigent will, which has become the plan of Zeus, and the humane concern which yields to Patroclus and the emergency. Now Patroclus goes, and quenches the fire.[58]

But from here on, the fire of the Plan of Zeus becomes ever less evident. Significantly enough, lightning does not appear in connection with Patroclus, brilliant as his deeds are, for Patroclus, who represents the human side of Achilles, could hardly be attended by the symbol of his wrath; nor would the lightning which betokens victory for the Trojans be appropriate to Patroclus, who momentarily repels them. Real lightning, in fact, returns only once. This is when the body of Patroclus is being dragged off by Menelaus, and the Trojans press forward, encouraged by one last thunderbolt, to drive the Greeks in rout.[59] Hector, still victorious, continues to be compared to fire, and so does the battle itself.[60] But the heavenly sign has disappeared. Actually, there is no longer any propriety in it, for when Patroclus set out, the wrath of Achilles, as he himself says, was already waning, and was now simply grief. Achilles' own indecisive period of waiting for Patroclus to return is reflected, perhaps, in a certain indecisiveness in Zeus' position. Since he does not yet know that Patroclus is dead, Achilles cannot foresee his own next move. Meanwhile, the wrath being partly abated, the plan of Zeus hangs in abeyance, though it is not formally declared at an end until after Achilles formally renounces the wrath.[61] But already before that, fire has begun to take new, and more miraculous forms, centering around Achilles himself. His breastplate, which he lends to Patroclus, is like a star, and the flash of it is seen several times, both on Patroclus and Hector.[62] But when Achilles goes to the trench and shouts, the fire of the hero himself appears. Athena crowns his head with a golden cloud from which flame shoots heavenward like the beacon of a besieged city.[63] The Trojans see it and quail.[64] The image of the besieged city foreshadows the end of the war, and the burning of Troy. This is the true fire, where the thunder and lightning signals had been deceptive.

The fire that shoots from Achilles' head denotes the *peripeteia* of the *Iliad*. The great battle which began in Book XI with the shout of Eris, holding in her hands the *teras* or "symbol" of war (which the Scholiast says was lightning) is ended by the shout and fire of Achilles. From here on, all deception breaks, the truth is out. Achilles is indispensable, but Patroclus is dead. Agamemnon was deceived, Hector was deceived; Pulydamas alone had read the omens right, and no one listened to him. Even Achilles, who foresaw so much about himself, did not foresee the death of his friend.[65] Now he has paid the price of human loss for his godlike intransigence. Once the issue is clear, with the return of Achilles to the field, the far-flung action of the *Iliad* begins to narrow to a single course, led on by the fire ignited by Athena around Achilles over the trench. All the associations of the image — death, rage, heroic greatness, the fall of Troy, and divinity itself — now play against each other constantly. From the vision at the trench, we pass instantly to the corpse of Patroclus, and shortly thereafter Achilles declares his plans for the pyre, with its human sacrifice.[66] Presently a fire is lit to heat water for bathing the corpse.[67] But the principal kind of fire in Book XVIII is divine fire, and when Thetis goes to Olympus, we meet the god of fire himself, Hephaestus.[68] The forging scene opens with twenty bellows blowing up the coals for the work to begin.[69] The *thorax* is brighter than the gleam of fire.[70] The great shield is too transcendent an image to be wholly dominated by fire images, but it includes them; sun, moon, and stars, the fiery bodies of heaven (to all of which Achilles, dressed in these arms, is later compared), occupy a prominent position together with the other three elements, earth, sky, and sea.[71] There are also the fires of wedding torches and of flashing men in arms.[72] But all things are in their places on the shield; the gift of the god is entirely true to the way things are. If Achilles, when he wears these arms, becomes all but identified with fire, it is because the gods' gifts are precisely those which lift a man perilously from his place and destroy him. In an agonized moment, Achilles wishes his father had taken a mortal wife;[73] as it is, he will pay the price of his half-divinity; he will put on armor wrought in Olympian fire, slay Hector and, therewith, himself.

The terror of the divine gift is apparent at once. Thetis puts the arms down in front of Achilles, and even the Myrmidons are unable to look at them. Fear seizes them. But rage seizes Achilles; his eyes gleam like fire, and he takes delight in handling the god's gifts.[74] It is not the supernal vision of the shield, the Olympian view of things as they are, which enters into him, but fire and fire alone; for this is the only one of the elements which applies to Achilles here — the most swift, short-lived, and dangerous. As he puts on the panoply, the motif of fire is closely conjoined with images of agony, lonely despair, and the heavenly bodies: in his eyes is the flash of fire, but in his heart his unendurable grief sets him in contrast to the other Myrmidons, under whose gleaming bronze the whole earth laughs.[75] The shield is like the glance of the moon, or like a distant forest fire seen by lonely sailors driven far from their friends by adverse winds.[76] The helmet glimmers like a star.[77] Moreover, the arms seem to weigh nothing, but lift their wearer like wings, an image provoked perhaps by the swiftness and upward course of flames.[78] The total vision of the hero armed is like the shining Hyperion himself.[79] Throughout the arming scene, the single symbol of fire connotes directly all the anguish, semidivine glory, and utter isolation of Achilles. Less directly, it still flickers with intimations of rage, loss, and imminent death.

During the great *aristeia* which follows, fire, though concentrated primarily on Achilles,[80] follows to some extent the general action. The plain is filled with the flash of bronze, Aeneas' arms gleam, and Hector, in a moment of retaliatory passion for the death of his brother Polydorus, faces Achilles "like fire." [81] There are remote references to the flame which will consume Troy,[82] and this foreshadowing of the city's doom is subtly associated with Achilles, who is compared to fire in a city.[83] But the really striking thing about Books XX and XXI is the contest between fire and water. The narrative in this section skillfully intertwines two actions, the *Theomachia*, or Battle of the Gods, and the River Fight. Released from the ban of Zeus, the gods take the field, pairing off according to their Greek or Trojan sympathies. Among the eminent Olympians appears the somewhat obscure figure of Xanthus, genius of the stream by Troy, who confronts Hephaestus.[84] Nothing is made of this at once, for the gods, always dependent on human action, interrupt their fight while Achilles pursues the Trojans who flee like locusts from a fire.[85] But when Achilles reaches the river, his *aristeia* is no longer merely that. It becomes a battle of the elements, in which the protective river of Troy rises up against the hero and attempts to drown him. Natural as it is for a stream choked with corpses to overflow,[86] Homer is not interested in leaving the scene on the naturalistic level. The river appeals to Achilles to desist, and he, as always, yields to a divine injunction; he tries to get up the bank, but the river pursues him. His footing is washed away, and in spite of appeals to Zeus and the help of Poseidon and Athena, Achilles is helpless to extracate himself from the flooding stream. The latter, no longer concerned merely for his own state, calls to his brother Simois to help defend Troy, lest Achilles sack it.[87] And now the meaning of the earlier confrontation of Xanthus and Hephaestus becomes clear, and with it the meaning of the whole *Theomachia*; Hera calls to Hephaestus:

> Up, lame-foot, my son, we deem that eddying Xanthus
> Rises in strife against you.[88]

Two things here deserve notice: first that the *Theomachia* had been suspended in the previous book, on the advice of Poseidon, because he felt certain of victory, and was content to let the mortals fight; he said, however, that if Apollo or Ares began a fight, or if any one held back Achilles from fighting, then the pro-Greek Olympians would show their strength.[89] Xanthus, by holding back Achilles, precipitates the battle of the gods, and Hera, the quick-to-wrath, calls upon Hephaestus. The second point is that Hera regards Xanthus' action *as river* against Achilles as identical with an attack *as personal god* on Hephaestus, his official opponent. Homer is seldom as directly symbolic with his divine figures as this, but he has a special reason. Xanthus threatens to quench the fire of Achilles, and fire itself must answer the challenge. Hephaestus "aims the divine fire" like a spear, burning first the plain with the bodies on it, and begins to restrain the water.[90] Trees and shrubs are consumed. The fish are tormented, and at last the water itself burns, or boils, and cries out in surrender. Achilles himself, in the middle of it, is untouched. All naturalism is here left far behind, and the basic imagery of the *aristeia* of Achilles has completely run away with the action. It is, in fact, an inversion of nature for fire to lick up water. But this is the fire of Achilles himself, which most recently has taken the form of arms made by Hephaestus, and the whole passage, like the *Theomachia* proper which follows it, becomes a dumb show of the taking of Troy. This fact is proven by the terms of Xanthus' surrender: he swears no longer to protect Troy, not even when the Achaeans burn it.[91] So the fire here is also prophetic.

The comic duels which follow this scene are a mere epilogue, for the real battle is won. Only Apollo is really serious in this scene. He represents the tragic valor of the Trojans, and, after refusing, out of respect, to struggle with his father's brother, he departs with intact dignity to defend Troy to the last. The threat of fire is upon it, and looking back, one can see how carefully Homer prepared for the duel between this inevitable fire and the waters of the Troad. Action and imagery are in accord throughout. As he hurls the body of Lycaon into the stream, Achilles utters a challenge:

> Perish, till we come to the citadel of holy Troy,
> You fleeing, and I behind you slaying.
> No help will the fair-flowing, silver-eddying stream
> Bring you.[92]

And again, after he has slain Asteropaeus, the son of the River Axius, his challenge to all the waters of the world is based on the lightning of his ancestor Zeus:

> Lie thus! it is hard for you, though son of a river
> To strive with the sons of Zeus.
> You say you are the offspring of a broad-flowing river,
> But I boast of the race of great Zeus. . .
>
> Thus Zeus is greater than rivers coiling seaward,
> And greater is Zeus' offspring than any river. . .
>
> With him (Zeus) not even lordly Achelous is equal,
> Nor the might of deep-channeled Ocean,
> From whom all rivers, all the sea,
> All springs and trailing rivulets flow.
> But even he fears the lightning bolt of mighty Zeus,
> And the dread thunder, when it crashes from heaven.[93]

Here the meaningful confrontation of deadly fire and its gentler opposite, water, is clear, as is the connection between the helplessness of the stream and the taking of Troy in the previous passage on Lycaon. These two particular passages can have been elaborated as they are for no other reason than to emphasize the imagistic structure. Neither does the threat to take Troy enter in any merely casual way. When Apollo goes to Troy at the end of the *Theomachia*, his concern is that the city should not be taken "beyond fate." [94] This "fate," *moros*, like all Homer's words for fate, indicates the process by which things are as they are; and part of the worldly process is time. Led by Achilles, the Achaeans now, as earlier in the *Patrocleia*, threaten to take Troy "beyond fate," or "before its time," [95] and Zeus had originally allowed the gods to rejoin the war in order that Troy might not be so taken.[96] This can only mean that the gods, especially Zeus, are in a way the keepers of the world process, custodians of time, though they themselves see things not as they happen, but entire, finished. In their own persons, they are absolute, and their gifts to man, such as the arms of Achilles, are tokens of man's own grasp of the absolute. Achilles' fire also is an absolute, hence it threatens to upset fate, or the temporal world process, even as it licks up the waters of Troy. Hence presumably, one may explain the fear of Aidoneus, the god of death, at the very beginning of Achilles' great attack. He feared the earth would be rent and the houses of death itself appear naked to all.[97] This is not merely grandiose rhetoric. It is on the one hand part of the cosmic imagery characteristic of these two books,[98] and on the other hand it reflects the pervasive fear of things happening beyond fate. To reveal death all at once would be to see it absolute, and not as the veiled end of the temporal process; yet such is Achilles' deathly earnest, so absolute is his fire, that this is precisely what he threatens to do. It may well be asked why, if that is so, did Achilles not take Troy; why did not this absolute fire, which consumes water, rush on unhindered? The answer of course is that nothing ever actually happens beyond fate; Achilles' absolute, like every heroic absolute, finds its *telos*, or fulfillment, not in dislocating the world as it is, but in self-destruction. Achilles' *aristeia*, since it destroyed Hector, did in a way destroy the city.[99] Hence the appropriateness of the symbolic shadow-show by which Homer implies what he does not narrate. But Achilles' own limit is also fixed. The all-destructive rage with which he assails the Trojans is directed in the last analysis against himself. Like Patroclus, he will have his meeting with Apollo. Homer does not narrate the death of Achilles, but in the scene where Apollo deflects him while the Trojans save themselves inside the gates, he symbolizes the limits of what Achilles can do.[100] Here Apollo has done exactly what he went to Troy to do. In delaying Achilles, he defends the *moros*, here "portion," or "lot," of Troy. Achilles angrily retorts that he would slay Apollo if he could. But this admission that there is anyone he cannot slay shows exactly where the limit of his great slaughter lies — in Apollo himself. And from this point on, the fire image begins to contract again, and to grow more confined to the action of the moment.

As Achilles turns from Apollo and races back toward Troy, Priam watching from the walls sees him in the likeness of a star:

Rushing over the plain, gleaming bright as a star,
The star that comes in autumn, and eminently its fires
Shine in the darkness of night, among the many stars;
That one they call by the name, Dog of Orion;
Brightest it is, and fashioned for a token of evil,
And brings much fever on suffering mortals. . .[101]

The comparison of a hero to a star does not occur only here. Diomedes, at the opening of his *aristeia*, is compared to a star — indeed the same autumn star — but how differently:

Fire exhaustless flamed from his helm and shield,
Starlike, the star of autumn, that gleams brightest
Washed in the ocean. . .[102]

In the latter case the traditional theme is compressed; the star is shorn of its threatening feverish association, and only its brightness is emphasized. In the former passage, the star partakes of the deadly significance of the moment. Hector also is compared to a star once, near the beginning of the great battle:

As a baleful star appears from the clouds,
Shining, and then dips back into dusky cloud,
So Hector sometimes in the forefront shone,
Sometimes marshaling the rear; and all in bronze
He shone like the lightning of the aegis-bearer, father Zeus.[103]

Though for the moment the lightning of the Plan of Zeus attends him, Hector's glory is intermittent; it comes and goes, which is in character for the man whose hopes are raised so high, and who lies so low at the end. It is in such instances that we can really see the poet's own work. Though the epithet may be a fixed, inherited lens through which to behold not individuals but heroic norms, themes of this sort — stock comparisons, as well as even episodes — are subject to great variation, and regularly in the work of Homer they take their shape from the individual concern of the action where they occur. Achilles' fiery star is of the same fire which we have seen springing from him and all but consuming the Trojan plain itself. It foretells the fire which will destroy the city. Now it is concentrated like a star, while Achilles is in the distance: as he draws nearer, the bronze looks "like fire or the rising sun." [104] The poet keeps to heavenly bodies, for the nonce, and a later comparison narrows the focus again, and even further, from Achilles himself to the spear point which he poises, looking for a chink in his opponent's armor:

> . . . And he lowered his head under the shining
> Four-plumed helm; and the fine manes tossed
> Golden, which Hephaestus set in abundant crests;
> And as a star goes among stars in the dark of night,
> The evening star, which stands in heaven the fairest star,
> So started the flash from the edged spear — [105]

Deserted by the gods, Hector faces Achilles alone. His noblest and fairest moment comes at the end of his long day of battle, with its glory and defeat; and the spear which transfixes him a few lines later is like the evening star. The fire of Achilles is distilled to a purposive and fatal point, and at the very last, as the star of the dying day, responds to the passion and beauty of both heroes.

The last two books of the poem are full of the sacrifice and funeral fires described earlier. Like a double frame, these natural but subtly intertwined forms of fire enclose the vast symbolic permutations which the theme undergoes in the main action. The first sacrifices and the first funerals of the *Iliad* were in general terms, the last are specific, tragic; and in this passage from the normative, formulaic motif to a particularized enlargement, without loss of the universal shape, we have only another form of that same artistic spirit which characterizes all classic art — the interdependence of the individual and the generic.

The foregoing analysis of the *Iliad*'s use of fire may seem somewhat to overbid the material. Torn from its context, this fire may seem even a little monotonous. Such treatment, however, may be excused as an attempt to give the case history of a single traditional motif in the hands of a supremely gifted oral poet. This image of fire stood in Homer's eyes, impelling and controlling his work; he could not read or write, but he could remember. Though interpretations might differ as to its significance in particular passages, the fact certainly cannot be denied that fire is the one clearly imagistic motif which continues throughout the poem, that it goes through more kinds of change and more varied association than any other. Yet — and this is most important — its symbolism is limited, in that there are things to which it might have been but never is applied, such as love. Like the metaphysical terms in philosophy, it transcends categories; it is also metaphysical in that it specifically connects the wrath of Achilles with the Plan of Zeus, and Achilles himself with the gods. Wherever it occurs in connection with heroes, it emphasizes their inspired energy and stress, and in Achilles' case it typifies his extraordinary self-identification with the absolute. These, and all the other associations of fire, — death, sacrifice, the fall of Troy, — coexist in each occurrence of it, or very nearly, but only in the *Iliad*. One would look in vain for any such associations in the *Odyssey*, where fire plays no very great role, and is in part supplanted by the continuing motif of the sea. These associations are the joint creation of the formulaic method and the poet's total vision. It is not to be thought that any preëstablished connection existed in Homer's mind among all the things which are connected in his poem with fire. It is simply that fire, or fiery objects such as sun and stars, was traditionally and in certain phrases compared to all these things, while of course it existed in its own shape as the natural destroyer of dead bodies, invaders' ships, and beleaguered cities. Its meaning grew with the song, but it could do so only if controlled by a master singer. And Homer's fire is never out of hand. Few themes in any art have been developed with such fullness and restraint.

One such symbolic pattern must be looked upon as the token of a concentrated ingenuity, haunted by an especially appropriate and supple image. If all the imagery of the *Iliad* were so developed, it would — supposing it were possible — point to a fantastically schematized and mannered conception of poetry. Most of the great similes come once and once only, and even the scenes and objects which appear in them are not, with the exception of fire, drawn into any strict pervasive rhythm. Yet a few images, especially the fundamental ones of earth, air, and sea, undergo partial, momentary elaboration. Although the treatment of them is far less extended, it does not differ essentially from the treatment of fire — where simple formulaic similes of warfare, such as "fighting like fire," or "flashing like fire," were carefully budgeted within certain associations until fire, having a symbolic life of its own, could act for itself and achieve its own climax. In a similar though lesser way, the formulae of earth, air, and sea behave not merely as units of speech but also of thought and structure, moving in and out of the factual bones of the story, and confusing themselves with them.

Although it seldom enters decisively into the emotional or dramatic scheme of the *Iliad* as it does in the *Odyssey*, the sea is always there as the vast backdrop of the poem. When Thetis on occasion comes from it wrapped in mist, her presence is primarily felt as that of goddess and mother; yet she is also the sea goddess, and there is even some hint of the *Urmutterschaft* of the ocean in Patroclus' accusation to Achilles: "Not Thetis, but the grey sea bore you," as also in the quasi-funeral of Book XVIII, when the Nereids form a lamenting chorus. Yet on one occasion the sea distinctly enters the action, first in the guise of Poseidon himself. At the beginning of Book XIII, Zeus momentarily turns his eyes from the war, and Poseidon, "keeping no sightless watch," swoops in three paces from Samothrace to Aigae, and thence drives his dolphin chariot to the coasts of Tenedos and the Troad.[106] For the space of the next two books he is, as we have seen, first in secret, then openly, the helper of the Greeks, who are battling desperately for their ships; during his presence on the field, the heroic fire changes from the Trojan to the Greek side, and the lightning flash of Zeus disappears in favor of a "sword like lightning" in the hand of Poseidon. But at the moment when Zeus finally dozes and Poseidon overtly leads on the Greeks in renewed strength, Homer suddenly injects this line:

And the sea crashed among the tents and ships of the Argives.[107]

This is the decisive moment. Not only in his personal form, but also in his elemental form, Poseidon assists the Achaeans, and the confusion between god and element is the same as in the case of Xanthus and Hephaestus in the *Theomachia*. For the moment, fire and water are on the same side, and Homer seems perfectly conscious of the fact, for in the splendid simile immediately following he links them closely: the din of the battle is compared first to breakers on the shore, then to forest fire in mountain glens, and finally (for good measure, and also because wind is a highly developed image in the Great Battle), to the wind in lofty oak trees.[108] These crashing breakers in a way complete an earlier sea image: Nestor, watching the battle, was indecisive as a billow that does

not break till Zeus decides its course.[109] Now the wave breaks — a
different wave, certainly, and not according to Zeus' decision, but
the sea wave is currently in the poet's mind, and may take on the
likeness of decision or of indecision. It remains in his mind, more-
over, even after Poseidon has left the Greeks and the tide turns
against them: two images of shipwreck, when the wave passes over
the swamped vessel, described the Trojans swarming over the
wall.[110] And thereafter, the sea ceases to participate in the battle,
either as god, element, or image.

The resistance of the sea god to the Trojan effort to burn the
ships is a little like the *Theomachia* in reverse: there, fire and
water were represented by Hephaestus and Xanthus, here by Hec-
tor and Poseidon.[111] There the triumph of fire foreshadowed the
fall of Troy; here nothing so far reaching is intended, but it is by
no means a fantasy to see in Poseidon's help something more than
the mere use of a god. The wave that crashes at his heels among
the ships and tents, and the prevalence of sea imagery, reveals the
tenor of the poet's thinking. To the polytheistic mind, the safety
of ships is the work of a benevolent Poseidon, a favoring sea. If
that favor is removed, shipwreck ensues. The difference between
the personal god and his element is merely a matter of aspect, as
usual in Homer. At other moments in the poem, other gods are
active in helping the Greeks, but when it is a question of the de-
fense of ships, even if the ships are drawn up on the shore, Poseidon
is the figure who naturally comes to mind, and with him a whole
train of images inevitable to the consciousness of a sea-faring peo-
ple. The poet scarcely needed to plan this; he merely had to keep
the scene before him. In the case of the *Theomachia* and River
Fight, a greater degree of conscious planning must be recognized.

Interwoven with the other nature imagery, especially in the
Great Battle, is the image of wind. It is joined often by clouds, dust,
rain, snow, or sea, and in general blows harder and harder as Hec-
tor's attack nears its climax. Before this attack begins, the Achaeans
withstand the Trojans like clouds on a windless day:

> Firmly they stood like clouds, such as the son of Cronos
> Stations in windless weather, over high-ranging moun-
>   tains,
> Motionless, while the might of Boreas sleeps and all other

> Violent winds, that ever with shrilling gusts
> Blow and scatter apart the shadowy clouds: even so
> Steadfast the Danaoi withstood the Trojans, nor turned
>   in flight. . .[112]

But when Hector and Paris rejoin the fight after their sojourn in Troy, they seem to their tired comrades like a favoring wind that Zeus gives to sailors.[113] A little later the seated armies, with their multitudinous spears bristling along the plain, are compared to the prickling dark patches of the sea under a freshening zephyr.[114] After the Interrupted Battle of Book VIII the wind is blowing in earnest: the consternation of the Greeks is like a sea storm aroused by Boreas and Zephyr; [115] they foresee the rout which the next day becomes a fact, when Hector, after the wounding of Agamemnon,

> Fell upon the battle like a hard-blowing squall,
> Which leaps down on the violet-faced sea and stirs it.[116]

He slays nine chieftains in rapid succession, then assaults the host in general:

> . . . as when Zephyr drives the clouds
> Of the clear south wind, smiting with a deep whirlwind;
> Many a swollen wave rolls, and aloft the spume
> Scatters in the howl of the far-wandering wind.
> So thick at Hector's hands fell the heads of the host.[117]

In the next phase of the struggle, the wind takes on more forms, from the brief formula comparing Hector to a blast [118] to the more developed description of the two Lapith brothers, sons of Pirithous, who make a stand against the Trojans, like mountain oaks resisting wind and rain.[119] Tree images are frequent for men who stand firm in battle, as tree-felling comparisons regularly characterize those who are cut down fighting. Here the generic tree faces a wind which has become in particular this special Trojan thrust. Later, when the Lycians support the Trojans, they too are like a black whirlwind.[120] Two similes of stones falling like snowflakes illustrate the different emphasis obtainable through combination of traditional motifs:

> . . . And they [the stones] fell to the ground like snow-
>   flakes
> Such as hard-breathing wind, driving the shadowy clouds,

> Pours down swarming on the full nourishing earth;
> So from their hands the missiles streamed, from Achaeans and
> Trojans alike; and the helmets rang out dully
> Smitten with the round stones, and the great-bossed
>   shields also. . .[121]

Here the wind is blowing hard, and the emphasis falls on the swift, violent flight of the stones, the smitten helmets and shields. In the other simile, there is no wind:

> . . . As flakes of the snow fall
> Thick on a winter day, when councillor Zeus is minded
> Sending down snow to manifest forth his shafts to men;
> Laying the winds asleep, he steadily pours, till it buries
> Towering mountains' heads, and the lofty headlands,
> Flowering fields and the rich ploughed lands of men;
> Even on the whitening sea it falls, on harbors and beaches,
> Curbing the billow that beats against it; all things else lie
> Wrapped from above, when the storm of Zeus falls heavy;
> So the stones flew thick, one side to the other.[122]

Here the silence of the windless snowstorm burying mountain and meadow, though compared to a fight when a great din arose, underlines the grimness and steady determination on both sides. Descriptions of two battle lines holding firmly against each other, neither having the advantage, usually prompt in Homer images of some very peaceful nature, and the effect is always a rather startling one.[123]

But now the wind begins to undergo variations. It combines with still other images which subsequently supplant it. Already it has appeared with sea, snow, and clouds — inevitably, of course, since wind is detected by what it blows. But from the middle of Book XII on, it becomes less casual and more associated with the activity of Zeus, and the confusions arising from the plan to honor Achilles. A line of Aeschylus nicely sums up the way human action, and with it its characteristic imagery, in Homer is taken up by the gods:

> God as well, whenever man himself takes action, joins with him.[124]

Homer's divinities depend on human promptings for their deeds; their knowledge is independent and transcendent, but their action as a rule is immanent in human action, or character. Hence all di-

vine participation has something of the effect of apotheosis, and
this is true no less of Homer's system of the continuing images than
it is of action itself. As Zeus' plan to honor Achilles is a kind of
apotheosis of Achilles, so too is the supernatural development of
fire in the later books, though the image had begun as a mere com-
parison. Now the vain, misled gallantry of Hector, which has re-
peatedly called forth wind images, draws toward a climax. Hector
again refuses to listen to the temperate advice of Pulydamas, who
has perceived the eagle of Zeus, and read therein the fruitlessness
of the Trojan effort. Hector trusts in the lightning flashes, and leads
his men forward. At this point Zeus rouses a blast of wind,

> Which bore dust toward the ships, and of the Achaeans
> He beguiled the mind, and gave glory to Hector and the Trojans.
> Lo, trusting in his signs and in their strength,
> They tried to break the great wall of the Achaeans.[125]

Actually, Hector is more beguiled here than the Achaeans, who are
simply suffering the consequences of the quarrel. The storm of
dust emphasizes the confusion on both sides, the weakening of
Achaean nerve, and the mistaken hopes of the Trojans. But the
wind still blows against the Greeks, and now it is divinely sent. The
wild wind of Hector's attack has become a daemonic moil, and the
cloud thus engendered becomes a motif which characterizes, with
sundry variations, the *mise en scène* of the next books. "Blinding
storm" might be the best description for the variety of phenomena
which occur. The two images of snowstorms and the assault of
the Lycians "like a black whirlwind" have already been mentioned.
At the beginning of Book XIII, wind and fire enter in brief com-
parisons, the two images of Trojan supremacy. But presently the
dust storm returns, this time around Idomeneus, whose inspired
counterattack repulses the onset of the enemy:

> As whenever the squalls of the shrill winds hurry
> On a day when the dust is plenty along the roads,
> Winds all together lift up a vast cloud of the dust,
> So to one place their battle came. . .[126]

Wind has not changed sides as clearly as the fire did, but it now
centers around a Greek hero, rather than around Hector. It has
also been joined by "mist" — a "mist of dust" — which will be

the next major modulation of the idea of "blinding storm." The Trojan rally at the end of Book XIII is marked by a simile of wind, lightning, and sea storm; [127] during the direct assistance of Poseidon, the comparable simile of the four elements which describes the noise of the battle has already been noted.[128] Such broad combinations of elemental imagery seem to occur when the battle is still undecided and raging on both sides.

Meanwhile, the idea of cloud or mist becomes dominant.[129] Balancing the dust-cloud on earth, with its motif of "beguilement" is the golden cloud which enwraps Zeus, now the beguiled, and Hera the beguiler on Mount Ida.[130] On the battlefield, the Trojans are no longer imaged as wind, but as a dark cloud.[131] It is now Patroclus, whose coming is like a clear sky after clouds:

> As, when from the towering head of a great mountain
> Zeus the lightning-gatherer moves the close-packed cloud,
> Hilltops all are revealed, and lofty headlands,
> Valleys too, and the boundless air of heaven breaks clear,
> So having thrust from the ships the deadly fire, the Danaoi
> Breathed a little. . .[132]

and later, he is like a whirlwind blowing away clouds:

> As when the cloud passes from Olympus melting into sky
> Out of the divine ether, when Zeus stretches out the whirlwind.[133]

The Trojan wind raised dust and enveloped the Achaeans; Patroclus is a clearing wind, for the time being. A little later, not in a comparison at all, but in the description of the Trojans fleeing and crowding the roads,

> The horses strained, and on high the wind
> Spread down from the clouds.[134]

Again the imagery is so far in the front of the poet's mind, he does not even make it a comparison. The cloud of dust, the cloud of Trojans, the clouds to which the Lycians were compared are all equally metaphoric clouds. Homer was not sure whether Patroclus was simply like a wind, or whether a real wind came with him.

The imagery of mist and wind continues consistent. Little need be made of the use of the formula for death, "mist wrapped his eyes," [135] but when the flight of the Trojans is compared to a rain-storm driven by a whirlwind, [136] Homer seems to add what is in his heart; the clouds of threatening but misled Trojans, and the veiled deceits of the Plan of Zeus, are about to be blown away. Perhaps for this reason, the storm of this simile is one which Zeus sends because he is angry with mortals for their injustice. It is a purgatorial storm, driven by a *laelaps*, a whirlwind. It clears the air morally.

But the clouds are by no means gone altogether. As the death of Sarpedon approaches, Zeus sheds a bloody dew in grief, and a little later draws a "baleful night" around the battle over his body. [137] Horror has taken a supernatural form consistent with the ever-darkening atmosphere which precedes the return of Achilles. This same darkness continues, or is renewed throughout Books XVI and XVII, and stands in acute contrast with the bright blaze of the *aristeia* of Achilles. When Patroclus is to fall, Apollo approaches him wrapped in thick fog, [138] and when he is dead, his body in its turn becomes the center of a battle in a blinding fog. [139] Mist, clouds, and darkness are again in the air; Patroclus could clear it only for a little. Twice the none-too-frequent formula "in his glowering heart," occurs; [140] Hector all by himself is called a "cloud of war," [141] and when his brother-in-law is slain, a "black cloud of pain enfolds him." [142] It is at this moment that Zeus for the last time signalizes a success by the lightning flash, as Hector leads one last drive at the Greeks; but simultaneously he wraps Mount Ida in clouds. [143] Thus literal and figurative clouds are mingled into one broad image of the confusion and agony of war. As the terror of the fight over Patroclus increases, the Achaeans are compared to a frightened cloud of starlings. [144] But this is merely an added touch, arising casually from the general cloud-imagery. The active climax comes a little before, when Ajax, peering into the mist, cannot find anyone to send to Achilles with the news of Patroclus' death; suddenly he prays to Zeus in words which Longinus took as a special example of sublimity:

> Father Zeus, save the sons of Achaeans from the mist,
> Make a clear sky, and let our eyes see;
> And slay us in the light, since that is your pleasure. [145]

And then finally the mist clears, the sun shines, and the whole battle-field becomes visible. By the sudden return of the light, Antilochus is sent to Achilles with the terrible news.

Image-making is basically a subrational process, and creates its own characteristic tenor differently in different poetic minds. In Greek epic, the process is predetermined to a degree by the formulaic material, which is the germinal of its imagery; but the selective principle, operating at high speed in oral composition, is the individual singer's own responsibility and opportunity. Beneath that selective principle, and directing it, must lie half-conscious or unconscious patterns of association and symbolific consistency which constitute at least one root of the poetic urge itself. Therefore, where the resultant images form a design consistent with and illustrating the action of a long narrative, and sometimes even supplanting it, it is difficult to see how more than one mind could have worked upon such a structure. However many bards may have sung its constituent episodes before, the *Iliad* which we possess is structurally and imagistically a single reconception of all that is in it, a unity in traditional terms, both in intention and in execution.

VIII

HOMERIC CHARACTER AND THE TRADITION

THE developed form of Homeric epic differs radically, as was stated earlier, not only from the primitive saga, but even from the most sophisticated evolvements of oral poetry found anywhere. The preferences of Augustanism, periodically recurrent, have created a tendency to see in Homer a vigorous and effective, but primitive art. Such an idea, however, confuses subject matter with treatment. Homer's tales are old, and there is savagery in them. They are not "expurgated," [1] but they are reconceived, and the Homeric reconception depends on as self-conscious an artistry as is to be found in literature. The poet's predecessors, answering as they could the changing demands of Greek taste, doubtless account for something, but it is imponderable. We must deal with Homer as we find him, reckoning with oral methods both in their limitations and their opportunities; and what we find is highly sophisticated, subtle, and contrived. The contents, like the contents of Geometric art, have an archaic look at times; but the touch is controlled, the intention steady, and the design ever present. If the festivals and what they implied for Greek culture in the eighth century provided the setting and conditions for such art, the nature of the art and its motivation must be sought in the poems themselves.

For a poet whose language and whole artistic medium is bound by the fairly rigid rules of an age-old tradition, the problem of originality is in great part one of formal mastery. But it also lies in the intellectual or intuitive penetration of the themes and character shapes which constitute the heroic typology. Parallels are not far to seek in early epic literature for the various kinds of valor represented by Homer. Everywhere can be found, reshaped according to shifting cultural standards, the ideal hero, *chevalier sans peur et sans reproche*, the crafty hero, the boaster, the grim and aging warrior, the slightly buffoonish hero, the aged king, the warrior virgin, the wise counselor, or the young reckless fighter. Action also falls into types: the typical siege, the brilliant trick, the hand-to-hand duel, imprisonment and release of a famous warrior, disappearance, and return. Such blueprints of character and action lie in the storehouse of Western culture, heavy with poetic implications. In selecting as the core of the *Iliad* the pattern of the hero who retires from the war, Homer probably did nothing extraordinary. The type surely existed, as the tale of Meleager shows.[2] But to build this theme into a study of heroic self-searching and the dark night of the soul was creativity in the highest sense, and a far cry from those glimpses of old Achaean rough-and-tumble which occasionally peer through the texture of Homer's work. Homer's genius is like a shuttle drawing the warp of profound self-consciousness across the woof of old, half primitive material, from the time when heroism meant chiefly physical prowess, murderous dexterity, colossal self-assertion. Yet it is also perhaps part of essential human equipment that the germs of a corrective to this self-assertion are not wholly lacking among the original types themselves. The hero who retires out of wounded honor, though he may not achieve the stature of Achilles, must nevertheless be in some degree a man of complex sensibility. There is an interesting brief episode in one of the Serbian epics which relates how one hero went out to slay a famous marauder; he accomplished his task, but then was stricken with remorse for having slain one better than himself, and disappeared forever into a cave. In the Arthurian legend, it will be remembered, Lancelot has periods of madness, when he is helpless, and Orlando too went mad. The consciousness of despair amid greatness and success was probably not originally the most popular theme for epic singing, but in Homer's hands, it grew to overshadow all else, and formulated, for the first time that we know of, the primal shape of tragedy.[3]

The problem of Homer's originality, raised earlier, is actually simplified rather than obscured by the oral theory. The only function denied Homer by the nature of his medium was, for the most part, novelty of phrase. All the larger aspects of his poetry were his own to form, character, structure, imagistic economy, and above all, point. It has actually been suggested that Hector and Patroclus are his own inventions.[4] It cannot, of course, be proved whether they are or not, and the assumption seems a little unlikely. On the other hand, it is also unnecessary, for beyond question Homer has shaped these two figures, along with all his others, to a purpose wholly his own; there is a strong probability that whatever Hector and Patroclus were earlier, in Homer they have become something new, and comprehensible only as parts of the *Iliad*. The careful and consistent identification of Hector with Troy itself, especially in the Andromache scene and the scene where his death symbolizes the fall of the city,[5] can have found its motivation only in a poem which aimed at drawing the significance of the whole epic tradition about Troy into the framework of a single dramatic action. So too, Patroclus, whether created from nothing or from a figure already existent, could never have attained his complex character outside a poem which required him to substitute for the dread Achilles on the battlefield, and at the same time to be the embodiment of gentleness and friendship.[6]

Similar observations could be made about practically all the characters in the *Iliad*. One cannot, for instance, imagine that Agamemnon always appeared in epic tradition as he does in Homer. The great king of Mycenae must have been represented as noble, at least at his own court. But Homer has handled him with the most subtle irony, as a foil to Achilles, using all his traditional eminence as a means of diminishing the man. Early in the poem, Nestor points the issue nicely, when he attempts to bring Achilles into reconcilement with the king:

> Do not you, Achilles, set your will at strife with a king,
> Hostile, for never a scepter-bearing king, to whom Zeus gives
> Glory, has stood in equal honor with other men

> If you are the mightier, and a goddess was your mother,
> Yet he is greater, for he rules over more men.[7]

Nestor has stated the case precisely as Achilles will not allow it. To the semidivine hero, the mere fact of ruling over more men does not constitute greatness, and as for glory from Zeus, Achilles will prove by example which of them has more. The contest between Achilles and Agamemnon becomes from the outset a contest between internal and external value, a little after the manner of Sophocles' last play, though of course more diffused. It is interesting to observe, for instance, that the dress and general appearance of Agamemnon are obsequiously described three times, besides lesser mentions, and always in strictly concrete and factual terms.[8] The dress of Achilles is never described, except when he puts on the miraculous armor of Hephaestus. His appearance is never described at all, though it is constantly reckoned with in imagery. Agamemnon's whole psychology is bound and limited by his own material greatness. The quarrel in the first place arises from his sense of outrage that he will be the only one of the Achaeans without a prize, if he should give Chryseis back to her father.[9] His demand for a substitute girl, who will be "just as good," further limns his emphasis on the cash value of things, and contrasts subtly with Achilles' statement that he himself really loves Briseis.[10] The king's proffered amends in the ninth book are of similar kind: cities, bronze, gold, tripods, women, a state-marriage. Achilles' refusal of them at first and his disinterest when they are finally delivered are both symptoms of his insistence on the spirit. In what a different mood does he accept Priam's ransom for Hector, together with Priam himself! And as if to give the whole issue a final touch, at the end of the funeral games for Patroclus, Homer makes Achilles award the great king a prize for spear-throwing — an honorary token, for which he has not even competed; twice earlier, Achilles had stated that Agamemnon never earned any of the honors and rewards which he received.[11]

In some of Agamemnon's scenes, one may recognize motifs which doubtless are traditional. His discouragement and proposal to go home may well be a stock attitude for the leader of a host under certain circumstances.[12] But Homer has used the theme to underline certain phases of the action and to illustrate the character of the king. It occurs three times, twice in identical words. His first speech

in the assembly of Book II is a falsehood contrived to test the spirit
of the army, and, more important, to test the validity of his dream
by stating the opposite of what he hopes and believes to be true, to
see if the gods will intervene:

> O friends, heroes, Danaoi, comrades of Ares,
> Zeus son of Cronos has mightily caught me in heavy doom,
> Wretch, who promised first, and nodded me acquiescence,
> I should sack Ilion, well-walled city, and turn home;
> Vile deceit he devised, and now as it is, he bids me
> Go ill-famed to Argos, when I have lost many soldiers.
> Likely such, I suppose, was the pleasure of the almighty
> Zeus, who indeed has shattered the crowns of many a city,
> Yes, and will shatter still; for his power is supreme.[13]

It can be no casual coincidence that, weeping like a dark-watered
spring, Agamemnon repeats this speech word for word in the night
council after the first day's defeat. He had spoken more truly than
he knew; now that the truth is out, he is ready to propitiate
Achilles. The latter's answer is, of course, a counterproposal that
he himself go home, not out of fear of failure, but out of resentment
at a breach of mutual respect among warriors. Diomedes' rebuke to
Agamemnon's flagging courage at this point is respectful but firm.[14]
That of Odysseus, when Agamemnon for the third time proposes
flight, is plainly contemptuous.[15] In these passages, a traditional
motif, familiar for the hard-pressed leader of a host, has been turned
and deployed to its full psychological worth.

So too with the *aristeia* of Agamemnon, which initiates the Great
Battle.[16] On the surface, but only on the surface, this series of ex-
ploits resembles all the others. The arming of the central figure,
violent death on the field, comparisons to fierce animals, and the
flight of the enemy are all familiar elements. But every Homeric
aristeia is a character sketch, and in this we see another side of Aga-
memnon. The arming scene is greatly inflated to include the de-
scription of the magnificent breastplate, gift of Cinyras of Cyprus;
the shield wears not the supernal, cosmic signals of Achilles' shield,
but a terrible-faced Gorgon, as motto for what is to come. Homer's
battles are full of images of pity and terror, but in this scene there is
a singular concentration of them. Here all is intensely grim. Bianor
is speared through the brain, and he and his companions stripped and

left naked on the field.[17] Two sons of Priam follow — Isus and Antiphus, the latter once a captive of Achilles who spared him for ransom; Agamemnon drives his sword into his ear, and is thereupon compared to a lion crunching with his strong teeth the helpless children of a deer.[18] One is reminded of the Thyestean banquet, and the eating of Pelops. Next come Pisander and Hippolochus, who sue for mercy; they are refused, on the ground that their father had advised against giving Helen back to Menelaus. Agamemnon cuts off the head and hands of Hippolochus, and hurls the head "like a quoit" through the host.[19] The flight and rally of the Trojans by the city gates leads to another image of Agamemnon "covered with gore," and a comparison again to a lion, this time frightening a herd of cows, slaying one, breaking its neck, and licking the blood and entrails.[20] At this point, Zeus begins to turn the tide in favor of the Trojans, but Agamemnon slays one more man before he is himself wounded. Iphidamas, son of Antenor, young and newly married, rushes at Agamemnon, and is slashed in the neck:

> Thus he fell, and slept the brazen sleep,
> Pitiable, helping the citizens, far from the modest bride
> He wooed, whose grace he saw not, though he gave much.[21]

Herewith the sequence of terrible and sorry images which surround Agamemnon reaches a climax. The brother of Iphidamas tries to rescue the body; he wounds Agamemnon, but is himself slain and beheaded. Then Homer adds a rarity: he describes the pain of Agamemnon's wound. External symptoms of pain — writhing, swooning, shrieking — often appear. But here, almost with satisfaction, the poet says that the keen pangs assailed the king's spirit like the pains of childbirth, and with this grotesque conceit, the exploits of Agamemnon end.[22] Unlike any other *aristeia*, this one achieves scarcely even a degree of victory, but only the first ironical phase of the long defeat which brings honor to Achilles.

However the words and formulae of this passage are epic stock in trade, the circumstances and description attending the wounding of Agamemnon are carefully designed somehow to be in character. Odysseus and Diomedes are also presently wounded, and reveal themselves similarly. Odysseus slays by trickery the man who has scathed him, and then, still fighting like a lion beset by jackals, prudently retreats under the shield of Ajax.[23] Diomedes, shot through the foot by Paris, high-heartedly taunts his victor with cowardice, and says he does not care about this wound, any more than if a woman or a brainless child had hit him.[24] The surprising simile of the birth-pangs lends an odd air to the case of Agamemnon; as if the Hellenic intuition of *nemesis* found it appropriate for this savage and merciless slayer, who eats the helpless children of deer, to balance his heritage of child-eating with the pains of childbearing.

The refusal of mercy, together with the motives implied, also prompts comparison with other passages. Achilles, in his *aristeia*, refuses the appeal of Lycaon; but the speech he makes says simply that death is the law of the world, that the good and bad all die, himself included, and there is actually no escape; calling Lycaon "friend," as if by the bond of mutual mortality, he slays him.[25] Such knowledgeable passion as this is not the fruit of a spite which remembers the hostile action of the victim's father. Whereas to Achilles, Lycaon is in some large sense a friend, to Agamemnon, the suppliants before him are simply enemies. The enemy deserves no quarter, and far from giving it himself, Agamemnon will not even allow Menelaus to give it. "Have they benefited your house?" he asks. "Let not one escape death at our hands," adding characteristically, "not even the boy the mother carries in her womb." [26] When Achilles wills death to all the Trojans, he wills it for all the Greeks too, except himself and Patroclus,[27] in a speech which will demand attention later, but the contrast in the treatment of a theme is evident.

Again, the scepter of the king of Mycenae was the symbol of the mightiest royal power in Greece. Homer describes it famously — forged by Hephaestus, given by Zeus, descended through Pelops, Atreus, and Thyestes to Agamemnon.[28] Yet this magnificent adjunct, so carefully brought before our eyes, is involved in some disillusioning contexts. Leaning on it, Agamemnon makes his deceitful proposal to return home and give up the war.[29] Odysseus, inspired by Athena, runs to Agamemnon and receives from him the "ancestral, imperishable scepter" as a badge of vicarious authority. With gentle words he restrains the leaders, but the common folk he rounds up like a herd, using the scepter physically as a goad.[30]

When the host is reassembled, the ugly and lowborn Thersites rises
and rails at Agamemnon; his words echo those of Achilles, in the
previous book, as he accuses the king of greed and unfairness, and
by a skillful turn he ends his harangue with a line which Achilles
himself had used to the effect that such a king as Agamemnon must
rule over "good-for-nothings," or he would presently be mur-
dered.[31] Few things are more subtle in the *Iliad* than the way in
which this "good-for-nothing," the social and physical antitype of
Achilles, reiterates the resentment of the hero: the theme of the
entire second Book is Delusion, and truth can appear only in the
mouth of a Thersites. He is silenced by Odysseus, with a violent
blow of the lordly scepter, while the other soldiers, unhappy as they
are, laugh at him.[32] What is Homer saying through these scepter-
passages, except that Agamemnon, himself deceived by Zeus, is de-
ceiving and bullying his people into disaster? The scepter is no mere
ornament; it enters into the actions of its owner, as the agent of
power misled and misused. How differently Achilles treats the
scepter which he holds when he makes his tense and furious oath:

> Yea, by this scepter, which never again shall put forth
> Leaves and branches, now it has left its stump in the mountains,
> Nor shall it bloom; for the bronze has lopped it round,
> Leaves and bark, and the sons of Achaeans bear it,
> Justice-deliverers, in their palms, who draw from Zeus
> Judgments; here, hark you, shall be a great oath:
> Yearning for Achilles shall surely come to the sons of Achaeans,
> All. . .
>
> So spoke the son of Peleus, and hurled to earth the scepter
> Studded with golden nails, and himself sat down.[33]

There is no need to labor the contrast between the scepter of kingly
violence, and the lopped and leafless scepter which is a symbol of
finality, hurled in contempt on the ground in token of Achilles' de-
fiance of external authority.[34]

In scene after scene, the character of Agamemnon, which one
might a priori expect to be massive and imposing, is undercut with
consistency throughout the poem. Yet the touch is everywhere
light, and Agamemnon is allowed to gain sympathy, if not respect.
His very weakness, the helpless way he stumbles against his own

limits and infinite pretensions, win him some measure of compassion. He usually offends those whom he addresses, except his immediate henchmen, who suppress their feelings.[35] A little scene with Teucer is most characteristic; Teucer is doing well in battle, and wins Agamemnon's praise:

> If ever Zeus the aegis-holder and Athena grant me
> To spoil the well-founded citadel of Troy,
> Into your hand I will put a token of honor,
> First — after myself. . .

Teucer impudently answers: "Why do you spur me on when I am working on my own account?" [36] and Agamemnon vanishes for the rest of the book. One of his best features is perhaps his solicitous care for Menelaus, yet this devotion is wholly unlike the high-hearted friendship of Diomedes and Sthenelus, the passionate unity of Achilles and Patroclus, or the studious and admiring love of Nestor for the gallant younger men. Agamemnon fusses over Menelaus and worries about him. When Menelaus is grazed by an arrow, Agamemnon's lament over the wound is almost hysterical.[37] No great warrior himself, Menelaus has a fine moment, when he rises to answer Hector's challenge, and hopes the rest of the Achaeans turn to "earth and water," for being so spiritless; but Agamemnon seizes him and makes him sit down in safety.[38] His very solicitude betokens more fear than love, even as his prayer for the army's safety, by contrast with the famous prayer of Ajax for death under a clear sky, accents his timorous nature, insecure in itself and a fuse of alarm to others.[39]

Homer's sense of character is always profound, but Agamemnon is a consummate masterpiece. There is no reason to believe that he was always drawn as Homer draws him; rather the opposite. As in the case of Patroclus and Hector, the man is envisioned within the framework of the total poem; his traditional kingly attributes, his primacy among peers, his position as marshaler of the spearmen, his personal exploits, and even his scepter, have all been used, but used with a difference, to establish him as the opposite of Achilles — the nadir, as Achilles is the zenith, of the heroic assumption. As Homer makes Agamemnon, he is a magnificently dressed incompetence, without spirit or spiritual concern; his dignity is marred by pretension; his munificence by greed, and his prowess by a savagery which is the product of a deep uncertainty and fear. Yet none of this is ever overtly stated. He is always the king, with honorifics ever present. If Thersites bawls at him, Nestor, that repository of courteous mores, instructs him. The mores must be kept by all except those able to transcend them. It is for Achilles to reveal their real transparency. If Homer had acted overtly in drawing the feebleness of Agamemnon, the *Iliad* would have been satire, not tragedy. It is part of the tragedy that Agamemnon never meets with full disgrace, or understands himself really at all.[40]

Such individual elaborations upon the heroic norm, and in particular the difference of value so implied, must be in some part the consequence of molding the large epic out of the short epic song. From the first, the various famous figures must have been characterized by certain individual traits, some perhaps more than others; but there could have been little motive to represent their special relationship to the heroic heritage, their comparative individual interpretations of its meaning. Nobility, *arete*, a value composite of personal, social, and military features, was the assumption for all, and, though in different times and districts it would have presented varying aspects, the implicit cultural aspiration was universally accepted without definition. An individual hero would receive his due of admiration in terms appropriate to the people or city to which he belonged historically; if a singer thought well of an action which was narrated of some other warrior, he could, if it were not too specifically pinned to someone else, expropriate it for the character he had in hand. The generalized epithets which form units with the personal names illustrate well the fundamental unity of the heroic tradition. These epithets, "strong," "swift-footed," "good at the war-shout," "plume-crested," "bronze-clad," do, as Parry once wrote, adorn not individuals, but the whole of epic verse.[41] They spring from a universally recognized ideal which in its early phase envelops character, rather than testing it or illuminating it. With the first attempt to weld the short tales of single exploits into a panorama of all the heroes, a new problem arises. The characters must either duplicate each other to the point of utter boredom, or their individual differences must begin to distinguish them. Once the latter process has begun, we are on our way toward that extraordinary roster of unforgettable individuals which Homer presents. His formulation is surely not the only one which ever could have been, though its self-completeness suggests as much. Any bard dealing with the amalgamation of epic traditions must have attempted something of the sort. But Homer's construction is the one which impressed the Greeks, and laid the basis for all subsequent conceptions of the figures of myth, both gods and heroes, as Herodotus says.[42]

But the process of distinguishing the characters of tradition involved more than merely letting the inevitable happen. It meant building consciously upon rudimentary data; it involved a shift of interest from merely what happened (to the greater glory of somebody) to how and why it happened, to whom, and through the agency of what sort of man. In the *Iliad*, at least, the question even arises as to what is the greater glory, and to whom can it come. It is naive to think that Homer celebrates all his heroes equally simply because his epithets do. The keen principle of dramatic selection is constantly at work in his exploration of the meaning of heroism. In Homer, many are called to the heroic trial, but in the last analysis, only one is chosen. Others achieve a partial glorification, and some are even consigned to the muster, not of heroes, but of ruffians. Agamemnon's character, with its grievous shortcomings, is saved from ridicule by the mores and by the more important necessity of giving Achilles an adversary of weight and seriousness. Some lesser characters are not so fortunate. Ajax the son of Oileus, for instance, appears only in the Great Battle, sometimes as companion to his great namesake, and in the Games for Patroclus. In the Battle, his deeds, like those of Agamemnon, involve a special insulting violence. He hurls severed heads like balls, and murders his captives.[43] When the Trojans momentarily break and flee before Poseidon at the end of Book XIV, Ajax is accorded the dubious distinction of being the best at overtaking and killing men who are running away.[44] His only other appearances are a couple of indifferent slayings and the footrace with Odysseus and Antilochus in the Games.[45] In this passage, Homer reserves the only low humor in the *Iliad* for Ajax; Athena makes him slip and fall headlong in the manure of the sacrificed cattle, and thus lose the race. Is it fanciful to see herein a foreshadowing of Athena's revenge on him for his rape of Cassandra in the sack of Troy, and the poet's contemptuous dismissal of him as a mere thug? As he picks himself up from the ordure, the Achaeans laugh at him, and the only other person laughed at in misfortune is Thersites. Whatever his reputation had been in his native Locris, in Homer he has become a sketch of mean violence, and Idomeneus' judgment, which seems to be also Homer's, adhered to him.[46] In this figure, as in one or two others in the *Iliad*, where the hero is submerged in the fighter, one may see a reaction from the primitive admiration for a man who kills his enemy. Idomeneus, though he is drawn more sympathetically than the Locrian Ajax, is another such. He is represented as slightly aging, but still efficiently deadly on the battlefield, where, in Book XIII particularly, he, with Poseidon, leads the counterattack. There is something noticeably grim about him, and also something coldly professional. In the midst of the battle he holds a long, cool discussion with his companion Meriones about spears and the proper behavior in battle and ambush.[47] He knows his subject well, estimating the symptoms of cowardice with precision, and praising his friend's valor with unemotional approval. This is the only occasion on which Idomeneus is allowed to speak, except for battle speeches of encouragement or challenge; he never utters a word in council. He reveals himself as a fighter, one of the most dangerous, but as nothing else, and all his deeds, successful as they are, are buried in an atmosphere of complete indifference.

The spirit of the epic was traditionally that of praise, and it is not surprising that the less favorably drawn characters of the *Iliad* receive, on the whole, brief treatment, while those who demand admiration are given many lines. The exception is, of course, Agamemnon, for obvious reasons. Aside from Achilles, the men who really interest Homer are Ajax of Salamis, Diomedes, Hector, Nestor, and, in the next rank, Odysseus, Paris, Antilochus, Priam, Helen, Aeneas, and Menelaus. One may well ask why Homer gives so much attention to Ajax and Diomedes; national considerations could have had little to do with it, for Homer's audience was the international one of the festivals. The tradition, the tales themselves, can account for what was actually told, perhaps. But only the poet's total intention can explain the selection of what he tells, and in particular his developed portraits of Diomedes' dashing brilliance, and the sound magnificence of Ajax. Each has a special atmosphere; one thinks of Diomedes as always in rapid motion, of Ajax as immovably fixed to the earth, and these two contrasting images, which persist although Ajax does move and Diomedes can stand still, typify two aspects of heroism which Homer has chosen to embody in these two figures, motion and rest, action and endurance. These are real heroes, in the sense of what the tradition transmitted at its best, and they are normative, in a way, for that cultural aspiration which the tradition enshrined. Where Achilles is snared in all its tragic implications, Diomedes and Ajax fulfill the ideal with a kind of saving simplicity which renders them children beside Achilles, but children of an admirable and fine grain.

One of the pleasantest features of Diomedes' character is reflected in his relationship with Nestor. The latter's age and eminence render him the acknowledged guardian of the ideals, as socially conceived and accepted. Nestor remonstrates on occasion with Achilles, and almost constantly with Agamemnon, but for Diomedes he has only praise. In its simple outlines, the great tradition of the epic lives in Nestor; hence his approval of Diomedes stamps the latter as a type of proper behavior. It may well be that Homer invented this whole relationship quite purposefully, and built it, as usual, upon a slightly altered strand of tradition. In the *Aethiopis*, Nestor's son Antilochus loses his life rescuing his father from a maimed and tangled chariot on the battlefield, and there are those who believe that the scene in the eighth *Iliad*, where Nestor is rescued by Diomedes, is based on this scene.[48] Certainly the episode preceded both poems, and was one of the traditional stories told of the gallant Antilochus, whom Achilles especially loved. In giving an identical action to Diomedes, Homer created a father-son relationship, which becomes quite outspoken in the *Embassy*, when Nestor, warming to a courageous speech of Diomedes, says:

> Son of Tydeus, verily brave are you in battle,
> Best also in council among all your equals in years;
> No one will blame your speech, of all the Achaeans,
> Nor will he contradict; yet you reach not the fullness of words.
> Well, you are young, indeed, and well might you be my own son,
> Youngest of all my brood; you utter prudence
> Unto the Argive kings, for you have spoken in season.[49]

Nestor's only criticism is that Diomedes' speech was not long enough; he himself will make up the deficiency. The remark about Diomedes as Nestor's own son perhaps reveals Homer's consciousness of having transferred the rescue episode from Antilochus, and certainly characterizes Diomedes as the fully satisfactory offspring of the epic ideal. Diomedes subordinates himself to this ideal in every respect, and his contentment with it is subtly indicated in his cheerful obedience to all his superiors. When Agamemnon unjustly reproves him, he is shamefaced and silent, and when Nestor wakes him out of a sound sleep by kicking him, his irritation takes the form of an admiring compliment to the old man's indefatigable energy and zeal.[50]

The longest book in the *Iliad* is the *aristeia* of Diomedes, a series of exploits surpassed in length and development only by the *aristeia* of Achilles himself, which stretches over four books (XIX–XXII). As the first and last *aristeiai* of the poem, they balance each other to a degree and prompt comparison. Right at the beginning, Diomedes in arms is compared to a star.[51] The comparison of an armed hero to the star Sirius is doubtless traditional enough; and it has already been pointed out how Homer applies it also to Achilles, but with additional lines which make it, in his case, a bright but deadly star, a token of evil, a bringer of fever, which rises under the weight of the whole tragedy of Troy and of Achilles himself.[52] Diomedes' star is simply bright, washed in the ocean; no extra vista of tragedy attends the work of Diomedes. His is the heroic pattern without thought, victory without implicit defeat.

A hero's display of valor offered a special opportunity for virtuosity, and Homer here has not missed his chance. Where the vigorous deeds of Patroclus and Achilles on the field sound the deepest and most central tones of the poem, those of Diomedes are a display for its own sake; yet many of the motifs are identical. A hero in action might often, we presume, struggle with a god. Patroclus is thrust back from the wall of Troy by Apollo three times before he yields, and the passage foreshadows Apollo's destruction of him later.[53] Diomedes also makes three assaults on Apollo, who is defending Aeneas, and is similarly thrust back.[54] But thereafter, Apollo retires to Pergamon, and sends Ares to quell Diomedes. This is a most telling difference, for Ares in the *Iliad* has always a certain grotesque buffoonery about him, and he is always defeated. Homer never allows the slightest indignity to approach Apollo, although he is on the Trojan side. But Ares is contemptible in all eyes, and Diomedes' victory over him, with Athena's help, is about comparable to his earlier victory over Aphrodite. Both of these triumphs are full of sound and fury, signifying, if anything, the inconsequence of what is done. Indeed, nothing is really done. Aside from motivating Hector's journey to Troy in the next book, Diomedes' *aristeia* has no effect on the war, and his enormous thunderings gradually fade away until he is wounded in Book XI. Almost all the gods appear in the course of his actions, yet nowhere else in the *Iliad*, not even in the *Theomachia*, are the gods presented more simply as figures of fairy tale, bright adornments of a gay, victorious fantasy. Diomedes is early wounded by Pandarus, but is promptly and magically restored by Athena.[55] The gods' miracles are never without some support in the realities of the situation, and one may say here, as Homer does, that "the arrow did not subdue him." Yet the cure is so quick, and the significance for the whole so slight, it seems almost as much a joke as the rapid cure of Aphrodite's wounded hand. Aeneas' wound is also hastily cured;[56] that of Ares heals like curdling milk.[57] Sarpedon's wound is more serious, but though it is not miraculously healed, it is forgotten.[58] Wounds in this book do not count for much. The emphasis is on the joy of battle, with its romantic high-heartedness. Brilliant descriptions and handsome similes decorate the action, such as the vision of the Achaeans "dusty as winnowers," or standing in battle unmoved as clouds on a windless day.[59] There are some fine inversions: blood drawn by an arrow spurts back like a javelin,[60] and Diomedes, himself compared earlier to a flooding river, quails before Hector's counter-attack like a man before a rushing river.[61] To what a different climax the motif of man versus river comes in Book XXI! Here only the external appearances are consulted, and some of them are superb. The description of the arming of Hera and Athena and their journey to the field in a fiery chariot, their horses leaping at each bound as far as a man can see over the ocean, is a marvel of extended imaginative vividness.[62]

Homer's method of characterization, as is well known, objectifies internal states into visible figures, often into gods. If the valor of

Diomedes is objectified in the figures of Hera and Athena, yet there is a difference here too. In the case of the more weighted figures of the poem, especially Achilles, the gods' participation on the whole follows a motivation in the human sphere, as will be shown later. But Diomedes is instructed by Athena right at the start in what he is to do and he simply does it. As she cures his wound, she takes the "mist" from his eyes, so that he can recognize gods, if necessary, and warns him not to fight with any except Aphrodite.[63] Obediently Diomedes goes and wounds Aphrodite. For a moment, he is carried away and tries to kill Aeneas in the arms of Apollo, but desists in time, and real conflict is avoided. The sight of Ares accompanying Hector causes him to retreat, until Athena rejoins him and assists him against the god.[64] Diomedes stays well within the rules, and nothing that he does suggests a will to break the framework, or show himself too stubborn in the face of war's alternations of fortune. In Book VIII, when the lightning of Zeus drives back the Achaeans, Diomedes yields more reluctantly than the others; but there is nothing in his character that bears the gods along with him, or qualifies in any way the limits and realities which they represent. They play on him, not he on them. He is the product, not the creator, of the heroic assumption, and as such he can state, more clearly than anyone else on occasion, the norm of high valor, without reference to any embarrassing complexities.[65] His performance in the horse race at the Games is a clean sweep to victory, and the poet turns away from it immediately to develop instead the revealing little scene of altercation between Antilochus and Menelaus. Diomedes is a success, and Homer throughout lets him pay the price of it.

Ajax of Salamis is a different matter. Constantly referred to as the greatest of the Achaeans after Achilles, he is nevertheless given no *aristeia*, and no scene of distinction which is his alone. Two stories in particular were traditional about Ajax: how he defended the corpse of Achilles, and how he went mad and killed himself, after the loss of Achilles' arms to Odysseus. Homer narrates neither of these tales, though he seems to have both in mind. The wrestling match in Book XXIII with Odysseus doubtless prefigures the Judgment of the Arms.[66] Ajax lifts Odysseus in the air, but the latter topples his opponent by trick. Odysseus cannot lift Ajax, but falls himself, dragging Ajax down a second time. At this point, Achilles interferes and awards equal prizes; but enough has been said. The man of force has hit the ground twice, the man of guile only once, and the results of the Judgment of Arms are distinctly hinted. It has also been persuasively argued that the fight over Patroclus' body in Book XVII is based on a poem about the defense of Achilles' body.[67] This is probably in some sense true; yet the seventeenth book was known in antiquity as the *aristeia* of Menelaus, and reasonably, since here Menelaus, standing "like a mother cow over her first-born calf," fights off the attackers for some time before he is joined by Ajax, and even then, he is by no means eclipsed by the latter. The action of carrying a comrade's body out of a hot melee must have been stock in trade, and for its final accomplishment, it called for teamwork; someone must carry the corpse while others cover his retreat.[68] In Homer's treatment, the idea of cooperation in battle becomes the dominant one for the whole section, transcending the more usual individualistic outlook of the heroes. Isolated at first, Menelaus is hesitant to face Hector, who seems god-inspired; but he reflects that with Ajax beside him he would fight even against a god.[69] Two images of animals protecting young suggest the tenderer side of heroic brotherhood, called forth by the fall of the gentle Patroclus.[70] In a singularly outspoken moment of fear, Ajax says simply that he is not so worried about the corpse of Patroclus as he is about his own head and that of Menelaus.[71] Later, as they look about for someone to take the terrible news to Achilles, Antilochus is drawn in as a climax of the picture of struggling, sorrowful survivors. As he hears of Patroclus' death, Antilochus' eyes fill with tears and he is stricken dumb for a moment before he turns to take the news.[72] Hitherto, we had heard nothing of any special love between Antilochus and Patroclus; but this is a book devoted to loyalties, the dependency of fellow soldiers on each other. As Antilochus leaves, it is remarked that his Pylians missed him, though frequently in the *Iliad* warriors leave the field for one purpose or another without any notice being taken of their departure.[73] The sense of loss and of loyalty penetrates everywhere, even to the Trojan side. In an angry speech to Hector, Glaucus demands that he get the corpse of Patroclus to use in exchange for that of Sarpedon, which has fallen, as Glaucus thinks, into the hands of the enemy.[74] Sarpedon's body had actually been spirited away, by Sleep and Death, to his home in Lycia, and the present passage has been pointed to as an inconsistency. But it is quite consistent with the book as a whole, with its peculiar concern with the comradeship and mutual obligation of allies.[75] If this book was modeled on an old poem about Ajax' stout deeds over the corpse of Achilles, it has certainly developed into something else, something, indeed, quite consistent with Homer's view of Ajax elsewhere.

In the *Iliad*, the word for responsibility to others, and a sense of their importance to oneself, is *aidôs*. It is *aidôs* that keeps Hector in the forefront of his troops.[76] For the greater part, the Homeric heroes fight for their own individual glory, but a few of them are further motivated by a feeling of duty. Menelaus, for instance, a peace-loving man,[77] self-effacing to the point of being at times ineffectual,[78] fights under the pressure of his personal loss, rather than for glory, and feels deeply the responsibility he owes to the Achaeans suffering in his cause.[79] Antilochus also, traditionally the rescuer of his father, shows a friendly concern for Menelaus, who admires the young man's spirit.[80] But more than any other figure on the Greek side, Ajax is the man of *aidôs*. Throughout the Great Battle, other heroes come and go, distinguishing themselves variously, though the most eminent are absent because of their wounds. But the poet keeps bringing Ajax in; he seems to go on forever, slowly beaten back, but steadily fighting without rest or haste, holding his post, and only changing it if some special danger threatens in another place. He is in his element, the pitched fight, in which "he would not yield even to Achilles," as Idomeneus, critically analyzing the situation, points out.[81] As the fifteenth book draws to its sonorous, orchestral close, bringing Hector to the ships and the Achaeans to the brink of destruction, Ajax calls out three times to his troops, each time with the brief and grim eloquence that characterizes him.[82] The first of these outcries begins with a call to *aidôs*, and the second is wholly given to it. It is impossible to translate with anything like the poetic force of the original this moving appeal to the soldiers not to break and flee, but to "reverence each other," and fight for each other's sake. Less pointed, but still insistent on the need for mutual and self-reliance is the great last speech:

O friends, heroes, Danaoi, comrades of Ares,
Be men, fellows, remember your rushing valor.
What? can we say we have any helpers behind us,
Any warlike bulwark, to ward destruction from men?
No, no city is near us fitted with towers
Where with an allied people we might be saved.
Here in the plain of the close-mailed Trojans we lie,
Toppling against the sea, far from the land of our fathers;
So in our hands is light, not in a yielding from war.

Words, one feels, are squeezed out of Ajax only with difficulty, and
these rise from grim depths indeed. It is his massive and steadfast
devotion, not brilliant display, which makes Ajax what he is, both
here in the Great Battle, and elsewhere. For all his clear personality,
the *Iliad* represents him primarily as a hero among heroes, a fighter
shoulder to shoulder with friends, mighty yet modest.

As such, the contrast with Achilles is, of course, sharp. In the
Embassy Ajax makes only one brief speech, but it is fully in char-
acter. While Odysseus proceeds with diplomatic tact and design,
and Achilles himself and Phoenix probe the deeper meanings of
the situation, Ajax stresses the simple social level. He rebukes
Achilles for his lack of human regard for his fellows, and calls
upon him to remember *aidós*:

. . . But Achilles
Has a wild, great-hearted spirit in his breast,
Wretch, and cares not for the love of his friends,
Wherewith we honor him above all by the ships,
Cruel. . .

. . . Do you put on a gentle spirit,
Reverence your roof; under your roof, take heed, we are,
From the host of the Greeks, desiring to be to you
Closest and dearest of all the Achaeans.[83]

By no means unmoved by the claims of humanity, Achilles grants
Ajax his point, but holds to his wrath. But the view which Ajax
expresses has been deliberately reserved for him by the poet, and
it is carried out subsequently in the way Ajax bears the chief brunt
of Achilles' defection. Odysseus, Diomedes, and Agamemnon come
off with slight wounds. Ajax suffers it out to the end, and, as if to
emphasize the contrast between the visionary exaltation of Achilles
and Ajax' desperate immersion in immediate realities, Homer slips

a brief glimpse of the battlefield between the long speech of Achilles in XVI and the arming of Patroclus. The speech ends with a weird and terrible wish for himself and Patroclus:

> Would, O Father Zeus and Athena and Apollo
> Not one man of the Trojans might flee death, many as they are,
> Not one man of the Argives, but we two, putting off death,
> Alone might break the holy crown of Troy.
> Thus they spoke such things to each other.
> But Ajax no longer was holding out; he was driven by missiles;
> Zeus' plan and the glorious Trojans were conquering him,
> Smiting and smiting; and round his temples his shining helmet
> Stricken rang terribly, and always the blows fell
> On his well-wrought visor; and his left shoulder sagged
> Holding still the painted shield firm; yet round him
> Crowding with missiles, they could not stagger him.
> Always his breath came hard, the sweat poured down
> Heavily from all his limbs, nor could he rest;
> Everywhere evil was piled on evil.[84]

If the poet chose to paint so vividly the plight of Ajax in this particular place, in the middle of a scene otherwise devoted to Achilles and Patroclus, it could only be because he wished to show that the wrath of Achilles, and the plan of Zeus, while bad for everybody, put the most suffering of all on the most loyal and innocent man in the host. The position of Ajax begins to take on almost tragic shape, foreshadowing the tragic function of Patroclus. A few lines later, the head of his spear is hacked off, and Ajax recognizes, with horror, the hand of Zeus in the Trojan victory. He retreats at last, and fire falls on the ships.[85] Throughout the poem, Ajax is unique in having no direct dealing with any god; the nearest approaches to such are, besides this passage, a few places where Zeus sends him an omen, or blows away the mist, when Ajax prays him to slay the Achaeans in the light.[86] When the other Achaeans are wounded, Ajax is not; instead he is cast into a momentary irrational fear by Zeus, and retreats confusedly.[87] It is always Zeus on these occasions, the Zeus who is favoring Achilles, a fact which further emphasizes Ajax' relation to the Wrath. But in general it is not his stance in regard to the absolute world of the gods which reveals the nature of Ajax; it is his relations with the other human characters, his fellow warriors.

In the early part of the *Iliad*, he appears little, and then more as part of the panorama than as a character. His description is surprisingly brief in the *Teichoscopia*, or View from the Wall, and his duel with Hector is not specially impressive.[88] Yet even in these two passages, confined as they are to mere externals, one gets a glimpse of the man, huge, broad-shouldered, of brief speech, and "smiling with his terrible eyebrows" as he stalks up to the lists. When this sketch is filled out in the rest of the poem, the figure of Ajax reveals itself, like that of Agamemnon, as an especial masterpiece of the transformation of traditional material into character.

Some Homeric characterizations are limited portraits, acutely drawn but confined to one or two scenes: for example, Paris and Helen, who scarcely appear except in Books III and VI; Pandarus, in early IV and early V; Andromache, only in VI, XXII, and XXIV, the elegiac books; Teucer, who is fully visible only in VIII and in three or four passages of the Great Battle. Others, such as Glaucus, Sarpedon, and Aeneas, have numerous recurrent appearances, but, consistent as they may be, their characters play no great role in the continuity of the poem. The characters analyzed above, together, of course, with Achilles and Hector, who will be treated elsewhere, have a great deal to do with the poem's continuity. Each represents a purposeful crystallization of a general heroic figure, specifically developed along lines appropriate to the *Iliad*, and no better proof exists of the unity of the poem than the unity of conception underlying not merely the primary figures, but even these secondary ones, subordinated as they are to the major action and the transcendent concept of heroism in Achilles. Ajax and Diomedes, both normative in a way, the one of heroic endurance and *aidôs*, the other of brilliant daring and glory; Nestor, the embodiment of the rules of the heroic game; Agamemnon, the king deluded by the pretensions of power, yet essentially helpless; Ajax son of Oileus, the violent ruffian; even Thersites, the truthful boor: these are all, after one fashion or another, brought into revealing contrast with Achilles, and through this contrast Homer has succeeded in unifying the panoramic aspect of the epic with the dramatic structure which he has imposed. There can be no question of large chunks of epic material thrust raw into an *Achilleis*; everything has been reconceived with minutest care. Given the same plot and episode, the Roman Lucan might well have made Ajax his principal figure; Virgil, one suspects, could have performed some very different wonders with Agamemnon. Homer fashioned Achilles, and refashioned all the other characters in the story to fit him.

One other character belongs to this group: Odysseus. In his case, we have the *Odyssey* to aid in understanding the latitude enjoyed by the composers of epic in the treatment of a traditional motif or character. For the moment it is irrelevant whether the *Odyssey* be by the same hand as the *Iliad* or not, because the common denominator of both views of Odysseus is easily discernible, and may be reasonably taken as the traditional core of the character. Resourcefulness and trickery form the essence of it, both implying survival by adjustment, either self-adjustment or a skillful manipulation of circumstances. Part of the fascination of Greek character, today as in antiquity, is the interplay of this quality with its opposite, heroic inflexibility. Each implies a distinct view of what reality is: Odysseus sees reality as the situation or problem before him; Achilles sees it as something in himself, and the problem is to identify himself with it completely, through action. In both *Iliad* and *Odyssey*, Odysseus is fully the man of survival by adjustment. In the *Odyssey*, however, his ability to survive is viewed not merely as resourcefulness, but also as a kind of tough, moral stamina in the resistance to adversity, the quality called *tlemosyne* in Greek, and repeatedly emphasized in the epithet "much-enduring." Moreover, his "many devices" now take on a more genuinely intellectual coloring, so that in the *Odyssey*, Odysseus is developed into the first Occidental prototype of the *uomo universale*, the man who has seen everything, can do everything, and understands everything.[89] Reality is that which he finds before him, but there is nothing trivial in what a penetrating man finds before him; Odysseus finds in his wanderings the vast archetypal patterns of the things which are — brute force in Cyclops, and its opposite in the finely civilized Phaeacians; kind hosts (like Aeolus) who feed and help you, and Laestrygonians who eat you; temptations to oblivion in the Lotus-eaters and those counterfeit Muses, the Sirens; sex in its dangerous and deathlike aspect in Circe, and in all its youthful delicacy in Nausicaa; death itself in the quest of Teiresias' knowledge of the unknowable. In such an expansion of the theme, Homer has turned his resourceful man into Man the Resourceful Indomitable Seeker of all things which are, anticipating Sophocles' famous ode in the *Antigone*. The theme of trickery runs throughout, but subordinated to this main idea, dominating chiefly in the later books, where the suitors are slain by trick.

The Odysseus of the *Iliad* is quite the same man in essence, but viewed differently. Resourcefulness and trick are still the cornerstones of his nature, but a different structure rises on them. The cleverest in the army, he is the right-hand man of Agamemnon, and "shares his thoughts with him." [90] As the deviser of the wooden horse, and the captor, with Diomedes, of the Palladium of Troy, he was, according to tradition, one of the most useful, if not the most useful, of all the Achaeans to the cause. [91] Both his basic characteristics contribute to this usefulness. In the second book, when the army rushes for the ships, it is the quick thinking of Odysseus, inspired as always by Athena, who restrains the men, and saves the face of Agamemnon. Immediately after this episode, he makes his first appearance as orator and chief diplomat of the host, in the long speech about the hopeful portent at Aulis. [92] In this capacity he appears again in Antenor's reminiscences of him, and in the *Embassy* to Achilles. [93] As the embodiment of craft, and the complementary antitype of Achilles, as well as of Ajax, he represents in the context of the *Iliad* one of the chief forces which took Troy. Achilles and Ajax are lonely figures, and combine with nobody; but the more flexible man of war, Diomedes, combines very well with Odysseus to form a deadly team in Book X (if genuine), where the theft of Rhesus' horses, like so many episodes of the *Iliad*, is possibly a transference of the theft of the Palladium into terms appropriate to this particular stage of the action. Guileful, and always ready with an adjustment, Odysseus never in the *Iliad* exposes himself to unnecessary danger. His contrast with Diomedes in this respect is subtly accented in Book VIII, when Diomedes, seeing Nestor in peril of his life and unable to flee with the others before the advancing Trojans, calls to Odysseus to help rescue him from the tangled reins of his horses. Odysseus prudently keeps running, and Diomedes alone comes to Nestor's aid. [94] Homer wastes no words condemning Odysseus' will to live on this occasion; rather the

opposite, for a few lines later he makes Nestor himself say to
Diomedes:

Son of Tydeus, turn again to flight your horses of cleftless hoof!
Do you not know that victory follows you not from Zeus?
Now Zeus son of Kronos ordains the glory to this man,
Today; but another time, if he wills, to us he will also
Grant it. . .[95]

Evidently the rule book included the specifications for living to
fight another day, without prejudice to one's heroic claims. Com-
mon sense was not to be excluded, and Odysseus in the *Iliad* has a
large share of it. And this common sense, which by no means marks
Odysseus in the *Odyssey* (his companions are always reproving
him for lack of it), is nevertheless the product of the same will to
live which motivates so much of the *Odyssey*. The tradition of re-
sourcefulness and adjustment has taken its own direction in the
Iliad. In the battle scenes, especially where he is wounded, his cool
wary outlook comes clear; he wins by a trick where he cannot by
force, and saves himself by keeping his head and getting next to
Ajax.[96]

Yet, if his common-sense view of reality can sometimes look like
cowardice, it has also its human and penetrating side. Agamemnon,
always ready to retreat, proposes launching the ships to keep the
Trojans from burning them; once launched, they might as well
be used to go home, under cover of night. Odysseus' reply is finely
sarcastic. Not only is Agamemnon's suggestion low-spirited and
unworthy of an Achaean king; it is also utterly unrealistic to think
that the ships could be launched and the Trojans held off at the
same time; even to try it would spell destruction. And he concludes
his speech by addressing the king with a formula which strikes the
ear with extreme irony, under the circumstances: "O marshaler of
hosts." [97] Humbled, Agamemnon asks for advice, and gets a more
spirited proposal from Diomedes.

But, as in so many other cases, the character of Odysseus in the
Iliad reveals itself most clearly in the scenes with Achilles. The
chief polarities of the *Embassy* lie in the speeches of Phoenix and
Achilles, so that here the latter's contrast with Odysseus is at most
lightly sketched, in the juxtaposition of Odysseus' skilled, effective
appeal and the chaotic eloquence of Achilles' reply. Odysseus be-

gins with a graceful compliment for Achilles' hospitality; he out-
lines the danger of the Greek army, then weighs Achilles' incurable
remorse in after time, if he does not rescue the host, with the
honor he will receive if he does; he repeats the long list of Agamem-
non's peace offerings; and the speech ends with another compli-
ment, a flattering appeal to Achilles' supreme valor.[98] It is perfectly
constructed oratory, with exordium, exposition, arguments and
peroration. Cool, supple and contrived, it moves Achilles not at all,
as do the speeches of Phoenix and Ajax,[99] and compared with it,
the hero's answer is like a storm at sea, as he ignores all the argu-
ments, and heaps scorn on Agamemnon's gifts.

The real conflict between Odysseus and Achilles comes in Book
XIX, the scene of the renunciation of the Wrath. Agamemnon,
admitting his fault, wants to give the amends he had promised, but
Achilles puts him off; he longs for the war without delay, and
Agamemnon may give his gifts some other time, or keep them.[100]
Odysseus intervenes with the argument that it is going to be a long
fight, and that the army will perform better on a full stomach;
first let the men eat and Agamemnon give his gifts and entertain
Achilles.[101] Achilles again refuses; he will touch nothing until he
has avenged Patroclus, whereupon Odysseus puts the claims of
common sense more movingly:

> O Achilles, Peleus' son, far the best of Achaeans,
> Greater you are than I, and better by not a little
> With spears; but I in thinking, I surpass you
> Much, for I am older and know more.
> So, let your heart endure my words.
> Swiftly on men comes a sick surfeit of battle-din
> Where bronze strews the ground with much straw
> And the harvest is least, when Zeus tilts the balances,
> He who is steward of the war of men.
> Not by a fast can the Achaeans mourn their dead;
> Too many and frequent every day they fall.
> When shall any get breathing-time from the toil?
> Him who dies we must bury, having hearts
> Firm, and weeping for him but on that day.
> Those who are left amid the hateful war,
> They must remember drink and food, that rather still
> Ceaselessly we may fight with our enemies,
> Clothing our bodies in weariless bronze. . .[102]

Achilles does not answer this, and though he allows the delay for food and gifts, he eats nothing himself, and is instead sustained by a divine distillate of nectar and ambrosia, brought by Athena.[103] The presence of Odysseus in this scene makes clear, as few other things could have done, that Achilles, in renouncing his wrath, has not returned to the same world from which he retired. The council, in which he quarreled with Agamemnon in the first place, had been called by Achilles, out of concern for the army's welfare: [104] he had then been integrally united with the others. Nothing is farther from his thoughts now; Odysseus must remind him of the limits of time and humanity. Nor is there any real reconcilement with Agamemnon; the gracious formalities are a bore. Only the battle counts. Yet the importance of food, even to those who mourn their dearest losses, is a motif which will arise again, when Achilles himself gently presses entertainment upon Priam. But again, Homer miraculously transforms the motif. What is simple sense to Odysseus becomes in Achilles a token of mysterious, infinite compassion:

> Hark you, your son is ransomed, old man, as you bade;
> He lies on a bier; you yourself, with the glimpse of dawn
> Shall see as you take him away; now, let us remember food.
> Even fair-haired Niobe remembered food,
> She whose twelve children perished in her halls,
> Six daughters, and six flourishing sons. . .
>
> Yet she remembered food, when she was weary of weeping.
> Now somewhere among cliffs, in the sheep-pastured mountains,
> Sipylus, where they tell of the couches of heavenly
> Nymphs, who dance around the Achelous,
> There, stone that she is, she broods on the gods' afflictions.
> Come then, let us also, divine old man, consider
> Food. . .[105]

There is a wonderful passage in the *Odyssey* where Odysseus meets the ghost of Achilles in Hades. They are profoundly courteous to each other. Odysseus, outlining his own toils, reminds Achilles that the supreme honor which the latter receives from all makes light of death; but Achilles, complimenting Odysseus on the magnificence of his adventures, answers that there is no consolation in death, for it is better to be the living slave of a poor man than king of all the dead.[106] Yet, it is hard to imagine Achilles as the slave of a poor man, and hard to believe that he is speaking a literal truth. He is emphasizing the cost of his greatness, the incurable sorrow of being Achilles. He is saying, I have suffered the worst, and identified myself with it; you have merely survived. And Odysseus, for his part, says: you are very honored indeed, but you are dead; I am doing the really difficult and great thing. In the retrospective air of Hades, Homer can thus summarize the gulf between the two men, and their characteristic views of life, in a few lines. But the same gulf appears in the *Iliad*, subtly limned in books IX and XIX.

We do not know anything substantial about pre-Homeric poetry, but the consistently warlike and generalized nature of the formulaic epithets, as well as of the stock-in-trade motifs of battle, council, secret exploit, discouragement, assistance by gods, sacrifice, and all the rest, which are Homer's material, indicate a vast array of malleable rudiments, out of which the singer made what he could. With singleness of vision and real mastery of the rudiments, a poet might so dispose and deploy his material that the generalized motifs, crystallized phrases, and traditional imagery fall into contextual groupings of great specific significance. This seems to be what Homer has done. At every point the tradition supplied him with an abundance of what might be said. We cannot always follow his selective process, or know what he omitted altogether; but what he chose to say was so timed in context, combination, and contrast that his characters, from the most primary ones to those fleeting personalities who appear only as they fall on the battlefield, possess a haunting kind of individuality, an individuality which forces its way, by the poet's skill, through the universal heroic type. Something, undoubtedly, was due to predecessors; but the consistent unity of these characters is Homer's own.

ACHILLES: EVOLUTION OF
A HERO

ARISTOTLE was the first to state in analytic terms the dramatic unity of the Homeric poems: no more than a single drama could be made from either, whereas a great many plays could be and had been based on the poems of the Epic Cycle.[1] The poems of the Epic Cycle, in the form read by Proclus and others, are undoubtedly later than Homer; but one may reasonably suspect that their loose, episodic construction continued the ordinary methods of oral singers of an earlier day. The fragments are too scanty to allow a decision as to whether they were orally composed; the earlier ones, such as the *Aethiopis* of Arctinus, supposedly a pupil of Homer, may have been. Eugammon of Cyrene, on the other hand, in the fifth century doubtless wrote the *Telegony*. But, written or oral, the structure and conception of epic which appear in these poems are certainly more primitive than Homer's; they suggest, in fact, the kind of simple series of events, chronologically more or less cohesive but otherwise lacking in organization, from which songs for an evening's entertainment might easily be selected by a singer like Demodocus or Phemius, according to the immediate tastes and preferences of his audience. If the songs of those minstrels, therefore, provide some picture of the actual performance of pre-Homeric singers, it is possible that the *Cycle* offers some vague idea of what the storehouse of pre-Homeric tradition was like.

Character, as far as one can tell, was sketchy and typological; great emphasis fell on plot, especially on who killed whom, and precisely when. There seems to have been little subordination of episode to major plan, but rather a concern with completeness, event following event in what the poet deemed the right order, paratactically arranged.[2] The contrast between this method and that of Homer is greater than has generally been estimated. Line by line, Homer's style is still paratactical, the "strung style"; but in its larger elements of structure and characterization, his work is profoundly organic. Particularly in the *Iliad*, Homer has subjected his material to strict categories of primary and secondary, subordinating all characters to Achilles, and all incidents of the Trojan war to the Wrath. Many incidents of the war are, of course, omitted altogether; but Homer has managed to suggest or symbolize a good many which his scenario excluded from actual narration.

A hero's temporary retirement from heroic activity is not a motif peculiar to Homer. In the *Shah Nameh*, Rustam retires out of annoyance with the king of Persia, and Phoenix' narrative of the wrath of Meleager shows that such tales were not unknown to Greek legend.[3] The Wrath of Achilles had probably been an epic subject for generations when Homer found it, and the germ of its meaning, the conflict between personal integrity and social obligation, must always have been inherent. But Homer's development of the theme squeezes the last drop of psychological and metaphysical meaning out of the old material, partly by virtue of the fact that he refuses the easy answer of Phoenix, that social obligation must take precedence. Achilles could never have been drawn as he is, if that were the assumption. Rather Homer approaches the matter as an insolubly tragic situation, the tragic situation *par excellence*. Personal integrity in Achilles achieves the form and authority of immanent divinity, with its inviolable, lonely singleness, half repellent because of its almost inhuman austerity, but irresistible in its passion and perfected selfhood. Yet the scale is not weighted in favor of this gleaming vision. Homer has allowed the human world the fullness of all its claims upon our sympathy, and at length even Achilles himself curses, as do all the others, the rage which set him apart from his fellows.[4]

When Achilles joined the Trojan expedition, his assumptions

about himself and the actions before him differed little, we presume, from those of the other princes. Battle and siege were the proving ground of valor, where the brave win unforgettable glory, manifested in the visible, tangible forms of loot, spoils, and captives, and preserved in epic songs.[5] Any expectable difference between Achilles and his associates was at first merely quantitative; his superior talents would naturally lead to a greater degree of glory, a larger collection of its tangible signs. Relations between virtue and reward, however, turn out to be not so symmetrical in the actual world, and though the imbalance may be loftily ignored for a time, the point is likely to come when the affront to superior ability sinks deeper than the surface, and raises the whole question of what is to be valued in a man. It is at this point that Achilles' difference from his fellows reveals itself as a qualitative one. He no longer is concerned with the rule book of heroic behavior, the transparent unrealism of overblown egos asserting themselves through various forms of violence. He reacts from the mere acceptance of a creed, and places himself on higher ground. He will not seek honor as the others seek it. He will have "honor from Zeus," by which he means he will risk all in the belief that nobility is not a mutual exchange of vain compliments among men whose lives are evanescent as leaves, but an organic and inevitable part of the universe, independent of social contract.

The steps by which Achilles comes to this position show a causal complexity very characteristic of Homer. Viewed from a later vantage point, the Quarrel between Agamemnon and Achilles appears completely inevitable, but as Homer narrates it in Book I, it seems like a series of merely unfortunate accidents. Agamemnon, characteristically, refuses to accept ransom for the girl Chryseis, captured in the raid on Andromache's city, Thebe-under-Placos.[6] Her father, a priest, begs Apollo to afflict the Greek host with plague. Apollo does so, and Achilles calls a council to find out what is to be done.[7] The fact that Achilles is the one to take the initiative is in itself significant: he feels responsibility and concern for the cause, and is more quick and zealous than the king himself. When Calchas is afraid to reveal the reason for the plague, it is Achilles who swears to protect him, even if he should offend Agamemnon.[8] So far, Achilles has done nothing that could not have

been done by any of the leaders; yet there is a latent inversion of
the expectable roles. It is not the king, whose responsibility it is,
who is turning stones to achieve the army's safety, but the most
distinguished warrior; and it is not the most distinguished warrior
who is asserting his right to keep a captive, as the tangible meed
of glory, but the king. When Calchas says that the plague is due
to Agamemnon's insult to the priest, the storm breaks. In high rage,
Agamemnon agrees to yield Chryseis, but demands a substitute,
and when Achilles mildly points out that he will have to wait till
Troy falls, there being no general reserve of substitutes, Agamem-
non accuses him of trying to cheat him:

> Not so, good though you may be, godlike Achilles!
> Cheat me not with your plan, you will not overreach or persuade me.
> What? is this your will, while you have a prize, that I sit
> Lacking mine, and you bidding me hand her back?
> Well, if the great-hearted Achaeans will give me a prize,
> Suitable to my taste, somehow of similar value;
> If they will not give one, then I will choose for myself,
> Yours or Ajax' prize, or Odysseus'; I will come,
> Take and lead off. And he will be angry, to whom I come.[9]

Agamemnon's threat at first hovers indecisively: "Yours or Ajax'
prize, or Odysseus'." Ajax and Odysseus are both presumably pres-
ent, but Achilles does not wait for their reactions. He takes the
general threat to the system specifically upon himself, and insists
on being the test case. In a furious denunciation of greed, he re-
minds the king that the quarrel with the Trojans is not his own
but Menelaus', that he himself has done most to advance the cause
and has gotten least out of it, while Agamemnon always collects
the lion's share. Now even what he has is to be taken away; he
will simply leave. How can the king expect obedience on such a
basis?[10] Achilles has by no means lost his head, in this speech. He
is saying, in his typically torrential way, that a federation of princes
such as Agamemnon was leading can hold together only on the
basis of mutual respect of each other's honor and rights. Hitherto,
Achilles has apparently helped willingly, and winked at the unfair
distribution. But now, it is not a question of marginal manipula-
tion; it is an overt and wholesale assault on the supposed social
system. In the face of such insult, Achilles' threat to leave the ex-

pedition is a little less fierce than might be expected. But Agamemnon has not finished. He accepts Achilles' resignation, and calls it "fleeing." [11] He adds that he hates Achilles most of all the princes, scoffs at his abilities, and scorns his resentment. He will take Achilles' prize, Briseis, as he says:

> . . . That well you may know
> How much better I am than you, and another may shrink
> To speak as my equal, or liken himself to me, face to face.[12]

This is not merely insult, it is challenge, and to answer it, Achilles must either slay Agamemnon, or else take refuge on a totally different level. He begins to draw his sword, but the sudden epiphany of Athena embodies his realization that there is something incommensurate between Agamemnon and himself, that the issue is larger than a sword thrust. Agamemnon said that he himself was better, and the question is, what does he mean? Nestor explains it later: Agamemnon is better because he rules more people.[13] All admit that Achilles is mightier, so there is no need to prove it by the sword.[14] But what is the force of this "better"? The eminence of the throne of Mycenae was enough to impress its possessor, and even Nestor; both imply that Achilles' god-given valor is a thing of slighter value; but the secret appearance of Athena, whom only Achilles sees, explicitly indicates that they are wrong; she says:

> Thrice so many in future shall be your glorious gifts,
> All for this insolence. Restrain yourself, and obey us.[15]

The contest of dignity and value must be played out on the highest level of authority. Agamemnon, easily dismissing Achilles, said others would honor him, especially Zeus. Achilles accepts the challenge, retires from the war, and lets Zeus make it clear whom he honors. At this point, as Athena's promise hints, Achilles still expects his vindication to come in the form of "glorious gifts," in greatly increased numbers. Before long, however, he will recognize that it is no more a question of gifts than it is of sword-thrusts. As the *Iliad* progresses, the compensations of true greatness appear less and less engaging, and the supreme hero is less and less the gloriously satisfied top of the heap, and more and more a lonely and haunted sojourner among men of inconsequence and half-hearted ideals.

One remark which Achilles makes in the last speech of the Quarrel indicates his intuition about the levels of action involved. He will not fight physically to keep Briseis, but he will fight to keep his other possessions.[16] This statement completes, in a way, the scene with Athena. Achilles herein makes it clear that by yielding Briseis he is by no means admitting Agamemnon's right to rob him at will, or even granting that the king can take the girl at all, unless he himself allows it. Briseis has become a symbol of Achilles' own integrity, a thing which does not depend on the king or the heroic system. She is not on the same level with the other possessions, therefore; she stands for something quite internal, which Agamemnon can trespass against, but not understand. Only by trying to take her and suffering the consequences can Agamemnon see how helpless is the exterior pomp of kingliness compared to the god-given courage of the "best of the Achaeans." It is often said that in Homer women, that is war-captives, are looked upon in the same light as all other chattels; Achilles puts them up as prizes in the Games for Patroclus.[17] But it must not be inferred, therefore, that Achilles' concern with Briseis is identical with his concern for his other things, for this passage proves otherwise. Agamemnon, demanding a substitute of "equal value" to the girl he is losing, illustrates the common attitude. Achilles clearly feels differently about Briseis, who is commensurate with, and can symbolize, his inner conviction about his own honor; the other possessions are commensurate with force and fighting, the mode of self-assertion which in Achilles had been supreme above all others, and now is inadequate to his need. Later we learn still more about his relation with Briseis. It is no mere master-and-slave affair; he uses a word of her which elsewhere means regularly "wife":

. . . from me alone of the Achaeans
He seized and keeps my lovely wife; beside her let him
Lie and enjoy! But why should the Argives battle the Trojans?
Why has he gathered a host and led them hither,
This son of Atreus? Was it not for the sake of fair-haired Helen?
Alone of mortal men do the sons of Atreus
Love their wives? Any good man and sane, whosoever,
Loves and cares for his own, as I also
Loved her from my heart, spear-captive though she was.[18]

This passage shows clearly why Briseis, unlike most female prizes, differs from Achilles' other possessions, and why the defense of his right to her takes the extreme form it does. He loves her, even as he loves Patroclus, and the love of Achilles, like his hate, is likely to have cosmic implications. In one way, love is an absolute assertion of the importance of another person, and Achilles' own nature seeks the absolute in all its concerns. His feelings aspire to exist free of all secondary reference, even as his actions aim at utter supremacy. If any part of himself is challenged or defied, it is characteristic that his whole self must respond, echoed and supported by the intransigent forms of the gods themselves.

Achilles' two loves, Briseis and Patroclus, thus on the one hand take the measure of his heroic grasp of the absolute, the inviolable commitment. On the other hand, they also typify his human side. In the *Iliad*, Achilles is more often rebuked for his uncompromising firmness than praised for his human warmth, but the latter is nonetheless there. The passage quoted above is a simple enough statement of emotion: "everyone loves his wife, and I love mine." The relation with Patroclus involves even greater complexities. But clearly it is the violation or loss of these loves which drives Achilles to the austere and fearful extremities which characterize him. All human relationships require compromise; their very nature, committed as they are to mortality, imply violation and loss, by death, if by nothing else. But to the man who seeks a perfected glory in the heroic stance without blot, such implication is intolerable, and this is the essence of Achilles' suffering. He cannot keep pure his commitment in this world; the king of men is a cheat.[19] The effort to avenge the deception costs the life of Patroclus. Beset with such facts, the direct simplicity of human relationships is lost; their proper emotions cease to have the form of stimulus and response, and become spiritual states, agonizing and inexpressible, but necessary, since they keep the purity, if not the object, of love. In short, they cease to be human relationships, and become part of the hero's relationship with the absolute.

The *Iliad* traces almost clinically the stages of Achilles' development. More than tragedy, epic makes real use of time; whereas Oedipus, for instance, reveals himself before our eyes, Achilles creates himself in the course of the poem. He progresses from young hopefulness, cheerfully accepting the possibility of early death with glory, through various phases of disillusion, horror, and violence, to a final detachment which is godlike indeed. Tragedy, especially that of Sophocles, slowly uncovers a character which is complete from start to finish, but Achilles is actually not complete until the poem is complete. He is learning all the time. He is learning the meaning of his original choice, mentioned in his great speech in the *Embassy* of Book IX, learning, in fact, how really to make it. The choice of Achilles is a traditional motif in Greek literature; it occurs in the tales of Heracles and is used as late as the second century A.D. by Lucian, to symbolize the self-conscious acceptance of one's own aspirations. Achilles speaks of the two fates which his mother prophesied for him: either he could go to Troy, win glory and die young, or stay home and live to a ripe but inglorious old age.[20] Actually, Achilles does not say which he chose; his presence at Troy intimates the former, but the fact that he does not state his choice, and his entertainment of the possibility that he can still go home if he wishes, indicate further that at this stage of the action, Achilles is not yet entirely sure who he is. In order to fulfill the first fate of early death with glory, one must embrace the idea of death more closely than Achilles has yet done. His human attachment to life is still strong:

> Not worth life to me are the fabled quantities
> Of wealth Troy kept, well-founded citadel,
> Once in the days of peace, before the sons of Achaeans came,
> Nor all that the stone threshold of the Archer guards,
> Phoebus Apollo, in Pytho of lofty cliffs.
> Plunderers' game are cattle and sleek flocks,
> Tripods are for the taking, and the tawny heads of horses.
> But for the life of man to return, not plunder nor seizure
> Avails, when once it has passed the teeth's enclosure.[21]

He envisions himself as having well-nigh sold his birthright for a mess of pottage, and not even gotten the pottage. The society of heroes is deceptive, glory is nothing. He can excuse himself of the whole ridiculous hoax. At least, so he puts it in his hotheaded answer to Odysseus in the *Embassy*. He does not yet know that his choice really is made, and that he is already well on the way toward finding out exactly what kind of glory he will carry to his early

grave. The inner necessity, which compelled him to defend his right
to Briseis as he did, is still at work, sapping away such youthful
simplicities as the love of life, with friends, wife, possessions, and
setting in their place the terrible gift of heroic self-realization.
Achilles was human enough at first. For all his ferocity in battle,
he was gallant and generous; he ransomed his captives, and though
he slew Eetion, he buried him with honor, and "the nymphs of the
mountain planted elms around his tomb." [22] This was the way
chivalric warfare should be, magnanimously endowing even de-
feat and death with an honorable beauty. But the Achilles who gave
Andromache's father a funeral is not quite the same as the Achilles
who dragged her husband by the heels before the Scaean Gates.
In the interim, he had been driven to feel that integrity and life are
irreconcilable. For man, the only absolute is death, and Achilles
wills his own along with all others'.

Some inkling of this insight seems to lie in his speech in the
Embassy:

> Equal honor is his who waits, and his who fights,
> Caitiff and noble are held in one regard:
> Equally dies the deedless man, and he who does much.[23]

But here Achilles, still with hopes of his life, misreads himself to
the extent of concluding that hereafter he might as well be a deed-
less man. It is mere disillusion at this stage, not yet despair. It is
also somewhat self-righteous; he feels he has been to the Atreidae
like an adult bird feeding its young, and going hungry himself.[24]
True as this may be, the simile is a pretension in the name of ac-
complishment, a demand for the very rewards which he is refusing.
If he was merely tired of going hungry, why should he not accept
Agamemnon's lordly amends? But the truth is, he is seeking some-
thing deeper, and does not yet know what it includes. The com-
plaint about unrewarded effort, like the threat to go home, frames
well enough his disappointment with the company he has chosen.
He has yet to learn that part of his greatness will lie in how he
meets disappointment with himself, disappointment with what even
the greatest man can achieve.

Achilles has often appeared like a spoiled child to readers, and
the source of this impression is primarily his rejection of the em-

bassy. Few will deny that he was justified in his resentment in Book I, or that Agamemnon's action, far from being the exercise of rights by a superior, was a high-handed and maddening insult to a valuable, independent ally. But when the king, taught by a day's defeat at the hands of Hector, offers magnificent amends — not only the return of Briseis, but also seven other girls, together with bronze, gold, horses, his own daughter in marriage, and a dowry of seven cities — it often seems ungenerous and egotistical that Achilles refuses. These are the very quantities of gifts which Athena had said he would receive as a result of the king's insolence, which means that they were exactly what he expected. Moreover, the envoys who come are, as he says, those whom he particularly likes and respects: Odysseus, Ajax, and his old tutor, Phoenix.[25] Nevertheless, though he receives them with the most warm and gracious courtesy, he rejects their suit. What, if any, is his justification?

Careful reading of the ninth book reveals two important but somewhat neglected facts. One is that the embassy does not fail entirely to move Achilles, and the other is that his rejection of Agamemnon's offer is not based upon mere sulky passion, but upon the same half-realized, inward conception of honor which moved him originally to vow his abstinence from the war. The first point is the simpler one, but in itself reveals a good deal about Achilles. When Odysseus has finished, Achilles announces flatly that he is going home on the morrow.[26] After the long speech of Phoenix, he is less sure; he says that tomorrow they will consider whether they will go home or remain.[27] Finally, after the brief and touching appeal of Ajax, there is no talk of going home at all; he announces that he will not fight until Hector reaches the tents of the Myrmidons, and begins to burn the ships; then in more positive terms:

> Hark you, here by my own pavilion and dark vessel,
> Hector, hot in the lust of battle, I mean to restrain.[28]

Oddly enough, this promise to fight at the last ditch, though remembered by Achilles, is forgotten by the envoys; Odysseus reports only that Achilles threatened to go home, and hence the whole venture seems to have failed.[29] Odysseus' mind, somewhat typically, is taken up by the immediate problem in hand, and he seems not to have noticed that Achilles has already wavered a little, and that as the speakers grew less clever, they grew more persuasive. Odysseus got nothing from him. Blunt Ajax unexpectedly got the biggest return, for his simple humanity. Yet it was Phoenix who drew the pattern, and sketched the role which Achilles adopts. After narrating the wrath of Meleager, Phoenix points out that because Meleager yielded and fought only at the last ditch, he received none of the gifts which he would have gained if he had yielded sooner, and he concludes:

> Do not you, for my sake, plan this in your heart, let not a god
> Turn you thither, dear fellow; it will be worse for you
> To defend flaming ships; rather, in regard for the gifts,
> Go, for the Achaeans will honor you like a god.
> But if, without gifts, you plunge into murderous war,
> War though you ward away, you will not be the same in renown.[30]

It is in answer to this speech that Achilles draws most explicitly the distinction between the externals of the case and the inner satisfaction he is seeking:

> . . . I do not need
> This honor. But I deem I am honored in Zeus' disposal,
> And here by the curving ships it will keep me. . .[31]

The pattern of Meleager, from which old Phoenix tried to dissuade him, appeals to Achilles: to fight only at the last, and without gifts, with honor only from the "disposal of Zeus." Phoenix achieves not what he intends; ironically he helps Achilles to know his own intention, and by the time Ajax has spoken, Achilles has embraced the example of Meleager, and states his decision. Though Odysseus fails to perceive it, Achilles' position has clarified itself considerably through the speeches of the *Embassy*, and the great diplomat reports it quite erroneously.

The second point which is often overlooked in this scene is a closely related one. The flat refusal which follows Odysseus' appeal is equally, though less explicitly, a demand for true honor rather than false. In a long speech which is one of the most extraordinary poetic triumphs of the whole *Iliad*, Achilles, passionately, and as yet dimly groping for something loftier than a system by which men pay when they must and steal when they can, maintains a peculiar suave mastery and beats Odysseus at his own game of subtleties. He begins with a remark which much resembles the habitual formula, "now I will tell you the truth, and speak unerringly," but it is expanded a little, and is somewhat more intense than usual:

> Now it behooves me speak my words without scruple,
> Just as I think, and how it shall be accomplished,
> Lest you sit dinning my ears, on each side one of you.
> Hateful to me is he as the gates of Hell,
> Who hides one thing in his heart, and says another.[32]

One may well ask why Achilles preludes his answer to Odysseus with this heartfelt denunciation of a liar. Odysseus has told no lies, and indeed he is free to interpret Achilles' words as simply a rather strong asseveration that he means what he says. On the other hand, Odysseus has hidden something in his heart, and by this *double-entendre* Achilles shows that he knows it. Odysseus has repeated Agamemnon's offer almost verbatim, but there was one important omission. Agamemnon had ended his announcement of the amends with the following peroration:

> Let him be prevailed upon — Hell is deaf to prayers, impervious,
> Therefore also to mortals most hateful of gods —
> And let him stand below me, so far am I the more kingly,
> So far also by birth I say I am his elder.[33]

It is perhaps only natural that Odysseus, in his recital of the king's speech, should omit these none-too-engaging sentiments. But the omission does not prevent Achilles from seeing that Agamemnon merely wishes to use him, and that the offer of amends shows no change of spirit from what had prevailed in their last meeting. Gifts may be offered, but the insult remains, one proof being that the king did not come in person.

> Always clothed in shamelessness, not even would he
> Dare, dog that he is, to look me in the face.[34]

Agamemnon's offer is a little like Chekhov's drunken *parvenu*, who shouts, "I can pay for everything!" He still must have submission from Achilles, even if he has to buy it. It is not, however, for sale, and as if Achilles had actually heard Agamemnon's remark about his own kingliness, he cries that he would not marry the daughter of Agamemnon if she were beautiful as Aphrodite and clever as Athena:

> . . . let him choose another Achaean,
> Someone suitable to him, someone who is more kingly.[35]

There can be little question that Achilles' rejection of the embassy is essentially a rejection of Agamemnon's gifts and the spirit in which they are offered. He returns to the point briefly in Book XVI, when he says he would have thrown back the Trojans long ago, "if Agamemnon would show me a friendly attitude." [36] One may well believe that had the gifts been offered together with some abatement of kingly pretensions and the abandonment of unsavory comparisons, Achilles must have accepted. Achilles has been called stubborn, but Agamemnon is the really stubborn one. Achilles simply refuses to accept false coin for true. For all his complaints about the distribution of loot and himself going hungry, it is not loot that he wants. In the speech to Odysseus, he cannot as yet state clearly what he wants, but he knows that he does not wish to be bought. After hearing Phoenix, he can distinguish more clearly, and frame his desire as "honor in the disposal of Zeus" — dignity before the universe — a thing which Agamemnon cannot give. Indeed, after the *Embassy*, Agamemnon ceases to be of any relevance to Achilles' concerns; his reconciliation with him is a mere formality, perfunctorily observed by Achilles with complete boredom, while the king makes long self-excusing speeches. The whole quarrel with Agamemnon was merely the match that lit a fire, the impetus which drove Achilles from the simple assumptions of the other princely heroes onto the path where heroism means the search for the dignity and meaning of the self. Is it an overinterpretation to see a symbol of this self-search in Achilles' song of the "glories of men"? [37] We are told that the passage indicates that in the heroic age warriors improvised epic lays, and this is doubtless true. But Achilles is the only one who actually does any singing in Homer, aside from the professional bards of the *Odyssey*, perhaps for the very reason that to Homer, the practice of epic singing was profoundly involved with the roots of early self-consciousness, the estimate of oneself in the light of the future's retrospect. The deeply brooding Helen says that she and Paris will be a subject of song hereafter,[38] and it is by no means impossible that Homer, before plunging Achilles into the first phase of the search for his true place in history, envisioned that search in terms of what poets, himself included, must sing of him, and so introduced him with a lyre in his hand, consulting and re-creating the heroic tradition to which he would add a new perspective.

The next phase of Achilles' development is divided from the *Embassy* by the long, carefully wrought Battle books. Far from being a mere indulgence in the more primitive aspect of old epic, this Battle is a shapely masterpiece, a panorama in which the earthly and heavenly effects of the Wrath are deployed in piercing detail, steadily inwrought with motivations of the approaching tragedy. The structure of Book XI has in particular been criticized, but those who see in it two poems unluckily tacked together fail to recognize the problem which confronted Homer in relating the defeat of the Achaeans. On the one hand, this defeat must be told for its own sake, since the concern is not with Achilles alone, but with the whole action; on the other, its effect on Achilles must be reckoned with, and in particular its effect on Patroclus, who, from this point on, begins to play a new role. After the shout of Eris, and the arming and exploits of Agamemnon, follows the episode known as the Wounding of the Chiefs. Agamemnon, Diomedes, and Odysseus are rapidly put out of action; Ajax is directly confused by Zeus, and retreats; two lesser figures, Machaon and Eurypylus, are hit, and escape the field, Machaon in the chariot of Nestor, Eurypylus on foot. At this point, Achilles, watching, no doubt with some satisfaction, the way things are going, sees Machaon in the chariot of Nestor, but, unable to identify him at a distance, calls to Patroclus to go find out. As Patroclus comes out of the tent, "equal to Ares," an odd epithet for this gentle person, Homer solemnly announces, "And this was the beginning of his woe." [39] Such a statement could easily have been saved for the moment when Patroclus actually puts on the arms of Achilles, but the poet sees the action far ahead and throughout its devious paths. The beginning of Patroclus' woe is his exposure to the direct experience of the defeat caused by Achilles. Before he returns, he will have changed his opinion of Achilles' wrath; Achilles will have changed also, but his change will be visible mostly through Patroclus.

Natural and realistic as it is for Achilles to send a vassal rather than go himself, this sending serves also a symbolic purpose. It allows Achilles, moved as he may actually be by the sufferings of his friends, to maintain in the eyes of all his exterior detachment and indifference. Patroclus can play his human side for him, activate the simple curiosity he feels, and respond with pity to the wounds and disgrace. Patroclus goes, identifies Machaon, and is about to return, lest Achilles be annoyed at any delay. But Nestor feels talkative. More than that, he feels like talking to the point, or at least partly so. He cannot resist the recital of a long exploit by himself which took place in Elis before any one else in the army was born, but it is all to indicate that, if he still had his youth, he would not behave like Achilles. He remembers, in fact, his first meeting with Achilles, in Phthia, and how Patroclus' father advised his son to keep the young lion in hand with wise counselings. Why has Patroclus forgotten this? Achilles "alone will get good of his virtue," and regret it later, says Nestor, if he continues thus.[40] Valor is not to be a private possession; it must be used publicly. Patroclus should tell him so, and persuade him. Still, Nestor is always ready to be fair; perhaps Achilles has been warned by Zeus or his mother to stay out of battle, and in that case, let him at least send Patroclus to stem the tide a little.[41] Thus, through Nestor's habitually clear, if lengthy, eloquence, the other side of the case is brought home to Patroclus. Heroism cannot be maintained in isolation, or it becomes nothing. Though the heroic nature partakes of the absolute qualities of divinity itself, and though the higher it looks, the less it can endure the compromises of the human level, still its human connections alone justify it as a human phenomenon. Achilles cannot "alone enjoy his virtue," and Patroclus is the living proof that even now he is not so indifferent as he seems.

The scene with Nestor rouses Patroclus, and he starts back; but Homer adds another telling little scene, which indicates that it is not merely the words of Nestor which stir Patroclus, but something in Patroclus himself, the gift of pity and gentleness which, as Menelaus and Briseis say later, he had for everybody.[42] Still feeling some haste to return to Achilles, he nevertheless allows himself to be delayed again by Eurypylus, who is staggering back to the ships with an arrow through his thigh. The wounded man appeals to him for medical aid, the knowledge of drugs which Chiron taught Achilles and which Patroclus has learned; the regular doctor, Machaon, is himself wounded.[43] Patroclus wavers a moment, and then the die is cast. Achilles can wait. Patroclus takes the wounded man to his tent, and begins to treat his injury. Already some of Achilles' heroic equipment, his medical knowledge gained from Chiron, has come to the help of the Greeks. The *Patrocleia* has begun.

The Battle now goes its own way, with the retreat to the wall, the counterattack led by Poseidon, in XIII and XIV, and finally the rout. All this time, Patroclus is with Eurypylus, and Achilles is waiting for the answer to his original question. When the Achaeans, however, break and retreat a second time inside the camp, Patroclus reappears. Smiting his thigh in alarm, he rushes off, not to tell Achilles that the wounded man was Machaon, but (and he even quotes Nestor's very words) to persuade Achilles to do something.[44] At the beginning of Book XVI, he stands before Achilles, "weeping like a dark-watered spring," from compassion at what he has seen. And now begins the most puzzling part of the *Iliad* — at least, the most puzzling part of Achilles' actions. Even those who forgive Achilles his rejection of the embassy find it difficult to forgive him for letting Patroclus take his place on the battlefield. Certainly Achilles never forgives himself for it. And yet, from the point of view of the conflict created within Achilles by the very nature of the heroic paradox, there was nothing else he could do. He had said that his honor was "from Zeus," and that he would fight only when the fire reached his own ship, and this was as much as to say: individual honor is a matter strictly between the transcendent aspect of man himself and the universe; he alone knows what it is and he alone can get satisfaction from it. But Patroclus has heard the opposite from Nestor, and the fact that Achilles listens to Patroclus' appeal, the fact that he had the curiosity to send him out in the first place, shows that Achilles himself knows that the opposite is also true, that the heroic spirit, if it is to exist as a reality, must act in this world. The hero's head may touch Olympus, but his feet can leave the earth only when he dies. At the beginning of Book XVI, Achilles has proved, through the activities of Zeus, that his head is in Olympus, that his honor is from Zeus, that a transcendent will can change the map of fortune. But how is he to deal with his

human responses, which stand before him in the person of his best
friend, begging him to act, to yield the last few inches of satisfac-
tion, and save the ships?

The whole tragic paradox of Achilles centers upon this scene,
and in order to understand it, it is necessary to remember that the
wrath of the hero is a search for himself which is complete only
when the poem is complete. Achilles' will, which appears so fixed
and single, is actually not fully formulated. The wish for life, which
he revealed in the *Embassy*, is now a little more attenuated, but
it is still with him, and the conflict within him is intense. For mor-
tal man, the will to be absolute entails, however unrecognized, the
will to die, and a life-wish obscures it. In the sixteenth book, Achil-
les tries to preserve both sides of his will, both human and divine,
both life and the absolute, and such a volitional split may, perhaps,
be deemed a weakness. Certainly here he does not show the mag-
nanimity, at once self-contained and self-abnegating, which appears
in the closing parts of the poem. He has not yet accepted or imag-
ined that the honor which is solely from Zeus is as lonely as it is.
He still sees himself as triumphant in the war, acknowledged by
all as the absolute hero, "best of the Achaeans." And for this reason
he answers Patroclus as he does:

> No, it is this dread grief comes on my heart and spirit,
> Whenever, see, a man wishes to plunder his peer,
> Take back a prize, because he exceeds in sway.
> Dread grief to me is that, for I feel its pangs in my spirit. . .
>
> Well, let the past be the past; it is impossible
> Ceaselessly to rage at heart. And yet, I said
> I should not cease from anger, save when the very
> Battle and shout came to my own ships.
> But you, put my glorious gear on your shoulders,
> Lead the war-loving Myrmidons to the fight. . .
>
> Yet obey, as I put the instruction in your mind,
> So may you gain me great renown, and glory
> From the Greeks all, and they may bring me again
> The lovely girl, and offer thereto glorious gifts.
> Drive them away from the ships and return. But further, take heed, if
> Hera's lord of the loud thunder gives you glory,
> Do not you apart from me seek to do battle

With the war-loving Trojans; you will make me the more dishon-
ored;
Nor, in the proud delight of war and struggle,
Slaying Trojans, drive on to Ilium,
Lest from Olympus one of the ever-living gods
Come upon you; dearly Apollo loves them, who works his will.
But turn back, when you have won at the ships
Victory, and let the others struggle throughout the plain.
Would, O Father Zeus, and Athena and Apollo,
Not one man of the Trojans might flee death, many as they are,
Not one man of the Argives, but we two, putting off death,
Alone might break the holy crown of Troy.[45]

Achilles' vow to fight only when the fire reached his own ships
constitutes the active terms in which he has framed the absolute
for himself. This is the heroic paradigm which he embraced from
the story of Meleager, and by it he willed any and every disaster
for the Greeks, though he would save himself and his ships, to
demonstrate his self-sufficiency. This was the concrete form of his
rejection of the world where a man wishes to plunder his peer.
But now his humanity, the side of Achilles which could spare his
victims for ransom and bury Eetion, conflicts with so absolute a
moral judgment. "It is impossible ceaselessly to rage." Compassion
is also large and worthy of a hero, and Patroclus' charge that not
Thetis, the gentle sea-goddess, but the gray sea itself was his mother
has its effect. Let Patroclus go and help, if he will; for Achilles
himself to go would mean the abandonment of his whole heroic
position, an admission that his retirement was an empty threat, a
mistake. But let Patroclus help them a little, and so preserve the
setting in which he himself may emerge triumphant, with girl and
gifts. Achilles will have justice tempered, but not vitiated, by mercy;
hence the strict counseling of Patroclus not to dishonor him by
winning the war in his absence. But mingled with Achilles' concern
for his own honor is also the fear for Patroclus himself. His careful
delimitation of his friend's actions is really a statement, full of in-
sight and foresight, of who Patroclus is. He says, in effect, "You
are Patroclus, and what you do, you do out of mercy and humanity.
But these qualities will not take Troy. Do not play me, and attempt
to fight the absolute way, or you will destroy yourself, and me
too." And then come the last four lines, with their strange helpless

outburst.[46] As if he realized that by acceding to Patroclus' wish he was losing a little of his personal supremacy, his will to absolute glory takes the peculiarly unrealistic form of wishing all the Greeks and Trojans might perish, and only Patroclus and himself, "putting off death" like a pair of immortals, remain as the conquerors of Troy. In these lines, Achilles makes his nearest approach to self-deception. Caught between the jaws of his self-esteem and his magnanimity toward others, he half foresees the insoluble tragedy of his position, and reels back from it, wishing that all the world were dead except himself and his friend. He still has hope, but it is growing less and less reasonable. In the end, he will assert death for himself too.

It is significant, also, that now for the first time he associates Patroclus with himself in his wish for absolute glory. Hitherto, he had seen only himself upon the pinnacle. Gentle Patroclus was no matter for absolute glory, now or hitherto, but Achilles' own compassion is so strong in him at the moment, that he includes his friend in his own role of absolute hero. This passage is in fact the beginning of a confusion of roles between the two men. Homer regularly externalizes a spiritual or mental state in the form of an image or a god. In the present case, he has externalized the humane side of Achilles in Patroclus, and the inclusion of the latter in the vision of lonely victory over Troy is a token of the hopeless paradox of Achilles' will. How could a man be such an absolute victor, having willed death to the rest of the world, so to speak, and still have with him his humanity, in the form of Patroclus, or any other? Yet this is what Achilles desires and wills, his whole self transcendent, his human love, its object, and all.

The highest heroes are not men of delusion. They are men of clarity and purity, who will a good impossible in the world and eventually achieve it, through suffering, in their own spiritual terms. It is the will to the impossible which resembles delusion until the terms are found in which it is possible. In the end, Achilles and Patroclus do stand in the aura of isolated victory and immortal friendship which Achilles envisioned; but instead of being the ones to survive, they were the ones to die, while all the other princes, except Ajax and Antilochus, were present at the taking of Troy. Homer takes account of both the supremacy of individual prowess and the immortality of friendship later in the poem. Achilles' great *aristeia* does not actually end with the fall of Troy, but, together with the *Theomachia*, it symbolizes the ultimate victory, and in any case by its sheer force reveals Achilles as a warrior like no other. And when the ghost of Patroclus appears later, his final demand is that the ashes of Achilles be mixed with his own, in the golden urn given by Thetis.[47] The absolute and the human meet, but only after death.

But if Patroclus embodies and externalizes (from Book XI on increasingly) the humane side of Achilles, it was essentially in character for him to do so; he was a loving and compassionate fellow from the first. When he puts on the armor of Achilles, a great change comes over him. The gentlest man in the army becomes a demon-warrior, who drives the Trojans headlong from the ships, slays the redoubtable Sarpedon, utters proud, insulting speeches over his fallen enemies,[48] and sets foot on the ramparts of Troy itself, threatening to take it. Just before he is killed, he makes three great charges and slays nine men in each.[49] He even is given new epithets at the climactic moments: elsewhere, his name is modified only by his patronymic or by *hippeus*, "knight"; but when he tussles with Apollo, he is "equal to a god," and the epithet is repeated just before Apollo destroys him.[50] Otherwise, only when he emerges from his tent to go on Achilles' errand does he have any warlike epithet. Then he is "like Ares"; but here the poet is looking forward consciously to the *Patrocleia*, as is shown by the remark, "this was the beginning of his woe."[51] There can be little doubt that the change in Patroclus' character and characteristic epithets is not due simply to his presence in a battle scene. A kind of double image, as in surrealistic painting, is involved. Patroclus is playing the role of Achilles. For the moment, he has become Achilles, and acts much more like the great hero than like himself.[52] When Achilles prays to Zeus for Patroclus' safety, he seems to ask, indirectly, whether his friend can play his role adequately or not:

> . . . Give him glory, far-sighted Zeus,
> Strengthen the heart in his breast, even that Hector
> May learn whether even alone this companion of ours
> Knows how to wage the war, or if then only his hands
> Rage resistless, when I myself go to the moil of Ares.[53]

Herein Achilles all but prays Zeus to let Patroclus be adequate to represent himself. Personality in antiquity was conceived in terms of partially predetermined roles, as Meleager's story partly predetermines Achilles', and when Patroclus receives from Achilles the arms and the leadership of the Myrmidons, he receives also the heritage of glory and early death, which are not naturally his own. He cannot, of course, play Achilles' role to the full; he cannot lift the Pelian spear,[54] or slay Hector. But he can kill Hector's charioteer, and Sarpedon, and precisely like Achilles, he can almost take Troy, and be killed by Apollo in the attempt.[55] And so he becomes involved in the tragedy of Achilles. As the embodiment of Achilles' humanity, he recognizes the plight of the Greeks and will help them. But as Achilles on the field, he loses all sense of human limit, and tries to take the city. Precisely so, as epic tradition elsewhere related, Achilles himself forgot his mother's warnings in the heat of avenging Antilochus, and dies assaulting the city wall. Thus, in fact, a certain psychological truth shines through Achilles' wish that he and Patroclus alone might sack Troy. Their two roles are becoming inextricably twined. The death of Patroclus is a shadow play of the death of Achilles, a montage of one image upon another, emphasizing with mysterious inevitability the causal relationship between Patroclus' fall and the final stage of Achilles' tragedy. When Achilles' crest drops from Patroclus' head and is stained with dust for the first time in its history, Achilles is already death-devoted, already dead.[56]

It is interesting to compare the difference between Patroclus' and Hector's assumption of Achilles' arms. Zeus shakes his head at Hector in disapproval: "Poor fellow, you wear the armor of a much better man." [57] Yet Hector, presumably, is better than Patroclus whom he slew. The real inappropriateness lies in the fact that Hector cannot play the role of Achilles, whereas Patroclus could. If Hector puts on that armor, he puts on his own death, and he will not die in any person but his own. Hector runs away in Achilles' armor, whereas Patroclus, momentarily Achilles, hurled aside all caution (as he who plays Achilles must) and found death in a moment of superhuman valor. Literally, by being Achilles, he transcends himself, and this self-transcendence is symbolized in a most unique scene, by Apollo. Nowhere else in the *Iliad* does a god

directly, with his own hand, overcome a hero. The passage where
Apollo approaches Patroclus like a mist is one of the most unholy
terror, a blinding vision of the identity of glory and death. But it
belongs to Achilles more than to the man who has only for the
moment assumed the tragic mask. It is consistent with Homeric
subtlety, as well as with the requirements of the chosen plot of
the poem, that the self-transcendence and death of Achilles achieve
their poetic and emotional due in the *Patrocleia* and in the mourn-
ful horror of the fight over Patroclus' body, rather than in any
scene involving the death of the hero himself. In this way, to a
degree, the universal element receives the emphasis: a fallen hero
is a fallen hero. More important, the bitterest poignancy in Achilles'
tragedy lies not in his own death, but in that of the friend who was
so far a part of himself that he played his mortality for him. Achil-
les accepted Patroclus as his proxy as a means of being at the same
time above all other men and yet one of them, and this was, of
course, impossible and incompatible with life. To achieve at once
his supremacy over and unity with all men, Achilles must play
his mortal part himself, and not merely his divinity. His mother
gave him not only divine valor, but also a golden urn for his ashes.
Yet it was impossible to will his own death as long as he had so
great a love as Patroclus, alive in this world. Once Patroclus is
dead, Achilles is trapped in the necessity of dying, but he is also
thereby freed of all expectation and dependency on human life or
the world of men.

When Antilochus brings the news of Patroclus' death, Achilles
falls in the dust, staining his head, as his crest had been stained.[58]
A moment before, he had recalled a prophecy that the best of the
Myrmidons would die, while he himself was alive, and, like all
prophecies or the scales of Zeus, this one represents the truth as
it really is.[59] Hence, when the news comes, it occasions not only
the Reversal, or *peripety*, of the action, but it is also the Recogni-
tion, *anagnorisis*, by Achilles of his true position. He lies in the
dust "great, greatly stretched out," a phrase generally reserved for
the dead, while the maidservants beat their breasts and form a chorus
of lamentation. It is a funeral scene, in form, differing from a real
funeral only in that Achilles is as yet only symbolically dead, and
Antilochus must hold his hands to prevent him from actual self-

slaughter. Presently the mourners are joined by Thetis and a long line of Nereids, who come up from the sea.[60] Patroclus had said that not Thetis but the gray sea was Achilles' mother, and now the whole gray sea seems to fill the background, in token of the changeless world which alone can respond to Achilles' extremity, and to which he is now wholly committed. At first, his thoughts are solely on vengeance and death. He will rush out and slay Hector immediately, and fall himself when Zeus wills. More significant, even, is the fact that he curses his own wrath and himself as a burden upon the earth.[61] His whole former positon has vanished; and there is no mention of waiting till the fire reaches his own ships, or further dictating the terms in which he will reveal the divine honor which he claimed. Human ties have vanished utterly, and what remains, the inner divine force, no longer needs to feel after its appropriate terms, but reveals itself coldly in an agonized, overwhelming will to death. Achilles had given himself with his armor to Patroclus, and now he has no self.

By degrees, his self returns, but from this point on, his phases of self-consciousness come exclusively from the gods. Human affairs, though he continues to take part in them, no longer affect Achilles. Thetis first reminds him that he has no armor, but that she will bring him arms from Hephaestus. In the epic tradition generally, arms had a high significance; they were part of the whole warrior, and to lose them, even in death, was to lose not an adjunct, but a part of the heroic personality. Homer develops the theme further, in several places, but nowhere with such full meaning as in the Eighteenth *Iliad*.[62] The lost arms were given by the gods to Peleus, at his wedding with Thetis.[63] They were remarkable, but symbolized both the mortal and immortal aspects of Achilles. The new arms are to be wholly immortal, a miracle suited to a man whose mortal part no longer concerns him. Thetis, in her quiet and sorrowful foreknowledge, promises her son an apotheosis of the divine and destructive valor which alone is left to him. There is no joy in this, but the dread satisfaction is grand, inevitable, and pure.

After Thetis departs, another divine messenger arrives: Iris, sent by Hera "secretly from Zeus" to rouse Achilles to rescue the body of Patroclus.[64] One must ask why and how she came secretly from Zeus. Hitherto, Zeus has not missed any of Hera's activities, or not for long. But the answer is actually simple. The Wrath has crumbled, and so has the Plan of Zeus. Neither has been as yet formally renounced, and hence no official permission has been given to the gods to participate in the war; but for all that Hera knows her cue, having been duly informed of the process of events in her last scene with Zeus.[65] A little later, Zeus remarks wryly on her alacrity, but with no anger,[66] and from this point on, and even a little before, the gods begin to take part again in the war, before the official removal of the ban. As Achilles returns to himself, little by little, and his will to destroy the Trojans increases, the gods are gradually freed for action. Achilles questions Iris anxiously: "Who sent you?" and she answers, "Hera, secretly from Zeus." So tentatively, as if unfamiliar with himself, Achilles approaches his re-entrance into action. He argues that he has no armor; but he need not wait for armor, for externals, or visible symbols. At Iris' instruction, he goes to the top of the trench, and as he goes, miracles gather round him. With the aegis of Athena across his shoulders and Olympian fire shooting in an aura from his head, he shouts at the Trojans and sends them reeling back, while the Achaeans pull the body of Patroclus to safety. The whole scene is a singular triumph of Homer's method of externalizing states into images and action. Here Achilles, helpless and deprived of his very identity, slowly rediscovers himself, in anxiety for the corpse of his friend, and does what any helpless man would do — he shouts. But the shout is a prophecy and a self-declaration, in token of which Athena, the image of his irresistible power, shouts also.

The making of the arms is usually regarded as an interlude, an abatement of passion and a retreat into a tableau of detached symbolism.[67] But the whole Eighteenth Book, as the Reversal of the action, is necessarily the still point of the *Iliad*.[68] Before it, Achilles' will is divided; after it, his will is unified, moving him unswervingly toward death. Hereafter, he is concerned with nothing but to activate his enormous prowess, not for the rewards which it may entail, but to redeem his honor, no longer a public thing, but the secret and bitter residue of a once-bright faith in himself. But the ironical paradox is still present. Formerly he had desperately wanted to satisfy the standards and wring recognition from all; now that he no longer cares for that, and yearns only to satisfy his own burning self-esteem, his prowess takes on an indescribable terror and glory which demolishes all resistance, but leaves him still seething, still unsatisfied, still yearning for greater self-proof. Only after abandoning all human hope does he at last, in the scene with Priam, achieve his greatest communion with humanity.

There is little need to analyze in detail the forging of the arms, or the familiar wonders of the Shield. At the moment when the hero, self-doomed, is about to plunge into the final fatalities of the action, the poet universalizes that action by giving him a shield which is a summary picture of the world. Between the ocean at its rim and the sun, moon, and stars at its center, lie the cities and occupations of men: work, war, death, justice, marriage, peace, and play. One is not quite sure whether the pictures on the Shield are static or alive, Homer, in fact, is not quite sure just what kind of pictures are made by Hephaestus, whose golden automata have mind and move by themselves.[69] He seems to stand a little bewildered between the realism of the finished panels, and the limitations of the material, and says in one place:

> . . . The oxen turned in the furrows,
> Straining to come to the end of the deep new-ploughed land;
> All lay black behind them, and looked like ploughed soil,
> Yet it was gold; indeed, a very wonder was wrought.[70]

We also meet with black clusters of grapes, made of gold, and hear the lowing of cattle made of gold and tin.[71] Throughout the description, the wonderful constantly excludes the factual, till it becomes a little idle to ask learnedly after the artistic sources of this miraculous shield.[72] Yet a simile in it perhaps points to at least one model which is in the poet's consciousness. Describing the dancers, he says, carried away by his vision of dancing boys and girls:

> Sometimes round they ran on their skillful feet
> Lightly and well, as when between his hands a potter, sitting,
> Tries his fitted wheel, if it will spin.[73]

Here one suspects that, in describing the frieze of dancers, a motif not unknown to Geometric pottery, the poet's mind has moved on to the related image of the potter himself, trying his wheel. In any case, the structure of the shield in general is inconceivable apart from the Geometric scheme of running friezes, broken by metopes presenting scenes.[74] But the intention of the Shield is wonder. It is the miracle of cosmic diversity focused into formal unity and order, as the proper adornment of the unified heroic will. When he first receives it, Achilles sees only the flash of its brightness, but before the *Iliad* is over, he lives up to the fullness of its classic implications — passion, order, and the changeless inevitability of the world as it is.

From the point of view of the character of Achilles, the *aristeia* which follows in the next four books brings nothing new; it merely reveals and reiterates in various ways what has happened. Never niggardly with detail, Homer unfolds the full horror in Achilles' soul from beginning to end, sinking him in deeds of blood that totally eclipse all previous battle scenes and finally in the gruesome mutilation of his dead enemy and the immolation of twelve young captives. Homer has suppressed no repugnancy out of a wish to make his hero superficially attractive; and far from approving all these horrors, he even steps out of his epic anonymity specifically to condemn the mutilation and immolation.[75] Yet to whatever repulsive depths his violence leads him, Achilles saves himself from contempt by the fierceness of his suffering. Before he could do these things, he had to will his own death, and forsake forever all hope of joy, everything except revenge. As he puts on his divine armor, he puts in his heart unbearable grief.[76] He will no longer treaty gallantly with Hector, as he once might have done, for honorable burial of the loser's corpse.[77] If Hector can win, he may do as he pleases. Vengeance, at least, shall be absolute.

In the face of such an attitude, Agamemnon's pitiable reiteration of his proffered gifts shows as the mockery which it is. It is not enough to say that Achilles no longer wants them; he scarcely takes any notice of them.[78] He is barely persuaded by Odysseus to allow the men to eat before they fight, and reluctantly he waits while Agamemnon and others perform a rite of purification to dispose finally of the Wrath. While the others feast, he mourns for Patroclus, and refuses mortal food; he has done with mortality, except for dying, and his sustenance comes from the gods, in the form of a distillate of nectar and ambrosia.[79]

The *aristeia* of Achilles, up to the duel with Hector, must be understood through its imagery. The principal agent is, of course, Achilles himself who irresistibly drives the Trojans before him to the city, slaying them in plain and stream. But since Hector, the chief bulwark of Troy, is to be the ultimate victim of the attack, Troy by implication falls in the two books preceding the duel, and these implications overshadow to a degree the actual deeds of Achilles. In the earliest fire-and-water symbolism of Western literature, the fire of Achilles overcomes the tutelary rivers of the Troad, while the battle of the gods plays its semifarcical mirror-show of the city's fall. The static symbolism engraved on the cosmic Shield is now answered in the dynamic terms of action with universal import, and if the *Theomachia* itself passes from solemn beginnings to the bombastic and finally to the ridiculous, it nevertheless serves to accentuate more poignantly the human tragedy of Achilles and Hector. It is they who have set these gigantic wheels in motion, and for them it is not sport but earnest battle for the highest stakes in the life of each. For Achilles, this is the death march, the bitterest phase of his conception of the absolute. It wills death not only for Hector and himself but for all the Trojans whom he meets. There is little rancor in such hatred, only an engrossing vision of death, which sweeps aside what are now mere trivialities — mercy, ransom, and hope:

> No, friend, die, you also. Why do you mourn so?
> Dead is Patroclus too, who was far better than you.
> Do you not see how I, even I, am great and comely?
> Born of a noble father, a goddess the mother who bore me,
> Yet, take heed, over me hang death and implacable fate.
> Dawn there shall be, or evening, or some high noon,
> When in the war some man will take life from me also,
> Smiting perchance with a spear, or arrow from the bowstring.[80]

Achilles speaks like the very angel of death; death only is purity. The last claim which life can assert over him is to end life in avenging Patroclus. His perspective is as yet narrower than it will be later, but he is at least one with himself.

In one way or another, Achilles' character reveals itself through relations, direct or indirect, with almost every character in the poem, but there are four primary relationships, which frame the four main phases of his development. The first may be called his relation either with Agamemnon or Briseis, since both are equally important in making clear the conflict between externalities and spiritual conviction. The second is, of course, the relationship with Patroclus, embodying the division of will between absolute and human claims. The third centers around Hector, and the last, Priam. Hector possesses such sympathetic charm, that it seems almost invidious to mention his limitations. Yet his gentle, knightly appeal, his loyal devotion to wife and city, his simple bravery, and even his one momentary failure of nerve, all of which make him so immediately understandable, have to a degree unjustly drawn sympathy away from Achilles, who is none the worse for Hector's virtues. Both men are, in one sense of the word, tragic: both experience action, recognition, and doom; both are moved by noble motives and both are caught in the consequences of their own decisions. But there are great differences also. Though both defend causes which are, in the end, lost, Achilles' cause, the achievement of an absolute standard in life, was from the first impossible, and, seeing that it is impossible, he wills the absolute standard in death. Moreover, his perception of his own position is, at every moment, as clear as temporal circumstances permit; he is never deluded or willfully blind. By contrast, Hector's cause was not an impossibility; cities do not always fall, and though Hector foresees his own death as likely enough, he behaves as though he well might win. And perhaps for this very reason, he is subject to delusion. The Plan of Zeus includes rousing in Hector the hope of pushing the Achaeans into the sea, and this is a delusion deliberately imposed on Hector by Zeus and fostered throughout the Battle.[81] But as a rule, the gods affect men through their natures, and the limits of Hector's insight are sketched as early as the exquisite scene with Andromache in Book VI. This scene, memorable chiefly for its presentation of man's world and woman's world, at first juxtaposed separately and then mysteriously unified in the images of the infant Astyanax and Andromache's laughter amid tears, is intimately bound to the rest of the *Iliad* in that it solemnly prepares the death of Hector, and treats him as one already dead.[82] The three women he talks with — Hecuba, Helen, and his wife — are the three chief mourners of the closing scene of the poem; after his departure, Andromache leads a choir of lamentation for him, "though still alive, in his own house," [83] and his own long, sorrowful speech is heavy with prophecy.[84] And yet for all that prophetic air, Hector immediately contradicts himself in the prayer for Astyanax. He prays that Astyanax may rule over the Trojans and be considered better than his father, rejoicing his mother's heart with the spoils of his enemies.[85] Clearly it is the poet, and not Hector, who feels the irony in this prayer. Hector has no clear knowledge of the future. He is doing his best for the city; he is realistic enough to know that he may well lose all, and brave enough to struggle on in any case, but he has no foreknowledge. He has hope, and his last words to Andromache are the truest: I will die when I die; do not be too afraid; let us return to our tasks.[86] He sees the present task; and not out of any transcendent vision of himself or anything else, but, as in the case of Ajax, out of loyalty and *aidôs* he performs what he can.

In Hector, the psychological soil is ripe, not, certainly, for any and every delusion, but for precisely the forsaken hope which possesses him during Achilles' absence from the field. The natural thought that victory is now possible becomes, after the first day's fighting, a boastful assurance, mingled with fear, even, that the Achaeans will run away during the night, and thus escape.[87] He sets watch-fires to prevent this, and in a long speech announces that dawn will bring the day that shall have no morrow:

> Hoping in Zeus and all the other gods, I declare,
> Hence from this place I shall drive these death-borne dogs. . .
> Early by light of dawn in war gear arming ourselves,
> We shall arouse by the hollow ships keen Ares. . .
>
> He [Diomedes] shall tomorrow know his valor, whether
> It will sustain my threatening spear; but among the first, I fancy,
> Wounded he shall fall, and with him many companions,
> When the sun rises on tomorrow. O would that I,
> Being immortal and ageless all my days, I might so
> Venge myself as Athena and Apollo take vengeance,
> Seeing this day now brings destruction on the Argives! [88]

Zeus' omens of thunder and lightning flatter this hope into a blinding obsession, so that Hector fails to see certain other omens betokening the fact that the Wrath of Achilles is not the whole truth, that the Achaeans will be saved in the end. And as if to emphasize

the persistence of Hector's delusion, Homer introduces a surprising
character, the commoner Pulydamas, who is not possessed by
princely presumptions but gifted with insight into omens. There
can be little reason for Pulydamas' existence in the poem except
for him to point out certain truths which are there to be seen, if
anyone cares to look. As the Trojans, having crossed the trench,
gather themselves for the assault on the wall, an eagle appears with
a snake in its talons. The Trojans are frightened, and Pulydamas
warns Hector that their attack will end disastrously. Hector sweeps
aside his counsel contemptuously, and bids him put trust in Zeus'
Plan.[89] Elsewhere, on two occasions, Hector takes Pulydamas' ad-
vice, with good results, and one of the other leaders who disregards
it is slain miserably.[90] He is obviously intended to be the man who
sees clearly, and in Book XVIII, Homer openly says so, altering
his usual epithet "blameless" to "prudent," and stating that he alone
looked both "forward and backward," the regular expression for
a balanced judgment.[91] On this occasion, Pulydamas warns Hector
not to camp on the plain now that Achilles has returned to the
fight. But Hector's mind is obsessed. He repeats his challenges of
the evening before and boasts that if Achilles comes out against him,
it will be the worse for Achilles; the Trojans shout their approval,
and Homer explains that Athena had robbed them of their senses.[92]
Then the scene suddenly shifts; the Achaeans are mourning for
Patroclus, and Achilles is saying:

> No, Zeus accomplishes not for men all their plans;
> Fated it is for the same earth to cover us both,
> Here in Troy, for never shall the knightly Peleus
> Receive me coming home again in his palace,
> Nor Thetis my mother, but here the earth will keep me.[93]

There could scarcely be a more pointed, and at the same time more
sympathetic, confrontation of delirious hope and true tragic fore-
sight.

Hector comes to the truth at last, but he seems reluctant to be-
lieve that it is as terrible as it is. A great part of his gallant courage
had been based on the hope of success, and when that hope is
shattered, he has to find new resources which are not forthcoming
at once. Pausing alone before the Scaean Gates, while the others
flee to safety, he remembers Pulydamas' words, and recognizes that

he himself is responsible for the present defeat. Rather than face the rebukes of his friends, he will face Achilles; but even as he thinks this, his mind veers from reality, and pictures in detail a scene of treaty with the terror which is approaching. He will lay aside shield and spear; he will offer Helen, gifts, everything the city contains, oaths, anything.[94] Then suddenly he remembers who his enemy is, and the dream vanishes:

> Not now can it be, that I of tree and cliff
> Prattle to him, such things as girl and youth,
> Girl and youth, prattle in each other's ear.[95]

Even as he recalls himself, the image of lovers intervenes and tempts his mind to linger on it, sapping away his resolution. Like a dove before a hawk he runs, past the watch tower, the wild fig tree by the wall, past the two springs where the women used to wash their clothes in time of peace. He passes all the tokens of his life and the life of the city which was his to defend; the very cause for which he has fought binds him to life in such a way that he cannot face this angel of death, and he must flee. Homer makes the pursuit seem interminable by inserting, besides the similes where time also stops, the scene where Zeus, in his eternity, is moved to pity and wishes to save Hector. But it is hopeless, and the nightmare goes on,

> As in a dream impotent a pursuer hunts one who flees,
> Neither can one escape nor the other catch.[96]

One almost hears Hector praying to wake up; it must be a dream. Then comes the final delusion. Athena, taking the form of Deiphobus, pretends to have come to help Hector. Hope wells up again, and he stands and faces Achilles, but even now he tries to bargain, to set the duel within the intelligible limits of humanity; let them guarantee each other decent burial, whoever conquers.[97] But Achilles no longer knows humanity, and appropriately enough retorts in images of wild animals:

> Hector, speak not to me, ruinous wretch, of agreements,
> As between lions and men there are no sacred oaths,
> Neither do wolves and sheep have like tempers,
> So between you and me no friendship.[98]

The battle is in terms which Hector has never before conceived. Though he could strip off Patroclus' arms and threaten to disfig-

ure his corpse in the heat of battle, the cold and balanced view
which could imagine such for himself had never been his, even as
there had been inconsistency between his gloomy vision of himself
dead and his wife in slavery, and the prayer for Astyanax. He is
too committed to life to see glory and death as one. The absolute
stands before him, and instead of grappling with it, he does every-
thing to avoid it. But he cannot avoid it, and it is only when the
false Deiphobus disappears that Hector's last delusion vanishes:

> Hector then understood in his heart, and he said:
> Ah then, surely the gods have summoned me to death. . .
>
> Verily now an evil death is near me, and not afar,
> Not to be shunned; for thus long since, even thus, it pleased
> Zeus and the son of Zeus who smites at will, who in former time
> Eagerly rescued me; but now my fate overtakes me.
> Yet, let me not in default of deed and glory perish,
> But doing something great, for future men to learn . . .[99]

And now the image of the dove is replaced by an image of an
eagle, as Hector, sword in hand, rushes at Achilles and meets his
death. In his last instant, he sees the whole truth; in the face of it,
the flaw which false hope had made in his courage is cured, and he
meets Achilles like an equal.

In presenting the *aristeia* of Achilles almost wholly through its
effect on others, and especially Hector, Homer has done not merely
what was most dramatic, but also the only thing he could do. We
know the absolute only as it impinges on human life, and the angel
of death can be seen only by him who dies. Yet the whole *aristeia*
is a revelation of Achilles himself, and a peculiar effect arises from
its varying perspectives. At first one sees Achilles only dimly, wad-
ing through water, obscured by the blinding glow of fire, or
glimpsed at a distance between the shadowy figures of the con-
tending gods. As Book XXII opens, he is clearer, but still seen at a
distance, racing over the plain. Then he is envisioned through the
various images of terror in Hector — hawk, race-horse, hunting
dog, nightmare, or the blazing and beautiful evening star. Only
when Hector lies on the ground does the tumult of imagery sud-
denly cease, and there in a glare of finality he stands, victorious
and dismissing the prophecy of his own death as a thing already

accomplished, an outworn truism. What slowly comes clear to Hector by the same road comes clear to the hearer or reader, the real supremacy of Achilles over himself as over all others.

If Homer had ended at this point, Achilles would still be a tremendous character, and the *Iliad* would still be a great poem. It would be a little like *Macbeth*, however, in presenting a man whose conviction of individual autonomy, fanned by images of supernatural authority, carries him to commanding stature, yet self-ruined, utterly isolated from the rest of humanity, and more than a little forbidding in his violence. But such an ending would be completely inappropriate to Achilles, whose violence, however terrifying, cannot be looked upon as criminal. It is the extremity of self-assertion in war; it is condemned by the poet and renounced at last by Achilles, but it is in no sense a transgression of the heroic code whereby to the victor belonged any and every right of spoil. Rather it is that code pressed to its logical conclusion, after which must come a new insight. And it is only in the last two books of the *Iliad*, where Homer frames the new insight, that the character of Achilles achieves its end.

In his *aristeia*, Achilles activated the absolute in the terms in which he had conceived it for himself, and these terms were: the vindication of his honor in avenging Patroclus, supreme victory over the enemy, and the final willing of his own doom. The absolute is the ability and right of the heroic individual to perceive — or better, to conceive — law for himself, and then prove his case by action. The Quarrel, Wrath, Plan of Zeus, and *aristeia* demonstrate Achilles' conception of the law of himself, and prove it to be true. But all such conception, though godlike, is not the work of a god, but of a human being. Its force and purity may define and shape the will of the gods, as the Wrath defines and shapes the Plan of Zeus, but the hero remains a man. The conflict of the *Patrocleia* was precisely this. The absolute will, the vision of supreme individual autonomy, conflicts with the sense of common humanity, and such a conflict, pressed to a conclusion, becomes the conflict between the will to death and the will to live. Once Achilles has abandoned the latter, as he does after Patroclus' death, he feels free to ignore his sense of common humanity, and he does so for a while. But the very fact that all heroic conception and action is only possible to the human creature cannot be forgotten. Patroclus is dead, but his ghost returns. Heroism is the paradox of permanence abiding in the ephemeral; the transcendent will is like a tall tree, but once it has blossomed, the human soil from which it grew takes on a new and unexpected beauty.

The warlike marvels which Achilles has performed bring him little satisfaction. He calls to Patroclus that he has done all that he promised, and hurls Hector's body prone before the bier.[100] The mourning goes on, and though Achilles takes some part apparently in the feast, he refuses to wash the blood from his hands.[101] Then he goes and lies on the seashore by night, but his sleep is disturbed by the ghost of Patroclus begging for burial:

> You sleep, but you have forgotten me, Achilles;
> Not in life were you careless of me, but now when I am dead.[102]

What can be the meaning of this accusation, when Achilles can think of nothing but Patroclus? While his friend was alive, Achilles had listened to him, considered his nature, yielding to his claim upon him. Now he is dead, Achilles' actions are appropriate to himself, but not to Patroclus. What the dead wants is burial, burial in human decency, and above all, burial with Achilles himself in token of everlasting friendship. Hardened as he seems, Achilles is agonized by the vision of his dearest earthly tie, and crying out, "Why did you come?" he promises all that the shade demands. He tries to catch it, but it vanishes and his hands meet each other with a clap.[103]

The funeral scene which follows bulges with the enormity of Achilles' grief. Indescribable amounts of wood make the hundred-foot-square pyre; the Myrmidons march in full array carrying the corpse to it; sheep and cattle are slaughtered on it; jars of honey and ointment, four horses and two pet dogs are brought; the twelve Trojan captives are immolated; Achilles lays his lock of hair, dedicated to the Spercheius for his safe return, in the hand of the dead, a final token that he will remain with his friend in Troy. Then, since the world at large must feel the pressure of such loss and grief, the pyre will not burn until special winds are summoned from far away. As always, the divine wheels turn when Achilles acts. At last, the winds come over the sea, raising great waves, the pyre burns, and all night Achilles pours libations and calls to the shade of Patroclus. At dawn he sleeps a little, exhausted, beside the dying flames, and is promptly wakened by the arrival of the other princes. But something has now at least partly spent itself; the embers are quenched at Achilles' direction, and "the deep ash falls in." [104] The deadly fire of the *Iliad* dies away, and the bones of Patroclus are laid at rest.

With infinite courtesy and detachment, Achilles now prepares the funeral games. The man who had resented being deprived of prizes and visible rewards becomes the dispenser of them, and he provides them in lavish and lordly quantities. He takes no part in the games himself, pointing out simply that he would take first prize.[105] Nobody gainsays him. Achilles has returned to society as its master, quiet-voiced, a little aloof, but just and generous, doubling the prizes freely and adding extra ones.[106] Possessions are meaningless, but the courtesy with which they may be given, the honor rightly accorded to ability, is the first law which Achilles observes after his return to his colleagues, and rightly, since it was the breach of this law which drove him away. If he had upset the balance, he now begins to restore it. Order slowly spreads around him in a widening ring. The full meaning of the Shield, which was order as well as passion, begins to come true, and in the light of it, all the principal figures of the poem rehearse their proper roles briefly in review, before the scene again confines itself to Achilles alone.

For all the emotional relief of the funeral and his controlled conducting of the games, Achilles is still far from being at peace with himself. The others all sleep:

. . . But Achilles
Wept for his dear companion, nor did sleep
Seize him, the all-subduer, but he turned hither and thither,
Yearning after Patroclus, his young manhood and good strength,
All he had ventured with him, and sorrows he suffered,
Wading through wars of men and grievous seas.
All this in his recollection, he shed full tears,
Sometimes lying on his side, sometimes turning
Face up, sometimes prone; then starting upright
Roving along the sea-strand he wandered, and the dawn appearing
Found him still along the sea and the headlands.

Then he would yoke to his chariot the swift horses,
Binding Hector to drag at the cart's tail,
Thrice around the tomb of the fallen son of Menoetius;
Then in his tent he would cease, and let the corpse lie
Stretched face down in the dirt.[107]

This passage begins as a description of the specific night after the funeral games, but the verbs become iteratives halfway through, and it is apparent that the situation went on for some time. Later we learn that it went on for nine days and nights.[108] Apollo and the other gods, except Hera, are angry, and want Hermes to steal away the corpse. Zeus points out that this is impossible, however, because Achilles' mother comes to him night and day.[109] This is a surprising remark, on the face of it. Thetis is by no means literally always present with Achilles; at the moment Zeus speaks, she is in the depths of the sea between Samos and Imbros.[110] Hermes cannot steal from Achilles because the divine, or absolute, side of the hero's nature, sometimes symbolized in Thetis, really is triumphant, and is as commanding as a god itself. Hera, in fact, states the case neatly in the comparison between the ultimate values to be set upon Hector and Achilles: Hector is a mortal and sucked a mortal breast, but Achilles is the son of a goddess, whom Hera herself fostered.[111] Or, it may be looked at this way: the gods have espoused the cause of Achilles' honor, except for Apollo, who represents the dignity of Hector; the same gods, therefore, cannot cheat the man whom they have vindicated. Yet, their timeless vision of things as a whole, especially in Zeus,[112] foreknows that Achilles will learn better than to torment the dull earth; they know more of his magnanimity than he does at the moment, but he himself must activate it.

Zeus' refusal to allow Hermes to steal the corpse is his assertion that Achilles is his own master, and deserves to be. Divinity shall act in him as before, but with a wider vision of the heroic self. So Thetis is dispatched to Achilles. Divine and humane at once, she is the proper beginning of Achilles' new outlook upon humanity, and she begins with motherly tenderness, reminding him of his own human needs, food and love. But when she tells him of the gods' attitude and their demand that he accept ransom for Hector, Achilles yields so quickly and easily that, once more, as so often in Homer, it is manifest that the gods can teach a man nothing which he has not already learned and willed.[113] The god in such scenes is the clear moment of insight and decision, and it is significant that Achilles never resists or argues with a god, except Iris in Book XVIII, where momentarily he is completely lost to himself. Here, he yields all upon the mere prompting, and even the point about food and love is taken up later.

But Hermes, however he is denied his function as a thief, becomes an important motif in the book. At the command of Zeus, he is to escort Priam safely to and from Achilles.[114] Iris first comes and prompts the old king to go to the Achaean camp, and Homer never makes more explicit than here the internal nature of the gods' messages, as Priam says to Hecuba:

Madam, from Zeus to me an Olympian messenger came,
To go to the ships of the Achaeans, and loose my son,
Bringing gifts to Achilles, such as will please his heart.
Come now, tell me this, how does it seem to your mind?
Terribly my own stress and spirit urge me of myself
Thither, to go to the ships in the broad camp of the Achaeans.[115]

The gods have again suggested only what Priam's own "stress and spirit" willed quite by itself. His decision is already taken, despite the apparent consulting of Hecuba, whose warnings he disregards. As he goes, however, the Trojans bewail him "as one going to his death," and from here on the journey takes a strange turn.[116] It takes the form of the journey to the dead, motifs from the familiar folk tale entering one by one. Hermes, the escort, does not appear at once; Priam and his herald meet him in the darkness by the tomb of Ilus, a sort of terminus between the two worlds.[117] After a cryptic conversation, in which Hermes reveals more knowledge than a stranger should have, Hermes agrees to be their guide, and boasts that they could have no better one.[118] But he is also the Guide of the Dead, Necropompus; for Hector lies in the camp in one sense, but he also lies in the land of the dead, and so does Achilles. Hence a double image evolves; the Scamander, which they must cross, becomes the river of folk tale between the living and dead, and the heavily barred doors of Achilles' courtyard, of which no mention has ever previously been made, doubtless arise from the forbidding triple walls of the city of the dead.[119] So too, the beautiful god-like master of that walled court then fills the role of the king of the dead, an image which is again applied to him in the Underworld scene of the *Odyssey*.[120]

In other mythological stories, as in that of Orpheus and Eurydice, when the king of the dead gives back one who has fallen into his realm, it is a token of the power of love to move the immovable, to create life out of death, and work miracle in the name of infinite compassion. Achilles is looked upon by all as being fully as iron-hearted as Hades,[121] and yet, when Priam appears in his hut, the immovable is moved. Since he has renounced his own life, Achilles can look, as it were, from a distance upon the living and their emotions, including his own. And the very detachment of his vision brings him closer than he has ever been before to a real communion with his human fellows. In a sense, Achilles has attained the truly classical ideal, which appears in all Hellenic art of the best period — that mysterious union of detachment and immediacy, of passion and order. Though Achilles gives up the excess of vengeance, which, in view of his humane side, had never been really appropriate to him, he does so without repenting or negating his nature as a whole. He is still the man of indomitable intensity and fierceness. He threatens Priam with death, if he should anger him; for this yielding to ransom is not to be considered a correction, but a completion of his quest for honor:

> Anger me not, old man, now; quite of myself I am planning
> Hector's release to you, and from Zeus a messenger came to me.[122]

Ransom is in the context of the same god as revenge had been. There is no repentance here, nor rejection of the divine self-assumption in favor of humanity. It is an expansion of the assumption to include humanity. And Achilles goes and personally supervises the decent arrangement of Hector's body, and finally, with supreme courage and self-mastery, lifts him with his own hands onto the bier, praying as he does so to Patroclus to understand.[123] Achilles has fulfilled himself: his divinity and his humanity are one, and though the shade of Patroclus does not answer, one feels inevitably that the share of the ransom promised him is a token which that gentle ghost can accept with approval.

The restoration of dignity to the human scheme revolves quietly around several central motifs. The first is, of course, parenthood.

It is Thetis who comes to Achilles; Hera weighs the two heroes in the scale of their respective mothers; Hecuba appears. Priam, as universal father, is more important. He beseeches Achilles in the name of his own father, Peleus, and Achilles finds the resemblance.[124] He builds upon it himself:

So also the gods gave glorious gifts to Peleus,
Right from his birth; for he excelled all other men
Happy and wealthy, and he ruled over the Myrmidons,
And the gods gave him, mortal though he was, a goddess for wife.
Yet, even upon him the god set evil, for not to him
Rose a race of flourishing sons in his halls;
No, he had one child, all out of season, nor will I ever
Care for him in old age, for here, far away from my land,
Here in Troy I sit, troubling you and your children.
You too, old man; we have heard you were fortunate once;
All that Lesbos northward, Prince Makar's land, contains,
Phrygia, too, to the south, and the boundless Hellespont —
These, they say, old man, you surpassed in wealth and sons.
Yet the heavenly ones have brought this sorrow upon you,
Always wars and slaughter of men about your city.
Up and endure, nor lament unceasingly in your heart;
It will avail you nothing.[125]

Life progresses from its beginning in hopeful assets, and proceeds generally to loss, misery and despair. Old men, fathers, have lived slowly through what Achilles has experienced in the few days' action of the *Iliad*, and the famous image of the two jars of good and evil is appropriate to this old man's retrospect.[126] Priam and Achilles see life whole, and with the freedom of men on the last verge of time, they forget the present circumstances, and admire each other's beauty.[127]

Three other motifs appear very subtly to restore the human scheme: food, sleep, and love. Thetis admonished the sleepless Achilles to eat, and Priam also has neither eaten nor slept.[128] Now Achilles, with deep tenderness, presses food on his guest, recounting the story of Niobe. Niobe too achieved an absolute, for her perfection of grief at length turned her to stone; nevertheless, all suffering is in a human cause, and Niobe remembered food as long as her humanity lasted.[129] Food is served, and sleep follows closely upon it; and then, in a single line, Briseis reappears, for the first time since her return in Book XIX.[130] Thetis' suggestion had gone unanswered in the earlier scene, but all things, Briseis as well, are now in place. Achilles can now, though on a different footing, take part again in the ephemeral simplicities of the brief life which remains to him.

The *Iliad*, and therewith the character of Achilles, is deeper than all analysis. It is the earliest and yet the completest unfolding of that heroic vision which motivated so much of Greek culture. At many points, it is possible to see how Homer has built his conception out of the old materials, and made the first tragic hero from assumptions and qualities inherent in the earlier heroes of more primitive epic. But the miracle remains that he, and apparently he first, imagined the transcendence of the older scheme by a figure who would typify, not material triumph, but the triumph of the spirit amid self-destruction, and that he could dramatize this paradox as the search for the integrity of the self against a panoramic background involving all the forces of the world, human and divine. To ask how much Homer created here for himself is to invite endless subjective speculation, but it is safe to say that the baffling vision of self-destruction with eternal glory was native to Greek air, and that Homer was the first to frame it in the symbols of poetry and canonize it for the succeeding ages of the Hellenic, and especially the Athenian, mind.

X

FATE, TIME, AND THE GODS

IT was said earlier that Homer often objectifies the internal states of his characters into visible objects, other persons, or gods. So the weariness and relief of Odysseus find expression, at the end of the Fifth *Odyssey*, not in direct self-revelation by the man himself, but in the contrast of the peaceful river and windless thicket with the storm and shipwreck that went before. So too, the madness of the suitors is objectified in a vision of judgment caught only by Theoclymenus the seer, who suddenly sees the walls streaked with blood, and the hall full of ghosts.[1] The god who assists a hero on the battlefield or elsewhere is, for the moment at least, no more than a symbol of that hero's ability, or of the special circumstances in which he finds himself. Yet any symbol involves a comparison of associated meanings which affect the mind simultaneously; a discursive analysis of them is never wholly satisfactory, because their shimmering, instantaneous effect is lost thereby, and that effect is itself part of the meaning. It is not enough to say, for instance, that Athena, in the Fifth *Iliad*, represents the valor of Diomedes; she also represents the limits of that valor, as we have seen, as well as, in a more general way, the idea of victorious battle; moreover, her personality as a divine being is never lost, for all the meaning of her associations. Perhaps there is even a touch of poetic justice in her, when she directs Diomedes' spear against the truce-breaker Pandarus.[2] Yet, when it is remembered that Pandarus was inspired by Athena herself to break the truce, one sees how little the figures of the gods were bound to any moral or theological idea. Their appearances, insofar as they can be explained as organic to the human situation, represent as a rule an extended access of power, a dimension momentarily transcendental, reflecting in various contexts and forms the deep-seated Hellenic association of heroic force with absolute being. In the case of Diomedes, the absolute is limited by special rules stated by Athena herself: he is to fight with no gods whom he cannot overcome, which is to say, he is forbidden to be tragic. Patroclus, on the other hand, meets the absolute in hostile form, and fulfills the tragic pattern. The form which the absolute takes in each case defines the hero's character; hence, even its absence, as in the case of Ajax, takes on meaning.

Homer certainly did not invent this method of objectifying states into divinities; such a process must be one of the formative elements in the growth of any polytheistic religion. If one asks wherein Homer's part lay, again it must be sought in the control imposed upon the complex possibilities of the traditional procedure. Like the characters of the *Iliad*, the gods of the *Iliad* are refashioned, within the limits of their assigned spheres, to fit the poem, and there is no reason to believe that they would not be different in a different one. Such liberty in dealing with the gods was always the rule with the Greek poets, and the differences between the Zeus of the *Iliad* and the Zeus of the *Odyssey* are no more evidence for a difference in age or authorship of the epics, than are the rather opposite conceptions of Zeus which appear in the *Prometheus* and the *Agamemnon* of Aeschylus. Very little in the way of generalities about theological attitudes in Homer's time or before can be made, therefore. The epics present the gods confined in poetic contexts, so that, apart from a few references to cults, we can know little about the official or popular religion. In the pre-Homeric phase, before the emergence of the long epic, there must have been a large body of local and partly contradictory material about the divinities; some traditions would be recent, some as old as Mycenae and even older, some foreign, or pre-Hellenic. If Homer and Hesiod named and defined the gods, as Herodotus says,[3] it must have been in the sense that by a process of selection they established certain views (and perhaps also names) which later became the preferred ones, and which could even be looked upon as, in a way, canonical. Yet, though Hesiod shows concern with systematic theology, the controlling principle in Homer's selection is not theological theory, but poetic context; and in this respect, he is entirely classical. As in the dramatists, and especially Sophocles, the gods of Homer are symbolic predicates of action, character, and circumstance.[4]

Perhaps the clearest example of what is meant to be found in the relation between Aphrodite and the two lovers who are the cause of the war. Paris diverges widely from the heroic norm, having few pretensions as a man of battle. What warlike successes he has, such as the wounding of Diomedes, or eventually, the slaying of Achilles, are due to his bow and arrows, with which he picks off men from afar, to the contempt of the stalwart fellows who stand up to their enemies with spears. He is regularly compared to a woman, for indeed women, not war, are his natural sphere.[5] Reproved by Hector in damning terms for quailing before Menelaus, he replies mildly, admitting his shortcomings, and offering to try to vanquish them. He contrasts himself with Hector, whose mind is "like an axe," describing his own nature as the gift of Aphrodite, about which he had no choice.[6] In this speech, for all the causative role which he assigns to the goddess in the formation of his temperament, Paris is saved from being a mere puppet by his self-consciousness; he can appreciate Hector's point, and can say of the gods' gifts, "No one would choose them willingly." And in actuality, the causative role here given Aphrodite is only apparent; Paris had, in some sense willingly, chosen the gift of Aphrodite when he awarded her the golden apple so that her power over him merely expresses the usual hindsight, by which also a successful man is regarded as "dear to Zeus."

An even more evident case is that of Helen. Helen no longer loves Paris, but she is trapped. The scene in which the goddess in disguise summons her to rejoin him in their chamber is one of intense and subtle poignancy, as Helen, in all her guilty nobility, tries to resist the consequences of her erotic liberty; Aphrodite describes the beauty of Paris, whom she has just saved from Menelaus:

Thus she spoke, and aroused the spirit in her bosom;
And forthwith recognizing the fair throat of the goddess,
Her breasts desire-laden, and her gleaming eyes,
Taken aback she spoke, and called her by name:
Lady, why do you so desire to deceive me?
Where will you, on and on among well-founded cities,
Lead me, in Phrygia or lovely Maeonia,
Thither wherever someone of mortal men is your darling?
Now because Menelaus has vanquished divine Alexander
And wills to lead me home again, me the hateful,
Therefore now with a crafty heart are you here?
Go, sit by him yourself, renounce the way of the gods,
Turning your feet no longer toward Olympus.
Whimper forever about him, and keep him safe,
Till he might make you his wife, or better, his slave.
Thither I will not go, for a great reproach it would be,
To come to his couch; and the Trojan women behind me
All will scold. And I have numberless agonies at heart.
Angrily then answered the divine Aphrodite:
Do not arouse me, wretch, lest in anger I cast you off,
Loathing you then as much as now surpassingly I have loved.
Lest I contrive you an ugly hatred amid both hosts,
Trojan and Greek alike, and you go down an evil path.[7]

In this scene, Aphrodite represents a great deal more than the mere
power of love. Though Helen yields and goes to Paris, she goes
not out of love at all, but out of the fear of her present position.
Her charm has won her the protection of the Trojans; even the
old men are touched and moved. But if she loses that protection,
rejects Paris, and relies on anything but her erotic supremacy, she
has little to look for except a grim punishment. Helen is, in fact,
driven by her guardian goddess to the depths of humiliation in
order to save her own life; yet the scene, as Homer has dramatized
it, follows with infallible precision the psychology in the woman's
mind, with its three phases of temptation, disgust, and finally fear,
as she remembers the trap in which she has put herself. If Helen's
will is overborne, it is not overborne by the simple, univocal sym-
bol of Aphrodite, as equal to sex. The goddess is used as a sounding
board for all the emotions which rise out of Helen's complex knot
of circumstances. Her reproof and even insult to Aphrodite is pre-
cisely analogous to her continued self-condemnation, and testifies
to the moral dilemma which confronts her throughout the poem.

As Homer has drawn her, Aphrodite is the predicative image of all Helen's deeds, attitudes, and circumstances; and if Paris claims that Aphrodite has made him what he is, certainly with Helen, the goddess derives her aspect from the woman.

In the *Iliad*, the most central and basic association between a god and a hero is that between Achilles and Zeus. It is commonly observed that Zeus in the *Odyssey* defends universal justice, while in the *Iliad* he is arbitrary, even violent, and controlled by nothing, except "fate," of which he is occasionally reminded by Hera, or Athena.[8] The statement is true enough, in a way, but like so many of its kind, it is a mere generality upon symptoms, without reference to causes or notice of exceptions. In the *Iliad*, for instance, Zeus is not wholly unconcerned with the idea of universal justice, in the social sense.[9] His arbitrary temper has been taken as proof of the poem's primitive outlook, in contrast to the more advanced and dignified conception of the *Odyssey*; but here again an important distinction must be drawn. The speeches which Zeus makes about his own power, the threats he utters, and his reminders of former violence, are primitive enough material; he can hoist up the earth by its golden chain, thrash Hera, maim his adversaries with lightning, hurl the gods about the golden house, or pitch them out of heaven altogether. Such visions give us perhaps a glimpse of what the Mycenaean Age admired and expected in its gods. But these are echoes. In the *Iliad*, Zeus maims nobody, and hurls no one out of heaven. He takes no part in the *Theomachia*, where his force would certainly be decisive. Hera's outright deceit and disobedience elicits a dire threat; but her husband accepts her very dubious oath of innocence, smiles, and appeals to her for more cooperation.[10] His other rebukes to her are, for the most part, mere verbal ironies, springing from weariness with her maniacal hatred of the Trojans. Indeed, for all his boasts, threats, and imperious commands, Zeus is remarkably patient with the repeated attempts to disobey him, and, with two or three exceptions, his utterances to the other gods show a firm but gentle dignity. The impression of arbitrary force and irresponsibility rests upon one, and only one, thing which Zeus does: his defense of Achilles' cause.

When Zeus promises to honor Achilles, a kind of identification with him begins to grow, and from this time on Zeus slowly ac-

quires the characteristics which have made him appear violent and
irresponsible. The so-called Plan of Zeus is the immediate offspring
of the Wrath of Achilles. Zeus in one place even speaks of the
Wrath as his own,[11] and all that is arbitrarily willful or passionately
intransigent in Zeus is simply a reflex of those characteristics in
the hero. In one place, indeed, Athena seems to say explicitly that
Zeus feels no obligation to behave with justice. Restraining the
aroused Ares from going to the field to avenge his son, she says:

> Instantly will he, Trojans proud and Achaeans
> Leaving, come upon us, and bringing tumult to Olympus
> Seize, one after another, guilty and guiltless alike.[12]

But Athena is speaking distinctly of Zeus' present behavior, incom-
prehensible to them all, the behavior by which he is accomplishing
his Plan. Moreover, the god seems to derive his failure to distin-
guish the innocent and the guilty from Achilles, of whom Pa-
troclus says earlier to Nestor:

> Well you know, god-nurtured old man, what sort he is,
> Fearful man; he could find fault even with the guiltless.[13]

But when Thetis comes to Olympus with her plea, Zeus is mild
enough, and a little concerned over having to irritate Hera, if he
complies.[14] With the partial yielding of Achilles in Book XVI, all
trace of violence disappears from Zeus, though he does not offi-
cially return to his customary detachment until the council at the
beginning of XX, which corresponds to Achilles' official renuncia-
tion of the Wrath. Within the limits of the Wrath, Zeus appears
to the other gods, or at least to those favoring the Greeks, as the
distorter of the order of things, recklessly imposing defeat upon
an army ultimately destined to be victorious. He ceases to reflect,
for the time being, what must happen because it ultimately did
happen, namely, the taking of the city; temporarily, he reflects
what must happen if Achilles retires. Zeus, who defends neither
side of the war in general, is the only god who could act in this
way: his detachment from any *parti pris* is a little like Achilles' own
before the Wrath:

> . . . Not at all are they [the Trojans] guilty in my sight;
> Never yet have they driven my cattle away, nor my horses,

Never yet in Phthia the fertile, mother of heroes,
Have they destroyed my harvest, for verily, many between us
Lie the shadowy mountains and echoing sea.[15]

Achilles' motive for coming to Troy is not enmity for the Trojans; his motive is glory, or himself as he is and must be, and his cause is appropriately adopted by the god of things as they are. Even the physical isolation of Achilles from his fellows is echoed in images of Zeus' isolation. When Thetis comes to Olympus, she finds Zeus sitting apart from the others, and, throughout the Wrath, he is for the most part alone on Mt. Ida, "retired at a distance," a phrase used only of Achilles and Zeus.[16] Near the climax of the Wrath, further identification of the god and the hero may be traced in the way Zeus watches for the first flame to rise from the ships.[17] We are not told when Zeus sees the fire; instead, we hear how Achilles, who was also watching, saw it, smote his thigh, and called to Patroclus to hurry.[18] Thus the two contrivers of the Greek humiliation divide the moment of climax between them, producing the effect of a peculiar volitional unity.

The Zeus of the *Iliad* is not conceived theologically as a god with an arbitrary and irresponsible temper, nor should his Plan to honor Achilles be regarded as a miracle, dispensed out of interested favoritism. Both the Plan and the nature of the god are analogous in function to the peaceful shores of Phaeacia which greet Odysseus, or to Athena's companioning of Diomedes. They objectify in concrete terms the force and consequences of the hero's rage, coexisting with it, limited by it, and disappearing with it. The mere absence of Achilles and his Myrmidons is sufficient to explain rationally the Greek reverses which follow his retirement. But the god's participation extends the scope of the hero's action to include an aspect of the absolute and irreversible, and places him in the context of divinity, as no other hero in Greek literature is placed. And this result is not the product of deliberate, conscious symbolizing, but rather of the wholly classical envisioning of the world's divine agents as executors of what was and is, and therefore must be. If Homer says often that the gods are better and stronger than men, and that no one can overreach the will of Zeus, he does not mean that the government of the universe lies at the whimsical beck of exalted demons. The superiority of the gods lies in the absoluteness of their being, which, since it is free of time, immortalizes the processes and actions of the world, and necessitates their final results before they take place. This is the "fate" to which the gods are bound; Zeus himself represents it more broadly than the others, whose functions are conceived in connection with a single character's efforts, or with the circumstances and events of a limited time or place.

Zeus' arbitrariness and his subservience to "fate," with their apparent contradictions, are actually mere appearances, modes of speaking. The "fate" which he must acknowledge is the poet's scenario viewed as ineluctable fact, and herein lies the real meaning of the frequent phrases, "according to fate" and "contrary to fate." If fate here implied anything like predestination, the suggestion that anything could happen contrary to it would be meaningless. But nothing of the sort is implied. When Homer says, "Then such-and-such would have happened contrary to fate, had not — " he says in fact little more than that it almost happened, but did not. The added meaning which one senses in the phrase is simply a reflection of the view of the gods, who know the end, poignantly juxtaposed to the effort of the mortals who do not. And this repeated reminder of the gods' timeless comprehension of human action casts a mysterious light of inevitability upon all that happens in the *Iliad*.

When Zeus champions Achilles' anger, he foresees and asserts as accomplished fact the consequences of the great hero's retirement. When the Wrath is renounced, Zeus foresees and asserts the natural course of things when a vengeful Achilles takes the field. He voices the fear that Achilles may take the city "contrary to fate," and dispatches the gods to the scene of the fighting to prevent this.[19] There is no real apprehension in Zeus' mind. The poet has simply suppressed the god's transcendent foreknowledge of the end (contained in the mere word *moros*, fate) under the forms of fear and command, and thus dramatically centered attention upon the actions which achieve the end, actions without which the gods would have nothing to foreknow. This dismissal of the gods to their posts leads directly to the *Theomachia*, with its overthrow of the Trojan divinities, after which Apollo goes to Troy, to defend it, lest it fall "contrary to fate" — that is, he went to defend it as long as it was actually defended.[20] Achilles' threat to the city was a real one, with every appearance of being carried out. That it was actually not carried out was due to a whole concatenation of persons and events which Homer does not narrate in full, but which he adumbrates powerfully in the figure of Apollo. The divinity, by his very presence, removes the aspect of chance or accident from those persons and events, and casts them in the shape of ineluctable reality. Unlikely as it is that Achilles himself should fail to take Troy, he did fail; and Apollo, the unerring but equivocal prophet, best symbolizes all that lies between a likely effort and its unlikely event. So too Patroclus seemed likely to take Troy, but Apollo knew the end:

> Yield, divine-born Patroclus! Not fated, take heed,
> Under your spear is the town to fall of the Trojan charioteers,
> Nor yet under Achilles', who is far better than you.[21]

This scene, together with the mysteriously terrifying vision of Apollo destroying Patroclus, says little more, in fact, than that Patroclus nearly took the city, but was killed in the attempt. But by implication, the end of Book XVI embraces all those unknowables of character and action which become clear only after the event. Never are the roles of the gods or the meaning of fate more clear than in the scene of Hector's death. Zeus lifts the scales — always the sign of what is true — and Hector's *Ker*, or fatality, descends toward Hades; Apollo, the genius of Troy's safety, abandons him to the mercy of Achilles, who is instantly joined by the victorious goddess, Athena.[22] All the pieces fall into their final positions, and the truth is revealed. In single combat, Hector must fall to Achilles, and all the hopeful, apparent delays of that meeting have only served to bring it about exactly when it happened. Homer's method is the most subtle imaginable mode of revealing both the freedom and the inevitability of action; nor are we justified in assuming that every singer of epic tales treated the matter in this way. Surely here the vision is Homer's own, carried consistently through the whole *Iliad*, wherever divine and human action meet. It is a system for expressing the interrelation of factual and metaphysical truth, so that it is no accident when Paris, admitting the facts about himself and attributing them to Aphrodite, begins his speech by saying:

Hector, since you reprove me according to fate, and not
beyond it . . .[23]

Returning now to the Plan of Zeus, and his behavior in connec-
tion with it, one can see that the whole episode has the temporary
appearance, to the other Olympians, of being "contrary to fate."
In restraining them from taking part in the war, he forbids them
their proper roles, for a reason which not even Athena compre-
hends. To all without exception, and especially to Hera, it seems
to be out of character for Zeus, whose impartiality elsewhere is
unruffled, to take an active stand on one side or the other; they
object in the same spirit as they do when Zeus sorrowfully wonders
if he cannot save Sarpedon and Hector. It is arbitrary, and opposed
to what really happened, in their limited view, for the Greeks to
be driven to the sea. But Zeus, as Homer says, is older and knows
more. The greatest of the gods, partly because of his very detach-
ment, can respond to the spirit of the greatest and most detached
of the heroes. With all the sonority of divine thunder, the genius
of the universe itself answers and affirms the genius of man himself.
The relation between Zeus and Achilles is the most extended and
subtle of all Homer's characterizations by divinity. It makes the
Iliad what it is by setting at its core the supreme dignity of the
isolated individual spirit. Sometimes it is said that Achilles vanishes
from the whole middle part of the poem, but this is not true. He
is there in the form of a translated Zeus, governing the phases of
the long battle with his lightning; his whole character, state of
mind, and relation to circumstances is enormously projected into
the concrete image of the god. And yet, for all his temporary
identification with Achilles, Zeus continues to reflect the totality
of things, and not the Wrath alone. He can shed a bloody dew in
lamentation for Sarpedon, and console the long-suffering Ajax with
an omen of ultimate victory.[24] One of the great virtues of Greek
polytheism, and of Homer's use of it, is that no god, least of all
Zeus, is ever a perfectly univocal symbol. Multiple meanings con-
stantly merge with one another as the facets of the divine nature
light up in response to the phenomena of the world.

The connection between Zeus and Achilles, with all its com-
plexities, permeates and to a degree shapes the central action of
the *Iliad*. The poetic context of the other gods is in each case sim-

pler, but conceived with equal consistency and felicity. We have already seen how Athena's help to Diomedes contributes to the expression of the particular quality of heroism in the man. Her behavior with Achilles is of a quite different character. When she restrains him by the hair from killing Agamemnon, self-awareness, of a kind appropriate to the deity of the arts and intellect, is clearly implied. The exact terms of that self-awareness, however, are stated by Achilles himself in his two speeches which follow. Reminded by the divine apparition of his own superiority to the other princes, he vows his retirement from the war; then later he refers to his rejection of violence, and draws an important distinction:

> Something else I will say, do you put it in your heart:
> Not with my hands will I contend with you for a girl,
> Neither with you nor with another; you gave her, you take her away.
> But of the other things which are mine by my swift black ship,
> Nothing of these will you come and retrieve without my will.
> Come then, come and try, that also all these may know;
> Soon will your dark blood spurt around a spear.[25]

It is clear from this threat that Athena's restraint does not forbid all violence toward the king. As explained in the preceding chapter, a distinction in the hero's scale of values is meant. The matter of Briseis is too serious for blows, an easy victory for Achilles. The justice which must vindicate his feeling lies on a higher level, and must come to pass through all the devious obliquities of the Wrath. The world itself must be affected; the gods must act. The epiphany of Athena prepares this attitude in Achilles. He had contemplated retirement before;[26] now he swears it. The goddess is not an act of conscience, or a symbol of divine law, reproving violence or murder; she is the sudden self-realization of Achilles in the moment of stress, the visible symbol of the way he must, of his nature, conduct himself.

In most of her many appearances in the *Iliad*, Athena is the genius of Greek victory, and as such she reflects its various phases. When Achilles shouts from the trench, she shouts with him.[27] When he overcomes Hector, she is present to hand him his spear.[28] On the other hand, while the Greeks suffer defeat, she is confined to Olympus, but not without a struggle. She can still be present in Book

VIII, in the first stages of the reverse, and her thwarted attempt
to reach the battlefield in spite of Zeus corresponds to the madden-
ing frustration of the Greek princes baffled by lightning, minor
wounds, and an apparently causeless confusion. On the other hand,
by her deception of Hector in his last fight, she seems like a last
mocking echo of that hero's delusion of appointed victory.[29] Finally,
in the Pandarus scene, for a moment she typifies not merely the
victory of the Greeks, but also the justice of their cause, for the
treacherous arrow which Pandarus shoots at Menelaus, and which
only "rouses him the more," is in a way a reënactment of the crime
of Paris — a breach of faith, and one directed specifically at Mene-
laus.

Athena is often linked with Hera in the latter's implacable hatred
of Troy; the judgment of Paris rankles interminably.[30] In this
aspect, both of them are especial protectors of the Atreidae, the real
avengers of the insult. But even so, their activities are peculiarly
confined within the limits of character of the two kings. Agamem-
non, as we have seen, is a pretentious man of external pomp. As
he sets out in all his gorgeous armor for the battle, what do his
two goddesses do for him? They make a big thumping noise, "to
honor the king of Mycenae, rich in gold." [31] It seems unnecessary
to labor the contrast between this meaningless uproar, and the di-
vine fire with which Athena clothes Achilles at the trench. But
Agamemnon is also a man of terrible violence; he would kill all
the Trojans, even the child in its mother's womb, and Hera's hatred
of Troy is of similar savagery. Zeus says to her:

> Ho, if only you might, passing the gates and long walls,
> Raw devour Priam and the children of Priam,
> And other Trojans all, then you might salve your fury.[32]

On the other hand, in relation to Menelaus, both goddesses take
on a somewhat different appearance. Menelaus is the most cared-
for man in the army. Agamemnon worries over him, and even the
youthful Antilochus goes to look after him in battle.[33] Athena and
Hera also appear in the light of this general attitude after the duel
between Menelaus and Paris, when Zeus twits them for allowing
Aphrodite to be more zealous on behalf of her favorite than they

have been for theirs.[34] More pointed is the simile that describes Athena's deflection of the arrow of Pandarus:

> So from his flesh she brushed it, as when a mother
> Brushes a fly from her child, when he lies in sweet slumber.[35]

Such casual, delicate reflections of human character by the gods differ only in degree from the larger and more obvious examples, such as the relation between Athena and Odysseus in the *Odyssey*. Truth, Kierkegaard said, is subjective, and the statement is very true of certain aspects of Greek religion. The subjective agent in Homer is the character, defining and in a sense achieving its fullness and finality in a divine image. It is no wonder that Xenophanes could complain that the gods of Homer were altogether too like human beings.[36] They were conceived to ratify and enlarge a human scheme in a poetic context, not to define the nature of divinity abstractly, in and of itself. Yet they do not merely ape human conduct, because the timeless and the temporal ways of envisioning things differ; moreover, the scope of each divinity is wider than that of a single human being. Each owns an arc, a portion of the total circle of all things, within which he can move appropriately, and beyond which he is meaningless. Apollo and Athena cannot reflect defeat or indignity. Aphrodite can rescue a favorite, but cannot bring him victory. Hera cannot embody magnanimity or greatness. Poseidon can assist the Greeks at the sea's brink or help Achilles in the river, but apart from the context of water he is rather helpless.[37] No complete summary of any god's potential range is possible, for we do not know the poet's full range of association, and there are some surprises. The most that can be done is to point out the consistency of the conceptions within a single poem.

For this purpose, incidentally, the *Iliad* is a much more fruitful source than the *Odyssey*. There very few gods are really active, and their symbolic participation is much simpler. The role of Zeus is detached and reflects distantly the basic assumption of right order achieved in time. Poseidon has lost much of the personality he owned in the *Iliad*, and is little more than the hostile sea; Helios, with his plundered cattle, involves more in the way of folk tale, its meaning buried in antiquity, than of humanistic symbolism. Hermes appears thrice, once in each of his primary roles — as messenger, as protector of the traveler on land, and as guide of the dead — but with little reference to any individual's character. Athena has almost entirely displaced the large roster of gods in the *Iliad*, and it is only occasionally that she reflects the action or character of anyone other than Odysseus, the most important exception being, of course, Telemachus.[38] The situation of the *Odyssey* arises, however, from the same cause as that in the *Iliad*: the nature of the scenario. The action of the *Odyssey* as conceived cannot make use of the same panoramic background of divine character, because it does not possess the same panoramic foreground of human character. In the *Odyssey*, the totality of things is not approached through psychological subtleties, but through the quasi-abstractions of the Adventures, as narrated to Alcinous. No gods are needed here to limit and illumine meaning, for the figures of the Adventures are themselves gods or demigods, envisioned not in relation to many men, but only in relation to Odysseus. And it is his response to them which is telling, not their response to him. The man of infinite adjustment holds the center of interest, and therefore the emphasis falls on his reaction before these essences, what he will do, how he will pass the danger. The demonic figures of the Adventures present another whole aspect of divinity, the world in its unchangeable selfhood and challenge. Only Athena behaves in character, and is defined by it. Yet for all the difference in final outcome, there is no difference of method in the two poems. The gods in both are fashioned to the poetic concern; only the *Iliad* emphasizes psychology and the metaphysics of individual heroism, whereas the *Odyssey* is more concerned with the typology of humanity and experience.

One of the most puzzling gods in the *Iliad* is Ares. The reason for this is perhaps that he is connected with no particular character whatever. For the most part, his name occurs as a simple synonym for war, and even when he appears in his own person, he is sometimes accompanied by figures of pure allegory: Phobos ("rout"), Deimos ("terror"), and Eris ("strife"). Moreover, unlike any other god, he changes sides, though he generally favors the Trojans. Here we have a divine conception different from, and actually simpler than, those which are defined by their relation to human agents. Ares is war; yet even so, war in what sense? His actual appearances are few. He first appears leading the Trojans, together with his three grim abstractions; [39] in the beginning of the *Diomedeia*, Athena persuades him, on the pretense of retiring herself, to refrain from the war; but in the middle of the book, he is roused by Apollo to go and repress Diomedes.[40] As Hera and Athena go to meet him on the field, Athena remarks that he has broken his promise to help the Greeks.[41] He is wounded and sent howling back to Olympus, where Zeus, in disgust, condemns him as the most hateful of the gods, taking after his mother, Hera; nevertheless, he acknowledges him as his own son, and heals his wound.[42] In the Great Battle, Ares' son Ascalaphus, a Minyan from Orchomenos, is slain by Deiphobus; Ares starts up to avenge him, presumably, by joining the Greeks, but is held back by Athena, who reminds him that Zeus has forbidden all interference in the war.[43] In the *Theomachia*, Ares joins the Trojans, and, together with Aphrodite, is overwhelmed by Athena.[44] He does not reappear, except as a picture on the shield of Achilles.[45]

In all these scenes, two points are of major significance. First, Ares always gets the worst of his conflicts, with utter loss of dignity; and second, he changes sides. Why, it may be asked, does he not keep his promise to help the Greeks? He is ready to do so when his son is slain by a Trojan; but when he actually joins the war, he helps (if his interference is help) the Trojans. The reason has nothing to do with the fact that some stories made Ares the paramour of Aphrodite, Troy's natural ally. The reason is that Homer has conceived Ares as war in its aspect of turmoil, defeat, and disgrace. He cannot, therefore, be associated with the victorious host of Achaeans, except briefly, when they are driven back to the ships; even then, he never reaches the field. But he is promptly on hand to receive and symbolize the brunt of Trojan defeat in the *Theomachia*; in fact, wherever there is rout and terror, Ares is appropriate. Thus in the course of any long conflict, he must change sides on occasion, even as Robert Frost remarks that the war god is

> . . . no especial dunce
> For always fighting on both sides at once.[46]

Zeus "who gives the victory" is harsh to Ares, and hates him, while he is always gentle to Athena; and in popular belief, a man who suffers defeat or misfortune is hateful to the gods.[47] Yet Zeus must acknowledge him, for without defeat there is no victory. Though Ares is accompanied by purely allegorical figures, it required no conscious abstract thinking to conceive him as Homer does. It required only a concrete image of the disgrace and terror of defeat; and this image enters naturally whenever defeat enters.

Apollo, however, though invariably faithful to the Trojans, is never allowed an instant's humiliation. He disappears before a defeat, not because the gods are fickle, but because Apollo is the genius of Trojan valor, especially Hector's. When the gods finally come to blows, in the *Theomachia*, and the Trojan deities are overcome, Apollo must naturally have fallen before his adversary Poseidon. But Homer does not allow this. Apollo gracefully refuses to bandy blows with his uncle, and retires to defend Troy to the last; [48] and this is not devised merely out of piety toward one of the most feared and respected gods of the ancient pantheon, but chiefly because Apollo answers to every excellence in Troy and in Hector, and never to any failure. It is he who preserves Hector's body when Achilles drags it behind his chariot, and it is he who first asserts the dignity of the fallen hero in the council of the gods.[49] Throughout the poem, Homer's images of Apollo are vigorous, solemn, and even frightening, from his first appearance, coming down "like the night" to inflict the plague, to the vast visions of him trampling the Greek wall, or giving Patroclus his deathblow. For the greater part, he is to be understood through the character of Hector, whom he assists and protects. The two are conceived together under the image of Troy's chief support. One can see the working of association in the poet's mind when Hector, like Apollo, bursts into the Achaean camp "like the night"; [50] there is no other use of this formula in the *Iliad*. One wonderful passage in the Battle, where Hector is wounded by a stone, illustrates the relation of the two.[51] Hector has been knocked senseless, and Zeus sends Apollo to revive him. But Hector is already reviving, and is sitting up when Apollo gets there. The god addresses him in terms that suggest the return of consciousness to a man who has been stunned and begins to remember what happened:

> Hector, son of Priam, why do you, far from the others
> Sit with failing strength? Does some misfortune assail you?

Then with little force answered helmed Hector:
Who are you, best of gods, who question me face to face?
Know you not how, by the sterns of the ships of the Achaeans,
Ajax, great of war-cry, smote me slaying his comrades,
Stone in the breast, and repelled my rushing might?
Surely I thought that I should behold the dead and the house of
    Hades
This very day, when I hearkened to my own heart,

Then again spoke the prince, Apollo who works his will:
Courage now. So great a helper the son of Kronos
Sends you from Ida, to stand by your side and defend,
Phoebus Apollo of the golden sword, who also of old
Guards both you yourself, and the beetling citadel.
Up now, on; cheer on your many knights,
Drive your swift horses to the hollow ships.
I, going on before, shall wear each path
Smooth for your horses, and turn in flight the Achaean heroes.[52]

Gods restore heroes elsewhere in the *Iliad*, but this scene has a
special difference. The question and answers have a dazed tone, as
of a man surprised to find himself still alive. It is very inward, and
Hector is talking, in a way, only to himself. Just before the con-
versation, Homer seems to betray his inward conception of it in
the rather exceptional statement that "the mind of Zeus was awak-
ening" Hector.[53]

Apollo's appearances without Hector are few. The plague scene
of Book I has its roots more in cult than in context, though even
here the priest Chryses mediates between the two. His one scene
with Achilles, brief as it is, sounds a deep note. The god, in the guise
of Agenor, leads Achilles astray while the Trojans escape, all except
Hector, into the city. Then Apollo reveals himself. This is the one
frustrating circumstance of Achilles' great *aristeia*, and he is pro-
foundly angered:

Wrong you have done me, who work your will, most baleful of all
    gods,
Turning me hither now from the wall; yea, many still would have
Taken the earth in their teeth before they came to Ilion!
Now you have robbed me of great renown, you have saved them
Easily, since you feared not at all my vengeance hereafter.
Vengeance on you I would surely take, if mine were the power.[54]

Defiant as Achilles sounds, he admits a final limit to his strength, and it is no accident that that limit is in the shape of Apollo. It is Apollo who will direct the arrow of Paris that is to slay Achilles, as Hector, prophetic in the moment of death, foretells.[55] Achilles here catches a glimpse of the fate which he is knowingly pursuing: the final glory which he will lose in not being the one to take Troy, and his own early death. It is as if he said, in the words of Cocteau's *Orphée*, "Tu es ma mort."

The complex network of symbolic relations between gods and men presents, in Greek epic, a bafflingly innocent superficies, and tempts the conclusion that all such oral poetry made use of it. But this cannot be true. Doubtless all oral epic used the gods, but in the *Iliad* we are confronted by a peculiar point of view, and one consistently developed, appropriate only to this poem. It involves those semiconscious, intuitive processes by which any poet works, especially when handling vast and various material; and in all poets, and in all poems, these processes differ. No secondary hand, taking up the tale, could continue his predecessor's precise approach; when it came time to introduce a traditional motif involving a god, he would violate the previous symbolism, either by not seeing the organic relation between divine and human action or character, or by seeing it all differently. It is the intuitive levels of imagery and divine machinery in the *Iliad* which reveal its soundness as the work of a single mind.

The gods are, in fact, a kind of imagery, and their uses parallel, in a way, the continuous play of figurative language on the action. Every appearance of a god amid the deeds of a hero is an implied comparison, formalizing the event or character in the light of something other than and beyond itself. As possessors of pure being in various aspects, the gods in their presences lend to all humanity a fourth dimension, not of time, but of eternity, the essence of the heroic vision of glory and permanent value. The dimension added by an image may be of a different nature, but its function is essentially the same: to make an object or event more comprehensible through the simultaneous presentation of another object or event, somewhat after the manner of stereopticon vision. The resulting phenomenon is neither the object itself, nor its immediate rational symbol — that is, its name — it is a third thing, an intellectual symbol, a unit of personal comprehension, differing within limits in all recipients thereof. Through the use of such lenses, all poets focus their meaning as exactly as possible, and Homer is no exception. Yet exactness is not the primary intention of such a mode of communication; like a prism, poetry refracts as much meaning as possible to a single point, but will sacrifice a degree of precision for a greater degree of suggestion. If it sacrifices too much precision, chaos ensues; if too little, prose. Homer's work is breath-taking chiefly because of his supreme discretion in handling the process of poetic refraction. The *Iliad* sustains, as scarcely another poem has ever done, the finest possible adjustment of sharp, clear image and vast connotative design.

The aspect of the gods that appears in their relation to the characters is not, however, the only one, either in Homer or in the tradition to which he belonged. The pious *Theogony* and the Homeric *Hymns*, though later than Homer, continue a tradition of singing of the gods themselves as persons, acting among themselves and apart from humanity. This material, partly folk tale, partly the mythology of the cults and rituals, is not wholly absent from Homer; it appears in the pictures of Apollo as giver and healer of disease, and of Hera as protectress of Argos — allusive references to the provinces of the gods quite apart from the poem. Such interests, however, are not primary in Homer; they are mere touches amid the more important functions of the divinities as images of character. On the other hand, there is still a third level of divine activity in Homer, the frequent scenes on Olympus and elsewhere of the gods among themselves, quarreling, deceiving, or making love. These are quite different from Hesiod's pious formulations of the gods' life together, and the explanation of them again must come, not from guesses about Homeric or pre-Homeric religion, but from the poems themselves. We have seen how an image, especially that of fire, can gain a life of its own and quite run away with the action, or rather represent the action by becoming it. Similarly also the gods in Homer gain a life of their own, different from that of the cults, and from that of other poets, and constituting an imaginative extension of the context of human action to which they owe their immediate aspects. The temporary violence of Zeus toward the other gods is, as we have seen, the divine reflex of the Wrath of Achilles; on Olympus it is carried into realms which

seem quite extraneous to its source. The spirit of gentle piety which
motivates the twenty-fourth book of the *Iliad* doubtless is respon-
sible for the piety attributed to the gods in burying the children
of Niobe, after Apollo had slain them.[56] Here the connection be-
tween the gods' burial of the children of Leto's adversary and Achil-
les' yielding of burial to the son of Priam is clear, and the attitude
of the gods throughout the book bears it out. On the other hand,
Hera's seduction of Zeus, as well as his threats to her, carry far
into the upper air the earthly concerns of the Trojan victory and
the honor of Achilles, which are the real cause of trouble between
Zeus and his wife. Yet those concerns are not really lost; they are
merely rarefied in this heavenly tension, viewed as a remote image
in a world where passion partakes of the scatheless freedom of
eternal being. It is idle to point to this scene of Zeus and Hera as
Homer's way of dragging in the Sacred Marriage myth of Argos,
and to say that it is an example of Homer's deep religiosity.[57] Actu-
ally, it required something more like blasphemy to represent the
Sacred Marriage as a deceitful seduction, followed by the threat of
beating; most of all, it required a poetic context where Zeus and
Hera were at odds. Only so could the image be blown up into
what it is.

Such extensions of the imagery sometimes achieve surprising re-
sults. The human concerns from which the gods take their basic
attitudes are matters of life and death to the human agents. Basic-
ally tragic, the *Iliad* teems with passions which, when transferred
to the gods, lose the costly element of destruction, and become
mere naked impetus. The gods can suffer pity, pain, anger, and all
human passion except the fear or foreknowledge of death; but this
makes all the difference. It is the universal limitation of death which
causes human beings to restrain passions, and Achilles' disregard
of that limitation is what allows him to carry his passion so far and
become more like a god than a man. The gods have no need for
such balance, except perhaps Zeus, who more nearly reflects all
things at once than do the others. But he can instill no mercy into
Hera for the Trojans; her hate is pure. He cannot shame Athena,
for she is victory, and he always gives her gentle words. The gods
can embody passions pure and free of all restraint, but they cannot
suffer the consequences of them. Deep in the consequences of his

folly, Agamemnon cries out that Zeus, Fate, and a Fury had sent him the goddess Até, Fateful Passion, and tells at length how Zeus himself had cast her out from Olympus to afflict men rather than the gods.[58] He is not just passing on the responsibility. The unreflecting, passionate pride which led him to insult Achilles was an emotion which only a god can afford to feel — hence, it was sent by Zeus. Achilles showed a similarly unqualified intransigence, but with a difference: while Agamemnon apologized and survived, Achilles proved his point, at the cost of his own life and that of Patroclus.

Thus, though the gods have weight, power, and being, in other respects their freedom from consequence sometimes emerges as ludicrous, by contrast with the human figures. The wounds of Aphrodite and Ares, so easily healed, are essentially jokes; Zeus and Athena laugh at Aphrodite, and Zeus jeers at Ares.[59] Dione's tale of the sufferings of the gods at mortal hands cannot make them seem more serious.[60] The seduction of Zeus, developed at length for its own sake, is entirely in the spirit of comedy, and, like all scenes between the king and queen of Olympus, it ends with a sort of rough-and-ready peacemaking for the moment, with Zeus conquering by force and Hera silently vowing her revenge. What is starkest tragedy on earth is often imaged in heaven as a light and sometimes slapstick comedy. Though the gods may surpass men in essential power and being, they are barred by their own deathlessness from the dignity of tragedy, or the greatness of self-mastery. They are, after all, the gods of the Greeks, a people who more than all others have always believed in the joy, greatness, and supreme importance of human life. Homer was perhaps the first to formulate this view of life in metaphysical terms, and, as a balance to the tremendous solemnity of his hero, to thrust the gods into the ridiculous postures they sometimes assume.

Itself a comedy, the *Odyssey* has no such running comic commentary in heaven. Rather the gods, insofar as they actually appear, answer to the more serious values of the poem, and give it its force as a view of ecumenical order. An exception is, of course, the song of Demodocus in Phaeacia about the amour of Ares and Aphrodite.[61] But here Homer returns for the moment to the method of the *Iliad*. Like the gods, the Phaeacians live scatheless and ten-

sionless, and the contrast between their soft ways and the rough
endurance of Odysseus permeates the whole eighth book. The song
of Ares and Aphrodite is appropriate to the Phaeacians; as their
king explains:

> We are not blameless boxers or wrestlers;
> Swiftly we run on foot, we are most excellent in ships;
> Always the feast is dear to us, and harps and dances,
> Changes of clothes, and warm baths, and beds.[62]

Only later, just before Odysseus is to reveal his identity, and as a
motivation for that revelation, does Demodocus sing a song appro-
priate to Odysseus: the tale of the last night of Troy, and the horse
of Odysseus' own devising.[63] The contrast in the two songs here
points a contrast between the hero and his hosts which is precisely
the same as that between the heroes and the gods in the *Iliad*. For
all their charm and real helpfulness, the Phaeacians are inconse-
quential and a little ridiculous compared to the man who lives life
whole.

And yet, as in the *Odyssey* the gods participate in the moral
concern with right order in Ithaca, so in the *Iliad*, though a for-
mula represents them as "amusing themselves with men," [64] they
are not wholly divorced, on all levels, from the world of suffering.
Zeus especially responds with deeply felt pity for Sarpedon, ex-
pressed through the fall of bloody dew.[65] The pious observances
of mortals sometimes at least win a degree of sympathy from the
divinities; [66] and on the other hand, the majestic shake of the head
which occasionally precedes or accompanies some act of retribution
upon an offender, suggests an emotionally moral indignation, not
merely the cold workings of a system. In such moments, the gods
appear much more as governors of the universe than as reflections
of it, but it is merely an appearance. As Hector puts on the armor
of Achilles, stripped from Patroclus, Zeus shakes his head and speaks
disapprovingly; and Poseidon, seeing Odysseus on the raft, shakes
his head and raises a storm.[67] Yet Hector has done nothing out of
the ordinary in putting on the armor of a conquered enemy, and
Odysseus' blinding of Polyphemus, which was his only offense
against Poseidon, was an act of self-defense, gory indeed, but easier
to justify than the Cyclops' cannibalism. Passages such as these,

where the gods seem moved by real moral disapproval, are in reality just as much hindsight as those dealing with fate, mere images of troubles and hostilities which follow, consequentially or not, upon the actions of men. If difficulties confront a man after or because of an act, the gods must have disapproved. But there is no systematic morality which the gods sustain. Zeus does not consistently disapprove of wearing an adversary's armor. He merely knows that Achilles will avenge it, and seems to reflect that even Hector might foresee that much. With broad and sorrowful detachment, he echoes in advance all the passions of the coming tragedy, as he watches the Trojan prince, blinded by the hope of victory, put on the arms in which he will die:

> Ah, wretch, not at all is death in your memory,
> Yet it is coming near you; and you don the deathless armor
> Of a great man, before whom others tremble.
> Yes, you have slain his companion, nimble and mighty,
> But the arms, not in good season from his head and shoulders
> Stripped away. Now this hour, I shall bring you great victory,
> Recompense, that from you, out of this battle returning never
> Shall Andromache receive the glorious arms of Peleus' son.[68]

Foreknowledge of death, the stripped arms, the universal fear of Achilles, the dead Patroclus dishonored, the momentary delusion of victory, and even Andromache's grief are all in this speech; these are its components, all things which are happening or will happen in the *Iliad;* and what Zeus states is not the law of the world, but the law of the poem. It is not by theology, but by a telescopic view of existence, that the gods mingle with and transcend the world of men.

Some figures seem to embody in themselves that mysterious union of divine and human which is the essence of heroism. Thetis in particular, the sea nymph whose husband was a mortal, constantly mediates between Achilles and the gods, carrying his fierce demands to them, and returning with their gifts or admonishments. When she comes to her son, she brings the breadth and eternity of the gods' world with her, coming as a mist from the ocean, or descending from the heights of Olympus; and when she is in the depths of sea with old Nereus and her sisters, she is, unlike the others, a *mater dolorosa*. The lamentation of Achilles penetrates to her marine caves, and causes her to cry out,

> Ah me, sorrowful that I am, ah, mother of grief and glory! [69]

She can foretell Achilles' fate, but cannot save him, for the reason that she knows only so much of his future as a man of such demands upon himself knows anyway. Hence she warns him of his own death in specific terms, but can only vaguely hint that of Patroclus.[70] When she intercedes with Zeus for him, and fetches the armor from Hephaestus, she aids and abets his fatal intransigence, representing the power he possesses to draw the absolute to himself; but her ever-present grief responds simultaneously to his perishable human side. Of all the superhuman figures of the *Iliad*, she is the most available to suffering, and in her reflection of the tensions in Achilles' soul, she all but becomes what is a contradiction in terms, a tragic divinity.

Of very similar significance are the immortal horses of Achilles, gifts of the gods to Peleus. Best and swiftest of all the horses at Troy, they attract Homer's attention most keenly in their motionless attitude of grief. When Patroclus is fallen, they stand stock still "like a tombstone," shedding hot tears and sweeping the dust with their manes.[71] Zeus pities them and, shaking his head, says:

> Ah, poor things, why did we give you to Peleus the king,
> Mortal, you being ageless and deathless?
> Was it that you might suffer pain with luckless men?
> Nowhere surely is there a sadder thing than a man
> Of all the things that breathe and creep upon the earth.[72]

Not only do men suffer from the gifts of the gods, as Paris hints, but the gifts of the gods suffer among men. Merely by being an attribute of the doomed house of Phthia, the immortal horses become images of eternal grief, like a tombstone. So grief comes even to the gods, the timeless mirrors of the world. The heroic nature receives the impress of the absolute in the form of a gift from the changeless world, and transforms it, by the tragic conflict it causes, into an image of eternal tragedy. As Achilles drives these horses forth to avenge his friend, Homer subtly recalls this passage, by having one of them prophesy the hero's death, his mane again

drooping into the dust.[73] It is appropriate also that the only fig-
ures who are so involved in both eternity and time as conflicting
yet inextricable forces are confined to the context of Achilles. They
are the symbols of Achilles' foreknowledge and tragic suffering.

Thus even the one quality which the gods cannot share with
mortals, their ageless, deathless being, is to some extent affected by
the pressure of the heroic soul. As images of all that happens in the
epics, the gods show many and various aspects, and sometimes it
pleases the poet, doubtless because it pleased the tradition, to repre-
sent them in causal relationships. But it must be recognized that
the gods can only cause what happened anyway, what was moti-
vated by character and circumstance. Any proposal to do other-
wise is countered by the phrase "against fate." This is true also of
the miraculous rescues of heroes from the battlefield, as Aphrodite
rescues Paris and Aeneas. Such scenes, like those in which the gods
converse or wrangle among themselves are, again, examples of imag-
ery supplanting action. Paradoxically enough, though miracles in
general are not everyday experience, few people are alive, or have
ever lived, who do not feel that they have had a miraculous escape
at one time or another. The phrase is a metaphor, a short cut,
obviating a series of causes, mostly imperceptible, and Homer's
miraculous rescues are equally metaphoric; also they are visualized
within the particular dramatic context, in that they regularly are
performed by the god most nearly associated in other ways with
the character who is rescued. Some, like the revival of Hector by
Apollo, are so psychologically transparent that the sense of the
supernatural all but disappears. If Zeus makes a big stone light for
Hector to lift, he can do so only because victory itself seems easy
for Hector, with Achilles gone.[74] The entrance of the supernatural
element is prepared and motivated by the poem itself, and often
develops, like other Homeric action out of a simple formula. The
difference is slight, for instance, between the formula used by Dio-
medes in prayer to Athena, "Stand beside me now and protect me,"
and the scene in which she actually stands beside him in his chariot,
brushing away the spears.[75] In the case of more intellectual prompt-
ings from divinities there is a similar correspondence between the
familiar phrase, "a god put it in his mind," and the occasions when
Athena — she in particular — appears to Odysseus, as in *Iliad* II,

for instance, and instructs him how to stem the soldiers' rush for the ships.[76] This epiphany, incidentally, seems even less like an intrusion of the supernatural in that the goddess, as Homer makes quite explicit, serves only to press into action the feeling of dismay at the army's defection which already filled Odysseus' mind. And so too with the glamorous rescues of heroes from the field in the arms of protecting deities, there is a corresponding formula: "Some one of the gods rescued and saved him." [77]

The gods' miracles, like many another Homeric scene of magic or mirage, are in fact little more than dramatic forms of the metaphoric speech. But that is no slight thing, nor are the miracles to be deprived of their wonder, or dismissed with a rationalistic shrug. Insofar as they act out the human mind's deep-seated attribution of all safety and success to the benignity of the gods, their content is a potent wish and love for life, appropriate to heroes. In form, once more like metaphor, they are more akin to magic, which is a mode of reaching toward a desired end by a declarative ritual, wherever danger or uncertainty has breached the steady flow of calculable experience and reliable knowledge.[78] Thus all three — metaphor, magic, and miracle (as Homer uses it) — by promoting as well as symbolizing action, by reflecting desire in the light of the inevitable, add a further dignity to the heroic conception. The miraculous cure of Glaucus' wound by Apollo is an image of resurgent valor, but one which connects such valor with a transcendent world.[79] When Hera sends the Sun God westward "unwilling" and ends the great battle, it is not only a way of saying that the day ended before its issues were decided, but also a way of implicating the universe in those issues, by involving the gods in time.[80] At the end of the previous day's fighting, night came upon the Trojans and found them "unwilling," because they wished to finish the fighting, while the darkness was "thrice-besought" by the Greeks, who were hard pressed.[81] Here both sides have hopes, and both are unwilling to cease fighting when the sun goes down; so the unwillingness is assigned to the sun itself, by the figure known as *hypallage*, or transference of epithet. The dramatic mode greatly enlarges the sense of the human potential in such scenes, and emphasizes, as do all the other uses of the gods, the relation between heroism and the absolute.

In the *Theomachia*, by a tremendous tour de force, Homer has brought together all the levels of the gods' activity. In some ways, nothing is more remarkable in the *Iliad* than this strange tragi-comic conflict, now that the Wrath and Plan are renounced, and the war is permitted to find its inevitable issue. On its most organic level, it is a dumb show of the fall of Troy, preluded by the duel between fire and water, in which the streams of Troy surrender and allow the fire to overwhelm the city. The god of defeat, Ares, is defeated by the goddess of Achaean victory, and with him falls the goddess of the cause of it all, Aphrodite; the god of Trojan valor yields the palm gracefully to the deity of the Greeks' sea-borne cause, and goes off to sustain the nobility of Troy to the end. But at this point again, the imagery runs away with Homer. Artemis pertly rebukes Apollo for not fighting, and is promptly punished by her stepmother Hera, who catches both her wrists with one hand, and whips her with her own bow with the other.[82] Artemis' arrows are all scattered about, an inversion of her epithet, "Arrow-scatterer." A late Greek vase shows a mother holding her little girl by both wrists and brandishing a slipper with the other hand, so there can be no doubt about the nature of Hera's gesture. The great battle of the gods ends with a spanking; Artemis flees off to heaven and, sitting on Zeus' knee, complains about stepmothers. Zeus laughs. The tragedy of Troy is lost in the timeless and way-ward imagery it has engendered. Yet when the poet returns to the tragedy, it is all the more moving by virtue of its contrast with the essentially scatheless gods.

A full summary of the functions of the Homeric gods would be a summary of all the action, viewed without time, plus the addition of lighthearted episodes dramatized to point the contrast between the careless ease of absolute being and the temporal struggles of the heroes who strive for it. Epic tradition supplied the singer with this flexible machinery, and Homer has risen to the task of shaping it to fill his needs. If the gods are designed to fit the characters and issues of the poem, and are even at times ludicrous, that does not justify the conclusion, however, that Homer was irreligious, or was merely toying, as an eighteenth-century English poet might, with Greek mythology. Comedy could deride the gods in a religious spirit, and, throughout the history of Greek polytheism, the existential, predicative outlook on divinity, resisting all attempts to reverse the process and see God as the self-moved mover, remained the popular one. It does not by any means imply that the gods are imaginary, or do not have actual existence. Images indeed they are; but all images are a kind of abstraction from, or extension of, observable experience, and as such possess intellective reality. One must believe in such abstractions if the original observation be true and precise, and for this reason Greek mythology continues to sway the mind as it does: Greek observation of experience was always singularly true and precise. In later periods, the intellectual terms in which the popular gods received belief grew more abstract, but Homer's original images always remained, as they still do, meaningful. Homer could have had no notion of how to treat the gods other than the way he did, as magnified images of his poetic material, sometimes tremendously dignifying men and their acts by the implication of eternity, and sometimes appearing, like the Phaeacians, trivial, because spared the ennobling struggle against the shadow of death. Such a view is profoundly religious in the way the Greeks are religious about life and the world. And if it is deficient in doctrine, nonetheless Greek polytheism is the greatest of all religions in the matter of its illimitable responsiveness to knowable experience. There were few places indeed where an ancient Greek could look and fail to see, not the work of God, but a god; and this is why everything in the *Iliad* happens twice, once on earth, and once in the timeless world of deity.[83]

XI

GEOMETRIC STRUCTURE OF
THE ILIAD

NOT only in the associations of images and conceptions of both divine and human agents does the *Iliad* reveal its unity, but also in the matter of external form. It is now time to look at the whole poem as a series of scenes, and observe how these scenes are related to each other. As indicated before, Homeric scenes are analogous to the formulae in that they follow a typology designed to assist the singer; scenes of battle, arming, debate, supplication, lamentation, and jubilant victory bear a formal as well as an ideational resemblance to each other, though in Homer a vast degree of variety and shading has been achieved through the expansion, compression, or modification of the basic motifs. This typology of the scenes in the poetry of Homer and other oral singers has been the subject of excellent studies, and one does well to keep in mind the warning of Parry not to find "falsely subtle meanings in the repetitions, as meant to recall an earlier scene where the same words were used." [1] And yet, though such echoes would be present in all singers' efforts, one of the traits of Homer's excellence seems to have been the gift to control these echoes more than other oral poets have done. For the fixed elements of the oral style are fixed only in themselves, and out of context. In context they inevitably change color and tone, and it is by no means implausible, on the face of it, that a skilled

singer, the scion of many generations of the tradition, should be-
come aware of the subtleties of shifting context and make some
effort to use them. Clearly, not every one could be controlled;
moreover, it must be assumed that, like so many processes of poetic
composition, much of this effort must have failed to reach the level
of full consciousness. Yet, insofar as the use of balancing, or echo-
ing, motifs contributes to the broad structure of the poems, con-
scious intent is probably to be assumed, since the design which
emerges bears the unmistakable stamp of the waking intellect. In
treating imagery, one had to deal with association and intuition;
here, in the matter of structure, one is confronted by a schematized
pattern, rationally worked out and altogether consistent with the
observable artistic practices of the Geometric Age.

Recently, critics have begun to take account of the artistic role
in Homer of the repetitive elements native to oral technique. Stereo-
typed themes and scenes, mere serviceable tools originally, and never
more than that in the hands of a poor singer, become in Homer
through varying context the vehicles of characterization and for-
mal design.[2] Thematic motifs, such as descriptions of sacrifices,
ship-launchings, feasts, funerals, arming, and combat, are on the
whole fixities of the poems, as indeed they were of the world from
which the poems arose, and the recitation of such passages is as
ritualistic, in a way, as were the performances of the acts which
they describe. It is natural and true for a society dominated by the
rigidities of ritual to represent its characteristic function in un-
changing formulae, normative and in a way eternal. Yet every such
thematic motif may be narrated in varying degrees of fullness.[3]
It is not always easy to say what determines how far a given one
may be developed, though the pace of the scene, and its purport
as a whole would, of course, be governing factors. When Achilles,
for instance, pours a libation and prays to Zeus for the safe return
of Patroclus, the process of libation is described in minute detail,
even to the cleansing of the goblet with sulfur.[4] But this is an ex-
tremely solemn and critical moment in the plot, and it would be
absurd to elaborate all the libations in the epic to the same degree.
Again, the scene of the sacrifice performed at Chrysa by Odysseus
on behalf of the Achaeans is one of the most complete of all de-
scriptions of such a ceremony.[5] Here perhaps more than mere litur-

gical solemnity is involved; for the arrival, debarkation, and return of the ship in which Chryseis is sent back are also lengthily described, in contrast to the more usual brief versions of such processes. The whole episode at Chrysa, in fact, has a leisurely air, in contrast to the packed dramatic scene which has preceded. And the reason probably lies in the fact that the poet here has to account for the passage of twelve days, until Zeus returns to Olympus and Thetis can present her plea for Achilles. Gaps of time are rare in epic and regularly avoided. It requires, therefore, a tour de force on Homer's part to fill an empty space when nothing particular happened. Odysseus spent only one day and one night at Chrysa, and the journey there and back probably did not take more than two more days; but the slow detailed pace of this rather neutral episode falsifies the time sense effectively, and one is prepared to accept without shock thereafter the brief summary of Achilles' inaction, and the resumptive line, "but when the twelfth dawn came," and return to the main action.

Apart from the variations in length, there are the variations in contextual significance. The *Odyssey*, for instance, probably has more descriptions of feasts than any other poem ever written. The traditional lines about feasting, therefore, sometimes may seem a little repetitious. Yet, because it makes a difference who is feasting, why, and at whose expense, the lines take on many different meanings, and cast shade upon shade of significance on the highly central theme of hospitality. Hospitality, itself a moral norm, finds its chief expression in the feast, a social norm, which is in turn represented by a set of fixed lines, a poetic norm. Actually, the "feasting" formulae of Homer are extremely numerous, but they are mere verbal variants and do not in themselves imply differences of action. Yet, who can miss the sharp dramatic contrast between the feast spread by Telemachus for Athena-Mentes and that enjoyed simultaneously at the other side of the hall by the suitors, and all in the space of twenty-two lines? [6] Similarly, one cannot fail to experience the effect on Telemachus when he passes from the grim, disorderly banquets of the suitors in Ithaca to the stately entertainment, almost suggestive of the Golden Age, to which he is invited by Nestor on the beach at Pylos, and the later one at the palace, both graced by the presence of Athena herself. [7] Nestor spreads a feast in its fullest moral and social significance; as a symbol of society in order, it is deeply appropriate to the educative intention of *Odyssey* 3, and as such also Nestor appeals to it when, in the Ninth *Iliad*, he instructs Agamemnon amid his chaotic fears to give a feast for the elders, as his simple kingly duty.[8] Far from suggesting revelry on the brink of doom, Nestor proposes a feast as the gateway to rational deliberation, the token of civilized, ordered life on the basis of which sane decisions arise. Yet the formulae of the feasts themselves are all closely similar, recurring numberless times, and not differing essentially even when Circe puts food before her guests. The function of a norm is to regularize; but the effect of experience at large is to refract upon the norm infinite lights and perspectives. Hence the variety of Homer, a variety which could not be so complex and subtle if it did not echo constantly from the normative columns of a ritualistic and formulaic fixity, transforming them into whispering pillars.

The principle or intention underlying such practices is perhaps not precisely a structural one, though it could be so called in that it relates to the continuity and interrelation of the stuff of the poems, and especially to the relation between the elements which are universal in the heroic tradition and those which are peculiar to the poem. Less involved with meaning, but more clearly formal and structural, is the phenomenon now known as ring composition.[9] This framing device, whereby an episode or digression is rounded off by the repetition at the end of the formula with which it began, had its origin undoubtedly in the oral singer's need to bind the parts of his story together for the sake of simple coherence. Like the retrospective summaries of preceding action so characteristic of epic, it took both the poet's and the audience's mind back to a point where the next event was to find its orientation. But it has been ably demonstrated that Homer uses this device not only to serve a practical need, but also as an artistic device to give shape and clarity to the sections of his work, which, composed paratactically and with almost equal detail and emphasis in every part, might otherwise fall into an intolerably unarticulated series.[10] Examples thus may be found of both functional and nonfunctional ring composition, and it is particularly common in the *Odyssey*. The famous scene where Eurycleia recognizes Odysseus by the scar on his knee is an example of the former.[11] Between the discovery of the scar and the old woman's instantaneous gesture of surprise, Homer inserts a seventy-five-line episode about the origin of the scar, returning with perfect ease to the moment in hand by the mere repetition of the single verb, "recognized." The minimal nature of such a repetition perhaps illustrates how little is necessary to achieve the purely practical end. At the opening of the same book, a far more striking example of ring composition serves no practical purpose at all. The episode wherein Odysseus and his son stow away the arms under the guidance of Athena is neither a digression nor in any sense detached from the direct and purposeful march of events; it is an important step in the hero's achievement of vengeance. Yet Homer frames it at the end by the full and identical repetition of the two lines which began it:

> Then in the hall, godlike Odysseus was left alone,
> Pondering with Athena death for the suitors.[12]

Here, of course, the effect is to give an extraordinary finality to the scene which preceded, to make it shine with the enclosed inviolability of a perfect circle, so that, however sequential it may be in the plot, it seems like a thing apart. As a prologue to the slaying of the suitors, and at that a prologue involving the miraculous presence of Athena herself, it stands on a slightly different level from the rest of the narrative and seems to have taken place not quite in time at all, but rather in the timeless sphere of the goddess. But it did not have to, nor indeed could it have seemed to, had the poet not so enclosed it in echoing formulae. Somewhat similarly, and from no merely functional reason at all, the shipwreck of Odysseus is enclosed by the repetition of the line where Poseidon shakes his head and mutters to himself, as he hurls the waves at the wanderer.[13]

Such a device as ring composition, especially as developed into an architectonic principle, is wholly consistent with Geometric art. The very name "ring composition" arises because such enclosure by identical or very similar elements produces a circular effect, the acoustical analogue of the visual circle; and circles, especially concentric circles, are prime motifs in Protogeometric art. In later Geometric, this design is not so common, but the idea of the circle is carried out in friezes of warriors or mourners running back into themselves, whose moving aesthetic principle is unbroken continuity, perfect and perpetual motion. One may indeed find a similar circularity penetrating all Homeric poetry, especially the *Iliad*, not merely in scenes, but in the poem as a whole; and again the root of the principle lies in a practical need. Ever since the time of Cicero, if not before, Homer's habit of returning to things previously mentioned in reverse order has been observed, and sometimes compared to the rhetorical figures of hysteron proteron.[14] This device, doubtless of mnemonic purpose to assist the singer to keep in mind what he had said before, is also pregnant with stylistic possibilities; like ring composition, it returns to its point of origin and effects circularity of design, while the inverted elements may also be spread out to include as a centerpiece a whole scene or scenes, as in a frame. Thus hysteron proteron and ring composition, too, suggest not only circularity, but also framing and balance.

Moreover, even as ring composition balances by similarity or identity the idea of inversion in hysteron proteron is simply a form of balance by opposites. Probably all aspects of formal symmetry depend ultimately upon these two categories of similarity and opposition, as Plato seemed to know when in the *Timaeus* he finished off his cosmology with the two spheres of Sameness and Difference, which revolve in opposite directions. A basic and highly refined intuition of these two categories, which are in a sense the a priori ground of all cognition, existed from the first in the classical mind, shaping especially its artistic and philosophic approaches to experience. All peoples of course must possess it, but in the Greeks from Homer on it rose to an extraordinary degree of conscious activity, causing in them a tendency to treat all things in the light of antithesis or identity. Of the two, antithesis seemed to be the more appealing, as perhaps the more dynamic. Sameness is static; antithesis embodies movement around a still point. Hence doubtless arise those myriad and various uses of the antithetical particles, *men* and *de*, "on the one hand," and "on the other," of which the greatest and most accomplished stylists, both in prose and poetry, never seem to tire. They are the hallmark of true Hellenic speech in the classical time, not from mere habit, but because they reflect the deep seated intellectual love of polarities, the outside limits of a thought between which somewhere lies a fulcrum of balance. Much has been said about Greek balance and the golden mean. But the concept is a passive one. The active elements were the two extremes, the *men* and the *de*, between which the mean was felt as a theoretical point. Aristotle devised his whole ethical system by reference to the extremes of behavior, between which, though not always in the exact center, lay the mean point which is virtue. For Homer the framework of identity and antithesis is fundamental. We have already observed its operation, on a profound psychological level, in the matter of the rigid typological scenes shifting meaning and effect under the influence of changing context. It exists also on many other levels, such as, for instance, the cultural antitypes of the wild Cyclopes and the overcivilized Phaeacians, who were, not surprisingly, formerly neighbors, since intellectually at least opposites attract each other. It is present also in the confrontation and interplay of the two great themes of the *Odyssey*: the homeward journey, *nostos*, is a fixed idea, an assertion of static singleness, which integrates the hero's personality and unifies his will; the Adventures plunge into the variety of experience in a sea as infinite as it is unpredictable, stretching to the "limits of earth," extremes of difference from the hero himself, and often conceived in antinomic pairs.

The principle of circularity, including concentricity, or framing by balanced similarity and antithesis, is one of the chief dynamic forces underlying the symmetry of Geometric vase design. In the *Iliad*, the old device of hysteron proteron has been expanded into a vast scheme far transcending any mere mnemonic purpose, a scheme purely and even abstractly architectonic. Not only are certain whole books of the poem arranged in self-reversing, or balancing, designs, but the poem as a whole is, in a way, an enormous hysteron proteron, in which books balance books and scenes balance scenes by similarity or antithesis, with the most amazing virtuosity. The very serious question arises, of course, as to whether the audience, listening to an oral presentation of the poem, could possibly have caught the signs of such "fearful symmetry," or whether it would have meant anything to them if they did. Granted that the procedure *abba* is useful in small compass to a singer, and perceptible as a structural unit to the audience, such can hardly be

the case when *ba* is separated from *ab* by many thousand lines. Yet
two things may be said regarding this point. The human mind is
a strange organ, and one which perceives many things without con-
scious or articulate knowledge of them, and responds to them with
emotions necessarily and appropriately vague. An audience hence
might feel more symmetry than it could possibly analyze or de-
scribe. The second point is that poets sometimes perform feats of
virtuosity for their own sakes and without much hope of under-
standing from their audiences, for one of the minor joys of artistic
creation is the secret which the artist buries in his work, the beauty
(if such indeed it be) which he has deliberately concealed amid the
beauties which he has tried to reveal and express. *Finnegans Wake*
and the ciphers and acrostics in late Medieval and Renaissance
poetry offer good examples, though an even better one is to be
found in the poem which serves as prologue to Dylan Thomas's
collected works. This poem, some four pages long, employs per-
haps the most imperceptible rhyme-scheme ever invented: the first
line rhymes with the last, the second with the second last, and so
on until a couplet marks the exact middle. Needless to say, the
couplet seems fortuitous to the reader, and the rest of the zealous
effort goes by unnoticed, unless it is pointed out by someone who
heard it from someone else to whom the author explained it. A poet
does such things to please himself, one must suppose. As for Homer,
his scheme is at least as evident as Thomas's, and demonstrably
serves a more real end. In any case, it should not be dismissed as
mere empty virtuosity; for if the oral singer was accustomed to
designing scenes, or at least some scenes, by means of hysteron
proteron, it is not unnatural that he should seek to give shape to
the large epic also in the same way, and especially if he had before
him the example of the huge vases of the Dipylon, wherein, with no
change of technique, the motifs and proportions of earlier Geo-
metric pottery were expanded and adjusted to monumental dimen-
sions.

There is nothing new in perceiving Geometric design in Homer.
His use of polarities as a structural principle has been traced in
certain contexts with convincing results.[15] His use of the magic
numbers three and nine has been compared, less convincingly, to
Geometric circles.[16] Long ago, the *Shield of Achilles* was analyzed

as a symmetrically balanced set of opposites, and manifestly a de-
signed balance was intended in the fact that the *Iliad* begins with
a quarrel and ends with a reconciliation.[17] The men who are recon-
ciled are not the same as those who quarreled, of course; the poem
has its own movement and does not end precisely where it began.
The formulaic types, Quarrel and Reconciliation, are employed as
balanced opposites, while the contextual difference, with all its
implications for the character of the hero, creates the poet's mean-
ing. Less meaningful but more surprising is the grouping of the
days involved in the poem's action. So far as elapsed, or narrated,
time is concerned, the night embassy to Achilles (with the *Doloneia*,
if genuine) forms the middle point, flanked on each side by a single
day's fighting: namely, the indecisive Interrupted Battle of VIII
and the extremely decisive Great Battle of XI to XVIII.242. These
are in turn framed by two groups of three days each, in which
the action is not only closely unified but also similar. Books II to VII
devote one day to fighting (II–VII.282), one to burial of the dead
(VII.421–433), and one to the building of the wall (VII.434–482).
The corresponding group includes three days, too: the day of
Achilles' *aristeia* (XIX–XXIII.58), the funeral of Patroclus (XXIII.
109–225), and the Funeral Games (XXIII.226–end). The day
groupings of I and XXIV then reverse each other neatly: Book I
has first the day of Chryses' appeal, followed by nine days of
plague, the day of the council and quarrel, and finally a twelve-day
gap till the gods return to Olympus; Book XXIV begins with a
twelve-day period during which the gods grow steadily more dis-
gusted with Achilles' excesses, followed by the day on which Iris
rouses Priam to go to the Greek camp; nine days are then devoted
to gathering wood for Hector's pyre, and on the tenth day he is
buried.[18] The scheme of days then looks like this:

Book I   Book XXIV

1–9–1–12 — 1–1–1 — 1 — EMBASSY — 1 — 1–1–1 — 12–1–9–1

                      Inter-   night   Great
                      rupted [Doloneia?] Battle
              Fight Battle   Fight
              Burial   Burial
              Wall   Games

This can scarcely have made itself felt to a listening audience; and yet, it can hardly be fortuitous. Homer seems to have been playing with abstract form for its own sake, and basing his conception of it on the hysteron proteron scheme. Its mathematical symmetry would appeal to any artist of the Geometric Age. If it seems far-fetched for such a pristine time, we must bear in mind that there is absolutely nothing primitive about Homer except some parts of his traditional subject matter. And if it seems pointless and imperceptible from the point of view of the general public of Homer's period, we should also ask how many of Mozart's original audiences appreciated the extraordinary economy of tonality in *Don Giovanni*, or caught the musical puns on horns in *Figaro* and *Cosi fan tutte*.[19] So too, not all the admirers of *Lohengrin* know that, with the exception of one passage near the end of the first act, the opera is written wholly in 2/4 or 4/4 time, a feature of inner unity of no consequence to the conscious receptivity of the layman, but a token for fellow artists, on the one hand, and an unperceived but effectual device, on the other. Music, indeed, abounds in such abstractions, yet aims at achieving its effect even on those who cannot follow them. To dismiss or judge adversely these technical procedures, however, because they are not readily seen by non-professionals, is to assail art and raise the banners of Philistia. The artist hopes, but does not insist, that his technicalities will be universally admired. He can be understood on many levels, and it is only an added pleasure to be caught red-handed in a secret technical virtuosity.

But the *Iliad's* Geometric form is not confined to the grouping of days. As said above in connection with the confrontation of the Quarrel and the Reconciliation, the *Iliad* presents a vast hysteron proteron of scenes, in which episodes, and even whole books, balance each other through similarity or opposition. In this system, the center is not the Embassy, but the Great Battle, and the responsion of parts is most obvious in the early and late parts of the poem. This fact is not surprising, since the technique is essentially one of framing or enclosing; one might even call attention to the later instinct of the rhetoricians and prose stylists, who paid much attention to the rhythm of the beginnings and ends of sentences, and let the rest be filled in less formally. So too, in Geometric pottery, the greatest tendency toward naturalism, imbalance, and loose design is to be found in the scenes or metopes of funeral or war which sometimes appear toward the center of the vase, while the flanking borders and friezes rely upon the strictest conventionalism and exact symmetry. Furthermore, while the beginning and end of the *Iliad* respond mutually throughout the first nine and the last nine books, certain books form separate systems, either singly, or in groups, within the larger system, wherever a section of the narrative achieves a partial self-completeness. Thus the form of Book I, for instance, is not in itself annular, since its action is introductory rather than rounded; but it forms a circle with Book XXIV. Books III to VII, however, whose content intervenes between the adoption and the activation of Zeus' plan, form a perfectly enclosed Geometric system of balancing scenes, framing the *aristeia* of Diomedes.

When one comes to regard the details, they are sometimes surprisingly precise in pattern. The principal scenes of Book I, for instance, are (1) the rejection of Chryses, with the plague and the funeral pyres; (2) the council of chiefs and the Quarrel; (3) Thetis with Achilles, consoling him and agreeing to take a message to Zeus; (4) Thetis with Zeus, where the latter adopts the hero's cause; (5) the disputatious assembly of the gods, where Hera opposes Zeus. Book XXIV takes up this scheme, but reverses it, beginning with (5) the dispute among the gods, with Hera still leading the opposition, though now in a different sense; (4) Thetis with Zeus, receiving notice that the gods no longer support Achilles in his maltreatment of Hector's corpse; (3) Thetis with Achilles, consoling him and bringing him a message from Zeus; (2) Achilles with Priam, where the magnanimous restitution of Hector's body inverts the selfish seizure of Briseis, and the compassion between technical enemies reverses the hostility between technical allies of Book I; and finally (1) the funeral of Hector in Troy, corresponding, though perhaps vaguely to the first funerals of the poem in the Greek camp..Two important episodes cause a slight asymmetry: the Chrysa-scene, and the coming of Priam. Both are journeys, both have propitiation as their purpose, though beyond this they have little in common; also, they do not fit the hysteron-proteron scheme; still, the pattern of the first and last books emerges as essentially Geometric.

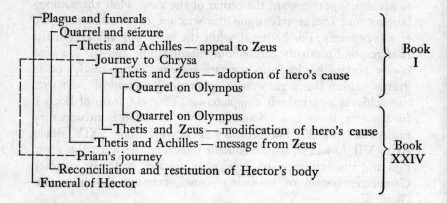

Here the balanced elements involve identity, or similarity, as in the funerals, or the people involved in the scenes; but the antitheses are actually more important. The case of Quarrel–Seizure versus Reconciliation–Restitution is the most striking, but the two scenes between Zeus and Thetis also offer a subtle contrast. In the first, Thetis is a secret suppliant to Zeus, and Hera regards her with a jaundiced eye. In the second, Thetis comes by invitation to Olympus; Athena yields her own seat to her, Hera offers her pleasant words and a goblet of gold, and this time it is Zeus who has the request.[20] Though his words are couched in the form of a command, he is, in a way, appealing to her, for, as he says, he is bound by his promise to her and cannot allow the body of Hector to be stolen. This reversal of positions between Zeus and Thetis deeply underlines the degree to which Achilles has added cubits to his own stature. He now holds the timeless world in the palm of his hand.

The next pair of books does not show an equal elegance of design. Their responsion is more broad and impressionistic, yet both are fundamentally similar in design, and both are Geometric. Book II is in two parts, the *Assembly* and the *Catalogue*, both of which deploy for the first time in the poem the host at large. Its spirit is panoramic and epic, rather than dramatic, and it offers a glimpse, rare in heroic poetry, of the feelings of the common soldiery in the person of Thersites, who is developed with bitter and rather low humor. The Assembly itself falls into two parts of opposing purport, first where the soldiers, misled by Agamemnon, rush to the ships to sail them home, and second where they are brought to heel by Odysseus with hopes of victory, equally misled, and shout vigorously for war at once. It is a disillusioned picture that Homer paints here, of a people deceived and hypnotized like sheep by leaders who are in turn deceived by Zeus. It is, in Jeffers' phrase, the "dance of the dream-led masses down the dark mountain," and the only person who speaks honestly in it is Thersites, the incarnation of the ugly truth.[21] In the perspective of a society driving to its ruin under magnificent but corrupt leadership, truth shows itself in a warped, repulsive form and is silenced by simple violence — a blow from the lordly but greed-ridden and deceiving scepter of the Pelopids. Thus at the center of this broad and brilliant display of the Achaean power stands Thersites, disgraced and weeping, not a little as Achilles also stands, stripped of his shirt as Achilles was stripped of his prize, by the self-willed decisions of the regime.

The two Assemblies are preceded and followed by two private gatherings of the princes, the first in which Agamemnon reveals his dream from Zeus, which is accepted as true by Nestor, and the second in which the king sacrifices a bull to Zeus for the fulfillment of the dream, and Zeus, accepting the sacrifice, refuses the fulfillment. The first part of the book thus falls into the following scenic structure.

Book II [without *Catalogue*]
Deceitful dream sent by Zeus
  Council of chiefs
    1 Assembly — conscious deception by Agamemnon
      Rush for the ships stemmed by Odysseus and Athena
    2 Assembly — unconscious deception by Odysseus and others
  Council of chiefs
Sacrifice to Zeus, and refusal of the prayer (affirmation of original deception)

Incidentally, the first speech of Agamemnon to the people is an important linking motif, for it is repeated in abbreviated form at the beginning of Book IX.[22] The words which Agamemnon first utters in falsehood, leaning comfortably on his scepter, he repeats in a dark hour in deadly earnest, groaning heavily and weeping "like a spring of dark water," when the truth begins to settle on him.

This first section is then followed by the marshaling, with its six fine similes giving the sense impressions of the host, and the *Catalogue*, giving the factual details of it. The *Catalogue* has been most unjustly despised. In its way, it is just as vivid as the famous similes which introduce it. No love is more deeply imbedded in the Greek soul than the love for places in Greece, with their names, the mountains, valleys, nooks, and rivers of the maternal soil. It is more than patriotic; the *Catalogue*, with its recounting of these place names, their leaders and their legends, has a religious love about it; it is a kind of hymnic invocation. When read aloud, its clear and easy stride seems resistless and inexhaustible, like the movement of an army on the march, and each contingent as it goes by is splendid with the retrospect of home, the continuous surprise of the familiar. At the close of each entry, a stock line gives the number of ships attending the leader, and these lines, varying a little, but all echoing each other, have the incantational validity of a refrain. In antiquity, a hymn to a god recounted his deeds; the hymn to an army recounts its constituents. The whole is ballad-like and brilliantly descriptive, freighted, like everything in Homer, with history and tradition, and touched with foreshadowings of the future. A hundred years or so later, Sappho listed an army as one of the things most beautiful in the world, and here we get some idea of what she meant.[23] If the first half of Book II gives an inner view of ugly truth and uglier deceit, the *Catalogue* is a simple vision of the Achaean panorama, seen from without indeed, but seen with clear precise sensibility, and utter mastery of the traditional and formal material.

The twenty-third book again, and for the last time, offers a panorama of the army, and again, its structure is bipartite: *Funeral* and *Games*. Like Book II, it involves a motivating dream, but unlike Agamemnon's dream, that of Achilles is true; that is, the shade of Patroclus appearing in his sleep urges him to do what indeed he should and must do — bury the dead. The pyre scene which follows is in outline the usual formula of such rituals, but enormously inflated with detail, and adorned with symbols of Achilles' devotion, culminating in the offering of the lock of hair, and of his savagery, in the immolation of the captives. It terminates with Achilles again falling asleep exhausted; the gathering and burial of the bones is briefly told, perhaps to balance the scene of the dragging of Hector which opened the book; and then follow the *Games*, linear in design, like the *Catalogue*, with one event following another as the contingents of the army had. Structurally, therefore, it is closely analogous to Book II, though with no reversal of order:

Book XXIII [without *Games*]

```
                                              to II (dream)
 ┌─Dragging of Hector and boast of no burial for him    ▲
 │  ┌─Achilles asleep — dream of Patroclus ──────────────┘
 │  │  Funeral
 │  └─Achilles asleep
 └─Gathering and burial of bones
```


So much for the externals, which are here less brilliant than elsewhere. In its import, however, the twenty-third book corresponds to and reverses the second book with peculiar subtlety. If the latter had shown the Achaean society deceived and disordered, dreaming of glories that were not to be, and mastered by either violence or fraud, this spirit is quite reversed in the *Games*, where for the last time all the main characters are passed in review. Musterings for war and festival are in themselves social polarities.[24] Agamemnon, wounded and still smarting with humiliation, is somewhat *hors de combat*; Achilles is the center of the Achaean scene. In contrast to what Thersites had said of Agamemnon's greed for booty, Achilles is the most lavish of prize-givers and, in pointed contrast to Agamemnon's former behavior, he awards the king a gratuitious prize. This is aristocratic society in order, where magnanimity and *noblesse oblige* operate as they should, and men's true abilities appear. Moreover, where Book II harked back to the portents at Aulis,[25] the panorama of the *Games* foreshadows the future in certain details, and draws into the scheme of the *Iliad* hints of the traditional events later told in the *Little Iliad*, *The Sack of Troy*, and the *Returns*.

The Judgment of the Arms is suggested by the wrestling match of Odysseus and Ajax; Diomedes' safe passage home can almost be foreseen in his easy success in the chariot race. The fate of the brave, but illegitimate, Teucer, who was driven away by his father when he returned without Ajax, seems implied when he is worsted in the archery contest by a lesser man, and comes off second best. Particularly interesting is the slip and fall of Ajax of Locris in the dung of the sacrificed oxen. Athena pushed him, she who later, for his rape of Cassandra, was to blast him with lightning on his return home. The Achaeans all "laugh sweetly at him," the same formula in which they had laughed at the discomfiture of Thersites.[26] These two episodes find their function in the accent they place on two contrasted views of the social order. In the world misled by kings deceived by Zeus and their own self-conceptions, the people laugh at the wrong thing — the vulgar but accurate speaker of the truth. In the world ordered by the law of magnanimity, and *areté*, they laugh rightly at the indignity suffered by one who is outwardly a prince, but inwardly, as Homer never is weary of showing, a ruffian and a boor.[27]

Thus in a way, Book XXIII offers a true panorama, and one illustrative of the characters of all, where Book II gave a picture at its best external in the *Catalogue*, and at its worst deceptive in the *Assembly*, where authority overrides the truth. Book II is dominated by Agamemnon and Odysseus, a syndicate designed to choose means and achieve ends; Book XXIII is dominated by Achilles and the shade of Patroclus, already an archetypal friendship, an end in itself, and a landmark of being.

As has long been recognized, Book III through VII form a natural group by virtue of the fact that during them the operation of the Plan of Zeus is essentially suspended, and very little notice is taken of the main theme of the Wrath. Only in Book VIII does Zeus forbid the gods their part in the war and begin to encourage Hector. For the space of five books, all that has been put in motion is temporarily set aside, and we find a series of episodes which cannot be regarded as in any sense a sequential narrative of events. The difficulties which arise in the plot are well known. The Greeks, according to plan, are supposed to be defeated in the absence of Achilles; but they are, on the whole, slightly more successful than the Trojans, so that the wall which they build at the end of Book VII to protect their camp seems not very well motivated by the day's events. The deeds of Diomedes, for all their brilliance, lead to no result, nor do the two duels, between Paris and Menelaus, Ajax and Hector. There is much motion, much coming and going, but no one of consequence is slain, except perhaps Pandarus, and the plot is not advanced at all. It has become a truism to point out also that the View from the Walls, where Priam has not yet learned to recognize the enemy leaders, as well as the duel of Paris and Menelaus, and perhaps that of Ajax and Hector, all belong naturally to the first year of the war, and are out of place in the ninth. The same should probably be said of the fortification of the camp, the episode of Glaucus and Diomedes, with its lofty chivalric tone, and of the council wherein a negotiated peace is contemplated in the possible return of Helen. Such attitudes occur when war is not yet a total commitment, and they scarcely accord with the dark and bloody determination of the rest of the *Iliad*. Clearly Homer has narrated events out of their natural order, and one must ask both why he did so, and how he dared, before audiences who must have known the tradition and had doubtless heard these episodes sung in their proper places, albeit in perhaps different versions.

If one looks at the structure of the five books as a whole, it is clear that this is no mere case of padding, but a most intricately designed, perhaps the most intricately designed, block of narrative in the whole *Iliad*. Homer has deliberately taken these episodes from their original context and rearranged them in the strictest Geometric pattern, which frames the *aristeia* of Diomedes as centerpiece. It is sometimes suggested that this *aristeia* presents Diomedes attempting to fill the gap left by Achilles' retirement.[28] But Achilles' absence is not yet really felt at all, for this whole section belongs to earlier years and different intentions. Diomedes' *aristeia*, packed with bright similes, high-hearted encounters with gods, and all the virtuosity at the command of a great master of the tradition, is a heroic comedy, which corresponds to the heroic tragedy of the *aristeia* of Achilles toward the end of the poem. It is a summary and a type, in part normative for the general view of the characteristic warlike achievements and pretensions of the Achaeans, in part strictly individual in its development of the personal nature of Diomedes, gallant, attractive, but limited. Like so many parts of the Homeric narrative, it falls into four primary phases, each developed with smaller episodes, and these lie symmetrically on either side of the brief meeting of the hero with Apollo. In the first and fourth of these phases, Diomedes is attended by Athena in person, in the second he is extremely successful, until he is thrust back by Apollo, while in the third he is steadily forced to retreat until rejoined by Athena. Preluded and punctuated by transitional passages of general warfare (*androktasiai*), these four main episodes have this approximate pattern:

Book V

Diomedes with Athena:
(a) Diomedes worsted by Pandarus
(b) Athena comes to his assistance
(c) Diomedes, with Athena's help, kills Pandarus

Diomedes *vs*. Aeneas: Wounding of Aphrodite [Greeks have advantage]

Diomedes turned back by Apollo

Diomedes *vs*. Sarpedon and Hector, led by Ares [Trojans have advantage]

Diomedes with Athena:
(a) Diomedes worsted before Ares
(b) Athena comes to his assistance
(c) Diomedes with Athena's help, wounds Ares

As an illustration of the singular kinds of inversion the epic motifs are subject to, it might be pointed out that in her first scene with Diomedes, Athena warns him not to fight with any gods except Aphrodite.[29] Diomedes observes this rule with care until it is countermanded by the goddess herself, who urges him to attack Ares.[30]

Books III to IV and VI to VII form a heavy frame around this paradigm of a Greek hero in action, more strict at the edges than elsewhere. Book III has three main episodes: a truce with oaths; the *Teichoscopia* or View from the Walls, where the Trojan elders sit with Helen, and, though their estimate of her is high, wish that she would go home; and the duel between Menelaus and Paris, to which is added the little domestic scene between the latter and his now disillusioned and reluctant mistress, who wishes him dead. Book VII corresponds with some exactness: it begins with a duel, equally indecisive as the former one, between Ajax and Hector, but, in contrast to the other, it ends in mutual respect and a chivalric exchange of gifts.[31] This is followed by a council of the elders of Troy, again though not now in her presence, deliberating about Helen and wanting to send her home. The book ends with another truce, with oaths, for the taking up of the dead to which is added the very brief narratives of the wall-building, the Thracian wine ships, and the nocturnal threat of Zeus' thunder. Books IV and VI correspond a little less exactly, from the external point of view, yet again three motifs seem designed with some parallelism. Book IV begins with an act of treachery on the Trojan side, when Pandarus breaks the truce by shooting Menelaus. At once the Greek army springs to action, and the episode which follows was called in antiquity the Marshaling of Agamemnon. As the battle begins, the gods, Athena and Ares, join in the fight. At the end of Book V and the beginning of VI it is noted that the gods have left the field. The general melee proceeds for a few lines, after which Hector at the instigation of Helenus rallies the beleaguered Trojans and drives back the Greeks somewhat.[32] Presumably this corresponds to Agamemnon's display of generalship in IV. The scene between Diomedes and Glaucus then interrupts the scheme, but connects with the *Diomedeia*, and the book closes with the episode of Hector in Troy, with Hecuba, Helen, and Andromache. This last reveals a very different aspect of the Trojans from that seen in the treachery of Pandarus. The one was the height of irresponsibility and villainy — *anaideia*, in Greek terms — the other offers the complete and winning picture of faithfulness, goodness, and *aidôs*. One seems to reflect the justice of the war, the other certainly mirrors its tragedy. But further, the scene of Hector and Andromache, the truly married pair, inverts the picture of the wanton lovers, Paris and Helen, both in the obvious matter of devotion versus lust, and even in some of the details of what they say to each other. Helen rebukes Paris for his lack of valor and wishes he were dead; Andromache fears above everything harm for her husband, and rebukes him for being too reckless.[33] Helen despises Paris for his lack of shame; Hector would be ashamed not to defend his city.[34] Thus

the scene of Hector in Troy answers not only to the Pandarus
scene, but also to the preceding one at the end of III; and the two
latter are thus linked in a way which has further implications.
The whole narrative from III.395 to IV.219 — that is, the scenes of
Aphrodite, Paris, and Helen, Menelaus in mad frustration hunting
for a vanished Paris, and finally Pandarus shooting Menelaus —
form a kind of compressed reënactment of the original treachery
which caused the war. Pandarus, a garrulous and irresponsible
archer, is not entirely different from Paris, and his target is, signif-
icantly, Menelaus; the armies move into battle as a result of his act
as the Achaean host mobilized at the act of Paris. Aphrodite is re-
vealed as an inward compelling force, and Menelaus is shown,
empty-handed, wounded, and raging with humiliation. In oppo-
sition to all this are Hector and Andromache, the noble sufferers on
the offending side, to whom the war brings unjustified destruction.
More than the typology of stock scenes is involved here; Homer
has created a montage of the motivating crime under the guise of
continuous narrative, and opposed to it a foreshadowing of its ul-
timate results. For the Hector–Andromache scene also is closely
allied with the closing books of the poem, and the lamentation for
Hector "while yet alive" pointedly indicates the tragedy to come.[35]
The pattern for the whole of Books III to VII stands as shown
below.

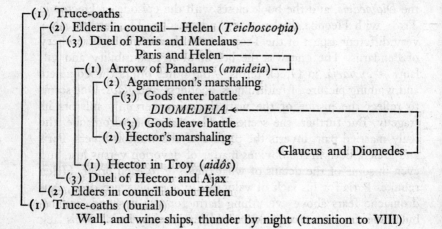

(1) Truce-oaths
  (2) Elders in council — Helen (*Teichoscopia*)
    (3) Duel of Paris and Menelaus —
              Paris and Helen ————————
      (1) Arrow of Pandarus (*anaideia*)——
        (2) Agamemnon's marshaling
          (3) Gods enter battle
              DIOMEDEIA ◄————————————————
          (3) Gods leave battle
        (2) Hector's marshaling
                                Glaucus and Diomedes —
      (1) Hector in Troy (*aidôs*)
    (3) Duel of Hector and Ajax
  (2) Elders in council about Helen
(1) Truce-oaths (burial)
          Wall, and wine ships, thunder by night (transition to VIII)

From what has been shown of the structure and import of this group of books, it is clear what the poet's concern must have been. Summary of antecedent events is a regular feature of epic technique; Odysseus' recollection of the portents at Aulis, or the long flashback about the scar in the *Odyssey*, and even some of Nestor's reminiscences are characteristic examples. But no real account of the earlier years of the Trojan War, or of its motivation, exists in the *Iliad*. It could, of course, be assumed that all knew it anyway, and such a deliberate narration would have been intolerable. On the other hand, Homer's intention was not simply to narrate the Wrath of Achilles, but to include a panorama of the war as a whole. To see in the unity of a single episode the summary and the implications of the total action to which it belongs, and somehow to subordinate these to the event selected as central, is one of the first premisses of the dramatic instinct. When one considers the skill with which Sophocles reveals the antecedent facts of the story in *Oedipus Rex*, it is obvious that Homer has no such native, supple, and developed gift for structural syntax as that; his style remains, of necessity, bound to the linear parataxis of epic tradition. Events are to be narrated in proper order, or at least they must seem to be. In the *Odyssey* the extremely rational and plausible device is adopted of allowing Odysseus himself to narrate the events of the preceding ten years.[36] In Books III to VII of the *Iliad*, Homer has selected representative scenes from parts of the story which must have been older, and retold them in the guise of sequential events. So far as the main plot is concerned, they remain static; dramatically they serve to expand enormously the tapestry of the poem and to bring within the scheme of the Wrath of Achilles a total view of the war up to that point. By dint of association of motifs whose typicality allowed them to include wider implications than they have in and of themselves, Homer has created a dramatic inset, a round summary of all the significant emotions, if not all the events, of the earlier part of the war: the crime of Paris, the sorrow and rage of Menelaus, Helen's position in Troy, the reactions of the Trojans to her, the attempt to negotiate peace and Paris' resistance to it, the early efforts to settle the war by duels instead of general bloodshed, the fortification of the beachhead, the misery and fear of the Trojan wives and mothers, and the fresh valor, lit by touches of chivalric generosity, of Diomedes and others, in a time before the action settles down to deadliest earnest. The device by which all this is pulled into the *Iliad* is a self-conscious one, and it is a little stiff. But it is Geometric to the core, carefully designed for its place in the poem, and indispensable to the totality which Homer intended. Viewed by the standards of the Geometric Age, it is a triumph of early syntax.

The corresponding group of books at the other end of the poem forms the completest possible contrast. Far from being static plot-wise, Books XVIII to XXII seem at last to put in motion the long-pent-up energy of deeds interminably motivated and anxiously awaited. When Achilles finally takes the field, one has the feeling that all the surge and motion of the *Iliad* hitherto has been nothing, so far does the hero's roused vitality surpass all else. More important, as the Group III to VII summarizes the first part of the war, so the *aristeia* of Achilles, as has been noted before herein and also by others, symbolizes the last of it in that it not only foreshadows Achilles' death, but also, in the *Theomachia*, in the surrender of Scamander, and in the frequent images of burning cities, the final fall of Troy. So the *Iliad*, ostensibly the tale of an event in the ninth year of hostilities (and not an extremely vital event at that for the general outcome), is made to embrace dramatically and by implication the entire epic tradition about the Achaeans at Troy; and the final touch, as has been suggested, is the foreshadowing, under the guise of athletic contests of Book XXIII, of events after the fall of the city.

Structurally, these books are not quite so elegantly devised as the group to which they correspond. This fact is not surprising in view of the difference in function between the two. The *aristeia* of Achilles advances the plot and must move from point to point, where the earlier group is a self-enclosed inset. Yet the separate phases of Books XVIII to XXII exhibit an attempt to impose the familiar system of balances by similarity and opposition. These phases may be regarded as either three or four in number, of which the first includes Books XVIII and XIX, the preparations for vengeance. When Antilochus brings the news of Patroclus' death to Achilles, the latter's reactions fall into the general pattern of a funeral, which is made more pointed by the great speech, "Let me die at once." [37] This theme of Achilles' death, now a certainty, is indeed touched on lightly by Hephaestus and Thetis,[38] but recurs with heavy emphasis only at the very end of Book XIX, when the horse Xanthus prophesies death to his master as he sets out. Prophecies by horses are calculated to arrest attention, and it is possible that Homer purposely chose to call attention to his motif in this way. It recurs, of course, in the mouth of the dying Hector, echoing both forward and backward.[39] Here it simply rounds off with the knowledge of certain death Achilles' resumption of the war. The principal motif of these two books is perhaps the divine armor. In answer to the speech, "Let me die at once," Thetis points out that her son's armor is lost, and promises him arms from Hephaestus. These he naturally puts on immediately before mounting his chariot when the horse prophesies. But the arms also form the centerpiece of these two books, in the pair of scenes where they are made by Hephaestus and brought to Achilles by Thetis. Before and after this centerpiece fall episodes which group themselves loosely under either Achilles' resolution and the eagerness for battle or the lamentations for Patroclus. These include the shout from the trench, the first laments when the corpse is brought back, the marshaling of the Myrmidons, the official renunciation of the Wrath, with its brilliant confrontation of the demonically possessed Achilles and the wordly-wise Odysseus, and then the further laments, including that of Briseis, over Patroclus. Some asymmetry occurs in two small scenes of the gods, and in the council of Trojans as they camp on the plain for the second time. The latter, of course is a link to Book VIII, and is quite symmetrical in the larger scheme of the whole. The design is therefore approximately as shown below.

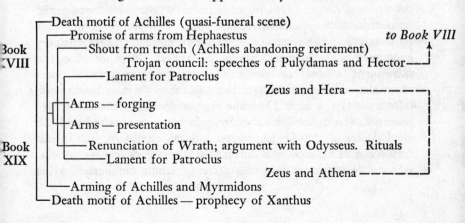

The next two books are very closely unified in action and design. The fight in the plain and the fight in the river actually form two somewhat contrasting phases of the *aristeia*, since Achilles in the second struggles with the river for a time almost as helplessly as his victims do with him in the first; yet since in their broad outlines the two books form a strict annular system, it is better to look at them together. A prelude on Olympus gives the official dissolution of the Plan of Zeus, and the gods are allowed to resume their activities in the war. This forms a link with the renunciation of the Wrath in XIX. The gods then repair to the Trojan plain and line up for hostilities. But no hostilities occur immediately. Apollo encourages Aeneas to meet Achilles, and then presently the gods, who had been so eager to participate, retire upon agreement to two separate vantage points to observe Achilles.[40] There follow two long developed scenes in which Aeneas and Hector both try to stand against Achilles, and both are whisked away to safety, Aeneas by Poseidon, and Hector by Apollo. The book closes with a general melee in which Achilles with the Greeks at his heels slays and drives the Trojans toward the river. This melee (*androktasia*) continues uninterrupted as Book XXI begins, and then two more developed scenes emerge from the confusion. This time the victims, Lycaon, son of Priam, and Asteropaeus, a leader of the Paeonians, are not so fortunate. Both are slain, in contrast to the two previous rescues; and, though it may be coincidental, like Hector and Aeneas, one is a Trojan prince, the other an ally, and at that, they appear in reverse order.[41] And now the divine forces begin to work again: through the natural blocking of the river's flow with corpses, the Scamander first appeals to Achilles, and then overflows and tries to drown him. The rescue of Achilles by Poseidon and Athena perhaps mirrors the former's rescue of Aeneas, but in any case, the subsequent outbreak of hostilities among the gods certainly completes the earlier scene where they had taken up their battle positions and then retired. The issue is now decided: the fire of Hephaestus, which Achilles also carries in his arms, has reduced the local deities of the Trojan rivers, and the city is to fall. In the final scene, the Greek gods defeat the Trojan gods, except Apollo, whose role continues only in a delaying action, betokened by his deception and deflection of Achilles, while the host of the Trojans escape within the walls.[42] The pattern is extremely strict.

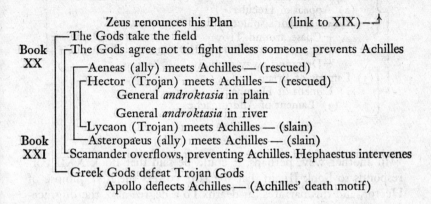

Zeus renounces his Plan   (link to XIX) —↲
  The Gods take the field
Book   The Gods agree not to fight unless someone prevents Achilles
XX
      Aeneas (ally) meets Achilles — (rescued)
      Hector (Trojan) meets Achilles — (rescued)
        General *androktasia* in plain

        General *androktasia* in river
      Lycaon (Trojan) meets Achilles — (slain)
Book   Asteropaeus (ally) meets Achilles — (slain)
XXI Scamander overflows, preventing Achilles. Hephaestus intervenes

  Greek Gods defeat Trojan Gods
    Apollo deflects Achilles — (Achilles' death motif)

Book XXII is linked to the preceding by the completion of the scene of Apollo's deception of Achilles, which subtly reminds one also of the hero's death motif, and thus connects with the last speech of Hector. For the rest, the book is designed rather simply, and is mostly self-enclosed. Priam and Hecuba, seeing Achilles' approach and Hector standing outside the gate, utter their appeals; then comes Hector's famous soliloquy. These three speeches are balanced at the end by the three laments of Priam, Hecuba, and finally Andromache; here all mere formality is transfigured by the inevitability of the speakers, and one may observe how perfectly the poetic economy is devised to fit the given material. As Achilles gets close, Hector flees, and the chase around Troy begins, to be balanced by the dragging of the body later. The poet in both connections emphasizes that these horrors were happening to Hector on his own home soil, a feature of special poignancy.[43] The next scene, that of the scales, the arrival of Athena, and the departure of Apollo, might be called asymmetrical, but the divine scenes frequently are mere extensions, either before or after the human ones, and this should probably be looked upon as part of the duel, which forms the center of the book. Thus one has for Book XXII the scheme detailed on the next page.

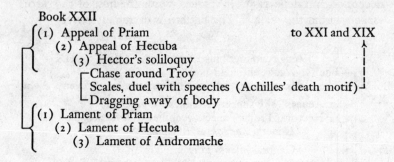

Book XXII
- (1) Appeal of Priam   to XXI and XIX
  - (2) Appeal of Hecuba
    - (3) Hector's soliloquy
      - Chase around Troy
      - Scales, duel with speeches (Achilles' death motif)
      - Dragging away of body
- (1) Lament of Priam
  - (2) Lament of Hecuba
    - (3) Lament of Andromache

In another way, perhaps, it could be said that Book XXII corresponds to Book III, in that the latter offers the first glimpse of Hector, and this narrates his death. To a degree also, the disgraceful and indecisive duel of Paris and Menelaus in III is balanced by this grave and catastrophic one, and the escape of the transgressor is somehow tragically answered by the fall of the unoffending hero. But one need not press matters too far. The correspondences and antinomies are clear and precise in any case.

After the compressed, "dramatic" time of Books III to VII, Book VIII returns to the original time level, or what might be called the "real" time of the *Iliad*. The Plan of Zeus is at last implemented, and the victory begins to go to the Trojans. Functionally, this book serves chiefly to motivate the *Embassy* to Achilles by bringing the Greek pride low, but it is also a masterly deployment of character and dramatic issues. The purport of Achilles' retirement from the war was simply that without him the Greeks could not withstand Hector.[44] Yet the fact that the Greeks ultimately were victorious, and without Achilles, was a complication which somehow had to be reckoned with; that is, this temporary but frightening defeat was not the final truth, and for that reason it appears in the light of peculiar unreason, especially to the pro-Greek gods and to that incarnation of success, Diomedes. Diomedes in retreat is almost a reversal of nature, and Hera's resentful anger reflects and enlarges this feeling of unaccustomed and almost inexplicable frustration. The Trojan victory must be seen, therefore, on two levels, as both natural and unnatural — natural, because Achilles' boast would be idle if the

Greeks could perfectly well have done without him, and unnatural because the heroes whose valor in the end did take the city must here be flung into confusion and despair. It would have been possible to tell the story simply on the first level, but Homer chooses to keep the perspective of the gods before our eyes, and to dramatize the passing moment against the background of events in their totality, which is Moira, or Fate. Diomedes' frustration and disgust, together with the seething rage of Hera and Athena, convey the responses of the long view; so also does the eagle which Zeus sends in answer to Agamemnon's prayer, an omen which recurs in the Great Battle with precisely the same meaning, that the despair need not be permanent.[45] The other level, which views Hector's triumph as a natural result, seems to be suggested in the symbol of the scales which Zeus holds up at noon when the battle is raging.[46] The scales, indicating here as elsewhere what is organically true in any situation, shift the causal responsibility away from Zeus; he consults the facts, so to speak, and the answer which the scales give puts a special coloring on the lightning with which the god proceeds immediately to encourage Hector and confound the Achaeans. The lightning is not a mere external miracle, but a miraculous emblem of what must be inevitably the case under the circumstances —Trojan victory if Achilles retires.

The individual reactions of the chiefs are wonderfully characteristic: Diomedes horrified and unable to believe that he is really being defeated; Nestor, though in grave danger, quite detached and ready to wait for victory on another day; Odysseus so concerned to save his own life that he leaves Nestor helpless; Agamemnon desperate and in tears; Ajax and Teucer grim, but steady and coolheaded, the nucleus of the brief resistance which the Greeks make. Hector, however, is the real masterpiece, as he gradually awakens to the fact that this is, unexpectedly, his day. His modest but sanguine temperament soon recognizes the lightning's import; he urges his men forward, and then calling to his horses, he reminds them of the grain which Andromache has given them in abundance.[47] This rather surprising mention of Andromache, recalling Hector's own scene with her and his warm intense loyalties, somehow poignantly prevents the mind from identifying the man too wholly with the delusion which, beginning at this point, leads him presently to grandiose expectations — the capture of Nestor's shield or Diomedes' breastplate, and finally total victory.

The delusive hope, loyalty, frustration, and dismay which attend the activation of Zeus' plan make up the spirit of the book. From the point of view of scenic structure, it is self-enclosed. It opens with a council of the gods, in which Zeus begins by boasting of his supreme strength, and then forbids the gods to participate in the war. As shown elsewhere, this mood in Zeus is not his natural one in the *Iliad*; it reflects the supremacy and absolutism of Achilles. In turn, its tone of arrogant self-assurance is echoed by Hector at the close of the council of Trojans, when they camp for the night on the plain. Two perhaps inconsequential passages seem to balance each other, where the armies take their meals before and after the battle. Then come the lightning scenes. With some difficulty, Zeus drives Diomedes back with flash after flash, and he finally yields, thinking of the Trojan taunts and wishing the earth would swallow him up.[48] This scene of direct frustration by Zeus finds its counterpoise in the one where he stops Hera and Athena halfway to the battlefield and sends them back with furious threats to maim them with lightning. Later, Zeus seems to point the correspondence neatly when he tells Hera that she too (like Diomedes) may plunge into the depths of the earth in helpless rage, and he still would not care.[49] When one remembers that these two goddesses were the ones who attended Diomedes in his *aristeia*, the connection becomes even clearer. In the center of the book is the attack and victory of Hector, interrupted by a short scene in Heaven,[50] Agamemnon's prayer with the omen and the brief resistance of the chiefs, especially Ajax and Teucer. At the outer verges of the book are two images of Dawn.

As observed earlier, there is a stricter tendency in the early books of the *Iliad* toward Geometric composition than in the later ones, Book XVII, the positional counterpart of VIII, shows no very clear-cut symmetry of outline. Itself a continuation of the Great Battle, it follows the general design of that section in having phases and episodes which bring matters to where they must be plotwise, but, since its action is not self-contained, it seeks no self-contained order. On the other hand, the implications of this book partly re-

Book VIII
Dawn
  Council of Gods with boastful speech of Zeus
    Lightning *vs.* Diomedes (also other chiefs; rescue of Nestor,
      and final retreat of Diomedes)
                                          "Let earth swallow me"
        Hector leads attack
          Scene in Heaven
          Agamemnon's prayer and omen
          Ajax and Teucer
        Hector drives Greeks before him
    Lightning *vs.* Hera and Athena
                                        "Plunge into the earth"
  Council of Trojans and boastful speech of Hector
      Trojans camp on plain; *cf. XVIII*
Dawn

flect and partly invert those of VIII. The atmosphere of frustration
is now pervasive, as both Trojans and Greeks strive vainly to pos-
sess the body of Patroclus. Still deluded by over-high hopes, Hector
tries to secure the horses of Achilles.[51] Moreover, his delusion is
reaching its climax, as Zeus reflects when Hector puts on the arms
of Achilles.[52] Most important of all, XVII reverses the Plan of Zeus
which began to operate in VIII. It is not, of course, formally re-
nounced until Book XX, but in XVII Zeus' mind reflects Achilles'
partly abated anger, and begins to waver. He envies Hector the
arms, pities Patroclus, and sheds mist over the battle to obscure the
sorrowful sight.[53] The other gods, who had been banned from the
field in VIII, begin to reappear: at least, Athena appears, sent by
Zeus himself to help the Greeks; "his mind changed," says Homer.[54]
But presently he changes it again, and for the last time, correspond-
ing to its first appearance in VIII, the lightning comes back to
hearten Hector.[55] Zeus is indecisive and so is the battle. The decisive
end can come only when Achilles learns what has happened; and
one of the prominent motifs of the book, a token of its vain effort
and helpless striving, is the reiterated fact that Achilles does not yet
know, and that someone must tell him.[56] The whole episode ends
only in the next book, when Achilles shouts from the rampart, the
Trojans reel back, and the Achaeans rescue the body. Thus part of

XVIII must be taken as the counterpoise to VIII, and here indeed one finds a pronounced circularity. As in VIII, the Trojans camp again on the plain, and Hector reiterates his boasts, in very similar terms.[57] The irony is obvious, of course, since now the Plan of Zeus no longer exists, Achilles is aroused, and only Pulydamas perceives where matters really stand. The responsion with its reversed import is clear, and the slight inconcinnity of position is necessitated by the plot which is now becoming imperious and putting difficulties in the way of perfect symmetry.

Book XVII

androktasia — Ajax and Menelaus over the body
Hector puts on Achilles' armor   **1**
Zeus shakes his head
mist   *androktasia* — Ajax and Menelaus over the body   **2**
Passage on Antilochus and
Achilles not yet knowing
Zeus shakes his head over the weeping horses
Automedon's deeds (456–542)
androktasia — Ajax and Menelaus over the body   **3**
Must tell Achilles
Prayer of Ajax
mist rises and blows away
Menelaus sends Antilochus to Achilles   **4**
"Achilles has no armor"
Retreat carrying the body

If Book XVII lacks extreme elegance of design, it nevertheless is extremely rich, as are all the battle books, in handsome similes. Compositional procedure here somewhat resembles also that in Book V, where four sequential phases of the *aristeia* were set off against each other by rather slight surface devices to produce contrast; in addition, Book V also abounds in dazzling imagery. Here the recurrent motifs, which set off to a degree the parts of the book, and lend a little order to the general melee and *androktasia*, are primarily: Achilles' arms, put on by Hector toward the beginning of the book and noted as lost by Ajax near the end; the theme of Achilles' ignorance of the tragedy and the need to tell him; Zeus shaking his head mournfully over the miseries of men; and the theme of mist. These motifs mark off somewhat vaguely four stages of the fight, in the first two of which the Achaeans have a slight advantage in spite of Apollo's presence on the other side, and in the last two of which the case is reversed in spite of Athena's presence on the Greek side. This is indeed the book of confusion, the dark hour before dawn, but such symmetry as it possesses might be analyzed as shown on the opposite page.

These parts can scarcely be called clearly articulated, and it remains that the chief elements which connect this book with VIII are the disappearance of the Plan of Zeus, and the Trojan council on the plain, which actually is reserved for Book XVIII.

The ninth and the sixteenth books of the *Iliad* are so obviously linked to each other as focal points of the main narrative that it is unnecessary to point out how the latter completes and in a way reverses the former. Achilles' rejection of the embassy, or at least of Agamemnon's offer, is here answered by his yielding to Patroclus. Yet in a sense he had yielded to Ajax also when, in contrast to his former threat to go home, he stated that he would fight when the battle reached his ships.[58] His further modification of his stand here continues to express the force of Achilles' sense of humanity, but also brings into final conflict the two irreconcilables which are rending his will. This conflict is felt and discussed in Book IX; in XVI it must be acted out, partly because the real urgency is now greater, but chiefly because the human demand comes home to Achilles much more closely. Perhaps the most beautiful and clearly significant repetition of a motif in the whole *Iliad* is the one of the "dark-watered spring" which occurs at the beginning of both IX and XVI.[59] When it first occurs, it is Agamemnon who weeps like a dark-watered spring when he cries failure and proposes abandonment of the war. His words are identical, though in abbreviated form, with those in which he had made the same proposal in Book II, but then speciously, himself deceived by Zeus. Now it is Patroclus who weeps like the dark spring in Achilles' presence, and the image, now weighted with its former associations and future implications, does more than link the two books together. It also reflects Achilles' torn emotions, his sense of grief, to which wrath has now given place. In Book IX, even to Ajax, he had said that his heart swelled with rage when he remembered the insult.[60] To

Patroclus, he calls his feeling "pain," and confesses that he cannot maintain ceaseless rage.[61] Accented by the repeated simile, the altered context gleams the more dramatically, and there is a close union between Achilles' mood and the tears of Patroclus.

Both IX and XVI are approximately of tripartite construction, though in the latter case, the traditional features of a battle scene lend themselves less readily to Geometric balance than does a series of speeches. Book IX is quite orderly, with its councils at the beginning and end, and the *Embassy* proper in the middle. Agamemnon's first speech is a link, as already noted, to Book II, and falls outside the design. Diomedes' brave retort to him, a paradigm of the simple valor which had been found wanting in the preceding day's fight, is echoed by that hero's restatement of his own value and intentions at the very end of the book. For the rest, the council speeches do not balance precisely, since three by Nestor and one by Agamemnon are answered by only one each of Agamemnon and Odysseus. The symmetry, however, makes itself felt. The *Embassy* proper is extremely formal, both in atmosphere and design. At the center lies the speech of Phoenix, the pattern of *sophrosyne*, to which is opposed, before and after, two speeches of Achilles which eloquently, if with some confusion and indirection, express the absolutism of his position, and his search for its appropriate expression. Phoenix is the only one of the envoys who understands the real and dangerous inner forces in Achilles, and these three speeches, the core of the *Embassy*, are the only ones relating to those forces. The appeals of Odysseus and Ajax are diametrically opposed, the one based on gain (*kerdos*) and self interest, the other on humanity, the claims of others, and *aidôs*. Achilles' answer to Ajax, with its partial acquiescence and at least theoretical approval of the claims of *aidôs*, is typical of his whole reception of the envoys, whom upon arrival he receives with all the formalities proper to the occasion, and, what is more, with real friendship. The reception of the envoys, therefore, and the answer to Ajax have the common denominator, friendship,[62] which, though set aside by the superior claims of absolute honor for the moment, becomes in Book XVI a force no longer to be denied. The following pattern emerges.

Book IX

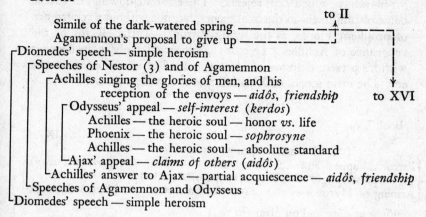

```
                                                          to II
    Simile of the dark-watered spring ————————↑————————┐
    Agamemnon's proposal to give up ————————┘          │
┌Diomedes' speech — simple heroism                      │
│ ┌Speeches of Nestor (3) and of Agamemnon              │
│ │ ┌Achilles singing the glories of men, and his       │
│ │ │    reception of the envoys — aidôs, friendship   to XVI
│ │ │ ┌Odysseus' appeal — self-interest (kerdos)
│ │ │ │ Achilles — the heroic soul — honor vs. life
│ │ │ │ Phoenix — the heroic soul — sophrosyne
│ │ │ │ Achilles — the heroic soul — absolute standard
│ │ │ └Ajax' appeal — claims of others (aidôs)
│ │ └Achilles' answer to Ajax — partial acquiescence — aidôs, friendship
│ └Speeches of Agamemnon and Odysseus
└Diomedes' speech — simple heroism
```

The design of Book XVI is somewhat simpler, but again with three main parts: the first extending to the departure of Patroclus, the second through the Sarpedon episode, and the last from Apollo's first opposition to the death of Patroclus. The centerpiece is the fight with Sarpedon, flanked by two scenes on Olympus having to do with the burial of the Lycian prince. The whole piece is enclosed by two scenes of general melee, the first by the ships and in the plain, the second where Patroclus tries to ascend the walls of Troy. Here Apollo intervenes, and Patroclus' star begins to set as the god first urges Hector on him and then attacks him in person. The last part may not seem very analogous to the first, yet both are full of heavy foreshadowing, and both emphasize powerfully the defection of Achilles. The scene which Homer has inserted between Achilles' speech and the arming of the Myrmidons, the scene of Ajax battered but still struggling faithfully, can only be intended to accent the desperate straits to which Achilles' retirement has reduced his friends. The death of Patroclus is, of course, the nadir of this defection, the point at which it becomes impossible even for Achilles himself to remain inactive. In a sense, therefore, Ajax' desperate hour prepares for that of Patroclus. Prophetic foreshadowings also frame the book, both in Patroclus' own speech, where Homer abandons his anonymity long enough to remark that he was begging for his own doom,[63] and in the prayer of Achilles for his safety, which Zeus rejects.[64] These foreshadowings of course come to fulfillment in the final scenes, but not without a recurrence of prophetic motifs, as the dying Patroclus warns Hector of the vengeance of Achilles.[65] Hector's lighthearted reply is, in keeping with his present delusion of victory, a kind of inversion of prophecy. The main scenes of XVI fall into the pattern shown below.

Book XVI

                                                                    to IX
                    "Dark-watered spring" simile ———————————————↑
⎧Patroclus' appeal and Achilles' answer   (foreshadowing)⎤
⎨   Desperate plight of Ajax (defection of Achilles)   │
⎩Arming of Myrmidons and prayer for Patroclus   (foreshadowing)⎦

    ⎡Fight at ships and on plain (to 393)
    │ ⎡Olympus — Zeus agrees to bury Sarpedon
    │ │   Sarpedon episode
    │ ⎣Olympus — Zeus sends Apollo to bury Sarpedon
    ⎣Fight at the wall   (foreshadowing, l. 693)⎤
⎧Apollo's opposition — pushing back Patroclus and encouraging Hector   │
⎨   Fight with Cebriones   │
⎩   Death of Patroclus (defection of Achilles)   │
 Prophetic exchange with Hector   (foreshadowing)⎦

So by this series of frames we are brought to the five books of the Great Battle which is the center of the *Iliad*. These battle scenes do not, apparently, fall into any particular system of balances; the hysteron-proteron technique makes its appearance in passages of small compass, but these seem to imply no attempt to spread the device into a principle of large design. In treating battle scenes, Homer relies on the unity of tone in the formulae themselves; the echoes are less planned, more chaotic thus, more suitable to the confusion of war. Yet even here, there is a touch of framing: the battle begins with the shout of Eris, and ends with the shout of Achilles.[66] Moreover the placement of Patroclus' scenes offers the possibility that these also were intentionally drawn toward the extremities of the battle: Patroclus might have been sent out by Achilles at any point, but actually he is sent fairly near the battle's beginning; and he does not return until near the end — strange behavior for a man who was expected to hurry.[67] But aside from these touches, the battle goes simply through its necessary phases, none of which provides sufficient contrast to balance another amid the general similarity of mood, except the Beguiling of Zeus, which forms a single relieving interlude.

The patterned regularity of the nine opening books and the nine closing ones might be pressed in more minute detail; but the object here has not been such detail; it has rather been to demonstrate how the native oral devices of hysteron proteron and ring composition, involving the balance of similarities and opposites, have been enlarged to provide concentric design for an enormously expanded heroic poem. Two special points must be noted. First, it will be recognized that this analysis of the *Iliad* assumes that the books of the poem, as we have them, existed in Homer's own time. As a rule, they are regarded as the arbitrary divisions of the Alexandrine scholars, but there is no reason to retain this view.[68] They are clearly the natural divisions of the poem, and most of them have very marked beginnings and ends, even when the narrative is continuous between them. Also, it has been recently estimated that these books average about the number of lines which it is possible for a singer to perform on a single occasion.[69] It is reasonable therefore to assume that the poem was conceived in terms of the books as we have them, and that the canonical division is not late. Secondly, the problematical Book X obviously does not belong to the Geometric structure as analyzed here, and this fact perhaps should be taken as an indication of its later insertion in the poem. Neither part of the battle, nor of the elaborate rings which enclose the battle, the *Doloneia* corresponds to nothing formally, and leads to nothing dramatically. It is the one part of the *Iliad* which can be omitted with no damage to the poem at all; the rest is from every point of view profoundly organic. On the other hand, the *Doloneia's* lack of any place in the Geometric pattern, though it creates a strong supposition, hardly seems sufficient proof for unauthenticity. Inconcinnities exist in the design in any case, even though none are so glaring as this would be; and in the last analysis the *Iliad*, coming from a tradition where parataxis, both in sentence and in scenic structure, was the rule, need not have departed from it so completely as to exclude all inorganic material. Moreover, Book X bears some significant resemblances to the rest of the *Iliad*, notably in its conception of the relationship between characters, such as Agamemnon and Menelaus, and in the continuation of the fire image. And yet, where everything else is so finely organized, this one episode does introduce a false note, a less mature procedure, with peculiar disregard for a symmetry which must have cost the poet some pains. Though the matter is hardly clear, it seems perhaps best to accept the dictum of the Townley *Scholia*, that this book was added later, perhaps even by Pisistratus.[70]

For the rest, the scenic structure, when laid out entire in a chart (see end of book), offers an extraordinary analogue to the rhythm and balance of the Dipylon vases. In the simple grouping of books, omitting X, one finds the relationship 2 : 5 : 2 : 5 : 2 : 5 : 2, a relationship frequently found also in the alternations of narrow and wide elements in Geometric ware.[71] Within this basic rhythm, if the details seem enormously complex, so are the works of the Dipylon, and their ornamentation depends similarly upon the deployment of traditional motifs in accordance with the first ripe development of the Hellenic sense of form. The underlying psychology of that sense in this early period has already been discussed, and it could only have been such a psychology, and such a conception of what form is, that led Homer to design the *Iliad* as he did, and to seek in his own materials of oral composition the means to impose order, suitable to a monumental work, on the loose parataxis of the heroic tradition. It is the spirit of the Geometric Age which is at work here, and the form which it produced would have been all but impossible in any other time.

XII

THE ODYSSEY AND CHANGE

A STUDY of Homer oriented, like the present one, through the *Iliad* is bound to differ widely from one whose focus is primarily the *Odyssey*. For all their identity of style, the contrast between the two poems is vast and obvious, and it is unnecessary to recall the numerous statements of their difference, from Aristotle's "passionate" versus "ethical," to more recent formulations such as "tragic" versus "comic," or "Aeolic" versus "Ionic." As to the last, there is certainly nothing Aeolic about the *Iliad* except perhaps, in origin, Achilles himself, and the numerous Aeolic dialectal forms, which occur equally in the *Odyssey*. In a more real sense the latter may be Ionic, in that the spirit of sea adventuring may have been stimulated anew as an epic subject by the colonization of Ionia. On the other hand, the character of Odysseus cannot in any sense be connected with the intellectualism and versatility which characterized the rise of Ionia later. In the time when the *Odyssey* must have been composed, the Ionians could have created as yet little of the civilization which is so admired in the sixth century. The character of Odysseus, as Homer received it, must have been of complex origin, a conflation of quasi-historical saga elements with the familiar folk-tale figure of the picaresque wanderer. What Homer made of it is again something else, for the *Odyssey* is no mere retelling of a traditional story.

It is, like the *Iliad*, a profoundly original creation, a vast expansion of a controlling poetic idea. It is the work of a master, though perhaps of a master whose zenith, as Longinus suggests, has gone by.[1]

Whether or not it was the same master who wrote the *Iliad* is a question which must probably remain unanswered, except in the personal convictions of individuals. Suffice it to say here that, for all the real and even extreme contrast between the two poems, there has yet to be produced a single cogent argument to the effect that they must belong to different hands, or different eras. Arguments drawn from minor points of subject matter, such as Phoenicians, the knowledge of riding astride of horses, familiarity with Egypt, and all such, provide intolerable examples of argument from silence, at best, and at worst betray convictions about Homer more positivistic than well-informed.[2] Attempts on linguistic grounds to prove the *Odyssey* later fail utterly; the epic language, save for what differences must exist because of the differences in the setting and the story, is the same for both poems, and in the *Odyssey* no neologisms exist of such a convincing sort that we must put the poem very much later than the *Iliad*. Also, on the grounds of oral theory, the *Odyssey* cannot be pushed very far into the period when literacy and a changing society were popularizing the various forms of lyric poetry, and relegating oral composition to the obscure corners of the Greek world. If the *Odyssey* belonged in any real sense to the seventh century, it must have been composed in some such obscure corner by a poet with old-fashioned tastes, bent on following in the wake of the *Iliad*, and essentially unmoved by the world around him. If such a poet existed — and many may have — it is hard to see how his work ever became known as Homer's. In the seventh century, the least of poets signed his work, and even the poems of the *Cycle* have names other than Homer's (and sometimes several) attached to them. To say the least, it is an uneconomical hypothesis to put the *Odyssey* so late. Both great epics belong to the most mature period of oral composition; both reflect the synthetic and formalized vision of the heroic Bronze Age in essentially the same way; both have ecumenical breadth, and tend to draw into their schemes large sections of the myth of Troy not immediately involved in the plot; both are complex, monumental, and retrospective; and both show much in common with the Athenian artistic approach, at once vivid, lucid, and subtle.[3]

Such basic similarities point to similar poetic concerns and a similar period of composition. But if one looks at certain differences of compositional approach, one may be able to guess the relation between the two poems a little more accurately. That the *Odyssey* is later than the *Iliad* most will agree, albeit the agreement is often based on the groundless assumption that the *Odyssey* is more "civilized," because more concerned with civilization as such, and the *Iliad* more primitive. The reverse could be asserted with equal truth, and, in any event, the *Iliad* penetrates further into the frontier mysteries of human psychology. But the relative outlooks upon character and experience cannot be decisive in such a matter. More significant is the relative structure of the two poems. The *Iliad*, as already shown, follows a strict Geometric design comparable to nothing except the sepulchral vases of the Dipylon. Very little of the sort occurs in the *Odyssey*, and where it does occur, asymmetrical elements are more frequent, the responsions less careful and less significant.[4] The antithetical polarities of the hysteron-proteron technique enhance meaning in the *Iliad*; insofar as they exist in the *Odyssey*, they are somewhat perfunctory, and the sense of form which one derives from the poem comes far less from repeated or inverted themes and episodes than from the substance of the narrative itself, its progress through time, and its achievement of a long-awaited end. The *Iliad* is tightly designed in every instant; the *Odyssey* sings itself, proceeding with a natural, leisurely pace, entirely suited to the prevailing mood of a large landscape with figures. For this reason, perhaps, the *Odyssey* has far fewer similes than the *Iliad*: the latter concentrates on one *mise en scène*, one major action, one monolithic idea of the heroic; visions of the rest of the world therefore knot themselves into hard images which cluster luminously around the rush of action. The *Odyssey* has a wider lens; it peers less deeply, but takes time to describe. Its object, like that of its hero, is often simply to see:

> Standing there, divine long-suffering Odysseus gazed.

And there is very little which Odysseus will not take time to look at. The same objective scrutiny falls on Cyclops, Circe, the suitors,

Eumaeus' steading, the gardens of Alcinous, the faithless maid-
servants, and weeping Penelope — "eyes like horn or iron."[5] The
Odyssey keeps building scenic episodes, typical and often static,
and in these lie its chief symbols, not, as in the *Iliad*, in continuous
and ever-shifting motifs.

This is not to say, however, that no evidences of Geometric de-
sign are to be found in the *Odyssey*. Certain parts, especially the
Adventures and the Phaeacian episode, show conscious scenic an-
tithesis and framing patterns. The *Adventures* are particularly ele-
gant, grouped as they are around the supreme adventure, the Jour-
ney to the Dead. This central episode, with its retrospect upon the
whole heroic tradition in the ghosts of Ajax, Achilles, Agamemnon,
and Heracles, and its mysterious prospect of peace at last and
"death from the sea" in the prophecy of Teiresias, is carefully
framed, first by the two Elpenor episodes, and then by the two
scenes with Circe. For the rest, the poet summarizes two out of
every three adventures rather briefly, and dramatizes one at greater
length, so that the pattern of Odysseus' narrative is as follows:

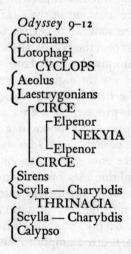

Odyssey 9–12

Ciconians
Lotophagi
    CYCLOPS
Aeolus
Laestrygonians
    CIRCE
        Elpenor
            NEKYIA
        Elpenor
    CIRCE
Sirens
Scylla — Charybdis
    THRINACIA
Scylla — Charybdis
Calypso

Calypso, of course, is dramatized in her own right in Book 5, but
not in the narrative of the hero. Book 8 offers, perhaps, a more
interesting Geometric structure. Here Odysseus is deliberately con-

trasted with his Phaeacian hosts, who grow more and more impressed and mystified by him until finally nothing will satisfy save the full narrative of his adventures. The whole book turns on the two principles of music and gymnastic, keynotes of civilization to the Greek mind, and both highly developed by the peace-loving and somewhat soft Phaeacians. Odysseus proves the supremacy in bodily arts of the lonely and experienced hero over those who dwell in the ivory tower on the edge of the world. As for music, he is not a singer, but he emerges as the living substance of the heroic lays of Demodocus, which are mere amusement to the Phaeacians. Of Demodocus' three songs, the middle one of Ares and Aphrodite, with its ring of Olympian laughter, is a lighthearted romance appropriate to the people who love warm baths and bed; the first and the last are Trojan songs appropriate to Odysseus, deeply involved with his identity, and prompting those tears which in turn lead to the full revelation of his experience. Few episodes in Homer are more skillfully handled than the Eighth *Odyssey*; form and purpose are truly one: [6]

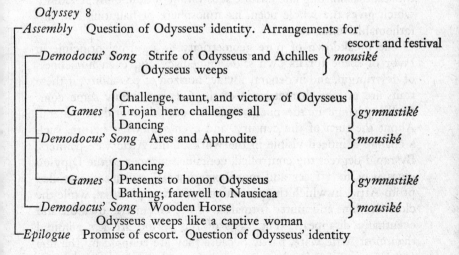

Odyssey 8

Assembly   Question of Odysseus' identity. Arrangements for escort and festival

Demodocus' Song   Strife of Odysseus and Achilles } *mousiké*
                   Odysseus weeps

Games { Challenge, taunt, and victory of Odysseus
        Trojan hero challenges all
        Dancing } *gymnastiké*

Demodocus' Song   Ares and Aphrodite } *mousiké*

Games { Dancing
        Presents to honor Odysseus
        Bathing; farewell to Nausicaa } *gymnastiké*

Demodocus' Song   Wooden Horse } *mousiké*
                   Odysseus weeps like a captive woman

Epilogue   Promise of escort. Question of Odysseus' identity

Other parts of the *Odyssey* might be shown to have comparable, though less perfect, symmetry of design, but wherever such is to be found, it is confined to sections and does not spread over the whole. Total design is no longer a matter of inner strains and balances; instead, it is achieved through scenes marking stages of the advancement of the story, and the effect is not annular, but linear. Antithesis is certainly omnipresent, but it centers around the primary moral concern of the poem, the goodness and evil of men, especially in the category of hospitality and in images of righteous and unrighteous feasting. Antithesis is, therefore, more concerned with explicit meaning in the *Odyssey* than with total external form, and hence the poem does not lead back into itself to enclose a single experience with finality, but proceeds to the point at which it wishes to stop. And even as the circular pattern was appropriate to the *Iliad*, as a poem of heroic being, the linear movement of the *Odyssey* is wholly inevitable for a poem of becoming. The line may be produced to infinity, and in some sense, the *Odyssey*, overshadowed by the prophecy of Tiresias, never really ends. The *Iliad* ends with a funeral, the symbol of utter finality, and the image of Niobe in stone, weeping forever. The *Odyssey* closes with Odysseus at home, but fated to wander still and at last to meet death from the sea, that shifting and chaotic substratum of boundless possibility which gives the whole poem its atmosphere of haunting and unfathomable romance.

The breakdown of pure geometricity as a formal principle in favor of scene for its own sake, immediacy and even homeliness of description, and in general a wider horizon of possibility, if these traits are in fact characteristic of the *Odyssey*, imply some comparable change in the poet's audience and his world in general. About the turn of the century, and even somewhat before, such a change is indeed visible in the work of the Attic vase-painters. By rapid degrees the controlled, contained manner of the Dipylon gives way to a freer and more experimental style, the so-called proto-Attic, in which the governing concern is pictorial, while the close rhythms and muted formalism of the Geometric dwindle and eventually disappear.[7] The vases of this period are less admired than most Attic ware, partly because they are eclipsed by the fine proto-Corinthian development, and partly because proto-Attic is essentially transitional, and leads to the triumphant Black Figure style. But the proto-Attic is not without its accomplishments. The manner is breezy, open, and slightly orientalizing. A new awareness of life in its immediacy, and not without humor, appears in contrast to the somber reserve of Geometric painting. Human and animal figures appear with new and sometimes realistic details; outline drawing is born, incision begins, and monochrome yields to the use of various new colors. It is clearly a somewhat undisciplined phase, where careless workmanship, especially in the traditional motifs maintained from the Geometric, often goes hand in hand with bold naturalism and realistic representation in the principal picture. The new techniques with color and incision are by no means mastered, and the glaze is far below the quality of proto-Corinthian or the better Geometric ware. Each pot seems a little more like a sketch than a finished painting. There is something also distinctly romantic about it, in contrast to the heroic austerity of the former period. There is no longer much concern, at least in most vases, to adjust the decoration to the shape of the vase. Subject matter wins the day more and more decisively, as the style progresses, until it is all refined into the new formalism of Black Figure. But in the earlier stages of proto-Attic, one feels the strong sudden impact of nature disintegrating the rigid rationale of the Geometric method, and especially in the human figure, which is no longer an anonymous bundle of sticks and triangles, but begins to swell with a kind of personality. The scene itself is all-engrossing; total design retreats. The old, sure-handed sophistication is gone, and if the new product is often naive, there is nevertheless tremendous spirit in it. The horizon is suddenly vast; almost anything can appear on a proto-Attic pot, and the subjects vary all the way from scenes of myth to the prosaic details of everyday life.

It can hardly be entirely fanciful to see in the change from the Geometric to the proto-Attic approach an analogy to the shift of outlook from the *Iliad* to the *Odyssey*. This is no mere matter of subject. It involves the whole instinct about the inner relationship of part to whole, of decoration to structure, as well as the basic conception of humanity and its context. The triumph of scenic episode over totality of design is perhaps the most striking parallel between the *Odyssey* and proto-Attic art. Yet the parallel extends also to many details of the creative approach. In the *Iliad*, battle scenes contain many summaries of unknown men slain by unknown men, *androktasiae*; these anonymities are, however, always named, and their little entries, as in the *Catalogue*, pass by with formulaic rigidity, like the rows of identical warriors on Geometric ware. Individuals become visible only through the shape of a norm. But in the *Odyssey*, the companions of Odysseus are treated differently. They fall into no formalized pattern of the whole, and only one or two are named at all. For the most part, they disappear until they have to do something, and are treated, in contrast to the brief tragic histories of the *Iliad*, as simple expendabilities. Proto-Attic art is not concerned to represent generalities of men, but particularities of event; and hence, instead of the typical scene, formulaic yet possibly individualized to a faint degree, there is either full individualization or nothing. Two of the companions emerge as people, the young, heedless and ill-fated Elpenor, and the presumptuous, sane, and slightly insubordinate Eurylochus. The rest are vapor. It is often said that the characters in the *Odyssey* are types, and some are. But they are regularly types of something in human experience, and never, with the exception of Odysseus himself, typical simply of humanity, as are the rows of names in the *Iliad*. No such generality runs through the *Odyssey*: its pictures seize the foreground and thrust out the binding continuous friezes.

Moreover, in the matter of characterization the methods of the *Iliad* and *Odyssey* differ. As described elsewhere, the secondary characters of the *Iliad* find their individuality through a series of subtle contrasts, either with the heroic norm, or with another character, usually Achilles. Personal details, especially of a trivial sort, play little or no part. But the *Odyssey* is directly descriptive, as a rule through illustrative action, sometimes even in minor detail. We learn the character of Eumaeus from his defense of the stranger from the dogs, from his manner of putting food before a guest, from his tears at the sight of Telemachus, from his strict obedience to orders, from his sedulous care of the swine, and a hundred other touches. Here is no characterization by reference to a single formulaic social norm. The poet is interested both in Eumaeus and in his total context; he wants to fill him out. He is interested in the behavior of dogs, too. In the *Iliad* they only tear dead bodies, a purely formulaic function. In *Odyssey* 16 they keep interrupting the progress of the plot with actions which the poet includes, presumably, out of a concern with naturalistic representation: they assail Odysseus, fawn on Telemachus, and whimper with fear at the apparition of Athena. These are real dogs, not symbols of death with disgrace, and they resemble in their vividness a fine proto-Attic sherd in the Agora Museum at Athens, showing a donkey's head, painted and incised, with mouth open in a most convincing and hilarious asinine grin.[8] So too of the details of personal appearance, one hears little or nothing in the *Iliad*, but in the *Odyssey* the hero's dark hair and stout limbs are often mentioned, especially in connection with his transformation by Athena. In particular, skin quality has newly impressed itself on the poet's imagination: Odysseus is darkly tanned, Penelope's skin is like cut ivory.[9] Such minutiae are unknown to the Geometric *Iliad*, though women in general are "white-armed"; but in the proto-Attic period, the vase-painters were beginning to represent flesh tones with different colors, white as a rule, but sometimes black for men, and it is perhaps no wonder that this new pictorial element has crept into the epic consciousness. Finally, in the matter of landscape and milieu, it is hard to find any descriptive passages in the *Iliad* comparable to that of the island of Calypso or the gardens of Alcinous. Here simple delight in the setting has tempted the poet to sing on and on, regardless of symmetry or waiting issues. New fields of content have revealed themselves, and the older concept of form has become attenuated amid the new preoccupation with the immediacy of life.

The change in epic, however, must not be looked upon as either sudden or radical. The traditional nature of oral verse precludes radical changes. It must be assumed that the bardic repertoire comprised in advance the formulae and other typological materials necessary to produce the *Odyssey* as well as the *Iliad*. The language of the *Odyssey* offers no foothold to the assertion that it is younger. But its motivating artistic concern is younger, and so is its idea of form. Hence it arises, once more, that the creativity of the poet in such a traditional medium consists in the deployment of his given material, which includes not only plot, but also the whole gamut of visionary, formalized detail which was the singers' thesaurus. It is a matter of selectivity and degree, operating in the service of a sharply focused artistic purpose. In the broadest sense, the *Iliad* draws upon the formulae of heroic warfare, the *Odyssey* upon those of peace, the norms of social existence, and of the adventures of long-existent popular folk tales. It is truistic to point out that the polarities involved exist side by side in the *Shield* of Achilles. The tradition embraced it all, and the poet needed to invent little or nothing in order to create either poem. But the principle governing his selection and emphasis must in some sense follow the artistic spirit of the age, and in the *Odyssey* one may observe the new suppleness, the naturalism, and even occasionally the carefree blunders of the proto-Attic times.[10]

If one attempts to fix the date of the poem more accurately, there is evident risk of pressing the argument too far. Yet there is some reason to feel that the *Odyssey* corresponds to the early stages of the proto-Attic period, and not to that phase, well on in the seventh century, when the style was already approaching Black Figure. Startling as some proto-Attic painting may be, it does not represent an instantaneous revolution. Some later Geometric vases show far less rigidity than the earlier ones; lines become sketchy, poses more supple, knees bend a little, the figures gain a little flesh on their bones; the contiguous warriors in a row may not be all in the same position.[11] One critic says eloquently: ". . . a strong wind seems to be blowing against the neat fabric and making it bend, totter and reel." [12] The change is rapid but the steps are observable. Moreover, the new animal motifs seem to be only partly the product of Oriental influence; partly they recall Mycenaean tradition.[13] Later, Orientalism triumphed, breeding sphinxes, griffins, and gorgons everywhere, and thrusting out the last traces of Geometric order. But at the end of the eighth century and beginning of the seventh century, the proto-Attic style clearly had its roots in tradition, and had by no means freed itself utterly from the Geometric. The *Odyssey* seems equally transitional. Geometric design, as seen above, has not totally vanished, but it does "totter and reel." The wind is blowing vigorously, but it has not yet blown away the epic form. If one were to choose a single vase as an illustration of the creative temper underlying the *Odyssey*, the best choice might be the famous Attic Analatos vase, dated about 700.[14] Geometric motifs are still present, notably the frieze of traditional waterfowl. But on the neck, the dance of long-haired girls and men, one with a lyre, responds with pristine freshness to the pictorial urge, the pressure of a new awareness in visual experience.

It is descriptive, not symbolic. Reserved space allows the picture to breathe, as in the *Odyssey* Homer gives his descriptions as much time as they want. The atmosphere is spring-like and unprejudiced by previous conceptions, and suggests a feeling of direct delight in life which is essentially foreign to Geometric painting. One cannot yet quite see, but one can foresee, the lyricism of the seventh century, the choirs of Alcman and Stesichorus, or the bright vignettes of Archilochus. The *Odyssey* and the Analatos vase both seem to stand exquisitely poised between two ages, not quite belonging to either, but drawing breath from both.

To arrive by such means at a date of about 700 B.C. for the *Odyssey* may seem both rash and impressionistic. Yet the phenomena involved are specific enough: the decay of Geometric design, the arrival at self-existent pictures for their own sake, greater variety and suppleness of individuation, a freer naturalism, and what might be called the opening of surfaces, whether by space in painting or by a more luxuriant expenditure of time in verse — all these are traceable facts and tendencies. What is more, they are tokens of attitude and motivation, the semiconscious theorizing of the artist as he sets to work, and as such they are hallmarks of a time, never quite to be imitated at any other time. When all the necessary allowances therefore have been made for the difficulty both of dating exactly the early pottery of Greece, and of comparing poetry and painting, the period around the turn of the eighth century still seems more reasonable for the *Odyssey* than any date which, by reason of tenuous and superficially more factual-seeming points of subject matter, would push the poem down to a time when it could only have been archaistic. The inner side of artistic creation is what must be decisive, for it alone is characteristic of its time.

One final comparison with the situation in vase-painting leads to broader considerations. The masterpieces of the Geometric Age were funerary, and their memorial purpose is revealed in the death-like quietude of their formality. They have the heroic death-consciousness which pervades the *Iliad*. The focus of the *Odyssey*, on the other hand, is life in all its variety and directness, and again recalls the more lyrical responses of proto-Attic art, where life as daily lived and observed, unmediated by anything but the senses, finds its first expression since the fall of the Bronze Age, and thereby lays the foundation of the so-called "Greek renaissance." Such a shift reflects a shift in the psychology of a people. Ordinarily it is said that the Greek renaissance was a period of rising individualism and the discovery of the self as such. Yet the *Iliad* is a poem of self-knowledge in every sense as much as the *Odyssey*, but whereas the latter exhibits a hero whose will is proverbial for its unity and tenacity, the *Iliad*'s hero is the first in our history to be divided by the metaphysical paradox of human nature. Achilles allies himself with equal intensity, both to his own human nature, with all its concern and commitments, and to that intuition of the absolute in being and value which is the besetting demon of the spiritual hero. These opposites can be joined only in the mysterious flame of a love at once detached and entire, self-discovery in self-destruction. Achilles stands representative in and of an architectonic world in which everything is known and in its place, except himself; his learning of himself is a creating of himself. Death is always imminently upon him, a formative limitation which reveals itself at last as the inevitable framework of his tragic being. By contrast, the life-consciousness of the *Odyssey* involves a vastly different view of the individual soul. In and of himself, the hero is a fixed personality, confronted by no hopeless division in himself; he is equipped, as if by magic, with every skill which any situation might require, so that he needs only to deliberate ways and means; in the whole course of the poem, his celebrated intellect deals with no problem which can even remotely be called intellectual, and least of all does he deal with that deepest of all intellectual problems, the self. He is himself — at least if viewed from one point of view. Yet from another point of view, the matter is more mysterious. Life's paradox now appears not in the man but in his external experience, and the adventures of Odysseus, both on the sea and in Ithaca, cast upon him a constantly shifting cloud of disguise, from which he never fully emerges until he has revealed himself to the last person to whom he must — Laertes. And it is by no means tactless of the poet to have saved Laertes till last, incidentally, for recognition by one's father is, in a way, the final legitimation which establishes a man in his world. And it is the world which is the overt concern of Odysseus. Achilles created himself; Odysseus creates his world, by risk, choice, tenacity, and action, and the world thus created reveals the selfhood of its creator. By contact with the "limits of the earth," Odysseus defines, rather than discovers, himself, each experience involving, and at last dissipating, a particular shade of that anonymity which overhangs a man until his context is complete. Hence in the first part of the poem Odysseus is regularly an unknown man to those who receive him, until by some word or action he makes his identity known. In the second part, his disguise conceals him, except at such times when the truth peeps out a little, for the astute to read. Mephistopheles promised to show Faust "first the small world, then the great," and through such experience Faust expands beyond the limits of his earlier self to a transcendent knowledge. The *Odyssey* exactly reverses this process. Odysseus begins, equipped with knowledge so various as to be in a sense transcendental, in the great world of magic and mysterious, absolute existences, and slowly by determination narrows it all down to the small circle of his own family household. And by contrast with the *Iliad*, where the world was architectonic and the hero the measure of the infinite, the *Odyssey* presents an infinite and rather amorphous world, under the image of the sea, out of whose mists any monstrosity or beguiling vision may arise, while the hero is the measure of fixity and definition. Perhaps for this reason the *Odyssey* has always seemed the more closely allied, of the two epics, to the classical period, for then too the prevailing outlook centered the legislating mind of the individual as the measure amid unpredictable experience, and infinite possibility. Indeed, it was precisely this view of the individual self, not the *Iliad*'s view, which began to take conscious shape in the seventh century, and to create the new lyrical forms. The *Iliad*'s view returns only in Sophoclean tragedy.

It is an unanswerable question how much of this view existed already in the tale which Homer found, and how much is his own emphasis. The nature of myth, or folk tale, is to reflect in external form the psyche's subconscious exploration of itself and its experience. Myths contain from the moment of their inception all the meanings which can be extracted from them. If Homer therefore created a poem in which the hero reveals himself, not so much directly as through the steady battery of experiences which rub against him, the reasons perhaps are, first that the tale he chose included the possibility of such, and second that such an approach would be welcomed and understood by his audience. The oral poet did not compose in solitude and publish at his own expense; he sang for gatherings of friends and strangers. And if one looks for the time when the stream of direct experience becomes of primary concern to the Greek artistic spirit and fills the foreground with the ideated shapes which to the archaic mind are knowledge, it is to be found precisely in this early proto-Attic period, when fragments of Geometric form, a few Orientalized motifs, and above all direct observations of life itself, merged, sometimes chaotically, sometimes into tapestries of vigor and finesse. All these elements merge also in the *Odyssey*, even to limited traces of the Orientalizing tendency,[15] but nothing is more characteristic than the ordering of the self from the point of view of external experience. And this is perhaps why the motif of self-revelation plays so large a part in the poem. To each of these adventures Odysseus must present and define himself, and he has various ways of doing it.

There is a kind of vague progress in the adventures themselves, the earlier ones, beginning with the sagalike attack on the Ciconians, being less fantastic than the later ones. The Ciconian adventure forms a link with the Trojan war; then Cape Malea is the last piece of genuine geography which Odysseus sights until he lands at Ithaca. Shapes of fantasy begin to appear, but in the Lotus-eaters, the Laestrygonians, and even the unlikely Cyclops, one sees only the milder exaggerations of sea adventurers who had, indeed, come upon sleepy shores and wild men of a cannibalistic persuasion. Aeolus also is a god of the Greek pantheon, a patriarchal king. It is only with Circe that one meets the truly magical, and from there on, the Land of the Dead, the Sirens, the Planctae with Scylla and Charybdis, and the island Thrinacia are the stuff of purest wonder in essence, though sometimes touched with the light of Greek rationalism. Odysseus plunges further and further into this realm, always with diminishing resources and friends, until he arrives at Calypso's isle, the utter submersion of identity, save for bare consciousness and the sea-locked will. This is the nadir, the quiet center of the magic world, "in an island girt by the waves, where the navel of the sea lies." [16] Delphi, the "navel of the world," is the seat of all true knowledge, and in making Ogygia the navel of the sea, Homer has given it an aspect of basic, interior truth.

A desperate struggle with the sea brings him again away from the deep world of faery to the Phaeacians, a people gifted with the especial ability to mediate between relative and absolute, human and divine; they live, as Homer says, at the edges of mankind, and close to the gods. Though they are drawn like an idealized Hellenic colony, their name means, or at least could only connote to Greek ears, "dusky" or "shadowy," and their ships are distinctly spectral. One need not labor the obvious resemblance in all this to hundreds of folk tales about heroes who reach fairyland and return only with difficulty, or having returned too rashly to the world of fact and mortality, go a long and racking journey to recover the sources of unfading quality and power.[17] The question is, what has Homer done? In the first place, he has envisioned all this experience as a paradox, as something to be both embraced and rejected not alternately, but somehow simultaneously; and secondly he has embedded it in a larger scheme of self-revelation and the restoration of right order. He has expanded all the psychological and moral implications of the myth into a parable of truth disguised and revealing itself in time.

Odysseus begins by having his choice. It is he who directs the attack on the Ciconians; in the lands of the Lotus-eaters, the Cyclops, and the Laestrygonians, it is his curiosity, not need, which prompts exploration, for the crew in all cases have already satisfied their needs on the shore; and it is the same in the case of Circe, as the companions already recognize to their dismay.[18] Odysseus is driven to these places, but it is he who chooses to explore them. But after Circe, choice vanishes; he is committed to the world of wonder and must go forward, as the sorceress foretells, nor does the power to choose come back to him until he has been with Calypso for seven years. There is a real difference between the reckless, self-reliant adventurer who comes to Circe, and the fate-driven, desperate wanderer who meets Nausicaa. The change, one may assume, lies more in the journey to the dead than in the arts of Circe herself, and it betokens the fading of an earlier and smaller self before the demands of an even more puzzling and vast world of possibility. After the years with Calypso, all former disguises are stripped away, and he arrives naked before Nausicaa, the genius of rebirth, only to begin a new series of disguises which this time he controls and will abandon in his own time.

To some of the denizens of the great world, Odysseus reveals himself, to others he cannot. The Lotus-eaters could not hear him in any case, the Laestrygonians are a mere nightmare. The friendly exchange with Aeolus does not need full narration. But Cyclops is a real test, and after the disguise of No-man, Odysseus cannot resist the hero's boast, and tells his name.[19] Cyclops and he have measured each other accurately, and the name is now in order. Circe, on the other hand, distillate of woman that she is, knows the hero by his power over her, and becomes, from a witch, a woman of gentle compassion who yields to Odysseus her body and her knowledge, and after restoring his companions comforts them with a sympathy unusual in goddesses.[20] When one thinks of Odysseus' tenacity of purpose, it is well to remember that, in this one case, he had to be reminded by his companions that he was on his way home. After such renunciation, the way home must lie through the Land of the Dead. And thereafter, Odysseus does not reveal himself until Phaeacia. The Sirens, who know everything, know him without being told.[21] The shades of the dead know him. In a moment of recrudescent boastfulness, he tries to face Scylla with shield and spear, and assert the self who fought at Troy, but he cannot even see her.[22] Troy and that whole world is past; he has just come from its ghost in Hades, where the panorama of the heroic life was reviewed in a dreamlike confusion. All that Odysseus has experienced when he comes to Calypso has defined him indeed, but defined him in lowest terms. Everyman has almost become No-man.

When he comes to Phaeacia, Odysseus is in no haste to tell his name. It is wrung out of him, but when it comes, it comes with the challenge of a man girt with knowledge and secure in it:

> I am Odysseus, son of Laertes, who live upon all men's
> Lips with my wiles, and my fame reaches to heaven.[23]

Having maintained his spark of identity in the devastating glare of the absolute, Odysseus is entitled to speak as he does. If he comes to the Phaeacians as a suppliant, he soon makes it clear that he is their master, or at least that he has a right to the service which they give him. Upon arrival in Ithaca, he begins to build, or rebuild, his world. In the depths of Hades, he has heard from Tiresias of the ruinous condition of his affairs at home. The beggar's disguise which Athena gives him is on the surface a practical device for reconnoitering and strategy, but it is also symbolic of a condition of the self. A beggar presents an image of humanity fallen, entitled by custom and religion to pity, but little more. The arrogant will not even grant pity, but the knowledgeable will grant much more, in deference to the changes of fortune and the community of all human things. Meanwhile, the self per se lies hidden. Odysseus can rebuild his world only out of those prepared by their own knowledgeability to penetrate the disguise, and he begins at the lowest rung with Eumaeus, the swineherd. And now the self-revelations begin again, not indeed with Eumaeus, but with Telemachus.[24] The modes of revelation tell more than the identity of the stranger; they rehearse his roles as father, hero, king, husband, and son. Telemachus, though he could have had no recollection of his father, had often imagined him.[25] The glorious shape which appears before him, when the disguise momentarily falls, seems at first to the young man like a god; when he hears that it is Odysseus, he believes, with youth's credulity, instantly without token or proof. He could not deny the substance of his imaginings; *certum est quia incredibile est*, it could not be too glorious. Argus the dog is just the opposite; to him there is not even a disguise, it is simply Odysseus.[26] Then comes a series of partial hints. Kicks and missiles bounce off the beggar, frail as he seems.[27] In the fist-fight with Irus, Athena once more fills out Odysseus' limbs, to the terror of his opponent, whom he presently half kills with one blow.[28] Odysseus has now established himself more or less firmly in the household, as the official beggar at the gate, presumably in Irus' place. As a quasi-domestic he is given somewhat better atention, and the courteous Amphinomus, who seems so out of place among the suitors, offers him wine. Odysseus, in a speech designed to conceal as much as it reveals, tries to warn him away from the approaching destruction:

Nothing more wretched the earth nourishes than mankind,
Out of all things that breathe and creep upon the ground.
Never a man declares he will suffer evil hereafter,
Excellence while yet the gods provide, and uphold his knees.
Yet when the happy gods accomplish misery,
This he also bears unwilling, with a spirit enduring.

Such is the mind of men that live upon the earth
As the day is which the father of gods and men leads on.
Once I myself had hope to be flourishing among men;
Many the wanton deeds I did, yielding to strength and violence,
Trusting in my father and in my brothers.
Therefore let not a man be wholly without law,
But keep the gifts of the gods in silence, whatever they give.[29]

On the moral level, Odysseus could not have been more explicit. He has all but said, "Do not be fooled by appearances or the mere present." He even goes on to condemn the suitors and urge Amphinomus to leave. But on another level, Odysseus has summarized the view of the self which characterizes the *Odyssey*: appearances are deceptive, yes; but the mind of a man is as the day Zeus brings. That is, the spirit is formed and defined by circumstances; Odysseus is now a beggar, but circumstances change, involving not only the dropping of disguise, but the reformation of the self. Amphinomus, troubled though he is, takes his place again among the blind suitors, and suffers in the end. Odysseus might conceivably have trusted Amphinomus with the facts of the case, if he really had wanted to save him. But the test is a moral one, and no one, not even Odysseus, can reveal his true identity to a blind man.

Then come the recognitions by the scar. This is a token which would mean nothing to Telemachus, but everything to Eurycleia, Eumaeus, and Philoetius, since they were present when Odysseus got the scar, and it is to them the emblem of the true king. One glance, and they are all convinced of the return of the young lord who slew the wild boar on his first hunt.[30] The sign serves to connect past and present for those of long memory in the household, and to assure them that this is the same master, the only master. To the suitors, there can only be one appropriate form of revelation — the bow. But the trial of the axes, and the stringing of the old formidable weapon recreate another of Odysseus' roles, that of the hero. The suitors are not like the men of old. The beggar whose limbs looked surprisingly stout now slips the string in the notches, plucks it so it sings like a swallow, nocks an arrow, and sends it through the axes. And thunder greets the falling of the disguise.[31]

So at the end of Book 22, the father, the true master, the touchstone of moral order, and the hero have all revealed themselves.

There remain the husband, and the son, or heir. One might well ask why, when Penelope hesitates to recognize her husband, does Odysseus not show her the scar, as he has to others, and as he later does to Laertes. The reason is that a scar may identify a person; but it is a poor sign by which to know a husband. Homer is dealing more subtly. The role of husband must be recreated, not merely the man made known. There can be little doubt in any case that Penelope's intuition has long since told her who the beggar is. It has been most persuasively argued of late that the conversation between them in the firelight, in Book 19, is in actuality a cryptic acknowledgment by Penelope of the stranger's identity.[32] No doubt the knowledge is not supposed to be wholly conscious, even at this point, but the intuition is sufficiently strong to induce her to set the trial of the axes and risk having to choose a husband. Earlier events had been conducive to her feeling, for it could scarcely be more than that. The prophecy of Theoclymenus at the beginning of Book 17, and the sneeze of Telemachus, a good omen which greets Penelope's casual words about the possible return of Odysseus, mingle religious symbols of truth with the queen's growing curiosity about the beggar.[33] When her son sneezes, she laughs — a rare thing for Penelope, but repeated later when suddenly, as she sits in her chamber, she laughs "foolishly," as Homer says, or for no reason, and conceives the unaccountable idea of adorning herself beautifully and maddening the suitors into giving her gifts.[34] As she stands before them, she says that she cannot be beautiful any longer since Odysseus is gone, that if he should return, her beauty and glory would be greater.[35] For whom are these words spoken? It is unthinkable that Penelope should deliberately fascinate a hall full of men whom she despises and wishes in their graves. She has adorned herself for Odysseus, and speaks to him, though the foolish, empty laugh shows that she does not really know it herself as yet. The episode ends in the suitors' giving gifts, and Athena, with a divinity's usual foreknowledge of how things came out in the end, treats this as more or less Penelope's motive; but the queen herself acknowledges no such motive, and states quite a different one.[36] The final proof comes when the suitors are trying the bow and refuse the beggar his turn. There is no reason why he should have a turn; queens do not marry beggars, and therefore Penelope says to the suitors, with quiet irony, that even if he should be successful, she will not marry him, but merely reward him with raiment and weapons.[37] But she insists that he must have his turn, and it is pressing the rule of hospitality too far to assume that she does so without knowledge of who he is.

Why then, if she knows him, does she not acknowledge him at once, when the suitors are slain? The reason is that the role of husband has yet to be recreated, and so, therefore, does the role of wife. The mere slaying of the suitors is no more adequate for this purpose than is the scar on the knee. Neither is the mere appearance of Odysseus in royal robes adequate, though it had been for Telemachus. Husband and wife have secret signs, which others do not know, says Penelope; and, somewhat like a new bride, she cannot speak or look at Odysseus.[38] Then comes the recognition of the marriage bed.[39] The motif can be paralleled elsewhere, but scarcely the treatment. Outwardly it is a test of the stranger, for only Odysseus who built it could know that the bed in Penelope's chamber was immovably fixed to a rooted olive tree. The stranger need only relate the history of the bed to recreate his role as husband. But even more pertinently, this scene is a test of Penelope, self-imposed, in order to recreate her role as wife. For she too must show him that she will have only the man who knows the nature of that steadfast bed and, therewith, her own nature. And to this end she has restrained her emotion and kept back her knowledge. Odysseus tells in full and leisurely detail the reason why the bed cannot be moved, and at the end asks:

> So now, I tell you this token. And yet, I know not at all
> Whether, wife, it still stands firm, that bed, or already
> Some one of men put it elsewhere, cutting off the root of the olive.[40]

Penelope has feigned much for a long time, and has lived in sundry false and inappropriate roles, but the burst of emotion which now overcomes her wipes them all away, and makes her a wife again.

In the scene with Laertes, the poet finds one more variation on the recognition theme. Odysseus shows the scar, but passes quickly on to a token more meaningful: childhood memories of following his father around the orchard. He names the trees which his father gave him as a child, thus in a way declaring his patrimony, his knowledge of the land, and his right to it.[41] He recreates, by continuity with the past and with the land, his role as the rightful and legitimate heir. And with this recognition Odysseus has, in a sense, restored his selfhood completely. Undoubtedly, the whole action of the *Odyssey* is involved with precisely this, but the scenes of self-revelation strike especially symbolic notes, in that each limns an aspect of the self in sharp focus, and somehow summarizes the hero's relationship to the person who recognizes him. The method is characterization by definition from without, and the self is conceived in terms of its personal and social limits.

Such externality, such objective observation is basic to the *Odyssey*'s wide range of realistic detail, from mill slaves, swineherds, and dogs to the structure of ships or palaces, brooches, belts, the tools of a craft, and the kinds of trees in a garden. The sense of the uncountable possibilities of existence carries with it an effort to mark off recurrent shapes of intelligibility, through the observation of functions and forms. And so also, the moral design of the poem, the somewhat schematized view of poetic justice announced by Zeus in the exordium, is far more an assertion of the validity of forms and quasi-ritual observances than a real exploration of the issues involved. The evil of the suitors is a house of cards, carefully piled up to be knocked down, with the appearance of justice, at the appointed time. In the case of Amphinomus and Leiodes, the poet seems to struggle with the story a little.[42] These two men, technical rather than actual offenders against Odysseus, are slain, their essential innocence being of no importance beside their position as suitors. On the other hand, Phemius the minstrel and Medon the herald, whose offices make them sacrosanct, are spared.[43] Clearly the slaughter of the suitors takes place on a level very far from that which views sin as lying primarily in motive and attitude. Its basis is a creed, the creed of the primitive clan, and if Homer has managed the character of Antinous so that one feels that his death is justified, the scene as a whole remains a massacre, an undiscriminating application of the univocal law of possession. It is very far from the psychological profundity of the *Iliad*, with its questioning of forms, and its insistence on the inner state of the individual. Here one feels that a primitive story — and the slaughter of the suitors corresponds to the ending of many an old folk tale [44] — has resisted the efforts of the poet to moralize and universalize it. It is meant to be a reëstablishment of right order, but an orgy of blood vengeance peers through the moral scheme, the less sympathetic for being committed, unlike the gory and self-destroying vengeance of Achilles, in the dispassionate conviction of moral rightness.

As outlooks change, some pieces of a tradition become less manageable, while others take on a new luminosity. Insofar as the *Odyssey* is, in outline, a folk tale told and retold in many ways, and here incremented by elements from the saga of Troy, it offered special problems which the simple, unified plot of the *Iliad* did not. The *Iliad* spins out, with infinite elaboration and formal perfection, an episode in itself so slight, that by comparison the *Odyssey* seems heavily encumbered by its masses of material, and leaning a little in the direction of that disunity for which Aristotle condemned the *Cycle*.[45] To dispose with skill and transform into meaningful image and scene so vast and varied a tapestry was to undertake, in a sense, to create a new form; and indeed, the *Odyssey* is not an epic in the same sense as the *Iliad*, but, with its openness to all detail, however homely, and its concern with social types and forms, something verging toward the novel. Perhaps for this reason it is the more popular of the two poems to modern taste. But as a work of ancient art, it lacks the perfection of its predecessor. The problems of disposal and transformation are not everywhere solved as one might wish, and whereas one thinks in the *Iliad* of a single miracle, in the *Odyssey* there are many wonders.

To return to the suitors, for instance, one may well ask if Homer's presentation does not fall somewhat between two stools. A few of them are vivid enough, yet originally they could not have been vivid at all. In the folk tale, such suitors are an immovable fixture, introduced merely to be the wrong men in contrast to the right man. Homer's interest in them, however, puts them on a different level, and his effort to make them real has led him to imagine them as young oligarchs. Doubtless he found adequate models of highhandedness and violence in the sons of the rich families of his own time, and the contrast between these essentially unheroic dynasts and the mythic individuals in the epic tradition would lend itself to the contrast between Odysseus and the suitors.

But the matter occasionally seems to be pressed further, to affect the whole position and purpose of the suitors. They do not, for instance, seem acutely eager for anyone to marry Penelope. As the latter indicates, their method of wooing is most improper, the reverse, in fact, of the usual procedure.[46] And whereas the assumption would naturally be that he who marries Penelope will be king of Ithaca, the idea of a restored kingship seems to be very far from their intentions, either for Telemachus, or for that matter, for one of their own number; the whole idea of "kingship" has become rather attenuated, so that Telemachus can speak of many kings in Ithaca, any one of whom might be king.[47] Clearly the title "king" is losing its meaning, and is taking on the one familiar in Hesiod, namely, "lord of an estate," or "nobleman."[48] Indeed, at one point Antinous proposes bringing the matter to a close: the choice, he says, is either to murder Telemachus and divide his possessions, giving the palace only as the share of the one who marries Penelope, or else to give up their present position, let Telemachus have his whole inheritance as king, and themselves woo the queen properly.[49] This is to say, that their current actions are leading not to the choice of a real king, but to a division, by force if necessary, of the regal inheritance among the dynastic families. The speech is delivered in a closed council, to which no one of the other inhabitants is admitted, a detail which reëmphasizes the earlier remarks of old Aegyptius about the scarcity of councils since Odysseus went away.[50] Such close communion is after the oligarchic fashion, and there can be little doubt that the original suitors of the tradition have been conceived by the poet somehow in terms of the oppressive oligarchies which supplanted the Mycenaean monarchies. To conceive them so was brilliant, in that their actions thus achieve a pointed vigor, especially to the poet's contemporaries. Yet, when it comes to their annihilation, they must all, after Antinous and Eurymachus, fall back into the shadows of the old tale, mere wrong men doomed from the first, yet now a little too real to be taken as such. The conflict between the material and the conception is not quite resolved. But perhaps it was in the effort to resolve it that Homer introduced the beginnings of civil strife in the last book, and rehearsed the problem in the second *Nekyia*. No one even thinks twice about the slain suitors in the folk tale. But Penelope's suitors have been rationalized into an all too familiar social scheme, and one must finish rationally: the dynastic families make reprisals under arms, and Homer is forced to bring the matter to a close by the direct interference of Athena and Zeus.

Such inconcinnity, little as one may feel it in actually reading the *Odyssey*, seems, like so much else in the poem's artistic conceiving, the token of slightly altered tastes, of new concerns entering and beginning to disintegrate older forms, even as one sees it in proto-Attic art. The form cannot as yet be called disintegrated, but one feels that, given a little more of this interest in the homely and the contemporary, a little more realism, a little more opening of the door to new impressions, and a new form must replace the epic, at least in its primacy. And indeed, the new forms came very soon, oral poetry yielded place to literature, and epic became a scholar's exercise.

But if the *Odyssey* marks the end of the great oral period of Greek literature, it is an end implied by the material, and a few symptoms of slackened technique do not prevent the poem from presenting a final apotheosis of the whole tradition. It is less intense than the *Iliad* and more external in its view of everything, not from disinterest in the profound, but from the distancing and detachment which comes of retrospect from new vantage points. Already by 700, the Greek world was showing a new face, and quicker changes were in progress than any which had taken place for centuries. Colonization, expansion of trade, contact with foreign parts, and hence wider geographical cognizance, the strong growth of oligarchy, a rising ethnic consciousness, and experimentation in all the arts — all these were forces energetically at work from the beginning of the seventh century, and all are, in one way or another, reflected in the *Odyssey*. The subject of epic was the past, but the approach, insofar as the traditional medium allowed, took on colors from the present. Some of these have been described, but the perspective which they create upon the heroic past, the real matter of the poem, is in itself one of the chief notes of difference between this poem and the *Iliad*. Here one is no longer in the midst of the heroic Achaean world; one follows instead a wanderer from that world, a wanderer who becomes more and more generalized through the first books into an image of Everyman in his experience, and in the last books, reparticularized into a commanding but somewhat altered personality in a world which is also changed. The old Achaean world reappears in Pylos and Sparta, in order to acquaint Telemachus with his heritage. One hears high tales of it from Demodocus, but the people to whom he sings are not of it, except for Odysseus himself. We see its representative string the great bow where the new men fail. But it is a thing of the past. Menelaus, Helen, and Nestor, active once, are now only receptacles of memory, glorious or sorrowful, of the deeds at Troy:

> There lies Ajax, scion of Ares, there lies Achilles,
> There also Patroclus, a councillor like the gods,
> There too my own dear son, both mighty and stainless,
> Antilochus, exceeding in swiftness of foot, and a spearman.[51]

If one seeks the Achaean world in the *Odyssey*, it is to be found far in the west, in the Islands of the Dead. The men of bronze slew each other, as Hesiod says, and Odysseus, nearly the last of them, is undergoing changes. The superb and panoramic dream of the *Nekyia* revisits and summarizes it all for the last time, fixing once more in deathly eternity the great persons of the tradition. Sad, but detached, it is an elegy for heroes who had lived in songs for future men; and now, the songs are changing. In the new world of Hellas, one sees them differently; they are still the verities of the culture, but the immediacy of life itself is already setting them further apart, while a new kind of man, and a new sense of artistic and intellectual form takes the foreground. The fierce purity of Achilles' spirit, disdainful of phenomena, yields place to a heroic conception more available to a time of widening horizons, the man who wades eagerly through the phenomena of experience, to define himself by the limits of action, perception and understanding. The tale of Menelaus and Proteus in Book 4 presents the paradigm: hold fast to the changing, chaotic shapes, and the truth will come in the end.

In the long run, both *Iliad* and *Odyssey* contributed their share to the perfecting of what we call the classical spirit. Embodying as they do the polarities of that spirit, they remain for us the archetypes of the Classical, the Hellenic, and like all Hellenic things, they stand by a structural tension of passion and form, at once mysterious and profoundly clear.

NOTES

TITLES ABBREVIATED IN THE NOTES

American Journal of Archaeology

American Journal of Philology

Annuario della regia scuola archeologica di Atene

Archäologischer Anzeiger

Athenische Mitteilungen

Annual of the British School at Athens

Cambridge Ancient History

Classical Philology

Classical Quarterly

Fragmenta Historicorum Graecorum

Harvard Studies in Classical Philology

Inscriptiones Graecae

Journal of Hellenic Studies

Mitteilungen der Deutschen Orientgesellschaft

Opuscula Archaeologica

*Pauly-Wissowa Kroll, Real-Encyclopädie der
    Classischen Altertumswissenschaft*

*Sitzungsberichte der Akademie der Wissenschaften
    zu Berlin*

*Transactions and Proceedings of the American
    Philological Association*

Roman numerals refer to books of the *Iliad*, Arabic to those of the *Odyssey*.

NOTES

1. See the excellent account of the "analyst" school in W. Schadewaldt, *Von Homers Welt und Werk*, 2nd ed. (Stuttgart, 1952), pp. 10–35; also M. Platnauer, *Fifty Years of Classical Scholarship* (Oxford, 1954), chap. I (account by E. R. Dodds). The old polemics, together with many old arguments, have revived, however, in D. Page's *The Homeric Odyssey* (Oxford, 1955).

2. See Robert Wood, *Essay on the Original Genius of Homer* (London, 1769); cf. Schadewaldt, *Homers Welt*, pp. 11f.; and R. Volkmann, *Geschichte und Kritik der Wolfschen Prolegomena* (Leipzig, 1874).

3. For bibliography of Milman Parry, see A. B. Lord, "Homer, Parry, and Huso," *AJA* 52 (1948): 43f. Lord's publication of the Parry collection is in progress.

4. The song of Avdo Međedović, soon to appear; see A. B. Lord, *Serbo-croatian Heroic Songs* (Cambridge, Mass., and Belgrade, 1954), I, 15f.; for a fuller account, see Lord, "Avdo Međedović, Guslar," *Journal of American Folklore* 69 (1956): 320ff.

5. See below, Chapter IV.

6. A. J. B. Wace, in the Foreword to M. Ventris and J. Chadwick, *Documents in Mycenaean Greek* (Cambridge, England, 1956), p. xxviii.

7. W. C. Greene, "The Spoken and the Written Word," *HSCP* 60 (1951): 24–31; and A. B. Lord, "Homer's Originality: Dictated Texts," *TAPA* 84 (1953): 124ff., answering attempts by Sir C. M. Bowra and H. T. Wade-Gery to correct Parry's view.

8. H. T. Wade-Gery, *The Poet of the Iliad* (Cambridge, England, 1952), p. 38. Cf. the well-known reaction of S. E. Bassett, *The Poetry of Homer* (Berkeley, 1938).

9. J. Whatmough, "ΩΣΠΕΡ ΟΜΗΡΟΣ ΦΗΣΙ," *AJA* 52 (1948): 50.

10. M. Parry, *L'Epithète traditionelle dans Homère* (Paris, 1928), pp. 114 and 227; *Les Formules et la métrique d'Homère* (Paris, 1928), pp. 50f., and *passim*.

11. M. Parry, "About Winged Words," *CP* 32 (1937): 59–63, in answer to G. M. Calhoun, "The Art of the Formula in Homer — ἔπεα πτερόεντα," *CP* 30 (1935): 215–217. Cf. Parry's general discussion of the function and force of epithets, *Epithète traditionelle*, pp. 146ff., esp. 156 and 158 on the much admired, and mistranslated φυσίζοος αἶα.

12. Parry, "The Traditional Metaphor in Homer," *CP* 28 (1933): 40.

13. 17.57; 19.29; 21.386; 22.398.

14. Cf. Ventris and Chadwick, *Documents*, and their earlier fundamental article, "Evidence for Greek Dialect in the Mycenaean Archives," *JHS* 73 (1953): 84ff. For theories before the decipherment, H. L. Lorimer, "Homer and the Art of Writing," *AJA* 52 (1948): 11ff. A history of the study of Linear B is given by S. Dow, "Minoan Writing," *AJA* 58 (1954): 77ff. For an attempt to refute Ventris, see A. J. Beattie, "Mr. Ventris' Decipherment

of the Minoan Linear B Script," *JHS* 76 (1956): 1ff. Beattie's attack, while it certainly exploits to the full the difficulties and shortcomings admitted by Ventris (*Documents*, pp. 26f.), scarcely does justice to the rigorous methods which underlie the decipherment; even less can it explain away the forty-odd pages of finely printed Mycenaean vocabulary at the end of Ventris' book. That Ventris' work has raised many problems is obvious; it would have been a case for real scepticism if he had produced a key to such ancient material which did not raise problems.

15. Cf. Whatmough, *AJA* 52 (1948): 47ff.; W. Lehmann, *Proto-Indo-European Phonology* (Austin, 1952).

16. U. von Wilamowitz, *Homerische Untersuchungen* (Berlin, 1884), p. 87.

17. V.655–697; cf. XII.101ff.

18. See also Chapter III, note 12.

19. See J. H. Finley, *Pindar and Aeschylus* (Cambridge, Mass., 1955), chap. I.

CHAPTER II. THE MEMORY OF THE ACHAEANS

1. Sir C. M. Bowra, *Tradition and Design in the Iliad* (Oxford, 1930), pp. 157f.

2. See Lorimer, *Homer and the Monuments*, pp. 38f., to whose summary of the evidence the present argument is much indebted.

2a. For the most recent formulation of the whole problem of the arrival of Indo-European in Greece, see J. Mellaart, "The End of the Early Bronze Age in Anatolia and the Aegean," *AJA* 62 (1958): 9ff. Unfortunately, this article appeared when my book had already gone to press; hence, it has been impossible to take full account of it, but the reader is earnestly referred to it for two cogently supported arguments in particular, which perhaps modify the view presented here: (1) the location of Ahhiyawa in the Troad, and (2) the coming of the Greeks from that region to Greece, by sea, around 1900 B.C.

3. See Sir C. M. Bowra, "Homeric Words in Arcadian Inscriptions," *CQ* 20 (1926): 168ff.; and "Homeric Words in Cyprus," *JHS* 54 (1934): 54ff.; C. D. Buck, *Greek Dialects* (Chicago, 1955), p. 7; L. R. Palmer, *Achaeans and Indo-Europeans* (Oxford, 1955), p. 3.

4. Ventris and Chadwick, *JHS* 73 (1953): 84; cf. S. Dow, *AJA* 58 (1954): 78, 120ff.; and A. J. B. Wace, "The Discovery of Inscribed Clay Tablets at Mycenae," *Antiquity* 27 (1953): 86; also, though more guardedly, G. E. Mylonas, *Ancient Mycenae: The Capital City of Agamemnon* (Princeton, 1957), p. 74.

5. Cf. J. Pendlebury, *The Archaeology of Crete* (London, 1939), pp. 224, 259ff., who notes Mycenaean elements in LM III, but whose conclusions must be reversed in the light of the tablets; more pertinent is A. J. B. Wace, "The Coming of the Greeks," *Classical Weekly* 47 (1954): 153.

6. See Lorimer, *Homer and the Monuments*, pp. 23–32, on LH II, and A. J. B. Wace, *Mycenae* (Princeton, 1949), pp. 22ff. O. Gurney, *The Hittites*, 2nd ed. (Penguin Books, 1954), p. 53, recognizes the Achaean thalassocracy from 1400 on, but it must have begun earlier; cf. Thuc. I.9.3–4.

7. V.43; noted by G. Murray, *Rise of the Greek Epic*, 4th ed. (Oxford, 1934), p. 221.

8. Dow, *AJA* 58 (1954): 126f.

9. The period is admittedly difficult. Miss Lorimer, *Homer and the Monuments*, pp. 19ff., speaks of possible plundering of Cnossos by Mycenae after the earthquake; also of Crete's remarkable recovery from the disaster in the period of the later Palace. The recovery is comprehensible in the light of Greek domination of Cnossos, the efflorescence of Minoan art on the mainland being then due to importation of skilled labor. For traces of a new, perhaps Greek, spirit in Minoan pottery of this period, see note 5 above, and Chapter V, note 28. In the Dark Age, according to the anachronistic passage of the *Odyssey*, 19.172–177, the Achaeans shared the island with the original Cretan population and with the Dorians.

10. See P. Kretschmer, "Zur Geschichte der griechischen Dialekte," *Glotta* 1 (1909): 6–59; C. W. Blegen, "Athens and the Early Age of Greece," *HSCP*, Suppl. I (Athenian Studies, 1940), pp. 8f.

11. Herod. I.56, 57 J. A. R. Munro, "Pelasgians and Ionians," *JHS* 54 (1934): 109–128; A. G. Laird, "Herodotus on Pelasgians in Attica," *AJP* 54 (1933): 97–119; Murray, *Rise*, pp. 41ff., summarizes the Pelasgian question. A. W. Gomme, *Commentary to Thucydides*, I, 94ff., rejects Herodotus' testimony, and identifies the Minyan culture as Ionian. The name Pelasgian remains obscure, both in derivation and in designation, though it can well be a Greek word. Its associations do not seem to be fundamentally Ionic, but rather Aeolic: in Homer it is connected with southern Thessaly (II.-681ff.), where the name survived into historical times as Pelasgiotis; with Dodona in Epirus, perhaps an Aeolic cult-center (XVI.233); with Crete and the highly Aeolic name Deucalion (19.177, 181); and with the Trojan allies from Larisa in Asia Minor (II.840ff., X.429, XVII.288), almost certainly an anachronism introduced after the colonization of Aeolis.

12. See the survey of its dialectal affiliations, Ventris and Chadwick, *JHS* 73 (1953): 101ff.

13. Examples of Linear B are so scarce from any districts except Pylos, Cnossos, and Mycenae (all of which may be assumed to have been Achaean in dialect), that there is no real evidence in any case. The point urged here is that, though Linear B reflects the vowel system and some of the particular features of both Aeolic and Arcado-Cypriote, but not the characteristics of Ionic, it must not be inferred that either (1) the three great divisions of East Greek had not to some degree taken shape by LH III, at least; or (2) the tablets represent a Greek which excludes Ionic. The latter, far from being the oldest of the dialects, is probably the youngest, and may not yet have developed the strong peculiarities which distinguish later Ionic and Attic, such as η for ā. If Linear B does eventually betray local dialectal differences, they certainly will not resemble those of four or five centuries later; so much is proved by the representation of the labiovelars alone. Such differences undoubtedly existed, but probably they were still too unpronounced, before the isolation in the Dark Age, to appear in the phonetically inadequate Linear B script.

14. Herod. VII.94, 95.

15. See Strabo IX.407; Paus. IX.24.2; Steph. Byz. *s.v.* Ἀθῆναι.

16. 11.235ff.; cf. the name "Minyeius," XI.722; see Sir J. L. Myres, *Who Were the Greeks?* (Berkeley, 1930), p. 311.

17. Buck, *Greek Dialects*, pp. 5ff., quoting Thuc. III.102 and IV.42.

18. R. Carpenter, *Folktale, Fiction, and Saga in the Homeric Epics* (Berkeley, 1946), pp. 27ff.

19. Hesiod, *Erga* 151.

20. Lorimer, *Homer and the Monuments*, p. 46.

21. Cf. W. K. Prentice, "The Achaeans," *AJA* 33 (1929): 206–218; probably correct, however, in the argument that the Hittite Ahhiyawa was in or near Asia Minor; see below.

22. See, for instance, C. A. F. Schaeffer, "Enkomi," *AJA* 52 (1948): 174ff., on both iron and bronze in Cypriote tombs, Enkomi nos. 6, 13, 16, from the period of the fall of Troy. For a general discussion, see Lorimer, *Homer and the Monuments*, pp. 111ff.

23. Ventris and Chadwick, *Documents in Mycenaean Greek*, pp. 375–381, 292–300; see also T. B. L. Webster, "Homer and the Mycenaean Tablets," *Antiquity* 29 (1955): 13. A similar revision of theory must probably be made in regard to greaves, once thought to be no part of Mycenaean armament, but now known from an example excavated near Olympia by the Ephor of antiquities, Mr. Yalouris; see Vanderpool, "News Letter," *AJA* 58 (1954): 235.

24. Ventris and Chadwick, *JHS* 73 (1953): 94; cf. L. R. Palmer, *Achaeans and Indo-Europeans* (Oxford, 1955), p. 4.

25. See Sir C. M. Bowra, *Homer and his Forerunners* (Edinburgh, 1955), pp. 18–30, for an excellent summary.

26. The details of this tormented question may be sought in Bowra, *Tradition and Design*, pp. 159ff.; Carpenter, *Folktale, Fiction*, pp. 35ff., 45ff., takes an extreme view indeed; Wade-Gery, *Poet*, pp. 33ff., a much more credible one; the real answer, or much of it, lies in Parry's remarks about the generic epithet εὐρνάγνια, *Epithète traditionelle*, p. 126.

27. Eratosthenes' date, 1184; the Marmor Parium favors 1209, Herodotus *ca*. 1250. For a convenient collection of ancient sources, see Wade-Gery, *Poet*, p. 75, n. 67, with a brilliant analysis of how Eratosthenes arrived at his date. For the historical basis of the Trojan War, see Lorimer, *Homer and the Monuments*, p. 36; H. Bengtson, *Einführung in die alte Geschichte* (Munich, 1949), pp. 98ff.; Wade-Gery, *Poet*, pp. 33ff.; it requires less credulity to believe in the historicity of the war than in some of the alternative theories, e.g., Bethe's exaggerated *Sagenverschiebung*, or R. Carpenter's effort to move the war partly to Egypt and partly to Teuthrania.

28. Language differences: II.804; 867; IV.437f.; 19.175; cf. *Hymn to the Delian Apollo*, 162ff.; *Hymn to Aphrodite*, 111ff.

29. Palmer, *Achaeans*, p. 20; cf. Bowra, *Homer and Forerunners*, p. 25, who, however, thinks that these are Greek names given to Trojans by Homer.

30. See C. W. Blegen, J. L. Caskey, M. Rawson, *Troy* (Princeton, 1950–53), III, 9ff.; adversely criticized in K. Bittel's review, *Gnomon* 28 (1956): 241ff., chiefly on the ground that pottery by itself is an unsafe criterion of ethnic affiliations; besides the pottery, however, there are now the personal names recorded in the Linear B tablets, and the traditional genealogies, asso-

ciating Greek and Trojan families. Cf. Lorimer, *Homer and the Monuments*, pp. 11, 13; H. Hencken, *Indo-European Languages and Archaeology* (*The American Anthropologist* 57, December 1955), pp. 36f. For a brief summary of Blegen's view, see J. L. Caskey, "A Preliminary Report," *AJA* 52 (1948): 119ff.

31. J. Lawrence Angel, "The Human Remains," *Troy*, Suppl. Monograph, pp. 26f., 31.

32. Lorimer, *Homer and the Monuments*, pp. 10f.; but the megara at Sesklo and Dimini may be earlier; cf. also H. Goldman, *Eutresis*, p. 37, fig. 42; for a good summary of the megaron problem, see E. Baldwin Smith, "The Megaron and its Roof," *AJA* 46 (1942): 99ff.

33. See Wade-Gery, *Poet*, pp. 35 and 80, n. 86. He also considers the Trojan-Etruscan equation proposed by Carpenter; but the "etymological bridge" is even flimsier than its author admitted.

34. XX.215ff.; XXIII.296.

35. Paus. VIII.24.3.

36. *Aeneid* VIII.130ff. Cf. the historians Callistratus and Satyrus in Dionysius Hal. *Ant. Rom.* I.68.2, and the curious tradition reported by Pausanias (I.4.6) about Arcadians who went to Asia with Telephus.

37. *Schol. T ad* VI.88; Clement Alex. *Protr.* 4.

38. Gurney, *Hittites*, pp. 18f.

39. See Gurney, pp. 117ff., for an excellent summary of the characteristics of Hittite, and its relation to other languages of Asia Minor; cf. also Hencken, *Indo-European Languages and Archaeology*, pp. 39ff., for a good collection of evidence, and various theories of Indo-European origins.

40. They may even have preceded it, if the *megaron* houses of Troy I and II are tokens of Indo-European habitation.

41. Herod. V.113; VII.90; Strabo XIV.682; Paus. VIII.5.2–3; Lycophron 586ff.; Hesych. *s.v.* Ἀχαιομάντεις; Steph. Byz. *s.v.* Γολγοὶ and Λακεδαίμων; cf. E. Gjerstad, *Studies on Prehistoric Cyprus* (Uppsala, 1926), and J. F. Daniel, "Two Late Cypriote III Tombs from Kourion," *AJA* 41 (1937): 82–83.

42. On the antiquity of colonies in Cyprus, see *Oxford Classical Dictionary*, *s.v.* Cyprus; Lorimer, *Homer and the Monuments*, p. 37; also P. Dikaios and Sir J. L. Myres, "An Inscribed Tablet from Enkomi, Cyprus," *Antiquity* 27 (1953): 103ff.; and Dikaios, "A Second Inscribed Clay Tablet from Enkomi," *ibid.*: 233ff., demonstrating the antiquity of the Cypro-Minoan script. For Rhodes, see Lorimer, p. 24; G. Jacopi, "Nuovi Scavi nella Necropoli micinea di Jalisso," *Annuario* 13–14 (1930–31): 253ff., and A. Furumark, "The Settlement at Ialysos and Aegean History c.1550–1400," *Op. Arch.* 6 (1950): 150ff., where it is demonstrated that a Mycenaean colony existed beside an earlier Minoan one.

43. XI.20ff.; 17.442f. Cf. J. A. Knudtzon, *Die El-Amarna Tafeln* (Leipzig, 1915), nos. 33–40.

44. This and most of the following identifications were first made by E. Forrer, "Vorhomerische Griechen in den Keilschrifttexten von Boghaz-Köi," *Mitt. Deutsch. Orientges.* 63 (1924): 1–24; and "Die Griechen in den Boghaz-Köi Texten," *Orientalistische Literaturzeitung* (1924): 113–118; they have been denied chiefly by F. Sommer, *Die Ahhiyawa-Urkunden*, (*Ab-*

handlungen der Bayrischen Akademie der Wissenschaften, Phil.-hist. Abt., Neue Folge 6, 1932), and *Ahhiyawa-Frage und Sprachwissenschaft*, (*ibid.*, 9, 1934); defended by P. Kretschmer; see his articles in *Glotta* 13, 15, 18, 21, and 24. See Gurney, *Hittites*, pp. 46ff., for a discussion of Forrer's views, and pp. 226f., for further bibliography.

45. See Forrer, *Mitt. Deutsch. Orientges.* 43 (1924): 7, 21; Gurney, *Hittites*, 57f.; Kretschmer, "Alexandros von Vilusa," *Glotta* 13 (1924): 205ff.; P. Giles, *The Year's Work in Classical Studies* (London, 1924–1925), pp. 119ff.; H. R. Hall, *The Civilization of Greece in the Bronze Age* (London, 1928), p. 250; C. J. Cadoux, *Ancient Smyrna* (Oxford, 1938), pp. 30ff.

46. Atreus could be in Hittite "Attarawas"; for "Attarissyas" the best conjecture is Bowra's "Atresios," but this could hardly be the original of Atreus. Is there a possibility in "Assaracus"? See Gurney's defense of Ah-hiyawa-Achaia, *Hittites*, 52ff.; phonologically, a little difficulty arises from the equivalence of -hh- with χ, which in Hittite cognates is generally represented by k or g: χείρ, *kesar*; χειμών, *gimmanza*. On the other hand, Sapir has suggested *hahru* as a cognate of ὠκύς and ὀξύς ("Indo-European Words for Tear," *Selected Writings of Edward Sapir*, ed. D. G. Mandelbaum, Berkeley and Los Angeles, 1949, pp. 296ff.) and one might compare Hittite *hanas*, "grandmother," with Lycian χῆνα. Moreover, we are here dealing with a loan-word of a special sort, i.e., a proper name, and not a cognate; see G. Hill, *History of Cyprus*, p. 34, n.3, with references to Forrer, *Klio* 30 (1937): 137, and I. Levy, *Mélanges E. Boisacq*, II (1938), 119ff. The case of "Millewanda" seems clear: The Hittite gives the general shape MLWT-, implying in early Greek *Μιλϝατος, which yields naturally Aeolic Μίλλατος (cf. Theocritus 28.21), and Attic-Ionic Μίλητος (cf. II.647, 868); *Hom. Hymn.* III.42; 180). The nasal infix in the Hittite seems of little consequence, since it does not universally appear; see Gurney, *Hittites*, pp. 55f., and G. M. A. Hanfmann, "Ionia, Leader or Follower?" *HSCP* 61 (1953): 5.

47. See Gurney, *Hittites*, 46ff., whose summary avoids wishful conjectures.

48. Ventris and Chadwick, *Documents*, p. 209, no. 78.

49. Gurney, *Hittites*, p. 55f. But "Tawagalawas" works much better as "Eteocles" than as "Deucalion."

50. Gurney, *Hittites*, p. 50, notes a tablet of Tudhaliyas IV, in which the name Ahhiyawa had been erased from a list of powers regarded as equals by the Hittite king. Gurney's explanation may be right, but it is also possible that the scribe inserted Ahhiyawa from a formulaic protocol of long standing, and then erased it because Ahhiyawa was no longer a great power in the East.

51. Hanfmann, *HSCP* 61 (1953): 4, 26, n. 11. More recently it is reported that the area around the Athena temple, at least, was occupied continuously from 1500 B.C. to Roman times; see M. Mellink, "Archaeology in Asia Minor," *AJA* 60 (1956): 381. Furumark, *Op. Arch.* 6 (1950): 252, risks the opinion that there were other colonies besides Miletus, though not as yet found. Cf. F. H. Stubbings, *Mycenaean Pottery from the Levant* (Cambridge, 1951), pp. 21ff.; 102ff.

52. Cf. Gurney, *Hittites*, pp. 38f.; H. R. Hall, *CAH* II, 281ff.; cf. note 67 below.

53. Lorimer, *Homer and the Monuments*, pp. 32–36. At Tarsus all Mycenaean pots are late intrusions, postdating the fall of the Hittite empire; cf. H. Goldman, *Tarsus* (Princeton, 1956), II, 63f., 205ff.

54. Wace, *Mycenae*, p. 18, on both shaft graves and tholos tombs; see also *passim* for further details of Mycenaean history. The earlier Grave Circle discovered by Mylonas and Papademetriou now dates the beginning of the shaft-grave dynasty before 1600; cf. Mylonas, *Ancient Mycenae*, pp. 128ff.

55. Mylonas, *Ancient Mycenae*, pp. 87f., 97f., brings down the date of the last *tholos* (Tomb of Clytaemnestra) from 1300 (Wace) to 1225.

56. Lorimer, *Homer and the Monuments*, pp. 32ff.; A. Furtwängler and G. Löschcke, *Mykenische Vasen* (Berlin, 1886), p. xliii; Wace, *Chamber Tombs at Mycenae* (*Archaeologia* 82) pp. 176ff. Slightly earlier dates suggested by S. Immerwahr, "The Protome Painter and Some Contemporaries," *AJA* 60 (1956): 137ff.; V. Karageorghis, "Two Mycenaean Bull Craters," *ibid.*: 143ff.

57. Perhaps Hittite; cf. Lorimer, *Homer and the Monuments*, pp. 32ff.

58. The present discussion follows the new dating of Mylonas, *Ancient Mycenae*, pp. 32ff., 118ff., based on the discovery of LH III B sherds and figurines under the foundations of the Cyclopean walls, Lion Gate, and Grave Circle parapet. Wace, *Mycenae*, pp. 133f., maintains a date almost a century earlier, and would extend the upper limit of LH III B to 1340. It is hoped that further evidence will produce an agreement of opinion.

59. See G. Karo, "Die Perseia von Mykenai," *AJA* 38 (1934): 128ff.; Lorimer, *Homer and the Monuments*, pp. 33ff.

60. Herod. IX.26.3; Paus. I.41.2; VIII.5.1; VIII.45.3.

61. Herod. VII.11; cf. G. Thomson, *Studies in Ancient Greek Society; The Prehistoric Aegean* (London, 1949), pp. 400ff. on Pelops, following the suggestion, no doubt, of G. Poisson, "Tantale, roi des Hittites," *Revue Archéologique*, ser. 5, 22 (1925): 75ff. The theory is a little extreme, but the legend of Pelops is doubtless connected with the Hittites. Cf. Murray, *Rise*, pp. 208ff.

62. On the increase in ivory in LH III, cf. Lorimer, *Homer and the Monuments*, pp. 61f.; it is frequently mentioned in the Linear B tablets.

63. Thuc. I.9.2; cf. R. Graves, *The Greek Myths* (Penguin Books, 1955), pp. 43f., 207ff., on Eurystheus and Atreus.

64. Mylonas, *Ancient Mycenae*, pp. 70ff.

65. Gurney, *Hittites*, p. 52.

66. H. R. Hall, "Mursil and Myrtilos," *JHS* 29 (1909): 19ff.; cf. note 61. Linear B shows that the change *-ti* to *-is* is very early in East Greek, Ventris and Chadwick, *JHS* 73 (1953): 102; "Myrtilos" must be the Dorian form of the name, generalized when Pelops was adopted by the Dorians; the name is "Myrsilos" in Aeolic.

67. See H. R. Hall, *CAH*, II, 281ff., for the Egyptian evidence in general; cf. also Hall, *The Oldest Civilization of Greece* (Philadelphia, 1901), p. 169 n., and "Keftiu and the Peoples of the Sea," *BSA* 8 (1901–02): 180; Sir J. L. Myres and K. T. Frost, "The Historical Background of the Trojan War," *Klio* 14 (1911): 447ff. The new Kara Tepe bilingual inscription does not necessarily upset the identification of Egyptian Danuna and Danaoi,

as Furumark concludes, "Ialysos," *Op. Arch.* 6 (1948): 243, n. 6. The inscription mentions *Danunim* living in Cilicia, and ruled over by Asitawanda of the "House of Mopsus"; cf. H. T. Bossert and U. Bahadir Alkim, *Karatepe, Second Preliminary Report* (Istanbul, 1946), pp. 25ff.; also A. M. Honeyman, "Phoenician Inscriptions from Karatepe," *Le Muséon* 61 (1948): 43ff. The inscription dates from the eighth or ninth century (Honeyman, p. 45; cf. H. G. Güterbock, "Die Bedeutung der Bilinguis vom Karatepe für die Entzifferung der hethitschen Hieroglyphen," *Eranos* 47 [1949]: 104), and cannot indicate much about the location of the Danuna six or seven centuries earlier. *Danunim, Danuna,* and *Danaoi,* likely enough, are all the same people, and there is nothing very surprising about having both the Danaoi and the House of Mopsus established in Cilicia, since Mopsus traditionally led colonies from Greece to various parts of Asia Minor, including Cilicia, in the thirteenth century; cf. W. H. Roscher, *Lexicon der griechischen und römischen Mythologie* (Leipzig, 1894–1897), *s.v.* Mopsus.

68. Lorimer, *Homer and the Monuments,* p. 27. Cf. Mylonas, *Ancient Mycenae,* pp. 14ff.; 124ff.; 168f.

69. Cf. Graves, *Greek Myths,* I, 28, 202; II, 30, 36; and J. B. Bury, *CAH,* II, 476ff., for a similar view; it appears also elsewhere, though with differences, and was probably first proposed by Tsountas.

70. Myres, *Who Were the Greeks?* pp. 308ff., 323ff. Bowra, *Tradition and Design,* pp. 169f., shows the general correspondence between the genealogical records and the dates fixed by Hittite and Egyptian sources for the Achaean hegemony between the middle fourteenth and middle twelfth centuries.

71. See Murray, *Rise,* p. 47, n. 1; E. H. Sturtevant, "Nouns of Relationship in Lycian and Hittite," *TAPA* 59 (1928): 48ff.; cf. Herod. I.173.4–5; Thomson, *Studies in Ancient Greek Society,* pp. 98, n. 52; 142.

72. Herod. VII.92; Paus. VII.3.7; Sarpedon, son of Zeus and Laodamia, grandson of Bellerophon, and cousin of Glaucus, can hardly be anything but Greek; if he came from Crete, it was as one of the Achaean overlords of the island, see above.

73. See V. Berard, *De l'origine des cultes arcadiens* (Paris, 1894).

74. Dionysius Hal. *Ant. Rom.* II, 1.

75. See P. Kretschmer, "Bellerophontes," *Glotta* 31 (1952): 92–103, esp. 101; an interesting study of relations between Lycia and Argos.

76. Miss Lorimer must be in some error to say that Mycenae was cut off from the sea by Diomedes' occupation of Tiryns (*Homer and the Monuments,* p. 35); Tiryns seems to have made no more use of the sea than did Mycenae, and commerce was on the wane everywhere. For the strategic argument, see also the next chapter, on the unity of Salamis and Athens.

77. See Viktor Burr, ΝΕΩΝ ΚΑΤΑΛΟΓΟΣ, *Klio, Beiheft* 49 (1944), substantiating T. W. Allen, *The Homeric Catalog of Ships* (Oxford, 1921); Wade-Gery, *Poet,* pp. 49ff., gives a convenient summary; but G. M. A. Hanfmann, "Archaeology in Homeric Asia Minor," *AJA* 52 (1948): 146ff., must also be right in saying that the *Catalog* could only have been composed in its present form in the eighth century; the general picture of Mycenaean Greece can only be traditional, whereas certain features, alluded

to by Hanfmann, could only have been thought proper in the eighth
century.

78. Hesiod, *Erga* 152–165.

79. 4.174ff.

80. IX.147ff.

81. XIV.84ff. Translation mine, as are also those that follow.

82. *Theogony* 27f.

83. 19.204; 17.518ff.

CHAPTER III. ATHENS, 1200–700 B.C.

1. The Cyclopean walls and the few stones of the palaces are about the
only Mycenaean remains noted in most earlier descriptions of Athens, and
they are generally called "Pelasgic." Evidence of Mycenaean cults in Athens
is treated by M. P. Nilsson, *Homer and Mycenae* (London, 1933), p. 212;
also *The Minoan-Mycenaean Religion and its Survival in Greek Religion*,
2nd ed. (Lund, Gleerup, 1950), pp. 474f., 488, 562ff.; *History of Greek
Religion* (Oxford, 1925), pp. 26f. See also B. Tamaro, "Culto miceneo sull'
Acropoli," *Annuario* 4–5 (1921–1922): 1–11; and G. W. Elderkin, "Cults of
the Erechtheion," *Hesperia* 10 (1941): 113–124, which is surprisingly sup-
ported in places by archaeological evidence in O. Broneer, "Excavations on
the North Slope of the Acropolis," *Hesperia* 4 (1935): 125ff. Cf. Schrade,
Götter und Menschen Homers (Stuttgart, 1952), p. 49.

2. For a good summary of the usual view of early Athens, see F. Jacoby,
Atthis (Oxford, 1949), p. 393, n. 22. The Pisistratean theory entered mod-
ern scholarship with Wolf's *Prolegomena*; fostered by Hermann, Bekker,
and Lachmann, opposed by Lehrs, and modified by Wilamowitz, *Homer-
ische Untersuchungen*, pp. 235ff., it has recently flowered again in G. M.
Bolling's attempt to reconstruct the text of Pisistratus, *Ilias Atheniensium*
(Lancaster, Pa., and Oxford, 1950).

3. Thuc. II.15. See A. della Seta's report of Italian excavations, *Bolletino
d'Arte* 4 (1924–1925): 88ff., and figs. 7–10; Doro Levi, "Abitazioni preis-
toriche sulle pendici meridionali dell' Acropoli," *Annuario* 13–14 (1930–
1931): 411ff.; G. E. Mylonas, "Ἡ Νεολιθικὴ Ἐποχή" (Athens, 1928), pp. 75ff.,
and "Athens and Minoan Crete," *HSCP*, Suppl. I (1940), p. 11.

4. H. D. Hansen, "Prehistoric Pottery on the North Slope of the Acrop-
olis," *Hesperia* 6 (1937): 539–570; cf. Mylonas, *HSCP*, Suppl. I (1940),
pp. 14–36, on continuity of Athenian civilization from Neolithic times on;
a more recent compendium is Ida T. Hill, *The Ancient City of Athens*
(Cambridge, 1953), pp. 1–31.

5. Hansen, *Hesperia* 6: 568ff.; cf. T. L. Shear, "The Campaign of 1937,"
Hesperia 7 (1938): 336–343; O. Broneer, "Excavations on the North Slope
of the Acropolis," *Hesperia* 2 (1933): 356–372; cf. R. S. Young, "Late Geo-
metric Graves and a Seventh Century Well," *Hesperia*, Suppl. II, p. 115, on
Minyan ware in the Agora.

6. See C. H. Morgan, II, "Terra Cotta Figurines from the North Slope,"
Hesperia 4 (1935): 189–213.

7. H. G. Lolling, *Das Kuppelgrab bei Menidi* (Athens, 1880); also, "Zum
Kuppelgrab bei Menidi," *Ath. Mitt.* 12 (1887): 139f.; from the Menidi tomb
come fragments of a boar's-tusk helmet, and a Mycenaean lyre of eight

strings, cf. Lorimer, *Homer and the Monuments*, pp. 212, 218, 456, 460; on Thorikos, see V. Stais, "'Ανασκαφαὶ ἐν Θορικῷ," Πρακτικὰ (1893): 12–17 and pl. B. O. Broneer, "A Mycenaean Fountain on the Athenian Acropolis," *Hesperia* 8 (1939): 416, suggests that Thorikos was the town from which the Laurion silver mines were worked in the Mycenaean period; see opposite view, Lorimer, *Homer and the Monuments*, p. 64. Close connection between Athens and Thorikos is implied in the legend of Cephalus, king of Thorikos, who married Procris, daughter of Erechtheus.

8. See T. L. Shear, "Discoveries in the Agora in 1939," *AJA* 43 (1939): 578ff.; cf. *Hesperia* 9 (1940): 274–291, and *AJA* 51 (1947): 270f., reported by E. Vanderpool; H. A. Thompson, "Excavations in the Athenian Agora, 1952," *AJA* 57 (1953): 24; Vanderpool, "News Letter from Greece," *AJA* 58 (1954): 231f., on chamber tombs elsewhere in Attica; those at Spata were long known, B. Haussoulier, "Catalogue descriptif des objets découverts à Spata," *Bulletin de Correspondance Hellénique* 2 (1878): 185ff.

9. See especially W. Kraiker and K. Kübler, *Kerameikos* (Berlin, 1939–1954), especially vols. I, IV, and V.

10. See O. Broneer, *Hesperia* 8 (1939), esp. p. 349; cf. pp. 423ff.

11. See C. W. Blegen, "Athens and the Early Age of Greece," *HSCP*, Suppl. I (Athenian Studies, 1940), pp. 1ff.

12. Exceptions: 19.177 (Dorians in Crete); Sparta as the regular home of Menelaus, rather than the Mycenaean sites of Amyclae or Therapne; Tlepolemus, son of Heracles, in II.653ff., is perhaps anachronistic, but not, of course, himself a Dorian. If the stories told of him reflect the Dorian colonization of Rhodes (cf. Lorimer, *Homer and the Monuments*, pp. 47f., 466, n. 2), there is no reason therefore to consider him an interpolation in the *Iliad*. All epic poety commits anachronism, Homer's not least; cf. the Pylos-Elis wars recalled by Nestor, though their events are perhaps to be dated two centuries after his death; see Wade-Gery, "What Happened in Pylos," *AJA* 52 (1948): 115ff.; F. Bölte, "Ein pylisches Epos," *Rhein. Mus.* 83 (1934): 319–347. On the other hand, Homer may, in the case of Tlepolemus, be following a different and more reasonable tradition than the one which makes Tlepolemus live over a hundred years and then colonize Rhodes. The latter was early colonized by Achaeans; Tlepolemus was an Achaean and belongs, according to the mythic genealogy, to the generation of the Trojan War. It may be that the Dorians later claimed him as the founder of their Rhodian colonies, by way of justifying their invasion of the island; cf. Cleomenes' remark to the Athenian priestess; Herod. V.72.

13. Plutarch, *Lycurgus*, 4.

14. See Bowra, *Tradition and Design*, pp. 181ff., quoting Meyer, *Geschichte des Altertums*, II, 400.

15. A. Fick, *Die Homerische Ilias* (Göttingen, 1886), and *Die Homerische Odyssee* (Göttingen, 1883).

16. For instance, Herod. VII. 91, on the colonization of Lesbos by Amphilochus and Calchas.

17. G. M. A. Hanfmann, "Archaeology in Homeric Asia Minor," *AJA* 52 (1948): 135ff., and "Ionia, Leader or Follower," *HSCP* 61 (1953): 1ff. The present discussion is chiefly indebted to Hanfmann; but others also have tended to his opinion, especially R. M. Cook, "Ionia and Greece in the

Eighth and Seventh Centuries B.C.," *JHS* 64 (1946): 67–98; also V. Desborough, *Protogeometric Pottery* (Oxford, 1952), *passim*, especially p. 304; cf. Wade-Gery, *Poet*, pp. 5, 9, and 66, n, 26. Also Lorimer, *Homer and the Monuments*, pp. 30f. with n. 5, suggests that the Greeks withdrew from Asia Minor, except Miletus, in the twelfth century and returned later. She recognizes the Carian occupation of Miletus; cf. Hanfmann, *AJA* 52:146. Miss Lorimer, pp. 458–459, also offers a very similar argument to the present one about the survival of the epic at Athens; cf. T. B. L. Webster, "Homer and the Mycenaean Tablets," *Antiquity* 29 (1955):14; cf. also C. Roebuck, "The Economic Development of Ionia," *CP* 48 (1953):9–16.

18. See Hanfmann, *HSCP* 61:3–8, on the difficulties of the Milesian evidence.

19. *Ibid.*, p. 15.

20. See Desborough, *Protogeometric Pottery*, p. 314, on the pottery and oval house at Smyrna, dated *ca.* 900, in the period said by Desborough to be the one in which Protogeometric spread from Athens to other localities. The oval (Geometric) house has a parallel in Athens, cf. Dorothy [Burr] Thompson, "A Geometric House and a Proto-Attic Votive Deposit," *Hesperia* 2 (1933): 542ff.; cf. Hanfmann, *HSCP* 61: 6. If the oval house at Smyrna had Athenian models, it might be remembered that Pylian refugees went to Smyrna (Mimnermus, 12. 1–6), and probably via Athens.

21. On the colonization of Aeolis by Orestes and his son Penthilus sixty years after the fall of Troy, and four generations before the Ionians, see Strabo IX.401, and XIII.582; *Schol. ad Pind. Nem. XI.* 34f. The son of Penthilus, Archelaus ("Echelas" in Paus. III.2.1), led the Aeolians to Daskylion near Cyzicus, and Lesbos was supposedly founded by Archelaus' son Gras. On Lesbos, cf. Herod. VII.91, colonized by Calchas and Amphilochus. Kyme was supposedly founded by Kleues and Malaos, descendants of Agamemnon. See W. Leaf, *Strabo on the Troad* (Cambridge, 1923), pp. 43ff., for a discussion. There are as yet no remains in Aeolis to bear out the tradition of such early Greek colonies; cf. Hanfmann, *AJA* 52:143–146; Wade-Gery, *Poet*, p. 79, n. 83.

22. O. Broneer, "What Happened at Athens," *AJA* 52 (1948):112. For material on the Dorian invasion, see Franz Miltner, *Klio* 27 (1934):54ff.

23. The pottery found in the abandoned houses resembled the Granary style of Mycenae, but is to be dated earlier by the commonness of the Kylix shape; see Broneer, *Hesperia* 2, esp. p. 372. Hence it appears that Athens was attacked before Mycenae was.

24. Broneer, *Hesperia* 2: 355f.; cf. Broneer, *AJA* 42: 450; cf. Lorimer, *Homer and the Monuments*, p. 458. Regarding the Kerameikos, see below, and cf. W. Kraiker, "Ausgrabungen in Kerameikos," *Arch. Anzeiger* 47 (1932): 206: "Vor allem geben sie [sc. the graves] Gewissheit für eine geschichtliche Entwicklung ohne Bruch-Wenigstens hier in Athen." Cf. G. Karo, *An Attic Cemetery* (Philadelphia, 1943), p. 7.

25. Cf. Morgan, *Hesperia* 4: 189–213. Note especially the remarks on the long continuity of the local clay, p. 189.

26. Cf. the early seventh-century "Snake-Goddess" plaque from the votive deposit on the northwest slope of the Areopagus in the Agora Museum. As in the figurines, the arms are raised, like the Minoan snake-goddess; see

Dorothy [Burr] Thompson, "A Geometric House and a Proto-Attic Votive Deposit," *Hesperia* 2 (1933): 604–609.

27. See Broneer, *Hesperia* 2: 367; cf. Kraiker-Kübler, *Kerameikos*, I, 175.

28. Broneer, *Hesperia* 8: 355 and fig. 30. This style is contemporary with the beginning of iron weaponry; cf. Kraiker-Kübler, *Kerameikos*, I, 174f.

29. On these motifs, cf. Broneer, *Hesperia* 8: 353–356; Kraiker-Kübler, *Kerameikos*, I, 127, 144, 174f., and pl. 50 and 51. The double-axe question is controversial; cf. B. Schweitzer, "Geometrische Stile in Griechenland," *Ath. Mitt.* 43 (1918): 56ff. For its occurrence on seals, Broneer, *Hesperia* 8: 414; Walters, *British Museum Catalog of Gems*, pls. IV–V; Young, *JHS* 48: 232, fig. 10; E. Buschor, *Greek Vase Painting*, pp. 7 ff.

30. See the brilliant article of G. W. Elderkin, "The Marriage of Zeus and Hera and its Symbol," *AJA* 41 (1937): 424–435.

31. Stirrup jars: Kraiker-Kübler, *Kerameikos*, I, 53ff., pl. 5–11; IV, 6f., pl. 4 Inv. 922; cf. Broneer, *Hesperia* 8: 389–392, figs. 69–72; Mycenaean armament on Geometric pottery, very common, e.g., Young, *Hesperia*, Suppl. II, pp. 69f., figs. 43 and 44; ridged foot: Kraiker-Kübler, *Kerameikos*, V, pls. 19, 20, 84, No. 4361; cf. Agora Museum *Inv.* P6605.

32. On the continuity, see also Kraiker-Kübler, *Kerameikos*, I, 131–177; Lorimer, *Homer and the Monuments*, pp. 40f.; esp. Peter Kahane, "Entwicklungsphasen der Attisch-Geometrischen Keramik," *AJA* 44 (1940): 464–482, pls. XVII–XXVIII; and Desborough, *Protogeometric Pottery*, pp. 1–4; A. Furumark, *The Mycenaean Pottery* (Stockholm, 1941), p. 581.

33. Cf. Broneer, *Hesperia* 2 (1933): 372.

34. See, for instance, Kahane's comparison of Attic with Samian Geometric, with its "close" style derived from Granary ware, *AJA* 44: 467. Cf. the situation at Delos, where the Purification ditch yielded only one Pregeometric vase; De Boccard, *Delos, fasc. XV (Vases Préhelléniques et Géometriques*, Publication of the French School at Athens, 1934), p. 8. Local Delian Geometric is chiefly a not-very-imaginative banded ware, see *ibid.*, pls. XXXIV–XXXVI, comparable to that frequently found in Delphi and northern Greece, and only later shows Attic influence; *ibid.* Text, pp. 39–44 and pls. XX–XXV.

35. Desborough, *Protogeometric Pottery*, pp. 125f. (Athenian origin); pp. 291f., 299, 302 (spread of Attic ware and even colonization). See pp. 294f. for his chronology of Protogeometric and Geometric periods.

36. Cyprus should perhaps be noticed here as an apparent exception to the whole foregoing argument. There Late Mycenaean culture merges into the Iron Age; the Granary style is at first imported and later imitated, and chamber tombs continue into Geometric times; see J. F. Daniel, "Late Cypriote III Tombs from Kourion," *AJA* 41 (1937): 57, 62, 67. But though the Mycenaean tradition continues, no such initiative is apparent as at Athens; Kübler's attribution of the half-circle design to Cypriote influence, *Kerameikos*, IV, 30 (cf. Young, *Hesperia*, Suppl. II, p. 68) can no longer be supported in view of Desborough's survey. Besides, as stated above, dialectal considerations exclude Cyprus as a possible locale for the survival of the epic tradition. No doubt it did survive there, at least for a while, but Cypriote bards could not have been the direct ancestors of the Homeric poems.

37. Desborough, *Protogeometric Pottery*, p. 299. Cf. Lorimer, *Homer and the Monuments*, p. 40, quoting Kraiker-Kübler, *Kerameikos*, I, 177.

38. J. Lawrence Angel, "Skeletal Material from Attica," *Hesperia* 14: (1945) 279ff. See especially the conclusions, pp. 318–331.

39. Angel, p. 323 and n. 107.

40. Cf. Kraiker-Kübler, *Kerameikos*, I, 253f., where little is made of the Nordic element, and the skulls of the Cerameicus are generally found to be affiliated with the *Urbevölkerung*. Cf. C. M. Fürst, *Zur Anthropologie der prähistorischen Griechen in Argolis* (Lunds Univ. Aarskr. N. F. Avd. 2. 26; 1930, No. 8), who discovered a strong Nordic strain in the Argolid Mycenaeans and identified them as Greeks; also in Arcadia, *Über eine neolith. Schädel aus Arkadien, ibid.*, 2 (1932), No. 13. Considerable typological mixture is characteristic of all Aegean civilization, see J. Lawrence Angel, "The Human Remains," *Troy* (Blegen and others), Suppl. Monograph, p. 25. Cf. C. W. Blegen, "Athens and the Early Age of Greece," *HSCP*, Suppl. vol. I (1940), pp. 1–9.

41. Desborough, *Protogeometric Pottery*, p. 126. Cf. Chapter V, notes 14 and 15; also Karo, *Attic Cemetery*, p. 7; R. S. Young, "An Early Geometric Grave near the Athenian Agora," *Hesperia* 18 (1949): 275ff. and H. A. Thompson, "Excavation of the Athenian Agora, 1940–46," *Hesperia* 16 (1947): 196 (ninth-century Areopagus tomb).

42. Cremation in Crete, like the use of iron, may be earlier than in Athens (*Kerameikos*, IV, 47), but it is equally Protogeometric; cf. Lorimer, *Homer and the Monuments*, p. 105, n. 3. It appears also early at Colophon and Assarlik; Lorimer, p. 106.

43. Lorimer, *Homer and the Monuments*, p. 105, suggests that foreign soil accounts for cremation, but on the ground that it provided protection against desecration. Land-poverty is more likely, especially in Attica. Refugees could hardly have acquired land of their own, at least for a long time, and burial on another's land would doubtless not be welcome.

44. See G. E. Mylonas' excellent study, "Homeric and Mycenaean Burial Customs," *AJA* 52, 1 (1948): 56ff.

45. 11.220f.; 24.189f.

46. Thuc. I.2.6.

47. Paus. VII.1.

48. Paus. II.18.8–9; VII.1.9. Note also that the Alcmaeonidae are traced in the first reference to Alcmaeon, a descendant of Nestor. Herodotus claims the same for the Pisistratidae, V.65, and notes the marriage of Pisistratus with the daughter of Megacles, I.61.

49. Aristotle, *Ath. Pol.* 346 (Kenyon) = Plutarch, *Thes.* 25.

50. See Paus. I.17.1; I.19.5; I.32.5–6; I.39.2; I.44.4.

51. 3.306–307. Note that Ἀθηνάων was changed rather arbitrarily to Φωκήων by Zenodotus.

52. But he is placed in the early twelfth by Scherling, *Paul. Wiss. Kroll RE*, s.v. Κόδρος.

53. Neleus, colonizer of Miletus: Herod. IX.97; Paus VII.2.1; *Schol. ad Iliad.* XX.404, quoting Clitophon, the historian. The traditional date for the Ionian Migration is either 1076 (*Marmor Parium*), or 1044 (Philochorus, Eratosthenes, Aristarchus); so far, neither can be made to agree with

archaeological findings. See *Vit. Hom.* VI, *Hom. Opera* V, App. critic. *ad* 31.

54. Herod. I.146.2.

55. Herod. I.147. See U. von Wilamowitz, *Über die ionische Wanderung, Sitz. B.* (Berlin, 1906), for the theory that the Ionians had no identity as such until about 700; cf. Clem. Alex., *Schol. ad Paidag.* II. 10, 114.

56. XIII,685ff. See Stanford's note to 6.162.

57. For instance, E. Bethe, *Homer*, 2nd ed. (Leipzig, 1929), II, 345ff., thought the *Iliad* had its origin in Athens.

58. *Vita Homeri* (Oxford), V, 7–8. See J. Wackernagel, *Sprachliche Untersuchungen zu Homer* (Göttingen, 1916), p. 89.

59. In Herodotus' list of contingents are Minyae from Orchomenus, and Cadmeians from Thebes; see note 74.

60. Strabo 333; cf. 392 and Aristotle, *Ath. Pol. fg.* 343 (Kenyon) = Harpocration, *s.v.* Ἀπόλλων Πατρῷς and Epit. Heraclid. 1.

61. Wackernagel, *Sprachliche Untersuchungen*, p. 89.

62. Lejeune, *Traité de la phonétique grecque*, pp. 204ff.

63. Richard Bentley, *Dissertation on the Epistles of Phalaris* (London, 1699), pp. 318, 400, was at pains to prove Attic elements in Homer to be old, and that Attic and Ionic differed little in the early period. Cf. Dionysius Hal., *De Thucydide*, 864. Whatmough, *AJA* 52: 48, dismisses Asiatic Ionic as impossible as the basic dialect of Homer.

CHAPTER IV. FESTIVALS, PISISTRATUS, AND WRITING

1. F. A. Wolf, *Prolegomena ad Homerum*, Chap. XXXIII; ed. I. Bekker (Berlin, 1872), pp. 86ff.

2. Plato, *Hipparchus*, 228 b 7; cf. Thuc. I.20.2.

3. Heraclides Ponticus, *FHG* II.210; Plutarch, *Lycurgus* 4; Dio Chrysostom II.45; Aelian, *V.H.* XIII.14. Cf. Strabo X.482.

4. Aristotle, *Ath. Pol.* XVIII.1.

5. Cicero, *De Orat.* III.34.137; *Anth. Pal.* XI.442. Paus. VII.26.13. Cf. Suidas, *s.v.* Ὅμηρος, and Lives IV and V of Homer (Oxford V, 245, 248). Fl. Josephus, *Contra Apionem* I.12.

6. Wilamowitz, *Homerische Untersuchungen*, I, 235ff.

7. P. Mazon, *Introduction à l'Iliad* (Paris, 1942), pp. 269ff. See also D. B. Monro, *Homer's Odyssey* (Oxford, 1901), XIII–XXIV, 402–410; J. A. Davison, "Pisistratus and Homer," *TAPA* 86 (1955), 1ff.

8. Murray, *Rise*, p. 190.

9. Passages suspected in antiquity: *Iliad* X entire: see *Schol. T.* in E. Maass, *Homeri Ilias, Scholia*, V, 341; Eustathius 697.41. This book was supposedly inserted in the *Iliad* by Pisistratus, but not for nationalistic reasons; II.558 or 546–558: Strabo IX.394; Plut., *Solon* 10 (whose source according to Wilamowitz, *Homerische Untersuchungen*, I, 235ff., is Hermippus, according to Mazon, *Introduction*, Hereas of Megara); Herod. VII.161; Quintilian V.40; Diogenes Laertius I.48; Aristotle, *Rhet.* I.15; Aeschines III.185 (epigram); II.573: Paus. VII.26.13, a conjecture by Pisistratus; I.265: omitted by Aristarchus = Hesiod, *Scutum* 182; cf. Dio Chrysostom, 57.1; Pausanias X.29.10; II.203: cited in a somewhat mysterious *scholium* as a remark which might be well said by Pisistratus; see Dindorf, *Scholia* I, p.

xxiv; 3.307: "Athens" changed to "Phocis" by Zenodotus; no reasons given; 11.602–604: added by Onomacritus, see *Schol. ad loc.*; cf. *Schol.* 11, 385; *Schol. Iliad.* (Dindorf), I, p. 2; 11.631: added by Pisistratus, according to Hereas of Megara; cf. Plutarch, *Theseus* 20; *F.H.G.* IV.426; 7.79, 80: suspected generally, see *Schol. ad loc.*; Tzetzes, *Alleg.* I, 7, 38; XII.372: athetized with preceding line by Aristarchus. The testimony of Dieuchidas of Megara is given in Diogenes Laertius I.57. It is clearly fragmentary, and has been variously filled out; cf. Mazon, *Introduction*, 279. The sense, however, is clear enough to indicate that Dieuchidas connected the Salamis lines with Pisistratus. Apollodorus, in Strabo 394, gives the alternative Megarian verses for II, 557f.

10. Mazon, *Introduction*, p. 272.

11. XII.351ff.; XIII.190ff., 685ff.

12. XII.372; athetized by the Alexandrines. Yet the whole passage in which it stands illustrates the alliance between Salaminians and Athenians. Cf. Paus. I.35.2, on the Athenian claim to Salamis through Philaeus.

13. Paus. I.35.3; I.42.4. Herod. VI.35.4; Plutarch, *Solon* 10.

14. Paus. I.28.11. Wilamowitz, *Homerische Untersuchungen*, p. 274, says that Ajax was originally an Aeolic hero, adopted by the Ionic bards. Telamon does indeed figure in the Aeolic sagas of Heracles, Argo, and the Calydonian Hunt, but Wilamowitz himself suggested that he was put there later. Pindar personally adopts Ajax, not for Aeolic, but for Aeginetan associations, as a symbol of Dorian nobility; but originally Ajax had no Dorian or Aeolic affiliations, but only Saronic ones. Mycenaean finds in Salamis are scanty so far; cf. D. M. Robinson, "A Small Hoard of Mycenaean Vases and Statuettes," *AJA* 54 (1950): 1ff.

15. G. E. Mylonas, "The Hymn to Demeter and Her Sanctuary at Eleusis," *Washington University Studies*, New Series No. 13 (1942); also "Eleusis and the Eleusinian Mysteries," *CJ* 43 (1947): 131ff.

16. See Paus. I.5.2–4; 31.2–3, on Eleusinian war; bequeathing of Megara, I.39.4. Cf. I.5.6; 39.6; IV.36.1 (Pylas founder of Pylos, cf. IV.1.5, introducing of Mysteries into Messenia).

17. Paus. I.19.5; 39.5–6. The tradition seems to have continued long: Nisus appears as one of four great Attic heroes on a red-figure vase of the 'Syriscos" painter about 460 B.C. The others are Pallas, Lycus, son of Pandion, and Orneus, grandfather of Menestheus.

18. Paus. I.39.5–6; 41.6; 42.1; 44.3.

19. See G. E. Mylonas, "Athens and Minoan Crete," *HSCP*, Suppl. vol. I (1940, Ferguson Studies), pp. 14–36.

20. Paus. I.42.2. Note also that the story of Leucothea–Ino is Megarian in origin (Paus. I.42.7) and that Calchas was Megarian by birth.

21. Paus. I.41.3. Bethe, *Homer*, II, 350ff., also regards Ajax as an Athenian hero, but as one adopted in the sixth century in connnection with the Salamis claim. See Lorimer, *Homer and the Monuments*, pp. 181f., for the opposite view that Ajax is a rootless and shadowy character.

22. Paus. I.42.6.

23. Paus. I.17.3–6. Cf. I.1.2; 23.8; II.25.6; III.18.5. Cf. the story of the capture of Aethra (Paus. I.41.4) who appears as Helen's handmaid in III.144, in a passage often called "Athenian."

24. Paus. I.43.3.

25. See Broneer, *Hesperia* 8: 352 (Peloponnesian connections), 391 and fig. 72a (kylix-based stirrup jar, local), 377f. (Cyprus); cf. small six-inch *lekythos* from the Areopagus chamber tomb, with concentric circle designs reminiscent of insular Mycenaean Geometric, as on the Cyprian jug in the Stoddard collection at Yale.

26. Thuc. II.15; Plutarch, *Theseus*, 24.

27. 3.278.

28. See Murray, *Rise*, pp. 312ff.

29. No Attic ware has been found on Corinthian soil before the seventh century, see C. G. Boulter, "A Pottery Deposit near Temple E at Corinth," *AJA* (1937): 217.

30. IV.405ff.

31. Especially those pointed to, apparently, by Aristarchus as evidence that Homer was an Athenian: see *Schol.* A *ad* II.371 (repeated formula in IV.288, VII.132, XVI.97; also *Schol.* T *ad loc.*, and *ad* XIII.827); cf. Aristonicus on XIII.197; V.700 (ἐπὶ νηῶν, supposedly Attic for ἐπὶ τὰς ναῦς).

32. See Eusebius on Olympiad 53.3 (566 B.C.); second *Schol. ad* Aristides, *Panathen.* 189.4.

33. Lycurgus, *In Leocr.* 209.102 (Bekker); Isocrates, *Paneg.* 74.

34. This law about singing in order is attributed to Solon by Dieuchidas, to Pisistratus by pseudo-Plato, and to Pericles by Wade-Gery, *Poet*, 30ff.

35. Mazon, *Introduction*, p. 270, by adopting the Hipparchan view, is forced to dispense with the transliteration of the poems from the Old Attic to the New Ionic alphabet (p. 275f.), for Hipparchus' manuscript would naturally be in the latter already. But for a scribe to write unmetrical ἔως at the beginning of a line for a metrical and comprehensible ἦος before him is not so natural as Mazon thinks; the argument severely violates the simplest principles of palaeography. If there is one "Attic" change in the text of Homer which is evident beyond all doubt, it is that the text was transliterated at some point, not necessarily after 403, into the Ionic alphabet from the old one. See Murray, *Rise*, Appendix I, p. 346f., for a good collection of the evidence on the point. Also, R. Herzog, *Die Umschrift der älterem griechischen Literatur in die ionische Alphabet* (Basel, 1912); cf. Wackernagel, *Sprachliche Untersuchungen*, pp. 83ff.

36. Thuc. I.126–135.

37. Wolf, *Prolegomena*, chaps. 45–49; cf. Grenfell and Hunt, *Hibeh Papyri* (London, 1906), I, 67ff., in answer to Ludwich's attempt to resist the theory, *Die Homervulgata als voralexandrinisch erwiesen* (Leipzig, 1898); most recently asserted by G. M. Bolling, *The External Evidence for Interpolation in Homer* (Oxford, 1925); *Athetized Lines of the Iliad* (Baltimore, 1944); and *Ilias Atheniensium* (Oxford and Lancaster, Pa., 1950), p. 3. Opposed by M. H. Van der Valk, *The Textual Criticism of the Odyssey* (Leyden, 1949). Since Aristarchus does not always agree with the vulgate, it is hard to see how he could have created it. He seems to have adopted a medium-sized text, doubtless Athenian, longer than that of Zenodotus, but shorter than the padded texts of the earlier papyri.

38. Murray, *Rise*, pp. 303f.

39. G. M. Bolling, *Ilias Atheniensium*.

40. See Wackernagel, *Sprachliche Untersuchungen*, 89ff.

41. Murray, *Rise*, p. 303; cf. Wilamowitz, *Homerische Untersuchungen*, pp. 286ff.

42. See Herzog, *Umschrift*, pp. 69ff.; a good case is made for Hesiod, but in the case of the later poets, dialectal problems and the question of Homeric imitation are ignored in favor of the monotheory. Despite Wackernagel's acceptance of Herzog, it is still highly possible that Wilamowitz was right (see preceding note) in saying that Ionic was the regular alphabet for literature by the end of the sixth century. But if that is true, the Pisistratids, in other respects so philionian, would surely have used it, had they been the first transcribers of Homer.

43. In any case 403 seems too late for the first transcription of Homer into Ionic letters; by that time, little confusion could have arisen between Ionic ἦος and Attic ἕως; at least Ionic forms in other early poets were not altered so as to make metrical confusion.

44. See Wade-Gery, *Poet*, p. 30 and especially n. 77.

45. *Ibid.*, *passim*. He gives many references.

46. *Ibid.*, pp. 15f. I think, however, that the Interludes would have been given at the end of the first and second day, as Sheppard would have it, rather than at the beginning of the second and third. It is un-Greek and bad theater to begin with a digression. Cf. Pindar, *Ol.* VI, pp. 1ff.

47. Murray, *Rise*, pp. 191f.

48. The Panionia was probably begun about 700; cf. Wilamowitz, *Über die Ionische Wanderung*, *Sitz. Ber. Berl.* (1906), pp. 38–57, 59–79. The Delia may be older, if referred to in the *Odyssey*, as Wade-Gery thinks, *Poet*, p. 3; in any case, it is well established at the time of the *Hymn to the Delian Apollo*. The Panathenaea began, according to Eusebius, in 566; but some such festival may have existed before that. Since all other early Ionian institutions were formed on Athenian models, it seems likely that their festivals were also. Certainly the cult of Heliconian Poseidon, originally Boeotian, was older in Attica than in Ionia; cf. Wade-Gery, *Poet*, pp. 3–5, 64. But if the Panionia, which was a feast of Poseidon Heliconius was not founded until 700, *ut Wilamowitz*, the cult could only have been known to Homer through Athens, or perhaps Boeotia, and not, as Wade-Gery suggests, in Ionia. Actually, XX.403ff. may have stood very anciently in epic repertoire.

49. See Notopoulos, *TAPA* 82: 87.

50. Cf. Lord, *Serbocroatian Heroic Songs*, I, 240f. and relevant notes.

51. The *Erotocritus* of V. Cornaros, written in the seventeenth century on Italian models of chivalric romance, is often recited whole with great precision in Crete. Avdo Međedović is an example of recomposing a written text; see A. B. Lord, *AJA* (1948): 42.

52. See T. W. Allen, *Homeric Hymns*, p. lxx, for statistics on the relative observance or neglect of the digamma in Homer and the *Hymns*; cf. Parry, *Formules*, p. 54.

53. Attic Dipylon Prize-Jug: see *IG²*I, 919; *Ath. Mitt.* 6 (1881), pl. III; and J. Kirchner, *Imagines Inscriptionum Atticarum*, p. 9, pl. 1; noted by Hampe, *Gleichnisse*, p. 30, to illustrate the currency of epic language in Attica in the eighth century. Hymettus sherds: C. W. Blegen, "In-

scriptions on Geometric Pottery from Hymettos," *AJA* 38 (1934): 10ff.; see esp. p. 26 for the dating, a little later than the Prize-Jug (cf. Lorimer, p. 129, n. 2). Other early examples of writing: Acropolis sherd No. 309, Graef-Langlotz, *Die Vasen von der Akropolis*, pl. XI, and Young, *Hesperia*, Suppl. 2, pp. 227ff.; T. L. Shear, "The Campaign of 1935," *Hesperia* 5 (1936): 33; Theran *graffiti*: *IG* XII, 3, 983f., 986ff.; *Thera* 2:63, fig. 217; Corinthian sherds: A. N. Stillwell, "Eighth Century Inscriptions from Corinth," *AJA* 37 (1933): 605–610, with the rather high date of 775–750; Boston Mantiklos Bronze, dated by S. Casson, "Early Greek Inscription on Metal," *AJA* 39 (1935): 512, to second half of the seventh century, but earlier date noted as possibility by H. Payne, *Perachora*, p. 263, n. 1, and *ca.* 700 suggested by Wade-Gery, *Poet*, p. 11; cf. Bowra, *Homer and Forerunners*, for other references, pp. 6ff. For various formulations and discussions of the matter, see H. L. Lorimer, "Homer and the Art of Writing," *AJA* 52 (1948): 18f.; and *Homer and the Monuments*, pp. 122ff.; Schadewaldt, *Homers Welt*, p. 94, n. 5; Wade-Gery, *Poet*, p. 10, and n. 28. The Phoenician source of the alphabet and of papyrus (word and article) is discussed ably by W. F. Albright, "Some Oriental Glosses on the Homeric Problem," *AJA* 54 (1950): 163ff. This article, and the remarks of Blegen in the above-cited article, pp. 27ff., seem to dispose effectively of the arguments of R. Carpenter, "The Antiquity of the Greek Alphabet," *AJA* 37 (1933): 8ff.; also, "The Greek Alphabet Again," *AJA* 42 (1938): 58–69; also, *Folktale, Fiction*, pp. 12–14.

54. Wade-Gery, *Poet*, pp. 11ff.

55. A. B. Lord, "Homer's Originality: Dictated Texts," *TAPA* 84 (1953): 129ff.

56. M. Parry, "Whole Formulaic Verses in Greek and South Slavic Song," *TAPA* 44 (1933): 181.

57. Cf. Schadewaldt, *Homers Welt*, pp. 91–92.

58. See W. C. Greene, "The Spoken and the Written Word," *HSCP* 60 (1951): 31, for the moderate theory that Homer must have used at least written notes. Wade-Gery goes further, *Poet*, pp. 9ff., asserting that Homer wrote the poem with his own hand. Cf. Bowra, *Heroic Poetry*, p. 240f. See the protest by A. B. Lord, "Homer's Originality: Dictated Texts," *TAPA* 84 (1953): 124ff.

59. A. B. Lord, "Homer's Originality," *TAPA* 84 (1953): 130ff.

60. J. A. Notopoulos, "The Warrior as an Oral Poet: A Case History," *Classical Weekly* 46 (1952): 17–19.

61. A. B. Lord, "Homer's Originality," *TAPA* 84 (1953): 131ff.

62. A. Einstein, *Mozart* (Oxford, 1945), pp. 247f.

63. See Murray's analysis of Plato's quotations, *Rise*, p. 293ff.; also, J. Labarbe, *L'Homère de Platon* (Liège, 1949).

64. Bolling, *Ilias Atheniensium*.

65. Myres, *Who Were the Greeks?* pp. 518ff.

66. E.g., the line which Zenodotus substitutes for XVI.93–96, where ἀπογυμνωθέντα somewhat implausibly assumes Achilles' foreknowledge of exactly what Apollo does to Patroclus.

67. See Notopoulos' forthcoming studies of modern Greek oral epic; also, Labarbe, *L'Homère de Platon*, pp. 423f.

68. See Lord's discussion of classes of formulae, "Homer's Originality,"

TAPA 84 (1953): 128f. The poem of Avdo Međedovič provides a perfect analogy for the process in question, of oral reproduction of a written poem. See note 51.

69. Wade-Gery, *Poet*, pp. 25ff., where by some skillful maneuvering, the date is made to come out to the eighth century.

70. Homer, *Vita VI*, 39 (Oxford), the ms. *Life*.

71. Cf. Suidas, *s.v.* Ἀρκτῖνος.

72. See Artemon of Clazomenae, *F.H.G.* (Müller), IV, p. 341.

73. See Jaeger, *Paideia* 1 (1934): 40, and "Tyrtaios über die wahre ἀρετή," *Sitz. Berl. Ak.* (1932), p. 540; Schadewaldt, *Homers Welt*, p. 93, n. 1; R. Hampe, *Frühe griechische Sagenbilder* (Athens, 1936); E. Buschor, *Vom Sinn der Griechischen Standbilder* (Berlin, 1942); cf. Bowra, *Tradition and Design*, pp. 256ff.

74. Cf. Schadewaldt, *Homers Welt*, 105ff. He gives a good summary of most of the salient points. Wade-Gery's notes, pp. 63–69 of the *Poet*, are also relevant; cf. Hampe, *Gleichnisse*, p. 5; Bowra, *Tradition and Design*, pp. 251ff.

CHAPTER V. HOMER AND GEOMETRIC ART

1. See Schadewaldt, *Homers Welt*, pp. 130ff.; R. Hampe, *Die Gleichnisse Homers und die Bildkunst seiner Zeit* (Tübingen, 1952); F. Matz, *Geschichte der griechischen Kunst* (Frankfurt, 1950), I, fasc. 1, 98ff.; B. Snell, *Die Entdeckung des Geistes* (Hamburg, 1946), pp. 21ff.; F. Stählin, "Der geometrische Stil in der Ilias," *Philologus* 78 (1923): 280ff.; Myres, *Who Were the Greeks?* pp. 511ff. For the best and most recent treatment, as well as further bibliography, see J. A. Notopoulos, "Homer and Geometric Art," *Athena* (1957), 65ff. Unfortunately this study appeared too late to be taken into full account here.

2. Desborough, *Protogeometric Pottery*, pp. 125f., 291ff.

3. See Furumark, *Mycenaean Pottery*, p. 504; G. Perrot and C. Chipiez, *Histoire de l'art dans l'antiquité* (Paris, 1898), VII, 206ff. (cf. the "Salamis" vases, *ibid.*, figs. 86 and 87); Buschor, *Greek Vase Painting*, pp. 14–16; F. Dümmler, "Mittheilungen aus der griechischen Inseln," *Ath. Mitt.* 11 (1886): 23 and Beilage II, 5; cf. Furtwängler-Löschcke, *Mykenäische Thongefässe* (Berlin, 1879), pl. XIX, pp. 136–139.

4. R. S. Young, "Late Geometric Graves," *Hesperia*, Suppl. II, 2–3.

5. Hampe, *Gleichnisse*, p. 32; cf. G. P. Shipp, *Studies in the Language of Homer* (Cambridge, 1953), p. 79, urging that, even linguistically, the similes reflect Homeric, not Mycenaean, times.

6. Hampe, *Gleichnisse*, p. 31.

7. Schadewaldt, *Homers Welt*, pp. 151ff.; and figs. 19 and 20.

8. Note folds of snake opening gradually to emphasize the neck curve of the hydria, Athens Nat. Museum No. 17497. Other snake motifs, plastic and painted: Young, *Hesperia*, Suppl. II, figs. 37, 38, 39, 130.

9. *E.g.*, Athens Nat. Museum No. 804, in Matz, *Geschichte der griechischen Kunst* I, fasc. 2, pls. 1 and 2; Athens Nat. Museum No. 990, in O. Rayet and M. Collignon, *Histoire de la céramique grecque* (Paris, 1888), pl. I; Athens Nat. Museum No. 223, in S. Wide, "Geometrische Vasen aus Griechenland," *Jahrbuch des Archäologischen Instituts* 14 (1899): 193, fig. 54,

and M. Collignon and L. Couve, *Catalogue des vases peints* (Paris, 1902), p. 41, No. 197, noting the asymmetry in the design.

10. Broneer, *Hesperia* 8:418. Cf. 353, 417.

11. E.g., the slight naturalism of the main figure in Kraiker-Kübler, *Kerameikos*, V, fasc. 1, pl. 87, No. 3366; cf. also No. 3238; pl. 110, No. 5354, with detail on pl. 141; cf. C. W. Lunsingh Scheurleer, *Grieksche Ceramiek* (Rotterdam, 1936), pl. III, 7.

12. I.267f.

13. Cf. Athens Nat. Museum No. 894, Perrot and Chipiez, *Histoire*, VII, fig. 58, with Wide, *Jahrbuch* 14:fig. 57; both types alternating in the same frieze, Kraiker-Kübler, *Kerameikos*, V, fasc. 1, pl. 69, No. 4923.

14. G. E. Mylonas, "Homeric and Mycenaean Burial Customs," *AJA* 52 (1948): 77; and "The Figured Mycenaean Stelai," *AJA* 55 (1951): 134–147.

15. See Lorimer, *Homer and the Monuments*, pp. 103–110, for a summary of the evidence.

16. 7.81; cf. II.547ff.

17. Nilsson, *The Minoan-Mycenaean Religion*, pp. 474f., 488. Schrade, *Götter und Menschen Homers*, p. 48, agrees, but states that in II.547ff., an actual temple is indicated.

18. See Lorimer's discussion of the passage, *Homer and the Monuments*, pp. 436, 502.

19. 6.41ff.

20. See Chapter VI.

21. On Achilles' raids, cf. Meyer, *Geschichte der Altertum*, II, 400; on the Pylian epic, see Wade-Gery, "What Happened in Pylos," *AJA* 52 (1948): 115–118; also *Poet*, p. 38.

22. XI. 750; cf. II.621; XIII.185; XXIII.638.

23. The oenochoe with crossed tubes, in the Agora Museum. See Young, *Hesperia*, Suppl. II, pp. 68–71; Hampe, *Frühe griechische Sagenbilder in Böotien* (Athens, 1936), pp. 87–88, who identified the figures of the Actorione, and gives a list of other early representations; cf. A. D. Fraser, "The Geometric Oenochoe from the Athenian Agora," *AJA* 44 (1940): 457–463.

24. XXIII.712f. Hampe, *Gleichnisse*, pp. 36f., compares the wrestling passage to the New York eighth-century hero-centaur group.

25. See Lorimer, *Homer and the Monuments*, pl. XXXII.

26. See Hampe, *Gleichnisse*, p. 30 and footnotes. Hampe suggests that the Attic oenochoe in Munich (*ibid.*, pls. 7–11) represents the shipwreck of Odysseus in the *Odyssey*. Cf. G. S. Kirk, "Ships on Geometric Vases," *Annual of British School at Athens* 44 (1949); R. Hampe, *Frühe griechische Sagenbilder*; Schadewaldt, *Homers Welt*, pp. 87ff.

27. Hampe's comparison, *Gleichnisse*, p. 33, of the fill motifs of Geometric to the particles of Homer is hardly this great critic's happiest thought. On the effect of Homer's particles, see Demetrius, *Style* II.54–57. But "Zielinski's Law" of epic narrative is relevant.

28. Cf. Kraiker-Kübler's *Kerameikos*, I, 175, on rhythms, as the most striking feature of Geometric style; cf. Myres, *Who Were the Greeks?* pp. 495ff. Some trace of this subordination of design to ceramic shape is found in Late Mycenaean and Late Minoan ware by Kahane, *AJA* 44:467,

and Buschor, *Greek Vase Painting*, pp. 7ff., 16. Cf. Broneer, *Hesperia* 8:383, and Kübler-Kraiker, *Kerameikos*, II, pl. 61, Inv. 533. See Chapter II on Greek domination of Crete in the Late Bronze Age.

29. Examples of ring composition, 19.1–52; cf. the opening and closing two-line formula. W. A. A. Van Otterlo, *Untersuchungen über Begriff, Anwendung und Entstehung der griechischen Ringcomposition* (Amsterdam, 1944); *De Ringcompositie als Opbouwprincipe in de Epische Gedichten van Homerus* (Amsterdam, 1948); J. A. Notopoulos, "Continuity and Interconnexion in Homeric Oral Composition," *TAPA* 82 (1951): 81ff.

30. W. Arend, *Die typische Scenen bei Homer* (Berlin, 1933); cf. A. B. Lord's "Composition by Theme in Epos," *TAPA* 82 (1951): 71ff.

31. J. T. Sheppard, *The Pattern of the Iliad* (London, 1922).

32. See Sir J. L. Myres' remarks, "The Pattern of the Odyssey," *JHS* 72 (1952): 1ff.; cf., however, below, Chapter XII, note 4.

33. S. E. Bassett, *The Poetry of Homer* (Berkeley, 1938), pp. 119ff.

34. 11.170–203.

35. Lorimer, *Homer and the Monuments*, p. 7; so too Etruscan-Bucchero ware. For other examples, see Broneer, *Hesperia* 8:372; also remarks by Furumark, *Mycenaean Pottery*, pp. 158f., 180, 204, 396, 402.

36. See the collection, W. Zschietzmann, "Prothesis und Ekphora," *Ath. Mitt.* 53 (1928): 17ff.

37. Hampe, *Gleichnisse*, pp. 25f.

38. Cf. Karo, *An Attic Cemetery*, pp. 10f.

39. Hampe, *Gleichnisse*, p. 8. See below, Chapters VI and VII.

40. For the old view, see B. Schweitzer, "Untersuchungen zur Chronologie und Geschichte der Geometrischen Stile in Griechenland," II, *Ath. Mitt.* 43 (1918): 1f.; for the more recent theory, R. S. Young, *Hesperia*, Suppl. 2 (1939), 4, 77–78. Corroborated by J. M. Cook, *BSA* 35: 165–219, who worked independently; and J. F. Daniel's review of Young, *AJA* 44 (1940): 159–161.

41. Nilsson, *Homer and Mycenae*, p. 126.

42. See final chapter.

CHAPTER VI. IMAGE, SYMBOL, AND FORMULA

1. See Finley, *Pindar and Aeschylus*.

2. M. Parry, "The Traditional Metaphor in Homer," *CP*, 1 ser. 28 (1933): 37. This small figure is due to the severely limited definition of metaphor which Parry uses in this article. His actual intention was to defend Homer from the charge of deficiency in metaphor.

3. XII.37.

4. IV.371, XI.160, VIII.378, 553, etc. The etymology of γέφυρα is unknown; hence it is impossible to say whether its use here is metaphoric, or represents some real, though vanished, meaning of the word.

5. E.g., metonymy: XIV.387 (δαΐς, "heat," for "strife"); synecdoche, VI.306; H. Schrade, *Götter und Menschen*, pp. 147f., fails to realize that synecdoche explains his "partial" epiphanies of the gods — hands, thighs, eyes, etc.; apostrophe, XVI.693; anaphora, 3.109ff.; personification (Eris), XI.3; onomatopoeia, 12.235–238.

6. S. Langer, *Philosophy in a New Key*, 3rd ed. (Cambridge, Mass., 1957), pp. 42ff. See chapters 2 and 4 in general. For this whole discussion of symbolism I am profoundly indebted to Mrs. Langer.

7. But see, in the aforementioned chapter, Mrs. Langer's defense of the whole mind as rational, to which the discursive and presentational modes appeal in ways which differ formally, but which imply no inner mental division between rational and intuitional. The symbolic process lying behind both modes involves the same selection from the steady barrage of sense impressions certain common denominators by which classes and "universal" concepts are formed. Both sense perception and formal reason depend upon such an organon of genus and species; hence ultimately there is no real opposition within the mind of the sensory and rational faculties. Their difference lies in mode of expression.

8. Langer, *Philosophy in a New Key*, pp. 68ff.

9. Schadewaldt's comparison of the Homeric simile to the definitions of philosophy, because of the simile's generic source, but specific relation to the texture, means not that the simile proceeds by the discursive logic of definitions, but simply that presentational symbols, like discursive ones, are comprehensible through classification by genus and species. See *Homers Welt*, pp. 148f.

10. *Henry IV*, part 2, IV.4.

11. I.52.

12. See for instance such a statement as: "Such a system could not be the work of a single poet: it must represent the effort of generations of singers, ever seeking and ever guarding the convenient expression, and using it when found, to the exclusion of all other formulae which could replace it." M. Parry, "The Homeric Gloss," *TAPA* 59 (1928): 242. Note the word "convenient."

13. See M. Parry, *passim*, e.g., *Epithète traditionelle*, p. 114.

14. Parry, *Epithète traditionelle*, p. 227, envisions three stages of stylistic development: (1) when the hexameter had not yet adopted unique noun-epithet formulae, but had an abundance of metrical equivalents; (2) when it began to adopt unique formulae; (3) when it created some analogical equivalents.

15. See A. B. Lord, "Composition by Theme in Homer and South Slavic Epos," *TAPA* 82 (1951): 71ff.

16. *Formules*, pp. 7–8, 22–23, 61; *Epithète traditionelle*, pp. 99, 103, 125–131.

17. See A. B. Lord, "Homer's Originality: Dictated Texts," *TAPA* 84 (1953): 127.

18. Cf. Parry, *Formules*, pp. 50–51, on the inevitability of the formula.

19. Parry, *Epithète traditionelle*, p. 196.

20. *Ibid.*, pp. 154, 172.

21. 8.230; XVIII.106; cf. XIX.218. Odysseus does win the footrace in XXIII, but the circumstances are special.

22. Parry denies it; *Epithète traditionelle*, p. 185.

23. Parry regards them as entirely traditional — *Epithète traditionelle*, p. 163–164 — noting, e.g., how πολύαινος, though used only of Odysseus,

is used of him in IX.673 and XI.430, before his adventures had earned the epithet for him.

24. 1.1; 10.330 (πολύτροπος); 3.310 (ἄναλκις). See Parry, *Epithète traditionelle*, pp. 196–198; 200ff., for a discussion with other examples.

25. A careless use of formulae probably accounts for ἀμύμων used of Aegisthus, 1.29; cf. the transference of "divine" from ἅλς, "sea" to ἅλς, "salt" in IX.214 (yet here it is θείοιο, never used of the sea, which is δῖος). Note also Odysseus felling "dry trees," 5.240, a formula better used of wood already felled and lying seasoned, 18.309.

26. XVI.705.

27. XVI.691, 693.

28. XI.604; cf. 644.

29. See for instance: Hampe, *Gleichnisse*, pp. 20–21, on the significance of the formula "man-slaying hands." Cf. Bowra, *Homer and Forerunners*, pp. 11f., on IV.66f.; 71f.; XXII.92; 2.246.

30. XXIV.572.

31. Schadewaldt, *Homers Welt*, p. 50.

32. 6.130–134.

33. XI.113ff.

34. 5.432f. The octopus takes the color of the rock he is clinging to, and is used by Theognis, 213–216, as a symbol of a ποικίλον ἦθος.

35. 8.523–530.

36. Homer is deeply conscious of the relation between the reality of action and the tradition of song which records it; cf. Helen's remark, VI.358. Action in a way exists for the sake of the poetic landmark, which is another way of looking at heroic κλέος. Action is the road to grandeur and eternity.

37. III.125ff.

38. 19.137–150.

39. See Schrade, *Götter und Menschen*, p. 221, on XXII.440ff. Purple as death, V.83; XVI.334; XX.477. Helen's web is also purple; the formula is identical in both passages: δίπλακα πορφυρέην. Helen's web, like her action, influences the web of Andromache as well as her fate.

40. 6.306.

41. 4.121ff.

42. 3.208; 7.197f.; XX.127f.; weaving council: IX.93; trickery: 5.356.

43. XIV.376–383.

44. See Odysseus' remarks earlier, XIV.95–102.

45. 19.392–468.

46. ἔδησε κελεύθου, 4.380; 469.

47. κατέδησε κελεύθους, 5.383.

48. 10.19f.; 23f.

49. 5.443.

50. 5.391, 452.

51. 5.291–296; 328ff.; 331–332; 368ff.; 469.

52. 5.478ff.

53. 6.20.

54. 6.131; 171.

55. 6.210; 212; cf. 7.282.

56. 6.43ff.

57. XX.95.
58. VIII.282; XVIII.102; XV.741; XVI.95.
59. 19.33ff.
60. See Stanford *ad loc.*
61. 20.351.
62. Wade-Gery, *Poet.*
63. V.310.
64. XVII.366–376.
65. XVI.459f., XI.53ff.
66. 12.394f.
67. See A. B. Lord, "Composition by Theme," *TAPA* 82 (1951), for a study of traditional scenic motifs. Also W. Arend, *Die typische Scenen bei Homer* (Berlin, 1933).
68. See Schadewaldt's excellent chapter, "Hektor und Andromache," in *Homers Welt*, 2nd ed., pp. 207ff.
69. *Epithète traditionelle*, p. 172.
70. See Aristophanes' parody, *Frogs*, 1016.
71. XVI.793–797.
72. X.262ff.; XI.632ff.; XI.19ff., respectively.
73. Lorimer, *Homer and the Monuments*, pp. 212–219 (boar's-tusk helmet); pp. 328–335 (cup of Nestor). It is surely pedantry to argue about how many doves and handles should be on the goblet, or whether πυθμένες can be the supporting stems of Schliemann's cup. A type is a type, and in Nestor's cup, the Mycenaean type is clearly described, though somewhat enlarged; see reference to Ventris, Chapter XII, n. 48, below. However, for the view that Nestor's cup and Schliemann's have nothing to do with each other, see A. Furumark, "Nestor's Cup and the Mycenaean Dove-Goblet," *Eranos Rudbergianus* 45:41–53.

CHAPTER VII. FIRE AND OTHER ELEMENTS

1. Parry, *Formules*, p. 61.
2. XII.432f.
3. XIII.137ff.
4. II.93, 340; IX.593; X.246, 547; XI.554; XVII.663; XVIII.492; XXII.150; XXIV.647. I have not wished to stretch the case, but it could be made to include at least some of these, such as the last two.
5. XII.177f.
6. I.40, 52.
7. I.462.
8. II.399, 402–429.
9. IX.206ff.
10. XI.771ff.
11. XXII.169ff.
12. XXII.510ff.
13. XXIII.175ff.
14. VI.417–420. Death, fire, and the magnanimity of Achilles are here first associated, in a most unique passage. Soon again, in the challenge of Hector, VII.79, the stipulation of honorable burial for the loser reflects the

same association. Cf. the threat in XV.350, where the reverse is implied. To give bodies to dogs, rather than to fire, is a threat of utter annihilation. See Schrade, *Götter und Menschen*, pp. 216ff. Terrifying as fire is in the *Iliad*, the denial of it is worse, for then glory is lost. In the context of funerals, and in the context of the Διὸς βουλή (see below), fire has much to do with heroic glory.

15. VII.323–441.
16. XVIII.336ff.; XXIII.24, 69ff.
17. XXIII.192–225.
18. I.103f.; cf. 200.
19. II.414. Though the *Iliad* never narrates the sack of Troy, the image of it constantly rises: VI.331; XX.316; XXI.375; XXII.410f. Suggested also in XVII.737.
20. II.455ff.
21. XV.608ff.
22. XIX.17, 365ff.; XVIII.110.
23. IV.75ff.
24. V.745.
25. XII.462–466. Cf. the bright Apollo, who also in a threatening moment comes "like the night," I.47. The night of Apollo's anger and that of Hector's victory are from the same source.
26. XV.690.
27. VIII.184.
28. XVI.287.
29. Tree-felling: III.482ff.; V.560; XI.86; XIII.178ff., 389; XVI.482, 633. Forest fire: XI.155; XV.605; XX.490ff.; XXI.12ff.
30. Apropos of the association of the Διὸς βουλή with the μῆνις, cf. V.34, where the phrase Διὸς μῆνιν occurs, referring to the ban on the gods' participation in the war, which has not yet taken place. Note too that Zeus and Achilles, during the Wrath, are both νόσφι λιασθείς, I.349; XI.80, a formula used nowhere else.
31. VII.476ff.
32. VIII.66–77.
33. VIII.130–136; cf. 169–170.
34. IX.32ff., 697ff.; XIV.110ff.
35. VIII.397–424.
36. VIII.150.
37. VIII.477ff.
38. VIII.171–176; cf. XII.235f., 256f.
39. VIII.246–250; cf. eagles and hare in Aeschylus, *Agamemnon*, 115ff.
40. XII.200ff.; XIII.821. Three omens seem to bear out the poet's explanation of the limits of Zeus' intentions, XIII.345–360, especially 348ff. But the whole passage indicates his meaning in allowing Poseidon to enter the battle.
41. VIII.509, 554; IX.77, 88 (where the Greek watchfires are also set on Nestor's advice), 234; X.12, 418. As Agamemnon looks at these campfires, his groans are like the thunder of Zeus, X.5ff.
42. VIII.181f., 217, 235.
43. IX.242, 347, 436, 602, 653.
44. XI.667; XII.198, 441; XIII.629; XV.417, 420, 597, 600, 702, 718, 744.

45. XIII.319.
46. XIII.688, 795 (here the Trojans are like wind driven by thunder); XVII.88; see below, and relevant notes.
47. XI.4, 184. In the first of these passages, the Scholiast suggests that lightning is what is meant by the τέρας πολέμοιο.
48. XV.377ff.
49. XIII.629, 688, 736.
50. XIII.242.
51. XIII.330, 471ff.
52. XIV.385f.
53. XIV.414.
54. XVI.113–129.
55. XV.464ff. Teucer also recognizes herein the operation of the Plan of Zeus.
56. XV.599–600.
57. XVI.124ff.; cf. XV.397ff.
58. XVI.287–293, 301.
59. XVII.595f.
60. Hector: XVII.88, 565; XVIII.154, 161; battle: XVII.253, 366, 737; XVIII.1.
61. XX.20–30, following the Μήνιδος ἀπόρρησις.
62. XVI.134; cf. the helmet, 70f., and also the appearance of Hector "flaming" in Achilles' arms, XVII.213f.
63. XVIII.205–214.
64. XVIII.225
65. XVII.404–411.
66. XVIII.232ff., 336ff.
67. XVIII.344.
68. XVIII.412.
69. XVIII.470ff.
70. XVIII.610.
71. XVIII.483ff.
72. XVIII.492, 510, 522.
73. XVIII.86f.
74. XIX.14–18.
75. XIX.362–367.
76. XIX.374–378.
77. XIX.381f.
78. XIX.386.
79. XIX.398.
80. XX.46, 371f. (note the emphatic repetition here), 490ff.
81. XX.156, 111, 423, respectively.
82. XX.316f., 375f.
83. XXI.522ff. Cf. Zeus' fear that Achilles will take Troy (XX.29f.), or Poseidon's that he will slay Aeneas (ibid., 336), ὑπὲρ μόρον. According to the Aethiopis, Achilles did make a furious assault on Troy, after slaying Memnon, cf. Schadewaldt and Pestalozzi.
84. XX.40, 73f.
85. XXI.12.

86. XXI.218ff.
87. XXI.308ff.
88. XXI.331f.
89. XX.134ff.
90. XXI.342ff.
91. XXI.373ff. See Schadewaldt, *Iliasstudien*, p. 156, n. 4, for a collection of references to the taking of Troy in the latter half of the *Iliad*.
92. XXI.128ff.
93. XXI.184–199 *passim*.
94. XXI.517; see also Chapter X, pp. 228ff.
95. XXI.544.
96. XX.29f.
97. XX.61–65.
98. Besides fire and water, earth and air are also constantly involved; cf. XX.494; XXI.21, 58f., 62f., 388; perhaps also the pun, XXI.6, ἠέρα δ' ῞Ηρη.
99. XXII.410f.
100. XXII.7–21.
101. XXII.26ff.
102. V.4ff.
103. XI.62ff.
104. XXII.135.
105. XXII.314ff.
106. XIII.10–38.
107. XIV.392.
108. XIV.394–400.
109. XIV.16ff.
110. XV.381ff., 624ff.
111. XIV.388–391.
112. V.522ff.
113. VII.4ff.
114. VII.63ff.
115. IX.4ff.
116. XI.297f. This and the following image, which also involves the sea, may already prepare the way for the identification of the Greek cause with the sea and Poseidon.
117. XI.305ff.
118. XII.40.
119. XII.132ff.
120. XII.375.
121. XII.156–161.
122. XII.278–287.
123. Cf. the honest woman measuring wool, XII.432f.; the shipwright with a chalk-marker, XV.410; the woodcutter at noon, XI.84ff.
124. Aeschylus, *Persae*, 742.
125. XII.254–257. Motif of θέλξις also at XV.317–322, and 594. Should Hector's wind be connected by paronomasia with ἀνεμώλια βάζειν?
126. XIII.334–337.
127. XIII.795ff. Note that for the third time, the stormy images of Trojan

victory (fire, lightning, wind, sea-storm) are here answered by the single symbol of ultimate salvation for the Achaeans, the eagle. Cf. note 37.

128. XIV.394ff. Wind also plays a part in the shipwreck images denoting the departure of Poseidon, XV.381ff., 624ff.

129. Dust is compared to mist, "better for a thief than night," in III.10ff.

130. XIV.343ff.

131. XVI.66. Is this cloud to be thought of as a contrast with φάος, safety, victory? See Ajax' prayer.

132. XVI.297ff. Achilles' horses which Patroclus drives run like wind, XVI.149.

133. XVI.364.

134. XVI.374f.

135. XVI.344.

136. XVI.384ff.

137. XVI.459ff., 567.

138. XVI.790. Contrast Athena who comes to the aid of the Greeks wrapped in a rainbow, XVII.547.

139. XVII.269, 368-377.

140. XVII.499, 573.

141. XVII.243.

142. XVII.591.

143. XVII.594.

144. XVII.755.

145. XVII.645ff.

CHAPTER VIII. HOMERIC CHARACTER AND THE TRADITION

1. Murray, *Rise*, pp. 125ff.

2. IX.529ff.

3. See Schadewaldt, *Homers Welt*, p. 37, on the problem of Homeric originality; p. 123, on the necessity of present considerations, not merely traditional ones, to enliven the material of the epic.

4. J. A. Scott, *The Unity of Homer* (Berkeley, 1921), pp. 205ff.; Schadewaldt, *Homers Welt*, pp. 177–181; cf. R. Scheliha, *Patroklos* (Basel, 1943); Wade-Gery, *Poet*, p. 36.

5. VI.403, 442ff., 492f.; XXII.410f. Cf. the overtones of the fall of Troy throughout XX and XXI.

6. On the contrast between such lines as XIX.300, and Patroclus' exploits in XVI, see below, chapter IX *passim*. Cf. Schadewaldt, pp. 179ff., on Patroclus as the soul of friendship.

7. I.277–281. See Palmer, *Achaeans and Indo-Europeans*, pp. 11f., for the implications of the terms καρτερὸς and φέρτερος, the latter indicating higher feudal rank.

8. II.42ff.; III.166ff., which perhaps give the traditional epic view of Agamemnon; XI.15–46. Cf. the purple cloak carefully noted in VIII.221.

9. I.118f., 133f.

10. I.136; cf. IX.340–343; note the ἐκ θυμοῦ.

11. XXIII.884–897. Cf. I.165ff.; IX.323–333.

12. Cf. the opening of the *Song of Bagdad*, Lord, *Serbocroatian Heroic*

Songs, I, 68. Here the theme serves to introduce the request for the help of Alija, as in *Iliad* IX it leads to the attempt to regain the help of Achilles.

13. II.110ff.; cf. IX.17ff.; XIV.74ff. The passage in Book II is a kind of divination by opposites, more familiar in the *Odyssey* (cf. 3.210–238 with 371ff.) than in the *Iliad*. Agamemnon has no intention that the army shall escape (cf. II, 75); he merely wants an additional sign from the gods, and gets it, as Odysseus solicits omens from the gods, 20.105ff. The modern Greek game of κλήδονας offers some analogy with the idea of saying the opposite of what you hope the gods intend. The most striking ancient example is in the *Odyssey*, 15.512ff., where Telemachus' suggestion, that Theoclymenus stay at Eurymachus' house, as the man most likely to succeed to Odysseus' inheritance, can only be interpreted as a solicitation of the omen which follows, by which it appears that Telemachus, and not Eurymachus, will be king.

14. IX.32ff.
15. XIV.83ff.
16. XI.15–283.
17. XI.92ff.
18. XI.101–119.
19. XI.122–147.
20. XI.172ff.
21. XI.221–243.
22. XI.267–272.
23. XI.434–488.
24. XI.367–395.
25. XXI.99–113. Refusal of mercy in battle is a stock motif, cf. Lord, *Serbocroatian Heroic Songs*, I, 112, where Budalina Tale slices his captives in two. But Homer has used the theme to illustrate character.
26. VI.45–65.
27. XVI.97ff.
28. II.101ff.
29. II.109ff. In the repetition of this speech, in IX, no mention is made of the scepter; instead it is introduced by the image of the dark-watered spring of tears; the scepter of deceit has been replaced by the tears of truth.
30. II.199.
31. II.242 = I.232.
32. II.265–270.
33. I.234–246.
34. Hurling down the scepter may be a regular motif in council scenes. Telemachus does it (2.80), but very differently, not as the solemn climax of rising tension, but after his very first speech of complaint against the suitors, and thereupon he bursts into tears. The same action may carry numerous overtones. As for the oath on the scepter, it seems to be a familiar folk-motif, and turns up again in the tales of Tannhäuser.
35. See the ἐπιπώλησις in Book IV, and note especially Diomedes' reply, 401–418; a passage taken rightly by Leaf to show that Diomedes, as ruler of Tiryns, was a vassal of Agamemnon.
36. VIII.287–294.
37. IV.155ff.

38. VII.96–119. One of the most cogent reasons for believing the *Doloneia* belongs somehow to Homer, and perhaps the *Iliad*, is the scene where Agamemnon deflects Diomedes from choosing Menelaus as a companion, 237ff.

39. Cf. VIII.236–244 with XVII.645ff.; see Longinus' remarks, *De Sublimitate*, IX.10.

40. See Schadewaldt, *Homers Welt*, p. 198, on Homer's humane contributions to the character of Agamemnon.

41. Parry, *Epithète traditionelle*, p. 172.

42. Herod., II.53.2.

43. XIII.203ff.; XVI.330ff.

44. XIV.520ff.

45. XXIII.754–783.

46. Note Ajax' rudeness, and Idomeneus' reply, XXIII.473–484, with Achilles' rebuke, 492–494. See Virgil, *Aeneid*, I.39ff.

47. XIII.249–294.

48. VIII.99–129; cf. Schadewaldt, *Homers Welt*, pp. 155ff., for a convenient summary of H. Pestalozzi's theory of the *Aethiopis* as the model for the *Iliad*; doubtless an earlier *Aethiopis*, not that of Arctinus.

49. IX.53–59.

50. IV.365–418; X.150–167.

51. V.5–6.

52. XXII.25–31. See Chapter VII, p. 143.

53. XVI.702ff.

54. V.434ff.

55. V.106–132.

56. V.305ff., 445ff.

57. V.902.

58. V.692ff. Sarpedon returns in XII without a scratch. It may not be a real inconsistency, for the time of Books III–VII is different from the time of the rest of the *Iliad*; see below.

59. V.499, 522ff.

60. V.113.

61. V.87, 597.

62. V.720–777.

63. V.124ff.

64. V.601, 702, 823–834. Diomedes is still of the same mind in VI.128f.

65. Note, for instance, his two speeches in IX.32ff. and 697ff.; cf. VII.-400ff.

66. XXIII.708–737.

67. See Schadewaldt, *Homers Welt*, pp. 155ff.

68. In the *Aethiopis*, Ajax is assisted by Odysseus; Odysseus in the *Iliad* is wounded, however, and is not on the field. It is hard to know who helped Ajax in the pre-Homeric tradition. In the *Aethiopis*, Ajax caries off Achilles' body (see Proclus, *Chrestomathy*) while Odysseus covers the retreat; in the *Iliad*, Menelaus and Meriones lift Patroclus and begin to carry him out of the missiles, succeeding only when Achilles shouts.

69. XVII.98–105.

70. XVII.4f., 133ff. These images are picked up in XVIII.318ff., where Achilles also, moved by a sense of shattered brotherhood, mourns for Patroclus.

71. XVII.240ff.

72. XVII.694ff.

73. XVII.704. Cf. 690, where the same formula occurs.

74. XVII.140–168.

75. A similar problem arises around XVII.364–365, athetized by Zenodotus. Yet these lines are a leitmotiv, a summary expression of one of the chief motivations of Book XVII, and it is hard to see where they might have come from except from the poet who conceived XVII.

76. VI.441ff.

77. XIII.620–639.

78. X.114–125.

79. III.99f.; VII.92ff. (a sort of inversion, but still motivated by αἰδώς); X.25ff.; XVII.91–95.

80. V.561–575; XV.568; cf. their friendly squabble in XXIII.

81. XIII.321ff.

82. XV.502ff., 561ff., 733ff. Cf. Nestor's speech, 661ff., also on αἰδώς, and resembling Hector's dutiful orientation.

83. IX.628–642.

84. XVI.97–111.

85. XVI.114–123.

86. XIII.821; XVII.645ff.

87. XI.544ff. One finds the poet perhaps at a slight loss here; he cannot have Ajax wounded, since he is necessary for the later scenes of the battle; but it is hard to make Ajax retreat unless he is wounded. The only answer is direct interference by the god of the Διὸς βουλή.

88. III.225–229; VII.185ff.

89. See Schrade, *Götter und Menschen*, p. 258.

90. IV.361.

91. Cf. Aeschylus, *Agamemnon*, 841ff., where Agamemnon says as much of him.

92. II.284ff.

93. III.204ff.; IX.225ff.

94. VIII.91–101.

95. VIII.139ff.

96. XI.401–488.

97. XIV.83–102.

98. IX.225–306.

99. IX.612, 645.

100. XIX.146–153.

101. XIX.155–183.

102. XIX.216–233.

103. XIX.305ff.; 349–354.

104. I.54–56.

105. XXIV.599–619.

106. 11.471–491.

1. *Poetics*, 1459b1.

2. On parataxis, J. A. Notopoulos, "Parataxis in Homer," *TAPA* 80 (1949): 1–23. I cannot, however, agree with the conclusions drawn about Homer's work as lacking organism, least of all with the interpretation of Aristotle's phrase πολύμυθον σύστημα as "inorganic unity." Unity is organic by nature, and Aristotle was actually saying that the *Iliad* had organic unity of plot, though the sentence structure was that of the λέξις εἰρομένη.

3. IX.529–599.

4. XVIII.107ff.

5. On Homeric honor, see Jaeger, *Paideia*, 2nd ed., I, 8f., 12f., 420 n. 27. On the view of Achilles presented here, see also E. F. Dolin, Jr., "The Realism of the Iliad" (unpublished Harvard Honors Thesis, 1950).

6. I.366–369.

7. I.54ff.

8. I.88ff.

9. I.131–139.

10. I.150f.

11. I.173.

12. I.185ff.

13. I.281.

14. I.178, 280.

15. I.213f.

16. I.298ff.

17. XXIII.261.

18. IX.335–343; taking "ἄλοχον" as referring to Briseis, not, as some think, to Clytaemnestra, who is quite irrelevant to the context.

19. IX.344, 375f. Agamemnon's consistent greed is emphasized by the iterative verbs, in IX.333.

20. IX.410ff.

21. IX.401–709. On Achilles' love of life, see Schadewaldt, *Homers Welt*, p. 369f.: "Even the heroic greatness of Achilles would not have been complete, had not the temptation of simple happiness crossed his path, and promised him, instead of his dear-bought fame, a peaceful existence amid the abundance of his possessions at home."

22. XXI.100ff.; VI.416–420.

23. IX.318ff.

24. IX.323ff.

25. IX.204. The question of the original number of envoys has been well discussed by Jaeger, *Paideia*, I, 423, n. 31. The use of the dual in 182 and lines following is a real slip on the poet's part, and probably indicates some familiar form of an embassy scene, such being quite traditional, where only two envoys are present. There is no need to assume a late contamination, however. Such a slip is characteristic of oral poetry; cf. the change in the number of generals slain with the Ban of Zadar in the *Captivity of Dulič Ibrahim*, Lord, *Serbocroatian Heroic Songs*, I, 108, 111. Lord's notes to the songs point out a considerable number of such slips, mistaken names, etc. See *Scholia ad loc.* and 8.48, where the dual is used with fifty-two people!

26. IX.356ff.

27. IX.618ff.

28. IX.650–655.

29. IX.682ff. Achilles repeats his promise somewhat wryly (γε) in XVI.-61f., at which point, however, he yields still further, and allows Patroclus to fight before the fire reaches his own ship.

30. IX.598–605.

31. IX.607ff.

32. IX.309–312.

33. IX.158–161.

34. IX.372f.

35. IX.391f. Contrast Achilles' remark to Phoenix: Ἶσον ἐμοὶ βασίλευε, καὶ ἥμισυ μείρεο τιμῆς, IX.616.

36. XVI.72f. Cf. the excellent article of D. E. Eichholz, "The Propitiation of Achilles," *AJP* 74 (1953): 138–148, who defends conclusively the unity of IX and XVI on grounds similar to those made here.

37. IX.186ff. Note that Phoenix repeats the phrase, IX.524, just before introducing the paradigm of Meleager, which actually provides Achilles with the personal model which he seeks.

38. VI.357f.

39. XI.604.

40. XI.762ff.

41. XI.790–797.

42. XVII.670ff.; XIX.295–300.

43. XI.828–836; note that ἤπιος is an epithet of both Patroclus and the drugs which he applies.

44. XV.390–404 (403f. = XI.792f.).

45. XVI.52–55, 60–65, 83–100.

46. Zenodotus and Aristarchus athetized these lines, suspecting their relevance, but all texts have them. It is hard to see how they could have been created by anyone except the creator of Achilles.

47. XXIII.83–92.

48. XVI.745ff., spoken over the body of Cebriones, is strangely out of character for the Patroclus who appears elsewhere.

49. XVI.785.

50. XVI.705, 786; cf. XX.447, where the three charges, and the epithet δαίμονι ἶσος, now used of Achilles, recall the *Patrocleia* and the identity of roles.

51. XI.604.

52. The *Patrocleia* is thought by Pestalozzi and Schadewaldt, p. 186, to be modeled on the death of Achilles in the *Aethiopis*. There can be no doubt that it is at least a montage on the traditional tale, if not on Arctinus' poem.

53. XVI.241–245.

54. XVI.140ff.

55. Both Achilles and Patroclus almost take Troy: XVI.698–709; XX.30; XXI.517.

56. XVI.794–800.

57. XVII.200ff.

58. XVIII.22–27.

59. XVIII.8–13.

60. The names of the Nereids are doubtless genuine, despite their absence from the Argolic text and the athetesis of Zenodotus and Aristarchus. It is all part of a Geometric picture. See Hampe, *Gleichnisse Homers*, p. 24. Their presence, if not their names, was traditional, from the funeral of Achilles, on which the scene is based; cf. 24.55ff.; Schadewaldt, *Homers Welt*, p. 166.

61. XVIII.98–126.

62. Cf. also XIV.376ff.; perhaps some idea of abstract valor existent in armor underlies such formulae as θοῦριν ἐπιειμένοι ἀλκήν, and δύσεο δ' ἀλκήν; at least, see XVII.210ff.

63. XVIII.84ff.

64. XVIII.166ff.

65. XV.49–77; cf. VIII.473–476, where Zeus outlines the future more cryptically to Hera. Such a passage makes it difficult to see Book VIII as an *Eindichtung*.

66. XVIII.356–367.

67. See Wade-Gery's analysis, *Poet*, p. 16, and Sheppard, *Pattern of the Iliad*, 83, 182. Probably, however, the shield passage closed the second day's recitation, rather than opening the third; but see Wade-Gery, notes 43 and 44.

68. Cf. Hampe, *Gleichnisse Homers*, p. 21, n. 9, on the forward and backward reference of this book.

69. XVIII.417ff.

70. XVIII.546ff.

71. XVIII.562, 574f.

72. Cf. Schrade, *Götter und Menschen*, p. 80.

73. XVIII.599ff.

74. See Myres, *Who Were the Greeks?* p. 519.

75. XXII.395; XXIII.24, 176.

76. XIX.366f.

77. XXII.265ff.

78. XIX.146ff., 199ff.

79. XIX.352ff.

80. XXI.106–113.

81. VIII.170–176.

82. See Schadewaldt's matchless analysis of this scene, *Homers Welt*, pp. 212–233.

83. VI.500. Cf. also in XXII.105, the echo of VI.442, where Hector's sense of duty destroys him, as Andromache feared.

84. Cf. also the consistency of Andromache's lines, VI.407 and XXII.457.

85. VI.476–481.

86. VI.486ff. There is actually more promise of life than foreknowledge of death in this speech. Contrast Achilles' speech, IX.320ff.

87. VIII.508ff.

88. VIII.526f., 530f., 535–541. Cf. 470 and 508.

89. XII.200–250. Cf. XIII.821ff., where Zeus' eagle appears greeting a bold speech by Ajax, but is disregarded by Hector, who confidently reiterates his boastful prayer of VIII.540f.

90. XII.60–87, 108–117; XIII.725–753.
91. XVIII.249–252, and the scene following.
92. XVIII.303–311. If one compares this, and the other passages on the deception of Hector, it seems best to accept as genuine XV.610–614, omitted by Zenodotus and athetized by Aristarchus.
93. XVIII.328–332.
94. XXII.99–121.
95. XXII.126ff.
96. XXII.199f.
97. XXII.254–259.
98. XXII.261ff.
99. XXII.296f., 300–305. Note the echo of the *Patrocleia* in the formula θάνατόνδε κάλεσσαν, 297 = XVI.693.
100. XXIII.19–26.
101. XXIII.42–56.
102. XXIII.69f.
103. XXIII.94–102.
104. XXIII.250f.
105. XXIII.274ff. The reference in 283ff. to the immortal horses still mourning for Patroclus is a telling image, reflecting indirectly Achilles' reasons for refraining from the games. Thus too the transition is made between funeral and horse race, with the image of the mourning horses between.
106. XXIII.558ff., 736f.
107. XXIV.4–18.
108. XXIV.107.
109. XXIV.71ff.
110. XXIV.78.
111. XXIV.58–61; note that Hera no longer objects to Thetis or her influence among the gods, but rather defends it.
112. XXIV.113f. Zeus "in particular" is angry, for he in particular sees the full context of things. In fact, it was Apollo who raised the issue, but Zeus, as the god of the universal at large, undertakes to see Achilles through to the fullness of his κῦδος; cf. 110.
113. XXIV.139f. In only two lines, with no argument whatsoever, Achilles gives up the whole thing.
114. XXIV.153.
115. XXIV.194–199.
116. XXIV.328.
117. XXIV.349–357; cf. Schrade, *Götter und Menschen*, p. 217f.
118. XXIV.439.
119. XXIV.453–456.
120. II.491.
121. IX.158; XVI.34f.; XXIV.206ff.
122. XXIV.560f.; see to 570. Cf. 572, where Achilles goes out like a lion.
123. XXIV.589–595.
124. XXIV.466f., 486ff., 511.
125. XXIV.534–550.
126. XXIV.527ff.
127. XXIV.629–632.

128. XXIV.637–642.
129. XXIV.601ff.
130. XXIV.676.

CHAPTER X. FATE, TIME, AND THE GODS

1. 20.351ff.
2. V.290.
3. Herod. II.53.2.
4. See W. Jaeger, *The Theology of the Early Greek Philosophers* (Oxford, 1947), p. 203, n. 44.
5. XI.384–395; III.39.
6. III.59–75.
7. III.395–417.
8. XVI.440ff.; XXII.178ff.
9. XVI.384ff. See Chapter VII on this passage.
10. XV.14–52.
11. XV.135ff.
12. XI.653f.
13. XV.72.
14. I.518ff.
15. I.153ff. Cf. Zeus' speech on the innocence of Hector, XXII.168ff.
16. I.498; νόσφι λιασθείς, XI.78 and I.349.
17. XV.599ff. (Zeus watching for the fire); cf. IX.650–653.
18. XVI.125ff.; cf. Chapter VII, p. 136.
19. XX.24–30.
20. XXI.517. Cf. Schadewaldt, *Homers Welt*, pp. 48f., who notes how the gods' will reveals itself little by little through human action. There can be only one reason for this, namely that in the poem, the gods' will is created by human action.
21. XVI.707ff.
22. XXII.208–214.
23. III.59.
24. XVI.459f.; XIII.821.
25. I.297ff.
26. I.169ff.
27. XVIII.217f.
28. XXII.276f.
29. XXII.226–246; 289–305.
30. XXIV.25–30.
31. XI.45f. Cf. also XX.310–317.
32. IV.34ff. Cf. the element of παιδοφαγία in Agamemnon's character, Chapter VIII; Aeschylus' development thereof, and the recurrence of the idea in Achaean history.
33. IV.148ff.; VII.107ff.; X.120ff., 240; V.565ff. (Antilochus).
34. IV.7ff.
35. IV.130f.
36. Xenophanes, 10–14.
37. An apparent exception to this is his rescue of Aeneas in XX.293–339.

Two points are relevant here: the terms of the gods' truce before the *Theomachia*, and Aeneas' future history. The gods had agreed not to fight unless some Trojan god began the fray or restrained Achilles (138f.). Apollo is the logical rescuer of any Trojan or ally, but for him to save Aeneas would have brought about the *Theomachia* too soon and before its main point, the ultimate fall of Troy, was thoroughly established. A Greek god would have to save him, and consent must be obtained of the chief opponent of Troy, Hera, before even he could do so. Poseidon is chosen, doubtless because by Homer's time the tradition of Aeneas' successful escape by sea and ultimate survival was already in existence. Cf. the prophecy of Capys, and the protection of Aeneas by Neptune in the *Aeneid*.

38. See Chapter VI on her role in the Nausicaa scene. Also, she bears some relation to Penelope, in the scenes where she appears in dreams or restores her beauty; for an excellent analysis of this relationship, see Anne Amory, "Dreams and Omens in Homer's Odyssey" (unpublished Radcliffe thesis, 1957).

39. IV.439f.

40. V.29–35 (here Ares seems to be the spirit of the Trojan counterattack after the death of Phegeus); 454ff. (Apollo calls on Ares).

41. V.832f. Cf. XXI.413f., where this breach of promise reappears, as a sin against his mother Hera. The scholiast of XX.67 emphasizes the brainlessness of Ares.

42. V.855–906.

43. XV.110ff. On Ascalaphus, cf. II.512; IX.82; XIII.518–525.

44. XX.38, 138, 152; XXI.391–433.

45. XVIII.516.

46. See Robert Frost, "Lesson for Today," in *A Witness Tree* (New York, 1942). The epithet ἀλλοπρόσαλλος probably means one who changes sides; cf. R. J. Cunliffe, *Lexicon of the Homeric Dialect* (London, 1924), s.v.

47. 10.72ff.

48. XXI.461ff., 515ff.

49. XXIV.18–54.

50. XII.463; cf. I.47; cf. XI.353, where it is said that Apollo gave Hector his helmet.

51. XV.236–261.

52. XV.244–261.

53. XV.242.

54. XXII.15ff.

55. XXII.359f.; cf. Chapter VII, p. 142.

56. XXIV.612.

57. Schrade, *Götter und Menschen*, p. 75.

58. XIX.86–138.

59. V.420–430, 889ff.

60. V.382ff.

61. 8.266–366.

62. 8.246ff.

63. 8.499–520.

64. VII.61.

65. XVI.459–461.
66. Hector, XXII.168ff.; XXIV.33ff.; Aeneas, XX.297ff.; Odysseus, 1.60ff.
67. XVII.198–208; 5.282–290, 375–379.
68. XVII.201–208.
69. XVIII.54.
70. XVIII.8ff.; cf. XVII.408ff.
71. XVII.434ff.
72. XVII.443ff.
73. XIX.405ff.
74. XII.450. Zenodotus, Aristophanes, and Aristarchus suspected this verse, because as a rule the preceding formula concludes passages about how a hero lifted a stone which no one now could lift. But the poet was quite well advised to put it in. It keeps freshly in mind the whole dependency of Hector's triumph upon the Plan of Zeus.
75. Cf. X.291 with V.850ff.
76. Cf. 5.427 with II.166ff. Cf. also Hera's mental prompting of Achilles to call the assembly, I.55, with Athena's personal restraint of Achilles, I.194.
77. XV.290; cf. XX.92f.; 22.372.
78. B. Malinowski, *Magic, Science and Religion, and Other Essays*, Selected with an Introduction by R. Redfield (Boston and Chicago, 1948), pp. 61f., 115f.
79. XVI.513–531; cf. B. Snell, *Discovery of Mind*, trans. T. G. Rosenmayer (Oxford and Cambridge, Mass., 1953), pp. 19f.; who, however, states confusingly that Homer took no such psychological view; rather that he attributed the healing to Apollo, but that there was nothing supernatural about it.
80. XVIII.239f.
81. VIII.485–488.
82. XXI.470–513.
83. On double motivation in Homer, see M. P. Nilsson, *History of Greek Religion* (Second edition, Oxford, 1952), pp. 122ff., and E. R. Dodds, *The Greeks and the Irrational* (Berkeley, 1951), pp. 13ff., esp. n. 90.

CHAPTER XI. GEOMETRIC STRUCTURE OF THE ILIAD

1. Parry, reviewing W. Arend, *Typische Scenen*, in *CP.* 31:360.
2. See especially J. A. Notopoulos, "Continuity and Interconnexion," *TAPA* 82:96, for repeated formulae affecting characterization, and an argument in general for the progress from functionalism to aesthetic purpose in Homer.
3. See A. B. Lord, "Composition by Theme in Epos," *TAPA* 82 (1951): 71ff.
4. XVI.220–232.
5. I.446–474.
6. 2.132–154.
7. 3.5–68; 430–472.
8. IX.78.
9. See W. A. A. Van Otterlo, *De Ringcompositie als Opbouwprincipe in de Epische Gedichte van Homerus* (Amsterdam, 1948), summary by

J. Tate, *Classical Review* 63 (1949):137–138; and *Untersuchungen über Begriff, Anwendung und Entstehung der Griechischen Ringcomposition* (Amsterdam, 1944); and a good description by Notopoulos, *TAPA* 82:97ff.

10. Notopoulos, 99ff.

11. 19.392–468.

12. 19.1f. = 51f.

13. 5.285 = 376.

14. See Chapter V and note 33.

15. See Schadewaldt, *Homers Welt*, pp. 51, 95, 115ff., and elsewhere. J. T. Sheppard, *The Pattern of the Iliad* (London, 1922). C.f. E. Buschor, *Von Sinn der griechischen Standbilder* (Berlin, 1942), pp. 10ff. Also especially Sir J. L. Myres, "The Last Book of the Iliad," *JHS*, 52 (1932):264ff. The present analysis of the *Iliad* was made independently of Myres, but equally on the basis of Sheppard. The interesting result is that neither scheme needs to deny the other; both can be true.

16. See Schrade, *Götter und Menschen*, p. 271.

17. Myres, *Who Were the Greeks?* p. 519. Sheppard, *Pattern*, pp. 204ff.

18. This was discovered, apparently, by J. U. Powell, see Myres, *JHS*, 52 (1932) 285. In XXIV some doubts arise, but they are more conducive to believing the poet's plan than otherwise. The gods are roused to action on the twelfth day (line 31), but later Zeus says, "for nine days we have been arguing" (l.107). Moreover, Priam asks for twelve days to bury Hector (ll. 664–667), but actually buries him on the tenth (ll. 785ff.). Perhaps the eleventh day is meant at 788 for the burial and feast, and in this case the scheme is broken a little. In any case the confusion over twelve and nine seems likely enough in oral composition; the poet knew that his opening involved these two time-gaps, and may have had some difficulty remembering, over such a space, which actually came first.

19. See Einstein, *Mozart*, p. 157f.

20. XXIV.100ff.

21. II.225ff.; cf. Chapter VIII, p. 161.

22. II.111–118 with 139–141 = IX.18–28.

23. Sappho 27a. See K. Marót, "La Béotie et son caractère hésiodique," *Acta Antiqua Academiae Scientiarum Hungariae* (Budapest), I (1951–2), pp. 261–323, on the word magic of the *Catalogue*.

24. See Schadewaldt, *Homers Welt*, pp. 115ff., and compare, of course, their use on the *Shield*.

25. II.299–332.

26. XXIII.784; cf. II.270.

27. See Chapter VIII.

28. Bowra, *Tradition and Design*, p. 205.

29. V.129–132.

30. V.819–834.

31. Perhaps there is in this half-friendly duel a reflection of the family connections between Ajax and Hector. Hesione, sister of Priam, was the mother of Teucer, Ajax's half-brother, who was therefore Hector's first cousin.

32. VI.102–115.

33. III.428–436 and VI.407–413.

34. VI.349ff. and 442ff.

35. VI.500. Cf. Schadewaldt, *Homers Welt*, p. 215: "Hektor steht schon hier im Tode."

36. Compare also the narratives of Nestor, 3.103–200; Menelaus, 4.333–592; Agamemnon, 11.405–434; incorporating much of the material of the *Nostoi*, not to mention other parts of the *Odyssey* summarizing events later told in the *Cycle*. On the *Iliad* as an epitome of the Trojan War, see Bowra, *Homer and Forerunners*, p. 40.

37. Cf. above, Chapter IX.

38. XVIII.440f., 464f.

39. XXII.358ff.

40. Apollo rousing Aeneas: XX.82–110; the retirement, 132–152. There could be no more pointed confession by the poet that the gods discover their appropriate offices through the reflection of heroic action, and can do nothing without it. The excuse for the retirement given in XX.153–155 is tacitly denied by the *Theomachia* itself.

41. Lycaon, XXI.34–135; Asteropaeus, 139–199.

42. See also G. Scheibner, "Aufbau der 20 u. 21 Buch der Ilias" (Doctoral dissertation, Leipzig, 1939); not available to me.

43. Cf. XXII.145–157 (the review of familiar scenes); 168–173 (Zeus' pity for Hector, on the scene of his many sacrifices); 403–404, "Zeus gave him to his enemies to torment in his own fatherland." Cf. Wade-Gery, *Poet*, pp. 40ff.

44. Hector is specifically mentioned in the oath on the scepter: I.242f.; again in IX.349–355. The Greeks of course took Troy without Achilles, but only after Hector's death.

45. VIII.245ff., XII.200; XIII.821.

46. VIII.68–74.

47. VIII.186ff.

48. VIII.150.

49. VIII.477–483; cf. Chapter VII, p. 134.

50. VIII.198–211. With the present analysis, compare Myres' slightly different one, "The Last Book of the Iliad," *JHS*, 52:274f.

51. XVII.75ff., 485ff.

52. XVII.201–208.

53. XVII.269ff.

54. XVII.544–546.

55. XVII.593–595.

56. XVII.378; 402ff.; 640ff.; 691ff.; 700ff.

57. XVIII.303f. = VIII.530f.

58. Cf. Chapter IX.

59. IX.14f. = XVI.3f., or almost.

60. IX.646ff.

61. XVI.55; 6of.

62. Cf. IX.198 with 642.

63. XVI.46f.

64. XVI.249f.

65. XVI.852ff.

66. XI.3–12; XVIII.217–242.

67. XI.604, and XV.390ff. See also Myres' analysis of the structure of Book XIV, "The Last Book of the Iliad," *JHS*, 52:276ff.

68. See Wilamowitz, *Ilias und Homer*, p. 32, n. 2; *Homerische Untersuchungen*, p. 369, for Zenodotus as author of book divisions.

69. Notopoulos, *TAPA* 82:86.

70. The present state of the evidence invites only guesswork about authorship: reference to the wrath of Achilles and the Trojan campfires on the plain show that the Dolon and Rhesus episodes were here being rehearsed not independently, but quite in keeping with the scheme of the *Iliad*. Moreover, as noted, the fire imagery, continued with the same associations as elsewhere, together with the relationships between major characters, indicates that the author of Book X had not only the general story of the *Iliad* before his eyes, but also its inner dynamics and artistic orientation. Here, as elsewhere in Homeric criticism, linguistic arguments against authenticity have failed to produce anything even remotely convincing; cf. Scott, *The Unity of Homer*, pp. 73ff. The animal skins used for clothing are, indeed, surprising; but Paris' leopard skin in Book III is not to be forgotten. The remarks, however, of W. Leaf (*The Iliad*, 2nd ed. [London, 1900–1902], I, 423f.) about the maneristic style seem to be entirely just. Whoever wrote Book X certainly strove for spectacular effects, and it seems impossible to reconcile the stage of creative maturity reached in this Book with that which characterizes the rest of the poem. Its taste is different. But since its language is the same, it is doubtless as old as, if not older than, the rest of the *Iliad*. It could have been an early work of Homer's, intended for the *Iliad*, but eventually omitted, only to be "restored," as the Townley *Scholia* suggest. Or a closely connected pupil of Homer's — such as Süssmayer was to Mozart — may have tried to emulate his master and improve his work: in either case, the point might be to draw a shadow play of the Palladium adventure of Odysseus and Diomedes into the scheme of the Wrath, as Homer had drawn shadow plays of the previous years of the war in III–VII, of the death of Achilles in XVI–XVIII, of the fall of Troy in XX–XXII, and some hints of the Returns in XXIII. If the poem was originally by Homer, the present version may represent an oral reproduction of it by another singer — a case, perhaps, of late eighth-century literary piracy. See the defense of Book X, A. Shewan, *The Lay of Dolon* (London, 1911).

71. See, for instance, the horizontal bands reproduced in the article of Myres, *JHS*, 52:272f.

CHAPTER XII. THE ODYSSEY AND CHANGE

1. *De Sublimitate*, 11.

2. The most recent of such arguments may be found in Wade-Gery, *Poet*, p. 62, n. 4. The chief points are four. (a) The *Odyssey* shows knowledge of Egypt, supposedly seventh-century knowledge and unavailable to the Greeks until then. But Wade-Gery himself knows of Greeks who went to Egypt before then, and there might have been others. More important, Homer's knowledge of Egypt is not seventh-century knowledge, but epic knowledge, namely, formulae, perhaps as old as the earliest Mycenaean con-

tact with Egypt. There is nothing very specific or authentic about it, and it perhaps should not be regarded as knowledge at all. Odysseus' men need not be regarded as hoplites; any army is helpless when surrounded; in any case, hoplite warfare seems to be implied in II.362ff. (b) The *Odyssey* shows knowledge of Cimmerians, and therefore of the North. Homer mentions the Cimmerians once, 11.4, and locates them in the West, near the Land of the Dead; hence it appears that he knew nothing of the Cimmerians, beyond their name. (c) The *Odyssey* mentions riding horseback astride. This occurs once in 5.371 (κέλης); aside from the dubious matter of X.513, the denominative verb κελητίζειν in XV.679 can only mean "ride" (see Cunliffe, *Lexicon, s.v.*), whatever equestrian acrobatics are implied by the simile; see Leaf, *ad. loc.*, quoting Aristarchus. Riding horseback is well attested on eighth-century Geometric vases, see Athens Nat. Museum No. 810, reproduced in E. Pernice, "Geometrische Vase aus Athen," *Ath. Mitt.* 17 (1892): 205ff., and pl. X; also Athens Nat. Museum No. 13038. Pegasus is not mentioned in connection with Bellerophon and the Chimaera in VI, but Bellerophon's horsemanship was well known to the mythography and art of the Geometric Period: see Perrot and Chipiez, *Histoire de l'art*, VII, 34 (cut of winged horse from the Dipylon); Hes., *Eoiae*, fg. 7, 16ff. On horseback riding in Geometric art, see Kraiker-Kübler, *Kerameikos* V, fasc. 2, p. 176, and note 168. (d) The *Odyssey* shows traces of shamanistic religion, in the *Nekyia* and the vision of Theoclymenus (cf. Wade-Gery, *Poet*, p. 75, n. 66). It is hard to see anything shamanistic in the *Nekyia*; as for Theoclymenus, see above, Chapter VI.

3. See Schadewaldt's excellent summary of the world view of the two poems, *Homers Welt*, pp. 96–129.

4. Sir J. L. Myres' attempt to erect a design for the *Odyssey* comparable to that of the *Iliad* seems to me to defeat itself by its sheer complexity and to prove almost the exact opposite; see "The Pattern of the Odyssey," *JHS* 72 (1952):1ff.

5. 19.209–212.

6. Cf. Notopoulos, *TAPA* 82:84.

7. For an account of the development and chief monuments of protoAttic pottery, see J. M. Cook, "Protoattic Pottery," *BSA* 35 (1934–1935): 165–219; also J. D. Beazley, *Development of Attic Black Figure* (Berkeley and London, 1951); and J. F. Daniel, review of R. S. Young, *Hesperia*, Suppl. II (q. v.), *AJA* 44(1940):159–161.

8. Museum of the Excavations of the Athenian Agora (Stoa of Attalos), Inv. P 22691; I am indebted to Miss Lucy Talcott for introducing me to this sherd, and for granting me permission to mention it. Cf. Cook, *BSA* 35:181f.; pl. 59; also F. Matz, *Geschichte der Griechischen Kunst* (Frankfurt, 1950), I, fasc. 2, pl. 188–196.

9. 16.175; 18.196.

10. These "blunders" are not found in the same places by all critics. Those discussed by Page, *The Homeric Odyssey*, seem to be based, like so many of the analytic arguments of the last century, on predetermined captiousness and ignorance of oral theory. The real formal weaknesses of the *Odyssey*, as compared with the *Iliad*, can be summarized under three headings: (a) occasional carelessness in the use of epithets or other formulae: e.g., ἀμύμονος

Αἰγίσθοιο, 1.29, or the feeble variants on VI.492f. to be found in 1.358f. and 21.352f.; (b) repetitiousness: e.g., overbidding of the hospitality motif, feasting, etc., and especially the genre scenes illustrating the violence of the suitors versus the piety of the faithful; a tendency toward "talkiness," in short (these passages are, as a rule, individually attractive enough, but in proportion to the whole, they are somewhat waywardly spun out); (c) an occasional awkwardness in handling the complexities of the plot: e.g., the directions of Odysseus to Telemachus in 16.281ff., bracketed by Zenodotus and Aristarchus, but undoubtedly the kind of slight inconsistency which is native to oral poetry. Examples of this last point can also be found in the *Iliad*; the first two appear to be traits of the *Odyssey*, and, together with the general relinquishment of Geometric structure, point toward a slightly altered poetic consciousness, a disinterest in older methods in favor of new. One might compare the proto-Attic deer, drawn in a basically Geometric style, but having two heads and six feet, in R. S. Young, "Late Geometric Graves . . ." *Hesperia*, Suppl. II (1939), pp. 176f., no. C119.

11. E.g., late eighth-century neck amphora, Athens Nat. Museum No. 894; see Perrot and Chipiez, *Histoire de l'art*, VII, fig. 58; cf. their figs. 65, 66, 98; cf. also A. Furtwängler, "Vasen Geometrischen Stils," *Archaeologische Zeitung* 43(1885):131ff.; figs. pp. 131, 139, and pl. 8; and F. Matz, *Geschichte der Griechischen Kunst*, I², pl. 12, 13, 15b.

12. Beazley, in Beazley and Ashmole, *Greek Sculpture and Painting* (Cambridge, 1932), p. 10. Cf. Beazley, *Development of Attic Black Figure*, p. 4.

13. Cf. Broneer, *Hesperia* 8:361: "One might almost say that the decorators of Protoattic pottery took up the animal designs where their predecessors of late Mycenaean times had left off. The similarity is very striking."

14. Athens Nat. Museum, 313. See Beazley, *Development of Attic Black Figure*, p. 5 and n. 11; J. M. Cook, *BSA* 35 (1935), pls. 386, 39; cf. pls. 43, 45, 46, 47.

15. E.g., the baldric of Heracles, 11.609ff.; perhaps the brooch in 19.226ff.; it is noteworthy, however, that the Sirens seem not yet to have become the bird-women of slightly later times. Had they been, the poet would hardly have missed the chance to describe them, as he does Scylla and Cyclops. They simply "sit in a meadow" and sing (12.45), and do not, as in later vases, fly around the ship.

16. 1.50.

17. See H. Zimmer, *The King and the Corpse* (Washington, D. C., 1948), pp. 76–88; 131.

18. 9.40, 44, 88ff., 171ff.; 10.100ff., 189–209.

19. 9.502ff.

20. 10.456–465.

21. 12.184.

22. 12.226–233.

23. 9.19f.

24. 16.154ff.

25. 1.115.

26. 17.291ff.

27. 17.233ff., 462ff.; Odysseus dodges all subsequent missiles.

28. 18.69ff., 90ff.

29. 18.130ff.

30. 19.392ff.; 21.221ff.

31. 21.404–423.

32. P. W. Harsh, "Penelope and Odysseus in Odyssey XIX," *AJP* 71 (1950): 1–21. For a more full and accurate assessment of the situation, see Amory, "Dreams and Omens in Homer's Odyssey."

33. 17.152ff., 541ff.

34. 18.158ff.

35. 18.180ff., 251ff.

36. 18.158–168.

37. 21.312–342.

38. 23.105ff. Cf. the withholding of her attention by Athene in 19.478f.

39. 23.165ff.

40. 23.202ff.

41. 24.331ff. Cf. Palmer, *Achaeans and Indo-Europeans*, p. 17, who points out that Odysseus' relation to the land determines him as the true king, according to the ancient caste system of the Indo-Europeans. In the light of this statement, the last book of the *Odyssey* can hardly be "late."

42. See above on Amphinomus; Leiodes 22.310ff.

43. 22.330–377.

44. See "The King of the Golden Mountain," J. L. C. and W. C. Grimm, *Grimm's Fairy Tales* (New York, 1917); "The Three Princesses of Whiteland" and "Soria Moria Castle," *The Red Fairy Book*, ed. A. Lang (New York, 1905).

45. Aristotle, *Poetics*, 1451a, 15–22; 1459b, 1.

46. 18.275ff.; cf. Antinous' speech, 2.123ff.; also 1.289ff., where it is clear that, even if Penelope marries one of the suitors, Telemachus will have to kill the others, in order to maintain his right.

47. 1.383–398; cf. 18.64.

48. Cf. Bassett, *The Poetry of Homer*, p. 96, on the βασιλεύς in the Shield of Achilles, and also IV.144 (more dubious); and Bassett, n. 18, referring to Eustathius 1162, 44, and *Etym. Mag.* 189, 12, where βασιλεύς has three meanings (1) θεός; (2) βασιλεύς; (3) οἰκοδεσπότης. Cf. *Schol. ad* 14.336 (βασιλεύς = δυνάστης); cf. Bowra, *Homer and his Forerunners*, p. 24, for evidence from Linear B, and Ventris, "King Nestor's Four-Handled Cups," *Archaeology* 7 (Spring 1954), on the terms βασιλεύς and ἄναξ.

49. 16.364–392; cf. 20.215f.; 3.331ff.

50. 16.361; cf. 2.25ff.

51. 3.109ff.

INDEX

INDEX

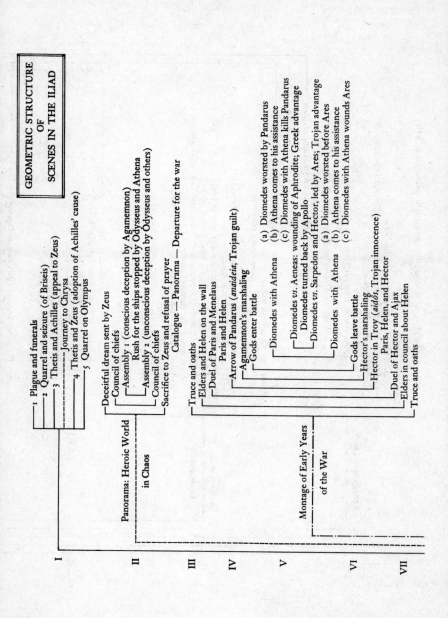

GEOMETRIC STRUCTURE
OF
SCENES IN THE ILIAD

I
1 Plague and funerals
2 Quarrel and seizure (of Briseis)
3 Thetis and Achilles (appeal to Zeus)
— Journey to Chrysa
4 Thetis and Zeus (adoption of Achilles' cause)
5 Quarrel on Olympus

II Panorama: Heroic World in Chaos
Deceitful dream sent by Zeus
Council of chiefs
— Assembly 1 (conscious deception by Agamemnon)
— Rush for the ships stopped by Odysseus and Athena
— Assembly 2 (unconscious deception by Odysseus and others)
Council of chiefs
Sacrifice to Zeus and refusal of prayer
Catalogue — Panorama — Departure for the war

III
Truce and oaths
Elders and Helen on the wall
Duel of Paris and Menelaus
Paris and Helen

IV
Arrow of Pandarus (*anaideia*, Trojan guilt)
Agamemnon's marshaling
Gods enter battle

V
— Diomedes with Athena
— Diomedes vs. Aeneas: wounding of Aphrodite; Greek advantage
— Diomedes turned back by Apollo
— Diomedes vs. Sarpedon and Hector, led by Ares; Trojan advantage
— Diomedes with Athena

(a) Diomedes worsted by Pandarus
(b) Athena comes to his assistance
(c) Diomedes with Athena kills Pandarus

(a) Diomedes worsted before Ares
(b) Athena comes to his assistance
(c) Diomedes with Athena wounds Ares

VI Montage of Early Years of the War
Gods leave battle
Hector's marshaling
Hector in Troy (*aidōs*, Trojan innocence)
Paris, Helen, and Hector

VII
Duel of Hector and Ajax
Elders in council about Helen
Truce and oaths

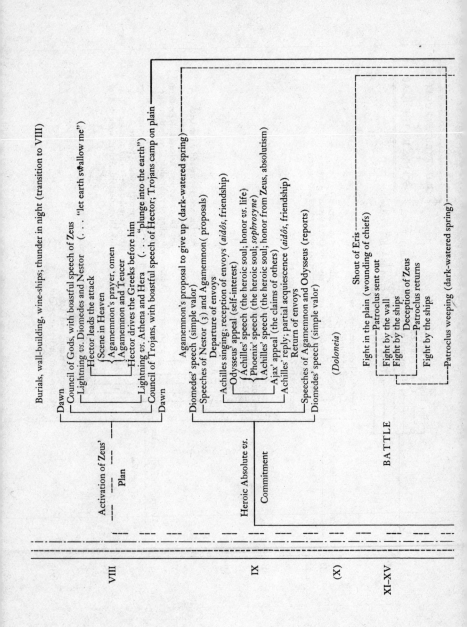

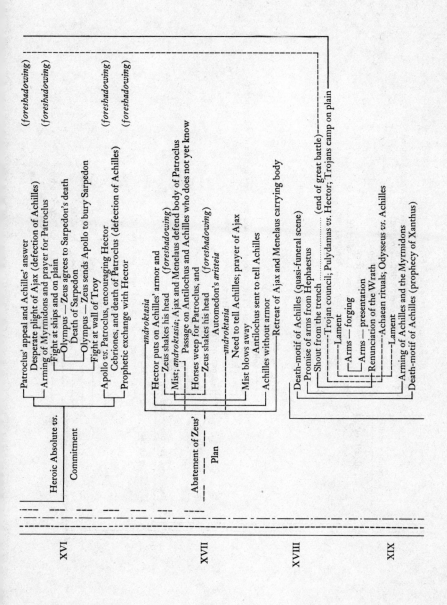

Renunciation of the Plan of Zeus
The Gods take the field
The Gods agree not to fight unless someone prevents Achilles
Aeneas (ally) meets Achilles (rescued)
Hector (Trojan) meets Achilles (rescued)
{ *androktasia* in the plain
{ *androktasia* in the river
Lycaon (Trojan) meets Achilles (slain)
Asteropaeus (ally) meets Achilles (slain)
Scamander overflows, preventing Achilles; Hephaestus intervenes
Greek Gods defeat Trojan Gods

Death-motif of Achilles — deflection by Apollo

Appeal of Priam
Appeal of Hecuba
Soliloquy of Hector
Chase around Troy; ended by scales-passage, and Athena as Deiphobus
Duel, with speeches; prophecy of Hector
Dragging of Hector's body
Lament of Priam
Lament of Hecuba
Lament of Andromache

Dragging of Hector and refusal of burial
Achilles asleep
Funeral of Patroclus
Achilles asleep
Gathering of bones and burial of Patroclus

Games — Panorama — The returns from the war
5 Quarrel on Olympus
4 Thetis and Zeus (modification of hero's cause)
3 Thetis and Achilles (message from Zeus)
Journey of Priam
2 Reconciliation and restitution (of Hector's body)
1 Funeral of Hector: laments of (a) Andromache
                                (b) Hecuba
                                (c) Helen

XX   Montage of the
          Fall of Troy

XXI

XXII

XXIII   Panorama: Heroic World
          in Order

XXIV

In the Norton Library

Victor Ehrenberg
The Greek State   (N250)

Guglielmo Ferrero
The Life of Caesar   (N111)

John Forsdyke
Greece Before Home   (N240)

Kathleen Freeman
Greek City-States   (N193)
The Murder of Herodes and Other Trials from the Athenian Law Courts   (N201)

Cyrus H. Gordon
The Ancient Near East   (N275)
The Common Background of Greek and Hebrew Civilizations   (N293)

Edith Hamilton
The Echo of Greece   (N231)
The Greek Way   (N230)
The Roman Way   (N232)
Three Greek Plays: The Trojan Woman of Euripides and the *Prometheus* and *Agamemnon* of Aeschylus, translated and edited by Edith Hamilton   (N203)

Homer
The Iliad: A Shortened Version, translated and edited by I. A. Richards   (N101)

D. W. Lucas
The Greek Tragic Poets   (N253)

Martin P. Nilsson
A History of Greek Religion (2nd Ed.)   (N287)
The Mycenaean Origin of Greek Mythology   (N234)

J. D. S. Pendlebury
The Archaeology of Crete   (N276)

Chester Starr
Civilization and the Caesars   (N322)

T. B. L. Webster
From Mycenae to Homer   (N254)

Cedric H. Whitman
Homer and the Heroic Tradition   (N313)

C. Leonard Woolley
The Sumerians   (N292)
Ur of the Chaldees   (N301)